Racial Profiling and Human Rights in Canada

Racial Profiling and Human Rights in Canada

The New Legal Landscape

EDITED BY LORNE FOSTER, LESLEY JACOBS,
BOBBY SIU, & SHAHEEN AZMI

IRWIN LAW

Published in 2018 by

Irwin Law Inc.
14 Duncan Street
Suite 206
Toronto, ON
M5H 3G8

www.irwinlaw.com

ISBN: 978-1-55221-482-4
e-book ISBN: 978-1-55221-483-1

Library and Archives Canada Cataloguing in Publication

Racial profiling and human rights in Canada : the new legal landscape / edited by Lorne Foster, Lesley Jacobs, Bobby Siu, & Shaheen Azmi.

Includes bibliographical references and index.
Issued in print and electronic formats.

ISBN 978-1-55221-482-4 (softcover).—ISBN 978-1-55221-483-1 (PDF)

1. Racial profiling in law enforcement—Canada. 2. Human rights—Canada. I. Foster, Lorne, editor II. Siu, Bobby C. Y., editor III. Jacobs, Lesley A., editor IV. Azmi, Shaheen, 1961–, editor V. Title.

HV7936.R3.R36 2018   305.800971   C2018-903670-2
                                                C2018-903671-0

Printed and bound in Canada.

1 2 3 4 5   22 21 20 19 18

Contents

Editors' Introduction

LORNE FOSTER, LESLEY JACOBS,
BOBBY SIU, & SHAHEEN AZMI[*]

A. RACIAL PROFILING AND PUBLIC DISCOURSE

Racial profiling is an uncomfortable topic of conversation for many Canadians. For starters, those who are racial minorities (in its sociological sense), and bear the brunt of profiling, report alienating or traumatic experiences. Not only are they angry and frustrated, but they also recognize that they do not have the same rights and freedoms as other people. These are the feelings that can resurface whenever the topic of racial profiling is raised.

And then there are those who strongly deny that racial profiling is anything extraordinary. They claim that it is normal to pay more attention to certain segments of the population because it is their job to set a priority on what needs to be done and focus on yielding tangible results. Shopkeepers, educators, marketers, salespeople, service providers, and law enforcement officers are often trained to target segments of the population (consumers, residents, students, patients, or children) for special services or treatment. They see themselves as professionals and profiling as nothing more than a competency that makes other people's lives better and is for the public good.

Profiling and being profiled yield two different sets of experiences and, incidentally, produce two different sets of results. People who do the profiling do not have the negative interpretations and experiences of

---

[*] Lorne Foster is a professor of public policy and equity studies, as well as the co-chair, Race, Inclusion and Supportive Environments, York University. Lesley Jacobs is professor of law & society and political science, as well as the director of the Institute for Social Research, York University. Bobby Siu is an adjunct professor of public policy and public administration, York University. Shaheen Azmi is the director of policy, education, monitoring, and outreach of the Ontario Human Rights Commission.

those who are profiled. The profilers may argue that their profiling produces good results: preventing crime, apprehending criminals, streaming students into specific educational paths, saving children from abuse or violence, enabling more consumption choices, serving customers more efficiently — and the list goes on. An increasing number of industries and professions are getting into the profiling business because it appears that racial and other types of predictive profiling bring positive results. In various social domains, profiling is associated with cost-effectiveness, gains in profits, community safety, child welfare, and domestic peace. However, the extent to which these results are considered to be beneficial to the public is debatable, which means that evidence on profiling results should be subject to closer scrutiny.

Recent academic research has noted that the belief in the predictive power of profiling may be illusory.[1] Despite its widespread use as a safety and security tool in Canada and around the world, there is no strong theoretical grounding or compelling scientific evidence that it is reliable, valid, or useful.[2] Meanwhile, the people being profiled represent a collective loss of human rights, dignity, and respect. This type of loss is what the *Charter of Rights and Freedoms* and human right laws were enacted to prohibit. Racial profiling, as it is being practised, violates the principles of human rights: freedom from discrimination, protection of individual dignity and worth, as well as equity rights and treatment. It also violates the principles of diversity and inclusiveness: respectful treatment, fairness, accessibility, and the value of individual differences.

So far, in the public realm, the multiple perspectives that people and institutions have regarding racial profiling have actually created a series of healthy discussions, albeit one with no conclusive consensus. Public dialogues have expanded from the traditional discussion on racial profiling in the police sector and other law enforcement domains (such as border security services and anti-terrorism efforts) to those in education, health care, and social services, as well as the commercial and retail sectors.

In the public arena, the Ethno-Cultural Council of Calgary's (ECC) definition of racial profiling seems to epitomize the emerging trend towards broadening the conversation. The ECC identifies racial profiling as an action that

---

1   Brent Snook et al, "The Criminal Profiling Illusion: What's Behind the Smoke and Mirrors?" (2008) 35:10 *Criminal Justice and Behavior* 1257.

2   Shannon Vettor, Jessica Woodhams, & Anthony Beech, "Offender Profiling: A Review and Critique of the Approaches and Major Assumptions" (2013) 6:4 *Journal of Current Issues in Crime, Law and Law Enforcement* 354.

reinforces differential, unfair treatment or scrutiny of individuals on the basis of race, religious belief, skin colour, ancestry, place of origin or a combination of these, and at the same time, extends the scope of focus of profiling practice to publications and notices, goods, services, accommodations, facilities, tenancy, employment, applications and advertising regarding employment, membership in trade unions, employers' organizations or occupational associations.[3]

Expanding the public discourse beyond law enforcement sectors has provided additional insights into the multi-faceted dimensions of racial profiling, and exposed new possibilities on policy and legal fronts. Recent discussions have included the following questions:

- Whether in business, social services, law enforcement, or other sectors, is the broadening of profiling based on race a direction that should be supported or rejected? Is racial profiling benefitting anyone?
- What can the legal system do to minimize the harm of racial profiling, especially when racial profiling is extending its reach to sectors other than policing?
- How can social scientists, educators, lawyers, and politicians expand the public dialogues on racial profiling and elevate understanding of the adverse impact of this phenomenon on segments of the population?

B. HOLISTIC PERSPECTIVES AND PRAXIS

Racial profiling is linked to a number of psychological concepts of which "stereotypes" and "prejudice" are central. Stereotyping is a cognitive process that helps people simplify life's complex reality and organize their thoughts. When people start simplifying what they see and grouping people together based on race, gender, and other constructs, there is a tendency to gloss over individual differences and generalize particular attributes based on the group affiliation. Such stereotyping is often the source of prejudice when the feelings towards the stereotypes are negative. In this way, stereotyping can lead to profiling. And although anyone can experience profiling, racialized persons are primarily affected.

Different shades of skin have traditionally been associated with different stereotypes. There are numerous stereotypes of racialized minorities,

---

3   Beth Chatten, ed, *Racial Profiling: The Lived Experience of Ethno-Cultural Community Members in Canada* (Calgary: Ethno-Cultural Council of Calgary, 2011) at 2.

but the association with criminality is the most damaging. When people have the image of racialized minorities as likely criminals, they react in a manner that often results in racial profiling. Hence, closer surveillance of racialized minorities in different social contexts such as shops, streets, public buildings, and neighbourhoods can appear to be warranted, which is a narrow way to interpret racial profiling. Yet, the psychological attributes of stereotyping and prejudice alone cannot fully explain complex subject matters like street carding, traffic stops, shop stalking, security surveillance, body searches, and other practices that are deemed offensive to racialized minorities. If it were that simple, a few educational and training sessions would make racial profiling disappear.

It is important to note that racial profiling does not exist in a social vacuum. Many of those who exercise racial profiling actions must be placed in an organizational context in which such actions are deemed to be not only acceptable, but acclaimed and rewarded. Law enforcement agencies have been crafting racial profiling strategies and tactics for many years and putting them into practice with official endorsement, encouragement, and enforcement.

As crime statistics and policing practices reveal, the more time police officers spend focusing their surveillance and intelligence gathering efforts on racialized minorities and their communities, the greater the chance that they will use their discretion to label "criminal" or "pseudo-criminal" elements. This practice reinforces the notion that racialized minorities are associated with some forms of criminality. More importantly, such behaviours further reinforce the notion that racial profiling is a legitimate and effective policing tool in ensuring community safety.

As racial profiling has become institutionalized and reinforced by a reward system in the law enforcement sector, this organizational trend has also been present in the political arena in which the desire to stop the expansion of racial profiling has been lacking for many years. The ideology that racial profiling is good for the community and the country as a whole, as it protects citizens, their properties, and well-being, has been simply too hard for political figures to resist. It is not that the Constitution, the *Charter of Rights and Freedoms*, and human rights legislation are too weak to challenge such ideology and practices; it is the lack of political will to enforce them.

The lack of political courage from politicians is also a reflection of the embedment of the ideology that racial profiling is a powerful tool to stamp out terrorism, criminal activity, and petty misconducts. There is no harm to politicians for continuing to support such ideologies and institutions as long as the general public is mostly silent on this issue. Silence, in this case, implies consent.

The outcry against racial profiling comes not from the broader, general public, but from smaller segments of the population. First, the targeted minorities, primarily members of the Black community, individuals who identify as Muslim, members of the South Asian community, and Indigenous peoples, have been angry about and vocal against such practices for a while. Second, civil liberties associations and progressive legal professionals have been lending their helping (legal) hands to further the legal battles on this issue. Third, human rights commissions, especially the Ontario Human Rights Commission, have devoted their resources to enable several sectors, primarily the law enforcement sector, to come to a realization that racial profiling is eroding human rights and that more effective policing may lie in community consultation and collaboration. Fourth, in spite of the general lack of resources devoted to research on racial profiling, a number of academic experts in this area have been relentlessly working to produce studies and collect empirical evidence to demonstrate the evils of racial profiling.

Public discourse and discursive narratives have been driving the need for a holistic multi-faceted approach to understanding the phenomenon of racial profiling and to pre-empt or eradicate this practice. As noted, a combination of psychological, sociological, organizational, political, and community perspectives and actions may well be an effective way to tackle the issue and promote social change. This holistic approach calls for praxis — a dialectic of theories and actions.

C. SOCIAL TRANSFORMATION

This book is designed to address some of the contemporary trends in the public discourse on racial profiling and to stimulate a broad-based and holistic understanding of the complexities of racial profiling in the Canadian context. This book has as its primary theme the notion of *transformation*. The modern concept of transformation can be situated in relation to the early Socratic epistemology of *aporia, elenchus,* and *anamnesis* — the intellectual and social process of recollection (re-collecting), rediscovery (re-discovering), and renewal (re-newing).[4] In contemporary parlance, transformative change involves the movement in thought and

---

4   Norman Gulley, *Plato's Theory of Knowledge* (London: Methuen, 1962) at 1–47; Alan F Blum, *Theorizing* (London: Heinemann, 1974).

action through interrogation and deconstruction and transgression of the forces of the status quo to the restoration and renewal of the whole.

In this collection of articles, transformation is about an engagement with diversity in a changing Canada, and it is also about changing Canadian diversity itself. Here, transformation is taken to mean gaining understanding in order to promote or direct positive social change. This requires recollecting, rediscovering, and renewing a commitment to cultural democracy and an inclusive society. It is this engagement of "transformation through inclusion" that is the common thread that weaves its way through the chapters in this book and which seeks to increase rational dialogues and critical perspectives; promote a holistic understanding of the intersections of race with gender, class, and power; and broaden conversations about the public good and community well-being.

Transformation requires a galvanizing of not only multiracial and multicultural groups, but also a broad range of stakeholders who are the movers and shakers of institutional changes and national movements. Stakeholders who develop structures and processes in public, broader public, and private sectors (such as law-making and enforcement, political apparatuses, civil service, social and community services, commercial and retail enterprises, school systems and post-secondary educational institutions, labour and trade unions, business associations, and advocacy organizations) have to play an active role in driving the transformation. This is easier said than done.

However, there are ways to get there. Stakeholders must interrogate their own personal values and those of their organizations in a framework of human rights and democracy and develop means to translate those values into policies and practices. Law enforcement agencies as well as others can reassess their own organizational structures — their performance management system, rewards and awards mechanisms, law enforcement strategies and tactics, human resources practices, and other processes — and transform them into a system that is better aligned with the principles of human rights and freedoms. This transformation may not need to be a change in social paradigm (as its democratic foundation is already in place); all it needs to move forward is reflection — and more reflection — on what has taken place in this racial and cultural arena, and for these organizational structures to take small steps towards progress.

The chapters in this collection represent some of these positive incremental steps from multiple perspectives. They provide mere appetizers for a social change that is hungering to take place. The articles are organized into three sections, mainly for the ease of use in discussions.

Each contribution interrogates the concept of racial profiling and where it is perceived to take place; each takes seriously the challenge of reconstructing and reorganizing understanding to shape the discussion of racial profiling in ways that can lead to transformative social change. Each contribution takes transformation through inclusion as its central lens by providing a measured approach to the comprehensive understanding of racial profiling, triangulating the examination of racial profiling around multiple sectors and settings, and connecting the reality on the ground to the systemic reality of Canadian society.

D. THE STRUCTURE OF THE BOOK

1) Deconstructing Racial Profiling

Part One of this book presents a series of chapters that examine racial profiling through an equality-as-transformation lens that provides an instructive background for the development of public policy and public law.

Bobby Siu, an adjunct professor in the School of Public Policy and Administration at York University, reviews the academic and government definitions of racial profiling with the aim of delineating the central conceptual issues, themes, and debates among scholars, lawyers, law enforcement, and other public officials in Chapter 1.

Shaheen Azmi, director of policy, education, monitoring, and outreach at the Ontario Human Rights Commission (OHRC), explains the human rights approach to addressing racial profiling in Chapter 2, and highlights the recent activities undertaken by the OHRC aimed at curbing and preventing racial profiling in various sectors and settings.

Sunil Gurmukh, counsel at the Ontario Human Rights Commission, further consolidates the human rights approach in Chapter 3 by describing how challenges to racial profiling are most substantive when they embody the values of the *Charter of Rights and Freedoms* and provincial human rights legislation.

In Chapter 4, David Tanovich, a professor of law at the University of Windsor, explores the application of the correspondence test in discrimination law as an important development for proving racial profiling.

2) Forms and Sector Analysis

Part Two broadens the scope of the discussion by exploring different manifestations of racial profiling, including the new shapes and forms of racial profiling emerging in multiple sectors and settings, as well as uncovering forms in everyday life that have been concealed and largely neglected.

In Chapter 5, Gary Melanson, senior director of legal services and risk management legal services branch, Waterloo Regional Police Service, examines "bias-neutral" policing practices and how they can guide police in their interactions with citizens.

In Chapter 6, Carl James, professor of education at York University, makes the case that Black youth who reside in the suburbs can be entangled in the relationship between race, space, and place that is conducive to profiling and outsider status, and examines the ways that the suburbs single out young Black males and facilitate special disadvantages.

In Chapter 7, Andrea Anderson, a PhD candidate at Osgoode Hall Law School and criminal defence lawyer, makes the case that the dominant paradigm of racial profiling fails to adequately address the experiences of Black women, and explores the ways in which racialized and Black women have been unjustly targeted and have had their rights violated by police officers.

Tomee Elizabeth Sojourner-Campbell, a mediator and diversity and inclusion consultant, provides a critical perspective on Ontario's retail environment with a view to increasing the visibility of consumer racial profiling in Chapter 8.

In Chapter 9, Tammy Landau, associate professor of criminology at Ryerson University, makes the case that discourses on racial profiling are typically "gender-free," as distinct from gender neutral, and the contexts in which women are racially profiled are both distinct and not limited to the state security apparatus.

3) Preventing and Responding to Racial Profiling

Part Three focuses on effective methods and strategies for the prevention and response to racial profiling, highlighting some transformative policy applications and equity initiatives.

In Chapter 10, Lorne Foster, a professor of public policy and equity studies at York University, and Lesley Jacobs, professor of law & society and political science at York University, examine the importance of collecting race data for the prevention of racial profiling and the promotion of inclusive citizenship.

In Chapter 11, Scot Wortley, a professor of criminology at the University of Toronto, makes the case that the consequences of racial profiling far outweigh the potential benefits, and that discretionary police tactics —

including police practices of carding and street checks — require monitoring mechanisms in order to ensure transparency and public accountability.

In Chapter 12, Lorne Foster and Lesley Jacobs examine how the development of police policy-making and service design might benefit from thoroughgoing two-way engagement with citizens and community groups.

Finally, in Chapter 13, Bobby Siu discusses a comprehensive model for ending racial profiling through the four pillars of strategic leadership, research, human resource management, and stakeholder engagement.

ACKNOWLEDGEMENTS

This book grew out of the partnership between the Ontario Human Rights Commission and the Institute for Social Research and the School of Public Policy and Administration at York University in Toronto. We are grateful and obliged for the support of many people at both the OHRC and York University. Renu Mandhane, chief commissioner of the OHRC, has provided steadfast support for this initiative. We would like to acknowledge the work of Ontario Human Rights Commission staff, especially Remi Warner, senior policy analyst at the OHRC, and Dora Nipp, a lawyer and human rights education and change specialist at the OHRC, for their rich and detailed feedback on the contents of this volume. At York University, we are grateful to Noel Badiou, the former executive director at the Centre for Human Rights, for his invaluable assistance and wise counsel throughout the numerous phases of the project. Our appreciation also goes out to David Rodrigues, who did excellent copy editing work on the contributions by individual authors.

PART I

Deconstructing
Racial Profiling

CHAPTER 1

Defining Racial Profiling

BOBBY SIU[*]

A. INTRODUCTION

This paper reviews the definitions of racial profiling as expounded in selected academic and government publications in Canada and the US. The review is not intended to be exhaustive, but it aims to delineate the central conceptual issues on racial profiling which have been the themes of debates among scholars, lawyers, law enforcement, and other public officials.

The paper highlights seven components in the definitions of racial profiling and variations in their scope, characteristics, strengths, and weaknesses. These seven components are: social domains, coverage, activities, rationales, triggers, psychological focus, and adverse impacts. Lack of common theoretical grounds, inconclusive empirical evidence, and competing values make it difficult to arrive at a consensus on the concept.

This paper is divided into four parts:

- Introduction
- Background
- Conceptual issues in definitions
- Observations

B. BACKGROUND

Police discretion based on extra-legal factors (such as racial prejudice) has long been the topic of discussion in criminal justice studies, but it was in the 1980s that race became a dominant feature in policing work as

---

[*]   Bobby Siu is an adjunct professor of public policy and public administration, York University.

well as the rest of the criminal justice system. The term "racial profiling" seemed to become in vogue in the 1990s.[1]

According to Withrow,[2] profiling has been used by the police to increase their chance of identifying criminals (especially the drug traffickers). Most racial profiling studies focused primarily on traffic stops.[3] It has been observed that some of these stops have been used as pretext stops for drug searches and some drugs have been specifically associated with certain ethnic groups such as Cubans, Colombians, and Thais in the US.[4]

American studies on traffic stops consistently showed that "minority drivers are stopped at disproportionately higher rates than they are represented in the community, . . . among licensed drivers, . . . and among actual users of the roadway" on a more local level.[5] Exceptions are noted among statewide studies, which showed that White drivers are more often searched, ticketed, and arrested than Black drivers. Overall, minority citizens are stopped and searched more often than non-minority citizens.[6]

Meanwhile, Tanovich[7] noted that racial profiling has been utilized as a law enforcement tool in Canada. Wortley and Tanner;[8] Bahdi, Parsons,

1   Rob Tillyer & Richard Hartley, "Driving Racial Profiling Research Forward: Learning Lessons from Sentencing Research" (2010) 38:4 *Journal of Criminal Justice* 657 at 658 [Tillyer & Hartley].

2   Brian L Withrow, *Racial Profiling: From Rhetoric to Reason* (Upper Saddle River, NJ: Pearson/Prentice Hall, 2006).

3   George E Higgins, "Racial Profiling" (2008) 6:1 *Journal of Ethnicity in Criminal Justice* 1 [Higgins, "Racial Profiling"].

4   Richard Bent et al, "Racial Profiling and National Security: A Canadian Police Perspective" [Bent et al] in Richard Marcuse, ed, *Racial Profiling* (Vancouver: BC Civil Liberties Association, 2010) 81 at 83 [Marcuse, ed, *Racial Profiling*].

5   Marielle Schultz & Brian Withrow, "Racial Profiling and Organizational Change" (2004) 15:4 *Criminal Justice Policy Review* 462.

6   *Ibid.*

7   David M Tanovich, "Using the *Charter* to Stop Racial Profiling: The Development of an Equality-based Conception of Arbitrary Detention" (2002) 40:2 *Osgoode Hall Law Journal* 145 [Tanovich, "Using the *Charter*"].

8   Scot Wortley & Julian Tanner, "Data, Denials, and Confusion: The Racial Profiling Debate in Toronto" (2003) 45:3 *Canadian Journal of Criminology and Criminal Justice* 367 [Wortley & Tanner, "Data, Denials"]; Scot Wortley & Julian Tanner, "Inflammatory Rhetoric? Baseless Accusations? A Response to Gabor's Critique of Racial Profiling Research in Canada" (2005) 47:3 *Canadian Journal of Criminology and Criminal Justice* 581 [Wortley & Tanner, "Inflammatory Rhetoric"].

and Sandborn;[9] Henry and Tator;[10] Tator and Henry;[11] Whitaker;[12] Eid, Magloire, and Turenne;[13] Wortley and Owusu-Bempah;[14] and Wortley,[15] citing research studies and minority perspectives, all maintained that racial profiling in one form or another is quite common in the criminal justice system.

Several human rights commissions, including the Ontario Human Rights Commission,[16] Alberta Human Rights Commission,[17] and Nova Scotia Human

---

9   Reem Bahdi, Olanyi Parsons, & Tom Sandborn, "Racial Profiling: B.C. Liberties Association Position Paper" [Bahdi, Parsons, & Sandborn] in Marcuse, ed, *Racial Profiling*, above note 4 at 31.

10 Frances Henry & Carol Tator, *Racial Profiling in Toronto: Discourse of Domination, Mediation and Opposition* (Toronto: Canadian Race Relations Foundation, 2005); Frances Henry & Carol Tator, "Theoretical Perspectives on Racial Profiling in Postmodern Societies" [Henry & Tator, "Theoretical Perspectives"] in Marcuse, ed, *Racial Profiling*, above note 4 at 55; Frances Henry & Carol Tator, "Rejoinder to Satzewich and Shaffir on 'Racism versus Professionalism: Claims and Counter-Claims about Racial Profiling'" (2011) 53:1 *Canadian Journal of Criminology and Criminal Justice* 65 [Henry & Tator, "Rejoinder"].

11 Carol Tator & Frances Henry, *Racial Profiling in Canada: Challenging the Myth of "a Few Bad Apples"* (Toronto: University of Toronto Press, 2006).

12 Reg Whitaker, "Profiling: From Racial to Behavioural to Racial?" in Marcuse, ed, *Racial Profiling*, above note 4 at 15.

13 Paul Eid, Johanne Magloire, & Michèle Turenne, *Racial Profiling and Systemic Discrimination of Racialized Youth: Report of the Consultation on Racial Profiling and Its Consequences* (Quebec: Commission des droits de la personne et des droits de la jeunesse, 2011) [Eid, Magloire, & Turenne].

14 Scot Wortley & Akwasi Owusu-Bempah, "The Usual Suspect: Police Stop and Search Practices in Canada" (2011) 21:4 *Policing and Society* 395 [Wortley & Owusu-Bempah, "The Usual Suspect"].

15 Scot Wortley, "Racial Profiling: Definitions, Data and Policy Options" (Paper delivered at the Human Rights Legal Support Centre, Toronto, 1 November 2012) [Wortley, "Racial Profiling"].

16 Ontario Human Rights Commission, *Paying the Price: The Human Cost of Racial Profiling – Inquiry Report* (Toronto: Ontario Human Rights Commission, 2003) [OHRC, *Paying the Price*]; Ontario Human Rights Commission, "Submission of the Ontario Human Rights Commission to the Independent Police Review Director's Systemic Review of Ontario Provincial Police Practices from DNA Sampling" (April 2014), online: www.ohrc.on.ca/en/ohrc-submission-office-independent-police-review-director%E2%80%99s-systemic-review-opp-practices-dna [OHRC, "Submission re DNA Sampling"].

17 Alberta Human Rights Commission, "Racial Profiling" (Information Sheet) (Edmonton: Alberta Human Rights Commission, 2012), online: www.albertahumanrights.ab.ca/publications/bulletins_sheets_booklets/sheets/protected_grounds/Pages/racial_profiling.aspx [AHRC, "Racial Profiling"].

Rights Commission,[18] further articulated the notion of racial profiling. Community and advocacy groups, such as the Ontario Federation of Indian Friendship Centres, Ontario Metis Aboriginal Association, Ontario Native Women's Association,[19] BC Civil Liberties Association,[20] and African Canadian Legal Clinic,[21] have expressed their strong stand against racial profiling.

This position was not left unchallenged. Harvey,[22] Melchers,[23] Gold,[24] and Gabor[25] argued that existing research studies are flawed in their research methodologies and the allegations of racial profiling are "inflammatory rhetoric" that "can undermine police services" and "serve to further alienate black and other visible minority people from mainstream Canadian society and reinforce perception of discrimination and racial injustice."[26] Melchers did not propose a definition of racial profiling, but he commented on the status of studies in racial profiling: "Most definitions and even general problem statements put forward about 'racial profiling' are fugitive or so insufficiently or even maliciously reasoned as to constitute non-falsifiable propositions."[27]

18   Nova Scotia Human Rights Commission, *Working Together to Better Serve All Nova Scotians: A Report on Consumer Racial Profiling in Nova Scotia* (Halifax: Nova Scotia Human Rights Commission, 2013) [NSHRC, *Working Together*].

19   Ontario Federation of Indian Friendship Centres, Ontario Metis Aboriginal Association, & Ontario Native Women's Association, *Urban Aboriginal Task Force: Final Report* (Toronto: Ontario Federation of Indian Friendship Centres, 2007).

20   Marcuse, ed, *Racial Profiling*, above note 4.

21   African Canadian Legal Clinic (ACLC), *Anti-Racial Profiling Toolkit: An ACLC Public Legal Education Resource* (Toronto: ACLC, 2011) [ACLC, *Anti-Racial Profiling Toolkit*].

22   Edward Harvey, "An Independent Review of the *Toronto Star* Analysis of Criminal Information Processing (CIPS) Data Provided by the Toronto Police Service" (2003), online: www.torontopolice.on.ca/publications/2003.02.20-review/pptpresentation.pdf [Harvey, "An Independent Review"].

23   Ron Melchers, "Do Toronto Police Engage in Racial Profiling?" (2003) 45:3 *Canadian Journal of Criminology and Criminal Justice* 347 [Melchers, "Toronto Police"]; Ronald-Frans Melchers, *Inequality before the Law: The Canadian Experience of "Racial Profiling"* (Ottawa: Royal Canadian Mounted Police, 2006) [Melchers, *Inequality before the Law*]; Ronald-Frans Melchers, "Comment on the Rejoinder of Henry and Tator to Satzevich and Shaffir" (2011) 53:1 *Canadian Journal of Criminology and Criminal Justice* 105 [Melchers, "Comment on the Rejoinder"].

24   Alan D Gold, "Media Hype, Racial Profiling, and Good Science" (2003) 45:3 *Canadian Journal of Criminology and Criminal Justice* 391 [Gold, "Media Hype"].

25   Thomas Gabor, "Inflammatory Rhetoric Undermines Police Service" (2004) 46:4 *Canadian Journal of Criminology and Criminal Justice* 457 [Gabor, "Inflammatory Rhetoric"].

26   *Ibid.*

27   Melchers, *Inequality before the Law*, above note 23 at 22.

Summarizing the current state of definitions of racial profiling and the difficulty in advancing knowledge and solutions in this field, Melchers[28] lamented that there was a tendency that "definitions by fiat, presumption of fact, misrepresentation of evidence, calls for acceptance of proportions on faith, appeals to anecdote, appeals to emotion, rhetorical *envoles*, characterization of any question as racist are all barriers to the emergence of any collective understanding of the problem and prohibit any possible solution."

As the academic literature, public debates, and media coverage suggested, the notion of racial profiling elicits strong emotion among people. This may be due to the observation that the social values and legal principles of privacy, freedom, and fair legal enforcement for all people are viewed as being undermined by the perception that law enforcement officials are treating people differently by imposing heavier surveillance and sanctions on racial minorities.[29] And then there is the issue of balancing the protection of basic rights and freedoms and the protection of national security and public order. People are concerned about the swinging of the pendulum and losing the balance.[30]

Being selected for greater scrutiny by the police has adverse impacts on racial minority members, psychologically, physically, socially, and economically.[31] Findings on racial disparities in traffic stops are important because they "represent a first entry point into the criminal justice system; if disparities are presented here, they set the stage for compounding effects as the individual continues through the system."[32]

Meanwhile, law enforcement officials merely believe that they are only doing their jobs professionally by "profiling" potential criminals. Racial profiling is merely one of their tools in law enforcement.[33] Currently in

---

28   Melchers, "Comment on the Rejoinder," above note 23 at 109.

29   Donald Tomaskovic-Devey, Marcinda Mason, & Matthew Zingraff, "Looking for the Driving While Black Phenomena: Conceptualizing Racial Bias Processes and Their Associated Distributions" (2004) 7 *Police Quarterly* 3 at 4 [Tomaskovic-Devey, Mason, & Zingraff].

30   Bent et al, above note 4 at 81.

31   OHRC, *Paying the Price*, above note 16; Eid, Magloire, & Turenne, above note 13.

32   Robert Crutchfield, April Fernandes, & Jorge Martinez, "Racial and Ethnic Disparity, and Jorge and Criminal Justice: How Much Is Too Much?" (July 2010) 100:3 *The Journal of Criminal Law and Criminology* 903 at 924.

33   Vic Satzewich & Wiliam Shaffir, "Racism versus Professionalism: Claims and Counter-Claims about Racial Profiling" (August 2009) 51:2 *Canadian Journal of Criminology and Criminal Justice* 199 [Satzewich & Shaffir]; Jimmy Bourque et al, *The Effectiveness of Profiling from a National Perspective* (Ottawa: Canadian Human Rights Commission and the Canadian Race Relations Foundation, 2009); Barbara Jackman, "Sustaining Inves-

Canada, racial minority communities and some of the police and security services are working through their different perspectives. If the police value of "community interaction and trust" is the global gold standard of police professionalism,[34] the distrust between the police and the communities that has been generated on this issue of racial profiling necessitates the urgency of resolving the issue, real or perceived.

The sensitivity towards racial profiling may not diminish soon, especially when the term racial profiling itself has a broad range of meanings, often conflicting. There are crosstalks over the notion, as there is no consensus over what should be included in that term. In the following section, definitions of racial profiling will be highlighted to illustrate the conceptual issues that have to be resolved prior to a healthier public dialogue on, more comprehensive theoretical articulation of, and sounder research methodologies on the phenomenon of racial profiling.

C. CONCEPTUAL ISSUES

At daily conversation or academic discussion, people tend to use the term racial profiling as if it has been well defined and well understood. Nothing is further from the reality.

The reality is that the term had been used in academic journal articles without offering explicitly clear definitions in many instances.[35] Examples may be found in Tillyer and Hartley's study[36], or Parker et al's study[37], which reviewed other scholars' work on racial profiling without finding their common elements and did not come up with their own definitions. Other scholars, using the term racial profiling loosely, discussed

---

tigations and Security Certificates through the Use of Profiles" in Marcuse, ed, *Racial Profiling*, above note 4 at 69; Daniel Moeckli, "Terrorist Profiling and the Importance of a Proactive Approach to Human Rights Protection" in Marcuse, ed, *Racial Profiling*, above note 4 at 99.

34   Paul Amar, "Introduction: New Racial Missions of Policing: Comparative Studies of State Authority, Urban Governance, and Security Technology in the Twenty-First Century" (April 2010) 3:4 *Ethnic and Racial Studies* 575.

35   Candice Batton & Colleen Kadleck, "Theoretical and Methodological Issues in Racial Profiling Research" (March 2004) 7:1 *Police Quarterly* 30 [Batton & Kadleck].

36   Tillyer & Hartley, above note 1.

37   Karen F Parker et al, "A Contextual Study of Racial Profiling: Assessing the Theoretical Rationale for the Study of Racial Profiling at the Local Level" (March 2004) 47:7 *American Behavioral Scientist* 943.

racial tension arising from policing,[38] pretext stops and racial disparities in traffic stops,[39] race-based policing,[40] and the inappropriate use of race in vehicle stops.[41] In addition, there are American publications that did not use the term racial profiling at all but focused on the differential treatment of minorities by police in the criminal justice system including the investigation of drug trafficking through traffic stops,[42] traffic stops as a pretext,[43] and probability of traffic stops experienced by racial minorities.[44] No explicit definitions of racial profiling were offered, and it is not clear whether they are referring to different forms of policing, racial or not.

This review of definitions of racial profiling covers American and Canadian academic journal articles and publications from government and community organizations from 1990 to 2015. It reviews only those that have explicit statements on the definitions of racial profiling. It does not claim to be exhaustive and it clearly excludes studies that do not have

---

38 John D Cohen, Janet J Lennon, & Robert Wasserman, "End Racial Profiling" (2000) 8 *Blueprint*, online: www.unz.com/Pub/Blueprint-2000q4-00062/.

39 David A Harris, "The Stories, the Statistics, and the Law: Why 'Driving While Black' Matters" (1999) 84 *Minnesota Law Review* 265; David A Harris, "Driving While Black: Racial Profiling on Our Nation's Highways" (1999), online: www.aclu.org/report/driving-while-black-racial-profiling-our-nations-highways.

40 Jim Leitzel, "Race and Policing" (2001) 38:3 *Society* 38.

41 Texas Department of Public Safety, "Traffic Stop Data Report" (October 2000), online: www.txdps.state.tx.us/director_staff/public_information/trafrep2q00.pdf.

42 American Civil Liberties Union, *Report of John Lamberth* (1996), online: http://homepage.divms.uiowa.edu/~gwoodwor/statsoc/lectures/w2/lamberth.html.

43 David Cole, *No Equal Justice: Race and Class in the American Criminal Justice System* (New York: New Press, 1999); Carl Milazzo & Ron Hansen, *Race Relations in Police Operations: A Legal and Ethical Perspective* (Paper presented at the 106th Annual Conference of the International Association of Chiefs of Police, Charlotte, NC, 30 October–3 November 1999); Samuel Walker, Cassia Spohn, & Miriam DeLone, 2d ed, *The Color of Justice: Race, Ethnicity, and Crime in America* (Belmont, CA: Wadsworth/Thomson Learning, 2000).

44 Steven R Donziger, *The Real War on Crime: The Report of the National Criminal Justice Commission* (New York: HarperCollins, 1996); David A Harris, "'Driving While Black' and All other Traffic Offenses: The Supreme Court and Pretextual Traffic Stops" (1997) 87 *The Journal of Criminal Law and Criminology* 544 [Harris, "Driving While Black"]; Joy James, "The Dysfunctional and the Disappearing: Democracy, Race and Imprisonment" (2000) 6 *Social Identities* 483; MT Zingraff et al, *Evaluating North Carolina State Highway Patrol Data: Citations, Warnings, and Searches in 1998* (Raleigh, NC: Department of Crime Control and Public Safety, 2000); Council on Crime and Justice, *Minneapolis Police Traffic Stops and Driver's Race: Analysis and Recommendations* (Minneapolis, MN: Council on Crime and Justice, 2001).

explicit statements on the definitions of racial profiling such as those mentioned above.

This paper highlights components mentioned in explicitly stated definitions and identifies the following seven components for discussion:

- Extent of social domains
- Coverage of grounds
- Range of activities
- Formal rationales and justifications
- Triggers
- Psychological focus
- Adverse impacts

Incidentally, these seven components are in line with Batton and Kadleck's view on the essence of racial profiling: realms of activity, characteristics of the incident, population of interest, aggregation level, and unit of analysis.[45] It is observed that not all definitions reviewed have all of these components. Most have some of them though. They may be described differently and their emphases are different too. The general conclusion of this review is that there is quite a divergence of ideas among these definitions and currently no consensus has been reached. This may explain why there are so many crosstalks on this topic.

1)   Extent of Social Domains

In this paper, the term "social domains" means social institutions and their agents. There have been changes in the definitions of racial profiling in the last twenty-five years. The scope of social domains covered has been expanding from police services in the 1990s to all social institutions in the 2010s. This does not mean that people in this field of study have been changing *en masse*. It means that more people have a broader definition now than before, and they have applied the term in expanding social domains.

In the 1990s and early 2000s, the term racial profiling was mostly used in a very specific manner. It was limited mostly to police services. Examples may be found in the definitions of Muharrar;[46] Taylor and

---

45   Batton & Kadleck, above note 35.

46   Mikal Muharrar, "Media Blackface: 'Racial Profiling' in News Reporting" (September/October 1998), online: FAIR https://fair.org/extra/media-blackface/ [Muharrar, "Media Blackface"].

Whitney;[47] Kennedy;[48] US General Accounting Office;[49] Ramirez, McDevitt, and Farrell;[50] and Wortley and Owusu-Bempah.[51] Even in the late 2000s and 2010s, definitions from police services still narrow the notion of racial profiling to policing only.[52]

In the mid-2000s and 2010s, the notion of racial profiling has extended broadly from police services to cover the entire law enforcement field, including the border security services and lately anti-terrorism agencies. In the law enforcement domain, some scholars defined racial profiling generically as "law enforcement surveillance activities"[53] or "the use of discretionary authority by law enforcement officers."[54] Some covered both police and security officers.[55] The Ontario Association of Chiefs of Police specified "an individual in an authority position" can cause racial profiling to occur.[56]

Along this trend line, it has been noted that the notion of racial profiling has been adopted in other fields beyond the traditional law enforcement and police services. Now, there is ongoing work on pharmacogenetical racial profiling activities in clinical medicine and health

---

47 Jared Taylor & Glayde Whitney, "Crime and Racial Profiling by U.S. Police: Is There an Empirical Basis?" (1999) 24 *Journal of Social, Political, and Economic Studies* 485 at 507 [Taylor & Whitney, "Crime and Racial Profiling"].

48 Randall Kennedy, "Suspect Policy" *The New Republic* (13 September 1999), online: https://newrepublic.com/article/63137/suspect-policy [Kennedy, "Suspect Policy"].

49 United States General Accounting Office, *Racial Profiling: Limited Data Available on Motorist Stops* (Washington: US General Accounting Office, 2000), online: www.gao.gov/new.items/gg00041.pdf [USGAO, *Motorist Stops*].

50 Deborah Ramirez, Jack McDevitt, and Amy Farrell, *A Resource Guide on Racial Profiling Data Collection Systems: Promising Practices and Lessons Learned* (Washington, DC: US Department of Justice, 2000) at 3 [Ramirez, McDevitt, & Farrell].

51 Wortley & Owusu-Bempah, "The Usual Suspect," above note 14 at 397.

52 Ontario Association of Chiefs of Police (OACP), *Anti-Racial Profiling Best Practices: A Self Audit to Minimize Corporate Risk* (Toronto: OACP Diversity Committee, 2009) at iv and 10 [OACP, *Best Practices*]; Ottawa Police Service, "Racial Profiling" (2011), online: www.ottawapolice.ca/en/news-and-community/resources/Racial_Profiling_Policy-27Jun11_FINALpdf.pdf [Ottawa Police Service, "Racial Profiling"].

53 Wortley & Tanner, "Inflammatory Rhetoric," above note 8 at 584.

54 Batton & Kadleck, above note 35 at 31.

55 Wortley & Tanner, "Inflammatory Rhetoric," above note 8 at 584; David M Tanovich, *The Colour of Justice: Policing in Canada* (Toronto: Irwin Law, 2006) at 13 [Tanovich, *Colour of Justice*].

56 OACP, *Best Practices*, above note 52 at iv and 10.

care fields,[57] consumer racial profiling in the retail sector,[58] and insurance racial profiling in the property insurance industry.[59]

In the 2010s, the term racial profiling has begun to be used in a very broad context, covering all people in authority positions irrespective of their social domains. Eid, Magloire, and Turenne's definition is quite broad: "Racial profiling is any action taken by one or more people in authority."[60] The Nova Scotia Human Rights Commission's definition also reflects this broadness.[61] Chatten's definition "extends the scope of focus of profiling practice to publications and notices, goods, services, accommodations, facilities, tenancy, employment, applications and advertising regarding employment, membership in trade unions, employers' organizations or occupational associations."[62] Henry and Tator's definition appears to be the broadest. It covers "all institutional sectors even in liberal democratic societies."[63]

---

57   Linda Hunt, Nicole Truesdell, & Meta Kreiner, "Genes, Race, and Culture in Clinical Care: Racial Profiling in the Management of Chronic Illness" (June 2013) 27:2. *Medical Anthropology Quarterly (New Series)* 253; Linda Hunt & Meta Kreiner, "Pharmacogenetics in Primary Care: The Promise of Personalized Medicine and the Reality of Racial Profiling" (March 2013) 37:1 *Culture, Medicine and Psychology,* 226.

58   Jerome D Williams, Geraldine R Henderson, & Anne-Marie Harris, "Consumer Racial Profiling: Bigotry Goes to Market" (2001) 108 *The New Crisis* 22; Shaun L. Gabbidon & George Higgins, "Consumer Racial Profiling and Perceived Victimization: A Phone Survey of Philadelphia Area Residents" (October 2007) 32:1–2 *American Journal of Criminal Justice* 1; Shaun L Gabbidon & George Higgins, "Contextualizing Public Opinion on Consumer Racial Profiling: A Marxist Approach" (2009) 7:3 *Journal of Ethnicity in Criminal Justice* 222; Shaun L Gabbidon & George Higgins, "Public Opinion on the Use of Consumer Racial Profiling to Identify Shoplifters: An Exploratory Study" (June 2011) 36:2 *Criminal Justice Review* 201; Shaun Gabbidon et al, "The Consumer Racial Profiling Experiences of Black Students at Historically Black Colleges and Universities: An Exploratory Study" (August 2008) 36:4 *Journal of Criminal Justice* 354; Kareem L. Jordan, Shaun Gabbidon, & George Higgins, "Exploring the Perceived Extent of and Citizens' Support for Consumer Racial Profiling: Results from a National Poll" (July 2009) 37:4 *Journal of Criminal Justice* 353.

59   Gregory Squires, "Racial Profiling, Insurance Style: Insurance Redlining and the Uneven Development of Metropolitan Areas" (2003) 25:4 *Journal of Urban Affairs* 391; Gregory Squires, "Trust, But Verify: A (Less) Spirited Defense" (2003) 25:4 *Journal of Urban Affairs* 423.

60   Eid, Magloire, & Turenne, above note 13 at 10.

61   NSHRC, *Working Together*, above note 18 at 109.

62   Beth Chatten, ed, *Racial Profiling: The Lived Experience of Ethno-Cultural Community Members in Canada* (Calgary: Ethno-Cultural Council of Calgary, 2011) at 2.

63   Henry & Tator, "Theoretical Perspectives," above note 10 at 55–56.

This broadening of social domains in which the term racial profiling has been used requires a decision on how far one may go in using the term. As noted by Williams,[64] not all social domains are created equal. The law enforcement domain has inherent coercive power that other social domains do not have. Law enforcement agents (including police officers) have coercive authority specified in legislation — people could be searched, arrested, handcuffed, charged, detained, or shot with the use of force by these agents. As the term is used increasingly in more social domains, one has to determine whether the current use of the term racial profiling carries with it the same coercive power as when the term was originally introduced to describe police intervention in the 1990s. Although there is a power component in each social domain, whether it is education, health care, goods, accommodation, insurance, or advertising, none is as coercive as law enforcement in the criminal justice system. As such, being racially profiled has different impacts on individuals in different social domains.

There are numerical questions arising from the drive for more conceptual clarity in racial profiling, keeping in mind that broadening the boundary of social domains does not necessarily make the concept clearer or, as a matter of fact, more useful for research, theoretical articulation, or practical application:

- Given the unique power dimension that the criminal law enforcement sector has, should the use of the term racial profiling be limited to that sector so as to demarcate its distinctiveness?
- If the term racial profiling is used in all other social domains, will it broaden the understanding of the phenomenon?
- What makes racial profiling different from racial stereotyping or racial prejudice?
- Should more appropriate terms be created to describe activities resembling racial profiling found in other social domains?

2) Coverage of Grounds

In this paper, the term "coverage" means the scope of prohibited grounds under human rights legislation. Similar to social domains, there have been changes in the extent of coverage through time. When the term

---

64   Christopher J Williams, "Obscurantism in Action: How the Ontario Human Rights Commission Frames Racial Profiling" (2006) 38:2 *Canadian Ethnic Studies* 1 [Williams, "Obscurantism"].

racial profiling emerged in the US in the 1990s, it was specifically focused on race, with occasional mentions of ethnicity.[65] An example from the writings of Harris[66] and Maclin[67] showed that "race or ethnicity" is viewed as "an indicator of criminal propensity, typically by law enforcement officers in the context of a traffic stop."[68]

Gradually, more grounds are covered in the definition of "racial profiling," such as "national origin."[69] The American Civil Liberties Union[70] added "religion" to the list. Ontario Human Rights Commission[71] expanded the range of grounds to include "colour," "ancestry," "religion," and "place of origin," over and above "race" and "ethnicity." This expanded list of grounds was adopted by Libby Davies' Private Member's Bill (Bill C-296) in 2004, Ontario Association of Chiefs of Police,[72] Ottawa Police Service,[73] Commission des droits de la personne et des droits de la jeunesse,[74] the African Canadian Legal Clinic,[75] Ethno-cultural Coun-

---

65   Taylor & Whitney, "Crime and Racial Profiling," above note 47 at 507; Peter Verniero & Paul H Zoubek, *Interim Report of the State Police Review Team regarding Allegations of Racial Profiling* (Trenton, NJ: Department of Law and Public Safety, 1999) at 5, online: www.state.nj.us/lps/intm_419.pdf [NJ State Police Review]; Kennedy, "Suspect Policy," above note 48; Minnesota Department of Public Safety, *Racial Profiling Report* (November 2000) at 2, online: mnclu.org/nr_racial_profiling.html; Samuel Walker, "Searching for the Denominator: Problems with Police Traffic Stop Data and An Early Warning System Solution" (2000) 3 *Justice Research and Policy* 63 at 64 [Walker, "Denominator"]; Jeremiah Nixon, 2000 *Annual Report of Missouri Traffic Stops* (Jefferson City, MO: Missouri Attorney General's Office, 2001) at 1 [*Missouri Traffic Stops*]; Vicky M Wilkins & Brian N Williams, "Representing Blue: Representative Bureaucracy and Racial Profiling in the Latino Community" (2009) 40 *Administration & Society* 775 at 785 [Wilkins & Williams, "Representing Blue"]; Frederick Desroches, "Peel Regional Police Racial Profiling and the Police" in OACP, *Best Practices*, above note 52, 27 at 28.

66   Harris, "Driving while Black," above note 44.

67   Tracey Maclin, "*Terry v. Ohio*'s Fourth Amendment Legacy: Black Men and Police Discretion" (1998) 72 *St John's Law Review* 1271 [Maclin, "*Terry v. Ohio*'s Legacy"].

68   Batton & Kadleck, above note 35.

69   Ramirez, McDevitt, & Farrell, above note 50 at 3; Tomaskovic-Devey, Mason, & Zingraff, above note 29.

70   American Civil Liberties Union (ACLU), "Racial Profiling: Definition" (2005), online: www.aclu.org/racial-profiling-definition [ACLU Definition].

71   OHRC, *Paying the Price*, above note 16 at 6.

72   OACP, *Best Practices*, above note 52 at iv and 10; Ottawa Police Service, "Racial Profiling," above note 52.

73   *Ibid.*

74   Eid, Magloire, & Turenne, above note 13 at 10.

75   ACLC, *Anti-Racial Profiling Toolkit*, above note 21 at 4.

cil of Calgary,[76] Alberta Human Rights Commission,[77] and Nova Scotia Human Rights Commission.[78] Tanovich[79] expanded the list of grounds further under racial profiling to include "Aboriginality," although it is not technically a prohibited ground.

It appears that the current notion of racial profiling covers more than race, and this raises a number of issues:

Concepts are abstractions of phenomena that enable people to communicate with each other what they think. They are also useful for theoretical articulation, empirical research, and application when they clearly describe the phenomena at stake. As a concept, race is already a fluid social construct with multiple meanings and changing boundaries. It is not a notion with broad consensus. Due to these characteristics, the notion of racial profiling with race as an identifier is likely to remain fuzzy in meaning. When the term racial profiling covers more than racial groups, it poses the issue of conceptual clarity. Clearly, ethnicity, colour, ancestry, religion, and place of origin are distinct concepts with very different meanings, and they imply different profiling meanings when applied in the real world.

Having a term that covers so much ground poses certain conceptual difficulties in the real world. As the current definitions of racial profiling are diverse and in need of a consensus, it may prove helpful to use a combination of grounds as a way to further conceptual confusion at both the academic level and practitioner level (as among the front-line workers). As Pratt and Thompson[80] have already noted, there is ambiguity on the centrality of race in racial profiling and the distinction between race and nationality, ethnicity, and religion. It is not at all clear that the front-line persons (such as police officers or border security officers) are able to distinguish the conceptual differences of these grounds, especially when they are now incorporated under the category of racial profiling.

What complicates the issue even more is the recognition that individuals may be subjected to differential treatment or greater scrutiny when race is connected with any of this broad range of grounds, along with age and sex (Alberta Human Rights Commission;[81] Ontario Human Rights

---

76 Chatten, ed, above note 62 at 2.

77 AHRC, "Racial Profiling," above note 17.

78 NSHRC, *Working Together*, above note 18 at 24 and 109.

79 Tanovich, *Colour of Justice*, above note 55 at 13.

80 Anna Pratt & Sara K Thompson, "Chivalry, 'Race' and Discretion at the Canadian Border" (2008) 48 *British Journal of Criminology* 620 at 620.

81 AHRC, "Racial Profiling," above note 17.

Commission[82]). This recognition of intersectionality appears to be confirmed by Wortley and Tanner's 2005 findings of Canadian students in which race and age intersected.[83] From an academic perspective, a broad coverage of multiple grounds intersecting with one another as noted earlier poses the issue of centrality for any one ground or a configuration of these grounds in a particular situation. It also raises the possibility that the impact of these grounds is cumulative or it could be interactive. For example, a combination of race, age, and sex (such as Black young men) may be an overrepresented population segment in traffic or pedestrian stops (an indication of racial profiling), but this particular population segment (combined race, age, and sex) may not be overrepresented in other situations (such as border security checks). This raises the issue of whether additional factors (such as organizational cultures or subcultures, internal training, media coverage, informational biases, individual appearance or behaviour) take priority over human rights-prohibited grounds in different law enforcement decisions. Is racial profiling actually race-centred, centred around other grounds, or centred even around non-racial factors depending on the contexts as suggested above? Answers to this question would help to conceptualize racial profiling, but it depends on research works in this field, which are currently quite scanty.

Any advance in conceptual clarity has to be made through more advanced research and better articulation with broad consultation. To avoid confusion, a new term may be needed to cover the expanding range of prohibited grounds in human rights legislation currently provided.

3) Range of Activities

In this paper, the term "activities" refers to formal or informal actions or reactions carried out in social domains.

In reviewing the definitions of racial profiling, it is noted that some definitions have very specific activities designated as racial profiling activities and some have only generic descriptions of what these activities are. It seems that generic racial profiling activities tend to appear in definitions that aimed to define the phenomenon in such a way that they are more encompassing and could be applied in a broader range of law enforcement activities. Meanwhile, specific activities in the definitions of racial profiling seem to appear in studies of traffic stops and activities in the post-stop stage.

---

82   OHRC, "Submission re DNA Sampling," above note 16.
83   Wortley & Tanner, "Inflammatory Rhetoric," above note 8.

Here are some examples of generic activities included in some definitions:

- Surveillance and treatment: "differential treatment";[84] "criminal justice surveillance";[85] "greater scrutiny or different treatment";[86] "heightened scrutiny";[87] "subjecting citizens to increased surveillance or scrutiny";[88] "differential, unfair treatment or scrutiny of individuals";[89] "suspect treatment";[90] "differential treatment or scrutiny."[91]
- Non-specific activities: "react with suspicion";[92] "intervene in a law enforcement capacity";[93] "practices ... that incorporate prejudicial judgments";[94] "any police initiated action";[95] "a category of governance";[96] "the practice of making law enforcement decisions";[97] "institutional mechanism for control and repression";[98] "any action";[99] "law enforcement practices";[100] "filtering information through the lens of stereotype";[101] "identify and target";[102]

---

84 Williams, Henderson, & Harris, above note 58.

85 Wortley & Tanner, "Data, Denials," above note 8 at 369.

86 OHRC, *Paying the Price*, above note 16 at 6; ACLC, *Anti-Racial Profiling Toolkit*, above note 21 at 4; AHRC, "Racial Profiling," above note 17.

87 Tanovich, *Colour of Justice*, above note 55 at 13.

88 Janet Chan, "Racial Profiling and Police Subculture" (January 2011) 53:1 *Canadian Journal of Criminology and Criminal Justice* 75 at 75.

89 Chatten, ed, above note 62 at 2.

90 Ottawa Police Service, "Racial Profiling," above note 52.

91 NSHRC, *Working Together*, above note 18 at 24 and 109.

92 Kennedy, "Suspect Policy," above note 48 at 11.

93 Lorie Fridell et al, *Racially Biased Policing: A Principled Response* (Washington, DC: Police Executive Research Forum, 2001) at 5.

94 Ralph Ioimo et al, "The Police View of Bias-Based Policing" (September 2007) 10:3 *Police Quarterly* 270 at 271 [Ioimo et al, "Police View"].

95 Tomaskovic-Devey, Mason, & Zingraff, above note 29.

96 Carmela Murdocca, "The Racial Profile: Governing Race through Knowledge Production" (Research Note) (2004) 19:2 *Canadian Journal of Law and Society* 153 at 153–54 [Murdocca, "The Racial Profile"].

97 George E Higgins, Gennaro Vito, & William Walsh, "Searches: An Understudied Area of Racial Profiling" (2008) 6:1 *Journal of Ethnicity in Criminal Justice* 23.

98 Wilkins & Williams, "Representing Blue," above note 65 at 785.

99 OACP, *Best Practices*, above note 52 at iv and 10.

100 Karen Glover, Miguel Penalosa, & Aaron Schlarmann, "Racial Profiling and Traffic Stops: An Examination of Research Approaches and Findings in the War on Drugs" (2010) 4:8 *Sociology Compass* 605 at 605 [Glover, Penalosa, & Schlarmann].

101 Bahdi, Parsons, & Sandborn, above note 9 at 31–32.

102 Bent et al, above note 4 at 81–82.

"applies a measure in a disproportionate way to certain segments of the population."[103]

Here are specific activities included in some definitions:

- "Traffic stops";[104] "stop African American drivers";[105] "pull over Black drivers";[106] and "suspect selection."[107]
- Series of concrete actions after stops: "any action taken by a state trooper during a traffic stop . . . ";[108] "questioning Blacks";[109] "stop, question, arrest, and/or search";[110] "stop, search, cite, or arrest a person";[111] "stop, question, or search minorities";[112] "stop and interrogate citizens";[113] " . . . discretionary traffic and field interrogation stops";[114] "stopping and citing";[115] "police stop and search practices . . . customs searches . . . police patrols . . . sting operations";[116] " . . . citizens are stopped, questioned, searched, or even

---

103   Eid, Magloire, & Turenne, above note 13 at 10.

104   Harris, "Driving While Black," above note 44; Maclin, "*Terry v. Ohio*'s Legacy," above note 67; USGAO, *Motorist Stops*, above note 49; PA Langan et al, *Contacts between the Police and the Public: Findings from the 1999 National Survey* (No NCJ184957) (Washington, DC: Bureau of Justice Statistics, US Department of Justice, 2001) at 20 [Langan et al]; Batton & Kadleck, above note 35 at 31; Washington State Patrol and Criminal Justice Training Commission, *Report to the Legislature on Routine Traffic Stop Data* (Olympia, WA: Washington State Patrol and Criminal Justice Training Commission, 2001) at 1 [Washington Routine Traffic Stop Data].

105   Walker, "Denominator," above note 65 at 64.

106   Henry & Tator, "Theoretical Perspectives," above note 10 at 55–56.

107   Ottawa Police Service, "Racial Profiling," above note 52.

108   NJ State Police Review, above note 65 at 5.

109   Taylor & Whitney, "Crime and Racial Profiling," above note 47 at 507.

110   Jim Cleary, *Racial Profiling Studies in Law Enforcement: Issues and Methodology* (St Paul, MN: Minnesota House of Representatives, Research Department, 2000) at 5–6.

111   *Missouri Traffic Stops*, above note 65 at 1.

112   Christopher C Cooper, "Subjective States of Mind and Custodial Arrest: Race-based Policing" (2002) 38 *Journal of Inter-Group Relations* 3.

113   Ronald Weitzer & Steven Tuch, "Perceptions of Racial Profiling: Race, Class, and Personal Experience" (2002) 40 *Criminology* 435 at 435 [Weitzer & Tuch].

114   Robin Shepard Engel, Jennifer Calnon, & Thomas Bernard, "Theory and Racial Profiling: Shortcomings and Future Directions in Research" (June 2002) 19:2 *Justice Quarterly* 249 at 249–50 [Engel, Calnon, & Bernard].

115   Albert J Meehan & Michael C Ponder, "Race and Place: The Ecology of Racial Profiling of African American Motorists" (2002) 19 *Justice Quarterly* 399 [Meehan & Ponder].

116   Wortley & Tanner, "Data, Denials," above note 8 at 369.

arrested ... ";[117] "apprehending a suspect";[118] "behaviour ... for disproportionate suspicion, surveillance, investigation and arrest."[119]

There are a number of conceptual issues related to how generic or specific activities are included in the definitions of racial profiling. The inclusion of generic activities enables the notion of racial profiling to be broader in scope and thus includes multiple components in a process within the criminal justice system, rather than mere isolated incidents subsumed only under the specific activities included in definitions.

When racial profiling is viewed as a broad-stroke process in a system, rather than a concrete incident, law enforcement is then framed as a series of multiple strategic decision points in the context of the larger criminal justice system, as Crutchfield, Fernandes, and Martinez[120] and Tillyer and Hartley[121] have pointed out. Stopping people who are driving or walking in the street has to be placed in the larger context; differential decisions may have already been made earlier in the criminal justice system, and racial profiling in traffic stops or pedestrian stops reflects the differential attention of law enforcement officers paid to specific neighbourhoods, segments of population, criminal activities, and law enforcement activities (such as arrests, searches, charges, uses of force, detention, court appearances, convictions, and sentencing). Stops are often viewed as the gateway to other steps in the larger criminal justice system. Their significance is undeniable. However, if one can manage to analyze and appraise the pre-stop and post-stop components and the role of law enforcement officers, one may be able to get a better picture of racial disparity or discrimination, if any.

4) Formal Rationales and Justifications

"Formal rationales" are officially stated reasons for activities performed at work in social domains. These rationales are usually related to organizational mandate and mission, and are often enshrined in legislation if the organizations are in the public sector.

Most definitions of racial profile in Canadian and American literature do not mention any formal rationales for profiling activities. The

---

117 Gabor, "Inflammatory Rhetoric," above note 25 at 457.
118 Higgins, "Racial Profiling," above note 3 at 1–2.
119 Bahdi, Parsons, & Sandborn, above note 9 at 31–32.
120 Crutchfield, Fernandes, & Martinez, above note 32 at 909.
121 Tillyer & Hartley, above note 1 at 657.

Ontario Human Rights Commission[122] made formal rationales one of the key features explicitly stated in its definition of racial profiling: "any action undertaken for reasons of safety, security, or public protection." Such position was adopted by Libby Davies' Private Member's Bill C-296 in 2004, Ontario Association of Chiefs of Police,[123] the Commission des droits de la personne et des droits de la jeunesse,[124], and Nova Scotia Human Rights Commission.[125] African Canadian Legal Clinic[126] also adopted these rationales for public education purposes. The reasons for such explicitness are not clear. It seems reasonable to believe that, for law enforcement officers, the official reasons have to be the enforcement of the law, whether it is stated in the definition or not.

Furthermore, the Ontario Human Rights Commission[127] provides a condition — reasonable suspicion — in which individuals could be singled out "for greater scrutiny or different treatment." This condition is also echoed in the definition offered by the Ottawa Police Service[128] as an exceptional reason for racial profiling: "racial profiling in policing occurs . . . except when looking for a particular suspect who has committed an offence and who is identified, in part, by their race." The definition of racial profiling offered by the Ontario Association of Chiefs of Police[129] does not have such a provision.

Moreover, the Commission des droits de la personne et des droits de la jeunesse adds another condition — factual grounds — for different treatment or scrutiny. These two conditions — reasonable suspicion and factual grounds — pose a number of loopholes for differential treatment or scrutiny of racial minorities.[130]

Suspicion is often built upon layers of assumptions that may or may not be groundless, subject to the availability of evidence. Reasonable suspicion may give legitimacy to the prevalence of stereotypes of racial minorities of law enforcement officers and their official claims for safety, security, and public protection. The notion of reasonable suspicion has its inherent flexibility of defining what being *reasonable* means.

---

122 OHRC, *Paying the Price*, above note 16 at 6.
123 OACP, *Best Practices*, above note 52 at iv and 10.
124 Eid, Magloire, & Turenne, above note 13 at 10.
125 NSHRC, *Working Together*, above note 18 at 24 and 109.
126 ACLC, *Anti-Racial Profiling Toolkit*, above note 21 at 4.
127 OHRC, *Paying the Price*, above note 16 at 6.
128 Ottawa Police Service, "Racial Profiling," above note 52.
129 OACP, *Best Practices*, above note 52 at iv and 10.
130 Williams, "Obscurantism," above note 64.

Being reasonable is often subject to the interpretation of the perceived invincible authority and knowledge of those in charge of law and order by the untrained eyes of trusting citizens or authorities. It may also mean that some traditional ideas such as "out of place," "shifty eyes," "nervous body movements," and "Black proneness to confrontation" need to be re-examined as proper reasons for suspicion.

The condition of factual grounds provides legitimacy of any information labelled as factual. Some information is indeed factual with evidence that is objective, impartial, and scientific in nature. This may not always be the case. Crime mapping (a tracking tool based on crime data that can be visually displayed on maps), neighbourhood reports of police patrols, socio-economic statistics, documents on individual family histories or single parenthood households, school behaviour reports, and information on individual associations or networks of peers and adults may all be viewed as factual, but they too may be based on incorrect or subjective assumptions and conclusions (regarding the connection between criminality on one hand and race, single parenthood, poverty, and relationships on the other), inappropriate methodologies, and unsophisticated interpretation of information or data.[131] The allowance of factual grounds as a precondition for differential treatment or greater scrutiny may be a problematic loophole.

Overall, these two conditions stated in these Canadian definitions of racial profiling may give legitimacy to law enforcement officers doing the wrong thing (profiling) for the right reasons (public safety, security, or pubic protection). Using these definitions, law enforcement officers in Canada may conduct differential scrutiny or treatment of racial minorities without fully knowing the extent of factual accuracy or the reasonableness of suspicion.

Some publications in the US observed that law enforcement practices (such as traffic stops) could be used as a pretext for other law enforcement activities (such as war on drugs or guns and gangs). Cooper mentioned that law enforcement officers may practice "using skin colour as a pretext to stop, question, or search minorities."[132] The term used may be *pretext* (and not reasonable suspicion or factual grounds), but the nature of practices is similar to different treatment or scrutiny.

It is important to note that just as any other forms of human behaviour, racial profiling is likely to cover a broad range of rationales, some of which are officially approved and are viewed as legitimate: stopping drivers

---

131   Amar, above note 34 at 586; Crutchfield, Fernandes, & Martinez, above note 32 at 912.
132   Cooper, above note 112.

or scrutinizing pedestrians due to perceived traffic violations, past and current information on criminal activities in neighbourhoods, deployment strategies of police departments, performance evaluation criteria of police officers, or perceived individual behavioural anomalies. And, as long as these rationales are officially sanctioned, they could be used to legitimize the behaviour of law enforcement officers. Therefore, official or unofficial rationales for police actions do not add much to an understanding of racial profiling; they merely serve to legitimize law enforcement activities that may be based on dubious reasons or grounds.

5) Triggers

"Triggers" means galvanizing factors that initiate activities related to racial profiling. These triggers could be one incident or action, or a series of factors that galvanize law enforcement officers to act or react.

Prior to police actions (such as traffic stops), it has been speculated that law enforcement officers must depend on or react to one or more factors that trigger their actions. What are these pre-stop factors? Is race the only or major factor, or are there other factors at work? In racial profiling literature, these questions have been raised.

The literature shows that there are definitions that are silent on the triggers of racial profiling, which means that they have no position on triggers or do not see the importance of stating the issue in their definitions.[133] However, for those definitions that have a formal statement on the issue of triggers, there are three camps.

One camp believes that race is the only factor in triggering police officers to take actions (be they stops, searches, arrests, etc.); the second camp believes that race is the major factor, not the only factor; and the third camp believes that race is only one of the many factors. The second and third camp believe that there are non-racial factors that trigger police officers to initiate their actions. All camps wrestle with the issue of finding the factors that impact the decision-making process of law enforcement officers before they take their actions.

Here are some examples of definitions of racial profiling from the first camp. They view race as a sole factor for police actions:

---

133 OACP, *Best Practices*, above note 52 at iv and 10; Glover, Penalosa, & Schlarmann, above note 100 at 605; Henry & Tator, "Theoretical Perspectives," above note 10 at 55; Wortley, "Racial Profiling," above note 15.

- Racial profiling is "the tactic of stopping someone only because of the color of his or her skin."[134]
- "Racial profiling refers to allegations that police officers stop African American drivers . . . on the basis of race and not because of legitimate suspicion of any law violation."[135]
- Racial profiling is "profiling (i.e., identification of target criminals) based upon one characteristic: race. It is an attempt to identify previously undetected criminals based upon the single factor of race."[136]
- Racial profiling is "a form of racial bias whereby citizens are stopped, questioned, searched, or even arrested on the basis of their minority status per se."[137]
- Racial profiling is an "institutional mechanism for control and repression of certain populations based exclusively on race."[138]
- "Racial profiling . . . occurs when law enforcement officials base their justifications for increased scrutiny on the characteristic of race without any additional evidence to implicate the individual in wrongdoing."[139]
- Racial profiling is "based on racial or ethnic factors."[140]
- "Racial profiling is said to exist when people are stopped, questioned or searched by the police because of their racial characteristics, not because of their individual behaviour or their actions."[141]

Some exponents of the camp on racial profiling who view race as a sole factor prior to police actions often use proxies for race as references. These proxies may include "social/religions/cultural identities";[142] or "a conglomeration of physical, behavioral, and psychological components" based on race to increase the probability of apprehending a suspect.[143] These proxies may consist of stereotypes of racial groups.

---

134 Kenneth Meeks, *Driving While Black: Highways, Shopping Malls, Taxicabs, Sidewalks; How to Fight Back If You Are a Victim of Racial Profiling* (New York: Broadway Books, 2000) at 4.

135 Walker, "Denominator," above note 65 at 64.

136 Gold, "Media Hype," above note 24 at 394.

137 Thomas Gabor, "Inflammatory Rhetoric," above note 25 at 457.

138 Wilkins & Williams, "Representing Blue," above note 65 at 785.

139 Bent et al, above note 4 at 81–82.

140 Chan, above note 88 at 75.

141 Wortley & Owusu-Bempah, "The Usual Suspect," above note 14.

142 Bahdi, Parsons, & Sandborn, above note 9 at 31.

143 Higgins, "Racial Profiling," above note 3 at 1.

The exponents of the second camp view race as the major factor, among others, in triggering police actions. Here are two examples:

- "using race as a key factor in deciding whether to make a traffic stop."[144]
- "the use of race as a key factor in police decisions to stop and interrogate citizens."[145]

The exponents of the third camp view race as only one of the many factors for police actions. Race is considered no more important than other factors. Here are two examples:

- "Racial profiling occurs whenever police routinely use race as a negative signal that, along with an accumulation of other signals, causes an officer to react with suspicion."[146]
- "Under the broader definition, racial profiling occurs when a law enforcement officer uses race or ethnicity as one of several factors in deciding to stop, question, arrest, and/or search someone."[147]

One of the key debating issues on racial profiling is whether individual law enforcement officers' special attention to minority groups is based on systematic analyses of crimes and intelligence and/or race. In other words, is racial profiling a function of race only, or a combination of other factors that may include race?[148]

What are these other factors? Solid answers to these questions are not easy coming. There are studies that attempted to find out non-racial factors which trigger police actions, and these factors include physical appearance, behaviour, time and place, information, organizational policies and tactics, systemic analyses of crimes and intelligence and/or race, and others.[149] Essentially, these studies assumed that there are numerous points in the decision-making process in which law enforcement officers have to assess the situation prior to taking action, and in this process,

---

144 USGAO, *Motorist Stops*, above note 49.

145 Weitzer & Tuch, above note 113 at 435.

146 Kennedy, "Suspect Policy," above note 48 at 11.

147 Cleary, above note 110 at 5.

148 Gabor, "Inflammatory Rhetoric," above note 25 at 458.

149 Robin Engel & Jennifer Calnon, "Examining the Influence of Drivers' Characteristics during Traffic Stops with Police: Results from a National Survey" (March 2004) 21:1 *Justice Quarterly* 49; Gabor, "Inflammatory Rhetoric," above note 25 at 457; Roger Dunham et al, "Transforming Citizens into Suspects: Factors that Influence the Formation of Police Suspicion" (September 2005) 8:3 *Police Quarterly* 366; Bahdi, Parsons, & Sandborn, above note 9 at 31.

non-racial factors are considered. This is indeed a debating point in racial profiling literature. Exponents of this "other factors" camp tend to believe that non-racial factors, including police intelligence or scientific studies of crime statistics, may be at work, and that law enforcement officers are merely doing their jobs in a professional manner even though their scrutiny or treatment of racial minority groups have been different from that of White people.

While all three camps include race in their conceptualization of racial profiling, the importance of race in triggering police actions is at stake. There are two scenarios in police actions: one views police actions as individual incidents requiring only one decision-making point on the part of the law enforcement officers, and the other views police actions as a series of incidents requiring multiple decision-making points from the same officers.

If police actions are viewed as isolated incidents (such as traffic stops), the first and second camps see race as paramount because it is the only or the main factor in the period before police actions. In the third camp, race may enter in the picture as one of several factors in the period before the incident of police actions. The importance of race in police decisions is debatable for each police action.

However, if police actions are viewed as a series of actions, the first camp views race as the only factor that triggers in every single police action (whether it is a stop, a question, a search, a warning, a charge, an arrest, etc.). The severity of police actions depends solely on race. The second and third camps view race as a more fluid concept in which its importance could be limited to one type or one stage of police action. The race factor appears or disappears depending on the centrality of other non-racial factors (such as rudeness in individual behaviour, warrants on individual records in police computer systems, etc.). The non-racial factors may take priority or replace racial factors when triggering additional police actions.

The implication of this demarcation is important because when police actions are viewed as the result of a series of decision points for law enforcement officers, race as the trigger (first camp) must be present prior to each police action, otherwise racial profiling does not occur. For example, if the drivers' racial features are not observed by law enforcement officers prior to traffic stops, non-racial factors may be present to trigger the stops. These factors may be considered to be "objectively reasonable grounds for suspecting that the individual is implicated in criminal activity."[150] This example therefore offers no evidence of racial profiling. However, if upon stopping the vehicles, law enforcement officers note the racial features of the drivers, and proceed to do searches based on their stereotypes of racial minority groups or prior information on drug trafficking in the neighbourhoods, then such searches may be interpreted as the result of racial profiling while the traffic stops were not.

Conceptually, the positions of these three camps on the status of race in triggering police actions are distinct. If racial profiling is viewed as a psychological issue, clearly the decision to include or exclude the triggering factors or to side with one of the camps in this debate has to be made in defining racial profiling. If racial profiling is viewed as a structural or organizational issue, a decision on the psychological triggers may not be necessary because it is the result of police actions and their impacts on racial minorities that count.

6) Psychological Focus

"Psychological focus" refers to the centrality of the psychological processes in explaining human behaviour. The psychological processes encompass many concepts including human feelings, cognition, motivation, and intelligence.

A significant component in many definitions of racial profiling is the psychology of individual law enforcement officers behind different treatment or scrutiny that is often labelled as racial profiling. The basic premise is that the mindset of law enforcement officers is one of stereotyping racial minorities and associating them with criminality. This stereotypical view of racial minorities is often related to prejudice and negative feelings. This psychological tendency is explicitly described in some of the definitions of racial profiling in the literature:

- Stereotypes and prejudice: "racial or ethnic stereotypes";[151] "race as a negative signal";[152] "stereotypes about race, colour, ethnicity, ancestry, religion, or place of origin";[153] "practices . . . that incorporate prejudicial judgments based on sex, race, ethnicity, gender, sexual orientation, economic status, religious beliefs, or age";[154]

---

150   Tanovich, *Colour of Justice*, above note 55 at 13.
151   NJ State Police Review, above note 65 at 5.
152   Kennedy, "Suspect Policy," above note 48 at 11.
153   OHRC, *Paying the Price*, above note 16 at 6.
154   Ioimo et al, "Police View," above note 94 at 271.

"relies on stereotypes about race, colour, ethnicity, ancestry, religion or place of origin";[155] "stereotypes about offending or dangerousness";[156] "negative stereotypes."[157]

- Association with criminality: "the expectation that [Blacks] are more likely than people of other races to be criminals";[158] "a fleeting suspicion that the person is engaging in criminal behaviour";[159] "suspicion of crime based on the individual's race, ethnicity, religion or national origin";[160] "association of racial status and criminality."[161]

The fact that psychological components are included in these definitions of racial profiling means that they are important to these authors. Their inclusion suggests that without stereotyping and prejudice of law enforcement officers, there may not be racial profiling in police actions. These psychological components are considered to be the driving force behind traffic or pedestrian stops, searches, and other police actions. They constitute a conceptual linkage between law enforcement officers and racial minority group members and are viewed as a precondition for police actions. In these authors' opinions, stereotyping of and prejudice against racial minority groups must take place prior to police actions. If the police action is a traffic stop, the stereotyping and negative feelings against racial minority group members must be there prior to the traffic stop. In other words, the psychological components are pre-stop prerequisites.

One of the features of these psychological components is that they could be the driving factor in racial profiling, "consciously or unconsciously,"[162] and that the practices based on these components could be "intentional or nonintentional."[163] The Ontario Association of Chiefs of Police also acknowledges that "racial profiling can occur without conscious intent."[164] Such feature makes it difficult to prove or disprove the existence of such psychological state and, as Gold and Melchers observed,

---

155　OACP *Best Practices*, above note 52 at iv and 10.

156　Ottawa Police Service, "Racial Profiling," above note 53.

157　AHRC, "Racial Profiling," above note 17.

158　Taylor & Whitney, "Crime and Racial Profiling," above note 47 at 507.

159　Meeks, *Driving While Black*, above note 134 at 4.

160　ACLU Definition, above note 70.

161　Glover, Penalosa, & Schlarmann, above note 100 at 605.

162　Tanovich, *Colour of Justice*, above note 55; Ottawa Police Service, "Racial Profiling," above note 52.

163　Ioimo et al, "Police View," above note 94 at 271.

164　OACP, *Best Practices*, above note 52 at iv and 10.

it is also an issue that the human rights tribunals and criminal courts have to struggle with.[165]

Such conceptual linkage between psychology (e.g., stereotyping) and police actions (e.g., traffic stops) is not without its blind spots. Amar observed that social scientists have a tendency to focus on personal perception, prejudices, and other psychological attributes in explaining policing with racial overtones.[166] This may be due to the prevalent cultural ideology of individualism and the theoretical framework of psychological reductionism. Individualism emphasizes individual initiation of actions and the accountability that comes with them. Psychological reductionism reduces the explanation of a social phenomenon, such as racial profiling, to individual psychology. The blind spots are the negation of organizational and institutional factors, power relations among people, socio-legal realms, racial hierarchy, and the historical-cultural environment under which racial profiling takes place.[167]

The psychological focus also reinforces research efforts to focus on police perception and how it affects decisions on each step in police intervention. For example, this line of inquiry is reflected in Dunham et al's study of police mental process, and reinforced by Johnson and Morgan's review of studies of how police officers develop suspicions about people across countries.[168] Both studies came to the conclusion that these police officers' stereotyping of criminal offenders, their sense of "out-of-place" reliance on involuntary non-verbal cues, and their knowledge of people's criminal pasts help them to decipher the likelihood of criminality. The continuation of a psychological focus of this nature in racial profiling studies has the effect of distancing police actions from the political context in which racial profiling takes place. That political context is the denial of liberty and justice through racial repression.[169] Incidentally, this also has the effect of disregarding or marginalizing the experiential

---

165 Gold, "Media Hype," above note 24; Melchers, "Comment on the Rejoinder," above note 23.

166 Amar, above note 34 at 579.

167 Glover, Penalosa, & Schlarmann, above note 100 at 605.

168 Dunham et al, above note 149; Richard Johnson & Mark A Morgan, "Suspicion Formation among Police Officers: An International Literature Review" (2013) 26:1 *Criminal Justice Studies* 99 at 99.

169 Glover, Penalosa, & Schlarmann, above note 100 at 605; Laura Khoury, "Book Review of *Racial Profiling: Research, Racism and Resistance* by Karen Glover" (2011) 81: 2 *Sociological Inquiry* 275.

knowledge of racial minorities and their actual experiences with law enforcement agencies.[170]

However, there are also definitions of racial profiling that do not have an explicit statement on psychological components.[171] Such omission may be interpreted in at least two ways: One interpretation is that such psychological components are not explicitly needed for defining racial profiling because available research results have not demonstrated conclusively the psychological "causes" of racial profiling, and therefore its "causes" remain largely unknown. The implication is that stereotypes and prejudice are not the necessary ingredients of racial profiling, therefore it is premature to include them in its definition. Such omission seems to suggest that racial profiling is a social and collective phenomenon, not an individual and psychological incident.

Another interpretation is that non-psychological factors may be more important for *causing* racial profiling. If racial profiling is not viewed as a psychological act, there is no need to find psychological evidences (stereotyping and prejudice) among law enforcement officers. Wortley and Tanner seem to suggest that, by summarizing the concept as used in criminal literature, racial profiling is "typically defined as a racial disparity ... racial differences ... increased police patrols ... undercover activities, or sting operations."[172] All these are not necessarily psychological indicators, but they may occur as the result of non-psychological factors with racial implications. Melchers has voiced his disagreement with such non-psychological definitions because data on racial disparities have not been properly collected, measured, or computed and these data do not imply racial stereotyping, prejudice, or discrimination.[173] Such position

---

170 John Reitzel & Alex R Piquero, "Does It Exist? Studying Citizens' Attitudes of Racial Profiling" (2006) 9:2 *Police Quarterly* 161; Glover, Penalosa, & Schlarmann, above note 100 at 611.

171 Cleary, above note 110 at 5; USGAO, *Motorist Stops*, above note 49; Ramirez, McDevitt, & Farrell, above note 50 at 3; Langan et al, above note 104 at 20; Washington Routine Traffic Stop Data, above note 104; Weitzer & Tuch, above note 113 at 435; Gold, "Media Hype," above note 24 at 394; Wortley & Tanner, "Data, Denials," above note 8 at 369; Batton & Kadleck, above note 35 at 31; Murdocca, "The Racial Profile," above note 96 at 153–54; Wortley & Tanner, "Inflammatory Rhetoric," above note 8 at 584; Wilkins & Williams, "Representing Blue," above note 65 at 785; Bent et al, above note 4 at 81–82; Eid, Magloire, & Turenne, above note 13 at 10; Chan, above note 88 at 75; Wortley & Owusu-Bempah, "The Usual Suspect," above note 14 at 397; Chatten, ed, above note 62 at 2; NSHRC, *Working Together*, above note 18 at 24 and 109.

172 Wortley & Tanner, "Data, Denials," above note 8 at 369.

173 Melchers, "Comment on the Rejoinder," above note 23.

has been raised earlier in Harvey's rebuttal of the *Toronto Star*'s findings of racial profiling in the Toronto Police Service.[174]

Non-psychological factors do not focus on stereotyping or negative feelings. They may include strategies and methods of governance.[175] Wilkins and Williams echo similar perspective on racial profiling: an "institutional mechanism for control and repression of certain population based exclusively on race."[176] These mechanisms may be operationalized in how police works are done: corporate anti-violence policies, community relations programs; police deployment strategies (on drugs, guns, and gangs); geo-mapping of neighbourhoods (using a variety of indicators including race); and crime data collection and coordination across jurisdictions. All these policies, programs, strategies, and tactics are not psychological in nature, but they may offer explanations to racial profiling.

Murdocca noted that racial profiling may be viewed as an issue of governance — the manner in which racial minorities are governed and often marginalized. Governance are non-psychological factors, and they may include police leadership and organizational issues such as leadership styles and commitment, corporate culture and subcultures, performance measurement and evaluation, succession management, and police training and development.[177] These organizational issues are not psychological in nature, but they have impacts on racial profiling as suggested by Bass, Batton and Kadleck, and Satzewich and Shaffir.[178]

Ioimo et al recognized the permeation of bias-based policing (of which the most common form is racial profiling) at different organizational levels in police establishments. They noted that it is carried out by "individual officers, supervisors, managerial practices, and department programs, both internal and nonintentional."[179] Such permeation corresponds to what Melchers has observed, racial profiling has been redefined as "more than individual bias, or even as improperly tolerated individual wrongdoing in an organization, but rather as the official policy and sanctioned practice of organizations."[180]

---

174   Harvey, "An Independent Review," above note 22.

175   Glover, Penalosa, & Schlarmann, above note 100. Wilkins & Williams, "Representing Blue," above note 65 at 785.

176   *Ibid.*

177   Murdocca, "The Racial Profile," above note 96 at 153–54.

178   Sandra Bass, "Policing Space, Policing Race: Social Control Imperatives and Police Discretionary Decisions" (April 2001) 28:1 *Social Justice* 156; Batton & Kadleck, above note 35 at 31; Satzewich & Shaffir, above note 33.

179   Ioimo et al, "Police View," above note 94.

180   Melchers, "Toronto Police," above note 23 at 360.

This divergence of psychological and non-psychological (organizational and collective) views is reflected in how racial profiling has been defined. As noted, such divergence has implications on theoretical articulation, research methodology, and practical application on racial profiling issues.

7) Adverse Impacts

"Adverse impacts" denotes negative results that are harmful or disadvantageous to human beings in various aspects of their life including physical, psychological, social, and economic. This negativism often spills over from individuals to communities and is even detrimental to the larger society.

There are authors who believe that it does not matter whether race and/or other factors are used prior to taking police actions or whether law enforcement officers have stereotypes of racial minorities or racial prejudice, consciously or unconsciously. For them, the important factor in racial profiling is its adverse impacts on racial minority groups. The Ontario Association of Chiefs of Police clearly states that "racial profiling is a form of racial discrimination."[181] Other examples of definitions that explicitly highlight discrimination: "discriminatory practice by police of treating Blackness (or brownness)";[182] "discriminatory practice . . . discriminatory omissions on the part of law enforcement";[183] "discriminatory behavior."[184]

Williams also alludes to the negative impacts of racial profiling on racial minorities by reinforcing White privileges, prestige, and power while, at the same time, making it difficult for racial minorities to be employed.[185] Henry and Tator maintain strongly that adverse impact is an important component in racial profiling as it creates "inequality for certain groups."[186] Melchers and Satzewich and Shaffir disagreed.[187] At points, they even use the notion of racial profiling interchangeably with racism: "Racism/racial profiling is to be judged primarily by its consequences in

---

181　OACP, *Best Practices*, above note 52 at iv and 10.

182　Muharrar, "Media Blackface," above note 46.

183　ACLU Definition, above note 70.

184　Henry & Tator, "Theoretical Perspectives," above note 10 at 55–56.

185　Williams, "Obscurantism," above note 64.

186　Henry & Tator, "Rejoinder," above note 10 at 66.

187　Melchers, "Toronto Police," above note 23; Melchers, "Comment on the Rejoinder, " above note 23; and Vic Satzewich & William Shaffir, "Rejoinder" (2011) 53:1 *Canadian Journal of Criminology and Criminal Justice* 125 [Satzewich & Shaffir, "Rejoinder"].

creating inequality for certain groups."[188] This is in line with Miller's position that racial profiling is a part in a broader context of systemic racism in the criminal justice system.[189]

The Ontario Human Rights Commission did not include adverse impacts of racial profiling as its definition of racial profiling, but its publications on the same topic clearly illustrate the adverse impacts.[190] As examples, the Commission states in one of its documents:

> People who have been racially profiled often suffer psychological effects such as humiliation, fear, anger, frustration and helplessness, and in some cases, post-traumatic stress disorder. Racial profiling can contribute to a community's deep mistrust of police and a reluctance to cooperate, which in turn can seriously hamper a law enforcement agency's ability to carry out its mandate and ensure public safety. Also, racial profiling contributes to the over-representation of African Canadians and Aboriginal Peoples in prison.[191]

While numerous studies have documented the damaging aspects of racial profiling on racial minorities, they have not included adverse impacts as a feature in their definitions of racial profiling.[192] In fact, the issue of adverse impacts is the least mentioned feature in all the American and Canadian definitions under review.

This silence on adverse impacts reflects the centrality of the psychological focus in the definition of racial profiling. Most definitions of racial profiling pay attention to the causes (stereotyping and prejudice) of racial profiling and the types of activities resulting from these causes (e.g., traffic stops or searches), but not their adverse impacts on racial minorities.

---

188   Henry & Tator, "Rejoinder," above note 10 at 66.

189   Jerome Miller, *Search and Destroy: African American Males in the Criminal Justice System* (Cambridge: Cambridge University Press, 1996).

190   OHRC, *Paying the Price*, above note 16; OHRC, "Submission re DNA Sampling," above note 16.

191   OHRC, *Paying the Price*, above note 16.

192   Scot Wortley, "Justice for All? Race and Perceptions of Bias in the Ontario Criminal Justice System — A Toronto Survey" (October 1996) 38:4 *Canadian Journal of Criminology* 439; Reitzel & Piquero, above note 170; Tanovich, "Using the *Charter*," above note 7; OHRC, *Paying the Price*, above note 16; Alnoor Gova & Rahat Kurd, *The Impact of Racial Profiling: A MARU Society/UBC Law Faculty Study*, Working Paper Series No 08-14 (Vancouver: Metropolis British Columbia, 2008); Eid, Magloire, & Turenne, above note 13; Louise Brossard & Evelyne Pedneault, *Racial Profiling and Systemic Discrimination of Racialized Youth: Report of the Consultation on Racial Profiling and Its Consequences: One Year Later: Taking Stock* (Quebec: Commission des droits de la personne et des droits de la jeunesse, 2012).

D. OBSERVATIONS

The multiple features of the concept of racial profiling as reviewed in the literature may be summarized as follows:

TABLE 1.1   Seven Components in Definitions of Racial Profiling

COMPONENTS	FEATURES
Social domains	• Police • Law enforcement • Health care • Retail sector • Property insurance • All institutions
Grounds	• Race • Ethnicity • Colour • Ancestry • Religion • National origin • Place of origin • Aboriginality
Activities	• Generic: surveillance, treatment, and other non-specific activities • Specific: traffic stops and post-stop activities (such as question, arrest, search)
Rationales	• Safety, security, and public protection • Reasonable suspicion • Factual grounds
Triggers	• Race as the sole factor • Race as the key factor • Race as one of the factors • Non-racial factors
Psychological focus	• Psychological focus: conscious or unconscious stereotypes, prejudice, and association of race and criminality • Non-psychological focus: institutional mechanism and governance
Adverse impacts	• Discrimination • Disparate or differential treatment • Inequality

This review of the definitions of racial profiling suggests that the concept has been evolving and has branched out in a few directions. Its evolution is not in a linear progress, but more like different directions competing with each other for dominance. This may be illustrated by the branching out of the notion of racial profiling in different social domains while the domain of the policing sector remains dominant. The concept acquired various features as it evolved, which made it even more difficult to reach a consensus among those who work in this field.

Every explicitly stated definition of racial profiling has something to say about three components: social domains, grounds, and activities. They appear to be basic concepts necessary for defining racial profiling. However, these definitions often don't consider rationales, triggers, psychological focus, and adverse impacts. For some authors of definitions, these four components are optional as they are silent on one or more of them. It is observed that most current definitions do not cover the issue of adverse impacts.

Meanwhile, while there are some broad commonalities among the definitions (notably in the focus on psychology and the relative omission of adverse impacts), there are also variations among them in the ways they deal with the issue of social domains, coverage of prohibited grounds in human rights, generic and specific nature of activities, formal rationales, and triggering factors.

Such diversity in the conceptualization of racial profiling illustrates the changing nature of the concept, as it remains fluid in its form and substance. There is no consensus on what constitutes racial profiling. Current definitions still have not grasped the defining characteristics of the phenomenon. It is "a rather elusive concept that lacks clear conceptual parameters. It is a term that assumes different meanings depending on the context in which it is used."[193] The implications of this conceptual fluidity is that there is no consensus on how best to do research on racial profiling.[194] There is also no consensus on the best way to eradicate the police actions that resemble racial profiling.

As noted earlier, there are unresolved issues in each of the seven components selected for discussion. Examples of these issues may be found in the role of race in triggering police actions, the broadness or specificity of activities, and the psychological or non-psychological ways of viewing racial profiling.

These unresolved issues are not disappearing anytime soon and the definition of racial profiling is therefore expected to be fluid for the near future. Three factors seemed to contribute to the lack of consensus on

---

193 Batton & Kadleck, above note 35.

194 *Ibid.*

what racial profiling is and how it works: (1) lack of common theoretical grounds, (2) inconclusive empirical evidence, and (3) competing values.

1) Lack of Common Theoretical Grounds

There is not a lack of efforts in explaining police actions loosely labelled as racial profiling, but not much progress has been made in articulating comprehensive frameworks. There were several academic attempts in understanding racial disparities (which some social scientists still maintain are not indications of racial profiling): legalistic, criminological, normative, and economic. Each perspective has its own views on focus, burden of law enforcement, individual behaviour, analytical techniques, and interpretations of findings. All four have their strengths and weaknesses when these perspectives are used to determine whether police officers make decisions based on citizens' race, but a common ground in utilizing all four perspectives is still missing.[195]

Another way to look at the situation of theoretical articulation is to check out the focus of social scientists in theorizing racial profiling from their levels of analysis. Four analytical levels have been noted — behavioural, community, organizational, and systemic — and they are usually conducted separately and not in concert with each other.

- Behavioural level: police actions as a behavioural pattern emerging from socialization heavy on negative stereotyping of racial minorities;[196] police actions as a psychological reaction to perceived racial threat.[197]
- Organizational level: This level of analysis focuses on the organizational aspects of the police establishments (such as their internal

---

195 Robin Engel, "A Critique of the 'Outcome Test' in Racial Profiling Research" (2008) 25:1 *Justice Quarterly* 1.

196 Michael R Smith & Geoffrey P Alpert, "Explaining Police Bias: A Theory of Social Conditioning and Illusory Correlation (2007) 34 *Criminal Justice and Behavior* 1262; Rob Tillyer, *Social Conditioning of Police Officers: Exploring the Interactive Effects of Driver Demographics on Traffic Stop Outcomes* (PhD dissertation, University of Cincinnati, 2008) [unpublished].

197 Hubert Blalock, *Toward a Theory of Minority-Group Relations* (New York: Capricorn Books, 1967); Allen E Liska, *Social Threat and Social Control* (Albany, NY: State University of New York Press, 1992).

policies, police deployment strategies, performance management models, institutional and senior management perspectives).[198]

- Community level: police actions as a translation into actions out of a suspicion of racial minorities seen not in the right place at the right time;[199] police actions based on the notion of criminal proneness in social disorganized communities;[200] police actions arising from race and urban disadvantaged environment;[201] and neighbourhood collective efficacy.[202]

- Systemic level: This level of analysis focuses on the criminal justice system (such as conflicting values and norms of authorities and citizens).[203]

It has been observed that most theoretical works are done at the behavioural and community levels, and less so at the organizational and systemic levels. This may be driven by research activities or the theoretical foci have been driving the research studies. In spite of the advancement, there are still a lot of disagreements on the strengths of these theories. Without a common paradigm for understanding and explaining police actions that could be loosely labelled as racial profiling, the concept of racial profiling therefore remains quite elusive.

2) Inconclusive Empirical Evidence

Many studies done in racial profiling are quantitative research that focuses on aggregating data on traffic stops. Most of these data show that racial minorities have been disproportionately stopped by police officers; however, some studies show otherwise. In the US, there are still debates

---

198 Engel, Calnon, & Bernard, above note 114 at 265–67; Tomaskovic-Devey, Mason, & Zingraff, above note 29.

199 Meehan & Ponder, above note 115.

200 Clifford R Shaw & Henry D McKay, *Juvenile Delinquency and Urban Areas* (Chicago: University of Chicago Press, 1942); Robert J Bursik, "Social Disorganization and Theories of Crime and Delinquency: Problems and Prospect" (1988) 26 *Criminology* 519.

201 William J Wilson, *The Truly Disadvantaged: The Inner City, the Underclass, and Public Policy* (Chicago: University of Chicago Press, 1987); William J Wilson, *When Work Disappears: The World of the New Urban Poor* (New York: Knopf, 1996).

202 Robert J Sampson, Jeffrey D Morenoff, & Felton Earls, "Spatial Dynamics of Collective Efficacy for Children" (1999) 64 *American Sociological Review* 633; Robert J Sampson, Stephen W Raudenbush, & Felton Earls, "Neighborhoods and Violent Crime: A Multi-Level Study of Collective Efficacy" (1997) 277 *Science* 918.

203 Engel, Calnon, & Bernard, above note 114 at 267–69.

on the soundness of research methodologies used in these studies, especially in the areas of research techniques (including sampling) and benchmarking. Some maintained that these studies were merely counting heads with no grounding in theoretical frameworks and therefore were unable to provide meaningful data or demonstrate the linkages between racial prejudice and police actions.[204]

The opponents of studies in racial disparities in traffic stops have a tendency to believe that the psychological focus is the central component of racial profiling. In their minds, without demonstrating that there is a racial bias among police officers, even the most robust data on racial disparities in traffic stops would not demonstrate racial profiling. Such mindset precludes the possibility of understanding racial profiling as a structural phenomenon and reduces racial profiling to a manifestation of individual biases that may result in police actions such as traffic stops. Meanwhile, the proponents of studies in racial disparities believe that racial profiling could be viewed in aggregate form, and that disproportionate data of police officers stopping racial minorities is a strong indication of their racial biases, whether they are conscious of it or not.

These two camps will continue to debate on the validity and usefulness of empirical evidence on racial disparities as long as both of them have different perspectives on psychological reductionism. In order to reconcile these two camps, the proponents of studies in racial disparities may need to conduct additional research on the psychology of individual police officers from which the data on racial disparities are derived; and the opponents may need to view the data in racial disparities as an aggregation of the behavioural skewness among police officers.

3) Competing Values

In spite of the lack of a consensus in interpreting data, American empirical data has been increasingly pointed to the direction of racial disparity in traffic stops, which many social scientists view as a proxy for racial profiling. At least in the US, the debate is now more focused on how extensive racial profiling is, and not on whether racial profiling exists or not. Meanwhile, in Canada, the debate is still centred around whether racial profiling actually exists or not.

It appears that the current discord on theoretical approaches or the meanings of empirical evidence is linked with the lack of alignment between

---

204 Karen S Glover, "Police Discourse on Racial Profiling" (2007) 23 *Journal of Contemporary Criminal Justice* 239; Engel, Calnon, & Bernard, above note 114.

two competing values: *law and order* and *democracy and freedom*. Usually these two themes are compatible with each other, except in this case.

The proponents of law and order tend to view this ideological theme as higher in priority than democracy and freedom. They believe that when police officers safeguard law and order, the long-term survival of democracy and freedom of the society and some short-term democratic rights and freedoms may need to be sacrificed. Being stopped by the police and having individuals' personal information gathered may be one of the sacrifices. According to this view, in enforcing law and order, the police officers are merely doing their jobs in traffic or pedestrian stops. Meanwhile, the proponents of democracy and freedom believe that people's democratic rights and freedoms are being withheld when police stop them without valid reasons or, worse still, on the basis of their race. This ideological theme is often echoed in racial minority communities (such as the African Canadian Legal Clinic) and civil liberties associations (such as the BC Civil Liberties Association).

These two ideological themes appear to underline the discord on the issue of racial profiling. Among social scientists in Canada, the debates on the issue of racial profiling based on the *Toronto Star*'s research findings in 2003–5[205] and those debates published in the *Canadian Journal of Criminology and Criminal Justice* in 2009–11,[206] while focused largely on conceptual issues and research methodologies, nevertheless embody the ideological clashes of the two schools of thoughts — one in defence of police actions (for their impartial and professional performance in enforcing law and order), the other in defence of racial minority communities (for their victimization and eroded democratic rights and freedom).

It is in this context that the lack of clarity and consensus on the definition of racial profiling is understood. Currently, definitions are constructed not out of a coherent theoretical framework or unquestionable research findings. Instead, they have been developed largely based on individual perception, public consultation, and research studies.

One of the unresolved issues is whether or not law enforcement officers have the stereotypical view of associating racial minorities with criminality and if their perception of racial minorities triggers their

---

205 Gold, "Media Hype," above note 24; Gabor, "Inflammatory Rhetoric," above note 25; Harvey, "An Independent Review," above note 22; Melchers "Toronto Police," above note 23; Wortley & Tanner, "Inflammatory Rhetoric," above note 8.

206 Chan, above note 88; Henry & Tator, "Rejoinder," above note 10; Melchers, "Comment on the Rejoinder," above note 23; Satzewich & Shaffir, above note 33; Satzewich & Shaffir, "Rejoinder," above note 187.

actions. This issue tends to create a divergence of opinions on racial profiling. When police actions are assessed on the basis of whether they have an element of racial stereotyping and race triggering, those actions without such psychological focus are not viewed as racial profiling. What further complicates this unresolved issue is the notion that stereotyping and race triggering could be "conscious or unconscious" or "intentional or unintentional." Such state of mind at the spur of the moment in some police actions, such as traffic stops, would be difficult to prove or disprove conclusively. At this stage of scientific inquiry, this issue may not be resolvable any time soon.

However, if the definition of racial profiling shifts its focus from individual psychology (that is, stereotyping and race trigger) to collective structure (that is, group and organization impacts), police actions (surveillance, traffic stops, searches, etc.) could now be conceptualized as organizational and systemic structures and processes that may have impacts on racial minorities. Such change in the focus in defining racial profiling would certainly open doors to newer ways to do research and theoretical articulation on racial profiling and move away from the historical fixation on trying to prove or disprove the psychological makeup of law enforcement officers prior to, during, or even post traffic or pedestrian stops. Data from research studies in counting heads, which had been collected in the US for the last few decades, could remain relevant, whether they demonstrate racial disparity or not. Racial disparity could now be viewed as an indicator of racial profiling, not because of its potential psychological roots in stereotypes, prejudice, and mental association of race and criminality among police officers, but because of its organizational and systemic roots.

This paper has reviewed many explicitly stated definitions of racial profiling in Canadian and American research studies in the last twenty-five years. The ways that definitions have been expressed give people the impression that racial profiling is a known phenomenon, where in fact, it is a yet-to-be-defined notion. Its accuracy and clarity in reflecting the real world could only be enhanced through more advanced research, theoretical articulation, and a rethink of competing values. For the time being, racial profiling could be defined and customized based on the best of our knowledge in this field and what we plan to do with the definition, whether it is for legislative changes, policy and program development, change management, or educational or training application.

CHAPTER 2

The Human Rights Approach to Addressing Racial Profiling

The Activity of the Ontario Human Rights Commission

SHAHEEN AZMI[*]

A. SUMMARY

In 2015 the Ontario Human Rights Commission (OHRC) embarked on a new round of activity in response to ongoing concerns of racial profiling. This activity came in the shadow of more than a decade of activity aimed at curbing and preventing racial profiling and growing recognition of new shapes and forms of racial profiling in multiple sectors and settings.

B. BACKGROUND TO CURRENT POLICY DEVELOPMENT

The Ontario Human Rights Commission employed multiple approaches in responding to racial profiling since 2002. Racial profiling has long been understood as a type of racism but its framing as a type of illegal discrimination in violation of human rights legislation was not significantly developed in Canada prior to the OHRC's work.

In 2002 a series of articles by the *Toronto Star* on race and policing in Toronto provided fresh evidence of the reality of racial bias in police activity by the Toronto Police Service.[1] In direct response to the controversy raised by *Toronto Star* articles, the OHRC announced that it would conduct an inquiry into the effects of racial profiling. Racial profiling was defined for the purposes of the inquiry as "any action undertaken for

---

[*] Shaheen Azmi is the director of policy, education, monitoring, and outreach at the Ontario Human Rights Commission.

[1] Jim Rankin et al, "Singled Out; *Star* Analysis of Police Crime Data Shows Justice Is Different for Blacks and Whites" *Toronto Star* (19 October 2002), online: www.thestar.com/news/gta/knowntopolice/2002/10/19/singled-out.html.

reasons of safety, security or public protection that relies on stereotypes about race, colour, ethnicity, ancestry, religion, or place of origin rather than on reasonable suspicion, to single out an individual for greater scrutiny or different treatment."[2]

The definition clearly frames racial profiling as a type of racial discrimination, which notably is not restricted to policing but to any context in which "safety, security, or public protection" is operative. The purpose of the inquiry was to "raise public awareness about racial profiling, to mobilize public action, to put an end to it and to bridge the divide between those who deny the existence of racial profiling on the one hand, and the communities who have long held that they are targets of racial profiling on the other."[3]

Although the immediate response from most police and political leaders was hostile, the OHRC Inquiry Report, titled *Paying the Price: The Human Cost of Racial Profiling*,[4] contributed to opening the door to a broad discussion that was previously limited in Ontario and in Canada more broadly. In the Inquiry Report, the OHRC committed to hold anyone engaging in racial profiling accountable in accordance with the Ontario *Human Rights Code.* Towards this end the OHRC committed itself to develop a new public policy on racial discrimination and to engage in activity to further this discussion and acceptance of racial profiling as a concern for police.

Following upon its commitment in the racial profiling Inquiry Report, the OHRC released its *Policy and Guidelines on Racism and Racial Discrimination* in 2005.[5] The Policy provided clearer guidance on the nature of racism as a feeder to racial discrimination and detailed different types of racial discrimination including racial profiling. It reiterated the definition of racial profiling first developed in the OHRC's inquiry activity. The Policy also identified an onus to collect race-based data where there is reason to believe that racial discrimination may be present. It argued that detecting some forms of racial discrimination including racial profiling may only be confirmed through collecting race-based data. The emphasis on data collection was in significant part related to calls

---

2   Ontario Human Rights Commission, *Paying the Price: The Human Cost of Racial Profiling: Inquiry Report* (Toronto: OHRC, 2003) at 6 [Inquiry Report].

3   *Ibid* at 67.

4   *Ibid.*

5   Ontario Human Rights Commission, *Policy and Guidelines on Racism and Racial Discrimination* (9 June 2005) at 4 [Policy], online: www.ohrc.on.ca/en/policy-and-guidelines-racism-and-racial-discrimination.

from racialized community groups for police to collect stop data based on race in order to identify and address racial profiling. To support the Policy's call for race-based data collection and provide concrete guidance on how to do this, the OHRC later developed and released in 2009 its guidebook *Count Me In: Collecting Human Rights-Based Data.*[6]

The OHRC's efforts to address racial profiling also included litigation that aimed at clarifying and promoting the legal interpretation of racial profiling. The OHRC's litigation activity contributed to several significant settlements and decisions that advanced the legal understanding of racial profiling and police activity in response to it.[7]

In the context of litigation activity, the most significant public interest remedy obtained by the OHRC was a human rights complaint settlement of a case alleging racial profiling with the Ottawa Police Service in May 2012 that required the collection of race-related police traffic stop data by the Ottawa Police Service for a two-year period. This data collection represented the first multi-year police stop data collection initiative undertaken by a Canadian police service to monitor for concerns of racial profiling.[8]

The OHRC has also been involved in several organizational development and training initiatives in the policing sector, which have included a focus on human rights and racial profiling. In this regard, notable partnerships have been undertaken with the Ontario Police College, the Toronto Police Service, and Windsor Police Service.

C. NEW ROUND OF RESEARCH AND CONSULTATION

Despite the many years of OHRC activity, concerns of racial profiling continue to be prevalent in Ontario. In the policing context concerns of racial profiling in street checks or the related practice of carding arose as

---

6   Ontario Human Rights Commission, *Count Me In: Collecting Human Rights-Based Data* (Toronto: OHRC, 2009), online: www.ohrc.on.ca/en/count-me-collecting-human-rights-based-data.

7   See, for example, *Nassiah v Peel (Regional Municipality) Police Services Board*, 2007 HRTO 14; *Phipps v Toronto Police Services Board*, 2009 HRTO 877; *Maynard v Toronto Police Services Board*, 2012 HRTO 1220.

8   Lorne Foster, Lesley Jacobs, & Bobby Siu, *Race Data and Traffic Stops in Ottawa, 2013–2015: A Report on Ottawa and the Police Districts*, Report for Ottawa Police Services Board (OPSB) and Ottawa Police Service (OPS) (October 2016), online: www.ottawapolice.ca/en/about-us/resources/.TSRDCP_York_Research_Report.pdf.

a major new area of concern over the last few years.[9] This development highlighted the contention that racial profiling in police work extends to many realms beyond the customary focus on traffic stop activity. Beyond police street checks there is concern that racial profiling is likely a factor in all areas of policing activity including surveillance, searches, arrests, charges, and data retention.

In response to these ongoing concerns, in 2015 the OHRC embarked on a new round of consultation and research on current experiences of racial profiling. The OHRC consulted with people and organizations representing diverse experiences including affected people from Indigenous, racialized, and Muslim communities; legal and academic researchers; educators; human rights practitioners; and police, among others. It conducted a caselaw review and an online survey, analyzed applications that alleged racial profiling made to the Human Rights Tribunal of Ontario, convened a policy dialogue conference focused on racial profiling, conducted focus groups with Indigenous peoples, and received written submissions. Overall, almost 1,650 individuals and organizations told the OHRC about their experiences or reactions relating to racial profiling in Ontario.

Following this work, in April 2017, the OHRC released *Under Suspicion: Research and Consultation Report on Racial Profiling in Ontario.*[10] This report reaffirmed the widespread experience of Indigenous and racialized peoples of being subjected to unwarranted surveillance, investigation, and other forms of scrutiny, punitive actions, and heavy-handed treatment.

Echoing the inquiry findings of 2003, this report reaffirmed that racial profiling causes considerable harm to individuals, families, and the social fabric of communities.[11] Members of affected communities stated that dealing with experiences of racial profiling and other forms of racial discrimination is exhausting because of its pervasiveness. Racial profiling is associated with negative effects, including effects on individuals' mental and physical health. It contributes to barriers that prevent Indigenous and racialized peoples from being able to achieve equal opportunity. Significantly, racial profiling — and the perception of racial profiling — severe-

---

9   Jim Rankin et al, "As Criticism Piles Up, So Do the Police Cards" *Toronto Star* (27 February 2013), online: www.thestar.com/news/gta/knowntopolice2013/2013/09/27/as_criticism_piles_up_so_do_the_police_cards.html.

10 Ontario Human Rights Commission, *Under Suspicion: Research and Consultation Report on Racial Profiling in Ontario* (April 2017), online: www.ohrc.on.ca/sites/default/files/Under%20suspicion_research%20and%20consultation%20report%20on%20racial%20profiling%20in%20Ontario_2017.pdf [OHRC, *Under Suspicion*].

11 *Ibid* at 80.

ly diminishes people's sense of trust in public institutions. This eroded trust undermines the effectiveness and authority of these institutions.

The report uncovered features of racial profiling not commonly recognized. It highlighted that racial profiling is not restricted only to law enforcement but finds manifestation in a wide array of other sectors like retail services, child welfare, education, transportation, heath, customs and border control, and national security.[12] For example, the report refers to the decision in the case of the *Peel Law Association v Pieters*, which highlights a situation where an African Canadian lawyer was aggressively scrutinized as he entered into a law association library.[13] The court's decision in this case shows that racial profiling can be a form of everyday racism. It is a phenomenon that is widespread in our society and has many faces.

The report highlighted that people may experience unique forms of racial profiling in specific contexts, depending on the sector where it takes place and stereotypes related to identities. People may be exposed to unique forms of racial profiling based on specific identities or intersections of identities. For example, common stereotypes of young Black men relate to heightened experiences of profiling in police stops, stereotypes of Indigenous people manifest unique experiences of profiling in health care, and stereotypes of Muslims connect to unique experiences of profiling in transportation and national security activity.

The report also highlighted that racial profiling is not only the result of biased officials but often can be traced to systemic elements of organizations such as institutional policies, practices, assessment tools, and decision-making processes.[14] This kind of systemic racial profiling is often unconsciously normalized as the proper way to do things. For example, police responses to violent crime have commonly been responded to by expanded traffic police deployment in racialized neighbourhoods, which has led to significantly disproportionate police stopping and ticketing of racialized people.

Also highlighted was the *pipeline effect* where a first incident of racial profiling may contribute to further instances of racial profiling by another institution or individual. An example is racial profiling that takes place in schools, which leads to child welfare and/or police involvement that compounds the initial impact of profiling.[15]

---

12   *Ibid* at 30.
13   *Peel Law Association v Pieters*, 2013 ONCA 396.
14   OHRC, *Under Suspicion*, above note 10 at 92.
15   *Ibid* at 22.

D. ALARMING PUBLIC ATTITUDES ON RACIAL PROFILING

OHRC polling of public opinion has demonstrated that shockingly large segments of Ontario's population support racial profiling activity by law enforcement. As part of a wider polling on human rights awareness and attitudes towards groups conducted in 2017, attitudes towards racial profiling were gauged.[16]

When asked about police profiling of specific groups, just under six in ten respondents or more (depending on the group) feel police profiling is never or rarely justified. However, around four in ten think it is at least sometimes justified for police to profile or target certain groups: Muslims, Arab people, Black/African Canadians, and South Asians. When asked about police profiling in general, two-thirds (65 percent) of respondents agree to some extent that police must treat everyone equally regardless of group identity, but one-third (35 percent) lean towards allowing police to profile communities that supposedly commit more crime.

When asked about specific groups, fully 45 percent of Ontario's population believes that it is sometimes (35 percent) or always (9 percent) acceptable for police to profile Muslims; 42 percent believe it is sometimes (35 percent) or always (7 percent) acceptable to profile Arabs; 40 percent believe it is sometimes (34 percent) or always (6 percent) acceptable to profile Black people; 39 percent believe it is sometimes (33 percent) or always (6 percent) acceptable to profile South Asians; and 37 percent believe it is sometimes (32 percent) or always (5 percent) acceptable to profile Indigenous people.

E. NEXT STEPS

The OHRC's latest work has demonstrated both that racial profiling continues to be widespread and that an alarmingly large segment of the population actually supports it as a practice to further safety and security. In this context the OHRC plans to continue activities to create better awareness of the manifestations of racial profiling; the fact that it is discriminatory, illegal, and counterproductive; and that it has a severe impact on the lives of many in the groups affected and on the fabric of society at large.

---

16   Ontario Human Rights Commission, *Taking the Pulse: People's Opinions on Human Rights in Ontario* (December 2017) at 25, online: www.ohrc.on.ca/sites/default/files/ Taking%20the%20pulse_Peoples%20opinions%20on%20human%20rights%20in%20 Ontario_accessible_2017_0.pdf.

The OHRC plans to develop specific policy guidance in sectors in which racial profiling is particularly evident to help individuals, community groups, and organizations understand how racial profiling can be recognized, prevented, and addressed. This policy guidance will review the definition of racial profiling to ensure that it is current and vital and will delineate manifestations of racial profiling in policing and law enforcement, child welfare, and court and correctional services. It will work with First Nations, Metis, and Inuit peoples to better understand Indigenous experience of racism and work towards the development of resources and tools to address Indigenous peoples' experience of racial discrimination including racial profiling. Where appropriate, the OHRC will continue to call for data collection to identify racial disproportionalities, launch public interest inquiries, intervene in cases and/or launch commission-initiated applications to the Human Rights Tribunal of Ontario to actively challenge cases of alleged racial profiling. Lastly, it will continue to work with community stakeholders to enhance public education on racial profiling.

CHAPTER 3

Interrogating the Definition of Racial Profiling

A Critical Legal Analysis

SUNIL GURMUKH[*][1]

A. INTRODUCTION

The Human Rights Tribunal of Ontario (HRTO) rarely determines whether an individual was a victim of "racial profiling." Instead, it focuses more broadly on whether there was racial discrimination.[2] Nonetheless, the definition of racial profiling matters. Clearly identifying the boundaries of a specific type of discrimination allows for the development of effective solutions. And there is no doubt that effective solutions to racial profiling are needed. It has a profound negative impact on Indigenous peoples, African Canadians, and other racialized groups.[3]

People who feel that they have been the victims of racial profiling often feel humiliated, frightened, frustrated, anxious, and helpless. As

---

[*]   Sunil Gurmukh is a lawyer at the Ontario Human Rights Commission.

[1]   This paper, prepared by a member of the staff of the Ontario Human Rights Commission, has not been formally approved by the commissioners. It is therefore not an official commission publication.

[2]   For a summary of significant legal developments in racial profiling jurisprudence in the ten years prior to February 2016 that may have an impact on, or be relevant to, interpreting and applying the *Human Rights Code*, see Sunil Gurmukh, "A Review of Racial Profiling Jurisprudence" (2017) 14:1 *Canadian Diversity* 9, online: Ontario Human Rights Commission www.ohrc.on.ca/sites/default/files/Racial%20Profiling%20and%20 Human%20Rights_Canadian%20Diversity.pdf.

[3]   *Peart v Peel Regional Police Services*, 2006 CanLII 37566 at para 93 (Ont CA) [*Peart*]; *McKay v Toronto Police Services Board*, 2011 HRTO 499 [*McKay*]; Ontario Human Rights Commission, *Paying the Price: The Human Cost of Racial Profiling* (2003), online: www. ohrc.on.ca/sites/default/files/attachments/Paying_the_price%3A_The_human_cost_of_ racial_profiling.pdf [*Paying the Price*].

the Ontario Human Rights Commission (OHRC) noted in its inquiry report *Paying the Price: The Human Cost of Racial Profiling*:[4]

> It is impossible to quantify the cost to these individuals, their families and friends, their communities and society overall of these psychological effects. Nevertheless it is clear that the emotional and psychological damage inflicted by profiling is significant and we as a society cannot afford to ignore it.

Racial profiling in policing is particularly destructive. It contributes to the overrepresentation of Indigenous peoples and African Canadians in the criminal justice system.[5] It also undermines effective policing,[6] the functioning of the justice system, and public safety by engendering mistrust in police. Frayed community relationships with police, fuelled by racial profiling, reduce the likelihood of civilians reporting crime, cooperating with police investigations, and providing evidence in court.[7]

This paper applies a critical legal analysis to definitions of racial profiling. In doing so, it considers many principles and developments in the caselaw that are relevant to interpreting and applying the Ontario *Human Rights Code*[8] and its defacto prohibition on racial profiling, including how:

- Racial profiling may be the product of stereotypes other than those about criminality and unlawful conduct;

---

4   *Paying the Price, ibid* at 47.

5   *McKay*, above note 3 at para 104; Scot Wortley & Akwasi Owusu-Bempah, "Crime and Justice: The Experiences of Black Canadians" in Barbara Perry, ed, *Diversity, Crime and Justice in Canada* (Don Mills, ON: Oxford University Press, 2011) 127.

6   *Peart*, above note 3 at para 93.

7   Chris Gibson et al, "The Impact of Traffic Stops on Calling the Police for Help" (2010) 21:2 *Criminal Justice Policy Review* 139; Lee Ann Slocum et al, "Neighbourhood Structural Characteristics, Individual-Level Attitudes, and Youths' Crime Reporting Intentions" (2010) 48:4 *Criminology* 1063; Tom Tyler & Jeffrey Fagan, "Legitimacy and Cooperation: Why Do People Help the Police Fight Crime in Their Communities?" (2008) 6 *Ohio State Journal of Criminal Law* 231.

8   RSO 1990, c H.19. The *Code* does not define racial profiling. The right to be free from racial profiling is captured, in effect, through the *Code*'s prohibition of racial discrimination in social areas. In *Nassiah v Peel (Regional Municipality) Police Services Board*, 2007 HRTO 14 at para 112 [*Nassiah*], the HRTO stated:

> Racial profiling is a form of racial discrimination. There is nothing novel in finding that racial profiling is contrary to the *Human Rights Code* and nothing turns on how it is defined. It is and always has been contrary to the *Code* for the police to treat persons differently in any aspect of the police process, because of their race, even if race is only one factor in the differential treatment.

- Proof of stereotyping is not required to establish discrimination;
- Racial profiling is a systemic problem in policing; and
- Racial profiling is not limited to the law enforcement context.

B. DEFINITIONS OF RACIAL PROFILING

The OHRC is considering modifying its definition of racial profiling in its forthcoming policy.[9] It currently defines racial profiling as:[10]

> Any action undertaken for reasons of safety, security or public protection that relies on stereotypes about race, colour, ethnicity, ancestry, religion or place of origin rather than on reasonable suspicion, to single out an individual for greater scrutiny or different treatment.

In *Québec (Commission des droits de la personne et des droits de la jeunesse) v Bombardier Inc (Bombardier Aerospace Training Center)*, the Supreme Court of Canada cited the OHRC's definition of racial profiling and quoted from a broader definition advanced by the Québec Commission des droits de la personne et des droits de la jeunesse:

> Racial profiling is *any action taken by one or more people in authority* with respect to a person or group of persons, *for reasons of safety, security or public order*, that is based on actual or presumed membership in a group defined by race, colour, ethnic or national origin or religion, without factual grounds or reasonable suspicion, that results in the person or group being exposed to differential treatment or scrutiny.
>
> Racial profiling includes any action by a person in a situation of authority who applies a measure in a disproportionate way to certain segments of the population on the basis, in particular, of their racial, ethnic, national or religious background, whether actual or presumed.[11]

The Court of Appeal for Ontario highlighted a narrower definition of racial profiling in its earlier decision of *R v Richards*. The definition was submitted by the African Canadian Legal Clinic (ACLC):[12]

9   Ontario Human Rights Commission, *Under Suspicion: Research and Consultation Report on Racial Profiling in Ontario* (2017) at 110, online: www.ohrc.on.ca/en/under-suspicion-research-and-consultation-report-racial-profiling-ontario.

10   Ontario Human Rights Commission, *Policy and Guidelines on Racism and Racial Discrimination* (2005) at 19, online: www.ohrc.on.ca/sites/default/files/attachments/Policy_and_guidelines_on_racism_and_racial_discrimination.pdf.

11   2015 SCC 39 at para 33 [*Bombardier*] [emphasis in original].

12   1999 CanLII 1602 at para 24 (Ont CA). See also *R v Brown*, 2003 CanLII 52142 at para 7 (Ont CA) [*Brown*].

Racial or colour profiling refers to that phenomenon whereby certain criminal activity is attributed to an identified group in society on the basis of race or colour resulting in the targeting of individual members of that group. In this context, race is illegitimately used as a proxy for the criminality or general criminal propensity of an entire racial group.

In *Peart v Peel Regional Police Services Board*, the Court of Appeal cited the ACLC's definition of racial profiling from *Richards* and added the following:[13]

A police officer who uses race (consciously or subconsciously) as an indicator of potential unlawful conduct based not on any personalized suspicion, but on negative stereotyping that attributes propensity for unlawful conduct to individuals because of race is engaged in racial profiling.

All three definitions delineate racially discriminatory conduct in the context of law enforcement or safety and security more broadly. This context is important and is assumed in this article when discussing racial profiling.

C.   RACIAL PROFILING MAY BE THE PRODUCT OF STEREOTYPES OTHER THAN THOSE ABOUT CRIMINALITY

It is trite law that racial discrimination is often the product of unconscious stereotypes.[14] While the OHRC's definition of racial profiling centres on actions that rely on racial stereotypes, the definition quoted by the Court of Appeal is narrower; it centres on assumptions about criminality and unlawful conduct. A review of jurisprudence reveals, however, that racial profiling may be the product of stereotypes about Indigenous peoples and African Canadians other than those about criminality and unlawful conduct.

1)   Stereotypes About Indigenous Peoples

McKay v Toronto Police Services Board is a racial profiling case involving an Indigenous man, Garry McKay. Mr McKay and his friend were stopped in

---

13   *Peart*, above note 3 at paras 89–90.

14   *Shaw v Phipps*, 2010 ONSC 3884 at paras 76–78 (Div Ct) [*Shaw* Div Ct], aff'd 2012 ONCA 155 at para 34 [*Shaw* CA]; *Peel Law Association v Pieters*, 2013 ONCA 396 at paras 111–15 [*Pieters*]; *R v Parks*, 1993 CanLII 3383 at para 54 (Ont CA) [*Parks*]; *Peart*, above note 3 at para 93; *R v RDS*, 1997 CanLII 324 at para 46 (SCC); *R v Spence*, 2005 SCC 71 at paras 31–33; *Briggs v Durham Regional Police Services*, 2015 HRTO 1712 at para 283.

a laneway in Little Italy in Toronto at around 4:30 a.m. by Officer Fitkin. There were concerns about break and enters in the area. At the time, Mr McKay and his friend were delivering flyers. The HRTO accepted that the decision to follow Mr McKay and his friend into the laneway, ask for identification, and conduct a records check were not discriminatory. However, the HRTO found that Officer Fitkin's decisions to pursue further investigation and arrest Mr McKay were discriminatory. They were tainted by his Indigenous ancestry.[15]

The HRTO's decision highlighted testimony from Mr McKay's expert, Jonathan Rudin, that over-policing of Indigenous peoples perpetuates negative police attitudes about them as "dysfunctional, dangerous and prone to criminal behaviour."[16] Mr Rudin also pointed to research from the Cariboo Inquiry that indicated that negative attitudes cause police to discount the veracity of explanations given by Indigenous people and adopt an "arrest first" approach. The respondents argued that the HRTO should not consider the specific stereotype of "lack of credibility" because they claimed that the expert did not testify on this point. However, the HRTO stated that even if Mr Rudin did not testify on the issue, the Supreme Court has accepted lack of credibility as a common stereotype applied to Indigenous peoples in *R v Williams*.[17] The Supreme Court observed that "[r]acism against aboriginals includes stereotypes that relate to credibility, worthiness and criminal propensity."[18] The Supreme Court quoted from stereotypes documented by the Canadian Bar Association in a report from 1988:[19]

> Put at its baldest, there is an equation of being drunk, Indian and in prison. Like many stereotypes, this one has a dark underside. It reflects a view of native people as uncivilized and without a coherent social or moral order. The stereotype prevents us from seeing native people as equals.

The British Columbia Human Rights Tribunal (BCHRT) highlighted various stereotypes affecting Indigenous peoples that may lead to racial profiling in the seminal case of *Radek v Henderson Development (Canada) Ltd (No 3)*.[20] The BCHRT found that Gladys Radek was discriminated against because of her Indigenous ancestry and disability. She was rudely

---

15 *McKay*, above note 3.

16 *Ibid* at para 103.

17 1998 CanLII 782 (SCC).

18 *Ibid* at para 58.

19 *Ibid*.

20 2005 BCHRT 302 [*Radek*].

questioned and followed when she entered the mall to get a cup of coffee. When she objected, she was told that she had to leave. When she refused to leave, more security officers arrived. She was repeatedly told to leave the mall and prevented from going to Starbucks.

The complainant's expert, Dr Bruce Miller, identified many stereotypes, including the following, which the BCHRT found to be of substantial assistance:

- Indigenous peoples are backwards-looking and stand in the way of social progress;
- Indigenous peoples are non-productive and live by donation/welfare, ungratefully taking more than their share of society's resources — the "deadbeat" image;
- All Indigenous peoples drink and are alcoholics — the "drunken Indian" image;
- Indigenous peoples are violent and prone to petty crime;
- Indigenous peoples are lazy and will not work or keep a steady job;
- Indigenous peoples are unhealthy and have a fatalistic disinclination to do anything about their health and other problems;
- Indigenous peoples are poor and live in a permanent under-class;
- Urban Indigenous peoples are decultured or disorganized; and
- Urban Indigenous peoples are degraded drug and alcohol abusers and sex trade workers (an image reinforced by publicity about the murder of many women from the Downtown Eastside, many of whom were Indigenous).[21]

2) Stereotypes About African Canadians

In *Sinclair v London (City)*,[22] Dr Frances Henry testified about stereotypes about Black men, emphasizing their sexuality, strength, and alleged propensity for violence or other criminal activity, which lead to racial profiling by various institutions in society, including media, schools, and employers. The HRTO accepted that racialization affects Black men through stereotypes of them as physically violent and more likely to be criminal, which may lead to heightened monitoring and racial stereotyping.

In *Nassiah v Peel Police Services Board*, the HRTO accepted Dr Scot Wortley's testimony that one of the potential causes of racial profiling is unconscious stereotyping. The HRTO held that Officer Elkington dis-

---

21   *Ibid* at para 135.

22   2008 HRTO 48 at paras 16 & 17.

criminated against Jacqueline Nassiah, a Black woman, by, among other things, threatening to take her downtown and subjecting her to an intensive, suspicious investigation for shoplifting because of her race. One of the factors that led the HRTO to conclude that the officer racially discriminated against Ms Nassiah was that the officer stereotypically assumed that a Black suspect may not speak English well. The officer's first question to store security was whether Ms Nassiah spoke English. She felt humiliated.[23]

The out-of-place phenomenon is a common stereotype that affects African Canadians in the context of racial profiling. For example, the possession of a luxury car or presence in a wealthy neighbourhood[24] are factors that can lead to racial profiling of African Canadians.

D. PROOF OF STEREOTYPING IS NOT REQUIRED TO ESTABLISH DISCRIMINATION

Discrimination analysis suggests that the Court of Appeal and OHRC's definitions of racial profiling are under-inclusive, unless they are applied in light of established human rights principles. This is because, unlike the Québec Commission's definition, the Court of Appeal and OHRC's definitions require action that relies on stereotypes. Proof of stereotyping is not required to establish discrimination.

In *Quebec (Attorney General) v A*, the Supreme Court of Canada held that "[s]tereotyping, like prejudice, is a disadvantaging attitude, but one that attributes characteristics to members of a group regardless of their actual capacities."[25] Requiring proof of stereotyping to establish discrimination "improperly focuses attention on whether a discriminatory attitude exists, not a discriminatory impact, contrary to *Andrews, Kapp and Withler* . . . . [I]t is the discriminatory *conduct* that s. 15 [the equality guarantee of the *Charter of Rights and Freedoms*] seeks to prevent, not the underlying attitude or motive . . . . [P]rejudice and stereotyping are neither separate elements of the *Andrews* test, nor categories into which a

---

23 *Nassiah*, above note 8 at paras 9, 129, and 166.

24 *Johnson v Halifax (Regional Municipality) Police Service*, [2003] NSHRBID No 2 at paras 11–43; *R v Khan*, 2004 CanLII 66305 at para 68 (Ont SCJ); *Brown*, above note 12 at paras 42–49; *Phipps v Toronto Police Services Board*, 2009 HRTO 877 at para 21; *Shaw* Div Ct, above note 14.

25 *Quebec (Attorney General) v A*, 2013 SCC 5 at para 326.

claim of discrimination must fit."[26] Similarly, in *Bombardier*, the Supreme Court reiterated that intent is not required to establish discrimination.[27]

The Office of the Independent Police Review Director's (OIPRD) systemic review into the Ontario Provincial Police's (OPP) practices for DNA canvasses[28] illustrates the danger of insisting on proof of stereotyping to establish racial profiling.

The systemic review followed a complaint filed by Justicia for Migrant Workers with the OIPRD. The complaint alleged that the OPP engaged in racial profiling when requesting DNA samples from approximately 100 Indo- and Afro-Caribbean male migrant workers near Vienna, Ontario, as part of a sexual assault investigation in October and November 2013.[29]

The OIPRD's findings demonstrate that there was racial discrimination.[30] First, the migrant workers identify with many race-related *Code* grounds, including race, colour, ancestry, place of origin, citizenship, and ethnic origin.[31] Second, the migrant workers experienced harm. The report states that the "workers were treated as potential persons of interest and asked to provide their DNA to authorities"; "the nature and scope of the DNA canvassing could reasonably be expected to have an impact on the migrant workers' sense of vulnerability, lack of security and fairness"; and that the sweep could "send the wrong message to others in the local community about how migrant workers, as a group, should be regarded."[32] Third, the OIPRD found that race was a factor in determining the scope of the DNA sweep. The report states:[33]

> The DNA canvass in this case was designed to obtain DNA from every migrant worker of colour . . . though a number of them could have easily been

---

26   *Ibid* at paras 327–29.

27   *Bombardier*, above note 11 at paras 40, 41, and 49; see also *Shaw* Div Ct, above note 14 at para 76; *Pieters*, above note 14 at para 60.

28   Office of the Independent Police Review Director, "Casting the Net: A Review of Ontario Provincial Police Practices for DNA Canvasses" (2016), online: www.oiprd.on.ca/EN/PDFs/OIPRD_Casting_The_Net_Systemic_Review_Report.pdf ["Casting the Net"].

29   *Ibid* at 1–4 and 22–23.

30   A discrimination analysis involves: (1) assessing whether a person experienced harm based on a protected ground (a *prima facie* case of discrimination); and if so, (2) whether a non-discriminatory justification can be provided. If no credible, non-discriminatory justification for the actions can be established, discrimination is made out; See *Shaw* CA, above note 14 at para 14; *Pieters*, above note 14 at paras 53–61; *Bombardier*, above note 11 at para 49; *Moore v British Columbia (Education)*, 2012 SCC 61 at para 33.

31   "Casting the Net," above note 28 at 15–17 and 50.

32   *Ibid* at 4–6.

33   *Ibid* at 54.

excluded based on the obvious and wide disparity between their features and the perpetrator's features, as described by the victim. Indeed, the evidence reveals that, in a number of instances, investigators reflected at the time that workers who were requested to provide DNA samples did not match the victim's description and raised no concerns as a result. . . .

I am also satisfied that a large number of migrant workers were unnecessarily asked to provide DNA samples and, as a result, a large number of DNA samples were unnecessarily taken.

Fourth and finally, the OPP was unable to provide a non-discriminatory explanation for its overbroad sweep:[34]

Investigators maintained that the breadth of DNA canvassing was appropriate since the perpetrator left items (shoelaces and a strip of clothing) at the crime scene . . . . In my view, this rationale did not provide sufficient justification for the decision to seek DNA samples from every local migrant worker of colour, regardless of his physical characteristics.

Despite the foregoing, the OIPRD did not find that there was racial profiling. Although the OIPRD adopted the OHRC's definition of racial profiling, it was applied narrowly, outside the context of human rights principles. The OIPRD's conclusion that there was no racial profiling seemed to rest predominantly on whether the OPP intended to discriminate, rather than on how the OPP's actions affected the migrant workers:[35]

I am satisfied that, in the particular circumstances of this case, the overly broad DNA canvassing was not based on stereotypical assumptions about migrant workers or persons of colour (and as such, did not amount to racial profiling) . . . .

All of the available information led the police, correctly in my view, to focus their investigation on the local migrant worker community. The description given by the victim of the perpetrator's skin colour and accent, her residence's proximity to orchards and bunkhouses where the migrant workers worked and lived, the nature of the typical traffic on the road, and the generally homogeneous population of Bayham all strongly pointed to the perpetrator as one of the black migrant workers who lived near the victim's house. This inference did not depend on any stereotypical assumptions or preconceptions about criminality and men of colour.

---

34   *Ibid* at 5.
35   *Ibid* at 5 and 50–51.

E. RACIAL PROFILING IS A SYSTEMIC PROBLEM IN POLICING

Stereotyping reflects another limitation of the Court of Appeal and OHRC's definitions. Racial profiling is a systemic problem in policing. However, certain institutional policies, procedures, and practices that contribute to systemic racial profiling in policing may not be the product (or sole product) of stereotypes. Again, this suggests that the Court of Appeal and OHRC's definitions of racial profiling are under-inclusive.

The HRTO and courts have repeatedly recognized that racial profiling is a systemic problem in policing.

In *Nassiah*, the HRTO stated:[36]

> What is new (in the last two decades) is the mounting evidence that this form of racial discrimination is not the result of isolated acts of individual "bad apples" but part of a systemic bias in many police forces. What is also new is the increasing acceptance by the Courts in Canada that racial profiling by police occurs in Canada and the willingness to scrutinize seemingly "neutral" police behaviour to assess whether it falls within the phenomenon of racial profiling . . . . Overall, the social science evidence establishes that statistically, racial minorities, particularly Black persons, are subject to a higher level of suspicion by police because of race, often coupled with other factors.

In *Peart*, the Court of Appeal for Ontario held that:

> The community at large and the courts, in particular, have come, some would say belatedly, to recognize that racism operates in the criminal justice system . . . . With this recognition has come an acceptance by the courts that racial profiling occurs and is a day-to-day reality in the lives of those minorities affected by it.[37]

Similarly, two years ago, the United Nations Working Group of Experts on People of African Descent stated that there is "clear evidence that racial profiling is endemic in the strategies and practices used by law enforcement" in Canada.[38]

The police deployment model is a theory of racial profiling that considers systemic or organizational factors rather than individual factors.

---

36 *Nassiah*, above note 8 at paras 113 and 126.

37 *Peart*, above note 3 at para 94.

38 United Nations Human Rights Office of the High Commissioner, News Release, "Canada: UN Expert Panel Warns of Systemic Anti-Black Racism in the Criminal Justice System" (21 October 2016), online: www.ohchr.org/EN/NewsEvents/Pages/DisplayNews.aspx?NewsID=20736&LangID=E.

According to the police deployment model, racial profiling is not necessarily the result of conscious or unconscious stereotyping. It is the result of where the police are deployed and how the police exercise their authority across different communities.[39] It combines greater police presence with more aggressive or proactive policing in minority neighbourhoods.[40]

The overrepresentation of African Canadians in Toronto Police Service (TPS) charges for marijuana possession recently examined by the *Toronto Star* puts the theory in context. The overrepresentation is consistent with systemic racial profiling[41] and may be at least partially explained by the police deployment model. It may not be the result (or sole result) of stereotyping and, thus, is an example that implies that the Court of Appeal and OHRC's definitions of racial profiling are under-inclusive.

The *Toronto Star* examined TPS marijuana charge and arrest data from 2003 to late 2013. There were 40,634 charges (34,646 arrests) for marijuana possession (possession of no more than 30 grams and possession for the purpose of trafficking) involving 27,635 individuals. Of all marijuana possession charges, 33.8 and 43.9 percent were against people with Black skin and White skin respectively. However, according to data

---

39   Donald Tomaskovic-Devey et al, "Looking for the Driving While Black Phenomena: Conceptualizing Racial Bias Processes and Their Associated Distributions" (2004) 7:1 *Police Quarterly* 3 at 19–20.

40   Research suggests that police officers are not deployed evenly across communities. Modern policing practices allocate a disproportionate share of police attention to crime "hot spots" or areas with higher than average levels of crime. Research demonstrates that recent immigrants and certain racial minorities are overrepresented in economically disadvantaged, high-crime communities, while Whites are overrepresented in low-crime communities. Research also suggests that the style of policing may vary across communities. Several studies have documented, for example, that policing seems to be more proactive or aggressive in areas with higher crime, and more reactive and less aggressive in areas with lower crime. *Ibid*; Jose Torres, "Race/Ethnicity and Stop and Frisk: Past, Present and Future" (2015) 9:11 *Sociology Compass* 931.

41   Researchers have long argued that Black overrepresentation in drug offences is "completely consistent with the racial-profiling hypothesis." Drs Wortley and Tanner stated:

Experts maintain, for example, that drug offences are often discovered by the police when they engage in racially biased stop-and-search tactics. This argument is supported by survey research that consistently reveals that although blacks are overrepresented in drug arrests, whites actually have higher rates of illegal drug use.

Scot Wortley & Julian Tanner, "Data, Denials and Confusion: The Racial Profiling Debate in Toronto" (2003) 45:3 *Canadian Journal of Criminology and Criminal Justice* 367 at 380–81; see also US Department of Justice, Civil Rights Division, *Investigation of the Baltimore City Police Department* (2016) at 55 and 58–61, online: www.justice.gov/opa/file/883366/download.

from the 2006 census, African Canadians made up only 8.4 percent of the population in Toronto while Whites made up 53.1 percent. Thus, African Canadians were 4 times more likely to be charged with marijuana possession than their representation in the population and 4.8 times more likely to be charged with marijuana possession than Whites. This was despite the fact that White and Black Toronto high school students who reported using cannabis in the 2015 Ontario Student Drug Use Survey conducted by the Centre for Addiction and Mental Health did so at rates resembling their proportion in the population.[42]

Where TPS officers were deployed and how they exercised their authority across different communities may explain at least some of the racial disproportionality.

First, the *Star* reported that neighbourhoods with the fewest marijuana charges were typically "whiter and wealthier." The TPS laid only 111 marijuana possession charges in patrol zone 325, the lowest number in a patrol zone. The north Toronto area includes "Hoggs Hollow, home to multimillion-dollar homes, and the Rosedale Golf Club. Nearly 80 per cent of the people who live there are white." In patrol zone 121, however, there were 550 charges for pot possession, the second highest in a patrol zone.[43] Zone 121 is "a pocket of the Weston–Mt. Dennis neighbourhood that has, proportionately, the largest Black population in the city at 27 per cent."[44]

Second, the high incidence of marijuana charges in the city's economically disadvantaged, more diverse neighbourhoods did not occur in iso-

---

42   Jim Rankin & Sandro Contenta, "Toronto Marijuana Arrests Reveal 'Startling' Racial Divide" *Toronto Star* (6 July 2017), online: www.thestar.com/news/insight/2017/07/06/toronto-marijuana-arrests-reveal-startling-racial-divide.html [Marijuana Arrests in Toronto]; "Preliminary Findings – Toronto Star Analysis of TPS Marijuana Data (2003–2013)" *Toronto Star*, (2017), online: www.scribd.com/document/353026454/Preliminary-findings-Toronto-Star-analysis.

43   Marijuana Arrests in Toronto, above note 42; it should be noted that the patrol zone data on where the arrests took place is missing for more than a quarter of charges laid (12,807 of 40,634).

44   In 2012, the *Toronto Star* reported that Weston–Mt Dennis was the poorest of the city's thirteen "priority" neighbourhoods. That same year, former chief of the TPS, Bill Blair, stated that there were twenty homicides since 2005 within the old boundaries of zone 121, the highest of all the city's seventy-two patrol zones. Jim Rankin & Patty Winsa, "Known to Police: Violent Crime in Weston–Mt. Dennis is Down, Youth Feel Harassed by Toronto Police" *Toronto Star* (9 March 2012), online: www.thestar.com/news/insight/2012/03/09/known_to_police_violent_crime_in_westonmt_dennis_is_down_youth_feel_harassed_by_toronto_police_1.html.

lation. They overlapped with high levels of carding,[45] which is associated with arbitrary detentions, unreasonable questioning, requests for identification, intimidation, searches, and aggression.[46]

Indeed, the relevance of the police deployment model in explaining the racial disparity in TPS marijuana charges is reflected in comments made by Daniel Brown, a Toronto-based criminal defence lawyer; Kofi Hope, executive director of the CEE Centre for Young Black Professionals; and even former chief of the TPS, Bill Blair.

> BROWN: "They didn't go into the parks of Forest Hill to shake down the rich white kids. They spent their time in the parks and community centres of the Jane and Finch corridor, and it was like shooting fish in a barrel."[47]

> HOPE: "There is not the same interest of police in controlling young people in Rosedale or Forest Hill."[48]

> BLAIR: "I think there's a recognition that the current enforcement disproportionately impacts poor neighbourhoods and racialized communities, and there's something unjust about that."[49]

F. RACIAL PROFILING IS NOT LIMITED TO THE LAW ENFORCEMENT CONTEXT

Another reason the OHRC's definition of racial profiling may be perceived as under-inclusive is because it relies solely on "reasonable suspicion" to exclude conduct.[50] Reasonable suspicion is a legal threshold[51] that is used

---

45 Marijuana Arrests in Toronto, above note 42.

46 Ontario Human Rights Commission, "Submission of the OHRC to the Ministry of Community Safety and Correctional Services on Street Checks" (2015), online: www. ohrc.on.ca/en/ohrc-submission-ministry-community-safety-and-correctional-services-street-checks-0; Deputation of the Canadian Civil Liberties Association to the Toronto Police Services Board (21 March 2012); Deputation of the Law Union of Ontario to the Toronto Police Services Board (23 January 2013).

47 Marijuana Arrests in Toronto, above note 42.

48 *Ibid.*

49 *Ibid.* See also Shannon Proudfoot, "Bill Blair: The Former Top Cop in Charge of Canada's Pot File" *Maclean's* (29 September 2016), online: www.macleans.ca/politics/bill-blair-a-former-top-cop-in-charge-of-canadas-marijuana-file/.

50 Despite the use of reasonable suspicion in the OHRC's definition, the OHRC recognizes that racial profiling is not limited to the law enforcement context. See *Paying the Price*, above note 3 at 6 & 7.

51 In *R v Kang-Brown*, 2008 SCC 18 at para 75, Binnie J defined reasonable suspicion as follows:

to justify certain actions in law enforcement, such as investigative deten-tions.[52] However, the caselaw suggests that racial profiling is not limited to the law enforcement context; it is a form of everyday racism.[53] It can occur, for example, in a law association lounge, school discipline, an investigation by a children's aid society, employment, an assessment of health and safe-ty risks associated with accommodating creed, and while shopping.

The Québec Commission's definition is broader than the OHRC's in this respect; it uses reasonable suspicion and factual grounds to exclude conduct. Although, as discussed earlier, the Court of Appeal's definition centres on assumptions about criminality and unlawful conduct, it too is broader than the OHRC's. Rather than using reasonable suspicion to ex-clude conduct, it relies on race being used "illegitimately" to include conduct.

1)   Entry into a Law Association Lounge

Peel Law Association v Pieters involved the treatment of two Black lawyers, Selwyn Pieters and Brian Noble, by a librarian in the Peel Law Association lounge in May of 2008. Only lawyers, articling students, and students of law were permitted in the lounge. The facts were consistent with racial profiling. The HRTO found that Mr Pieters and Mr Noble's race and col-our were factors in the librarian's questioning of them because, among other things:

> The "reasonable suspicion" standard is not a new juridical standard called into exis-tence for the purposes of this case. "Suspicion" is an expectation that the targeted individual is possibly engaged in some criminal activity. A "reasonable" suspicion means something more than a mere suspicion and something less than a belief based upon reasonable and probable grounds.

Justice Binnie's definition of reasonable suspicion was subsequently quoted by the Su-preme Court in *R v Chehil*, 2013 SCC 49 at paras 26 & 27 [*Chehil*]. The Court also stated the following about the relationship between profiling and reasonable suspicion (at para 38):

> In my view, it is unhelpful to speak of profiling as generating reasonable suspicion. The term itself suggests an assessment based on stereotyping and discriminatory factors, which have no place in the reasonable suspicion analysis.

52   *Chehil, ibid* at paras 23 & 24.

53   Of course, an absence or lack of caselaw in specific sectors, such as child welfare, does not mean that racial profiling cannot and does not occur therein. See, for example, Québec Commission des droits de la personne et des droits de la jeunesse, *Racial Profiling and Systemic Discrimination of Racialized Youth: Report of the Consultation on Racial Pro-filing and Its Consequences* (2011), online: www.cdpdj.qc.ca/publications/Profiling_final_ EN.pdf.

- The librarian interrupted her planned trip to the robing room to stop and question them;
- She approached them in an aggressive and challenging manner and asked them to produce identification. The librarian did not identify herself and interrupted Mr Pieters on the phone. No one else in the lounge was questioned and asked for identification; and
- The librarian falsely claimed that the reason she singled them out for questioning was because she knew everyone else in the lounge. There were two other people in the lounge who had never been there before and whom she did not know. One was not a lawyer.

Reversing a Divisional Court ruling, the Court of Appeal found that the HRTO was reasonable in concluding that the claimants were discriminated against because of race and colour in the lounge.[54]

The Divisional Court took issue with the HRTO's resort to previous tribunal decisions that involved racial profiling by police officers, including *Nassiah*. The Divisional Court stated that "there is a significant difference between what occurred here and a police investigation."[55] The Court of Appeal held that the Divisional Court should have deferred to the HRTO's greater expertise in assessing whether the difference between what occurred to the lawyers and a police investigation was so significant that *Nassiah* was unhelpful.[56]

The OHRC intervened in the case and argued that racial stereotyping will usually be the result of subtle, unconscious beliefs, biases, and prejudices, and is not limited to the law enforcement context. The Court of Appeal accepted this as a "sociological fact" and held that the proposition that "implicit stereotyping can affect the manner in which individuals continue to deal with others after an encounter begins does not seem . . . to be a matter that would provoke much controversy."[57]

2) Shopping

The HRTO found that Mary McCarthy, a Black woman who was represented by the Human Rights Legal Support Centre, was subjected to racial profiling by an employee of a Shoppers Drug Mart franchise in *McCarthy*

---

54 *Pieters*, above note 14 at para 128.

55 *Ibid* at para 109.

56 *Ibid* at para 122.

57 *Ibid* at para 123.

v Kenny Tan Pharmacy Inc.[58] The HRTO held that race was a factor in her being rudely approached, accused of trying to shoplift, having her backpack searched, and not being apologized to. Evidence that supported the inference that racial profiling occurred included the following:[59]

- The employee did not see the applicant put a store product in her bag, but strongly believed that she had done so, which was completely illogical. She was unable to offer a reasonable explanation for this strong belief;

- The employee was rude to the applicant from the outset of her interaction with her by not identifying or introducing herself to the applicant, speaking to her in an elevated voice, and demanding that she open her backpack;

- The employee's action in directly confronting the applicant and searching her backpack inside the store was contrary to the respondent store and Shoppers Drug Mart's policy on dealing with suspected shoplifting;

- Despite having been employed by the respondent store for almost five years, and having had to deal with shoplifting incidents during most of her shifts, the employee was unable to provide a single example where she directly confronted and searched the bag of a non-Black individual inside the store;

- After discovering that there was no store product in the applicant's backpack, the employee continued to be rude to the applicant by not apologizing to her. She was unable to offer a reasonable explanation why she did not apologize, and her behaviour was contrary to how she normally behaves, which is to be polite;

- The employee lied when she testified that the incident occurred shortly after midnight when the respondent store was closed; and

- The employee tried to evade the applicant's allegation of racial profiling and discrimination by falsely testifying that she did not notice that the applicant was Black when she first saw and spoke to her in the respondent store.

---

58 2015 HRTO 1303 at para 97.

59 *Ibid* at para 90; see also *Radek*, above note 20, which is another example of racial profiling while shopping.

G. SCHOOL DISCIPLINE[60]

Although there does not appear to have been a successful application at the HRTO that is consistent with racial profiling in school discipline, the testimony of the applicant's expert and the resulting non-binding recommendation of the HRTO in *BC v Durham Catholic District School Board* raised serious concerns about the phenomenon at the school board.[61]

BC was one of the first cases of alleged disproportionate imposition of discipline on racialized students that was addressed by the HRTO. The applicant, BC, a Black woman, alleged that she was discriminated against with respect to services because of race by the Durham Catholic District School Board (DCDSB), the Durham Regional Police Services Board, and a police officer. The events giving rise to the applications stem from an incident in 2008 when the applicant was a sixteen-year-old high school student at All Saints Catholic Secondary School (ACSS) and was alleged to have slapped and bullied another female student. BC was suspended for three days and was also arrested for assault. The criminal charges were withdrawn. The applicant alleged that race was a factor in the decisions to suspend and arrest, the manner in which she was removed from school, and in relation to certain comments alleged to have been made to her.[62]

The applications were dismissed. The HRTO's decision ultimately turned on its assessment of the credibility of the applicant and her

---

60   *JB v Toronto District School Board*, 2011 HRTO 1985, is another example of two unsuccessful applications that alleged racial profiling in school discipline. Two Black students alleged that the principal and school board engaged in racial profiling following an alleged verbal and physical altercation. Three decisions were at issue: the decisions to telephone police; to deny the students permission to call a parent or guardian, contrary to settlement of a prior complaint; and to suspend the students for five days. According to the HRTO, there was no evidence that the decision making was informed by the applicants' race. Staff acted in accordance with the Safe School Policy in calling police in response to the victim's complaint and request. The decision to call police was not based on a prohibited ground, but on the victim alleging serious assault causing bodily harm and threats of further menacing harm. There was no evidence that school staff had knowledge of the settlement agreement requiring that parents be contacted. The police may not have complied with their own parent-contact protocols, but it was apparent that school staff followed policy. There was no apparent discrimination in the imposition of discipline; the applicants were less involved than others, but they were implicated in the attempted intimidation. Discipline was well within the range of penalties under the Safe School Policy.

61   2014 HRTO 42 [*BC Final Decision*].

62   *Ibid* at paras 1–6.

witnesses.[63] The HRTO accepted that the school board and police officer provided non-discriminatory explanations to support their decisions to suspend and arrest that were credible on all the evidence.[64]

Dr David Osher was called by the applicant as an expert witness to testify about "disparities that result from the application of school discipline policies, particularly as they affect members of racialized groups."[65] He testified that the approach taken to student discipline under the Ontario *Education Act* and the school's student discipline policy were consistent with zero tolerance, which focuses on punitive and reactive approaches and includes policies that are discretionary. Based on his research in the US, Dr Osher testified that zero tolerance student discipline policies have increased the rate of suspension and expulsion for all students, but even more so for Black students. Because race-based student data is not collected in Canada, studies in Canada and Ontario are often qualitative and anecdotal rather than quantitative. Nonetheless, Dr Osher testified that what is reported in Canadian and Ontario studies is "very consistent" with US research. In doing so, he made reference to racial stereotyping and unconscious bias, including the assumption that Black students belong to street gangs.[66]

In an interim decision, the HRTO ordered the respondent school board to disclose the identities (redacted only to initials), yearbook photos, length of suspension, and other documentation for all students at the school who were disciplined for fighting and/or bullying in the 2007–08 school year. The HRTO also ordered disclosure of the school yearbook

---

63   The HRTO had significant problems accepting their evidence due to, among other things, diverging accounts, changes in testimony, inconsistencies, contradictions by other witnesses, and video evidence. The HRTO preferred and accepted the evidence of the respondents' witnesses.

64   The HRTO found that the school board provided a legitimate, non-discriminatory explanation to support the suspension decision that was credible on all the evidence. It concluded that the decision to suspend the applicant was made by the vice principal on the basis of the initial statement by the victim that she had been slapped hard by the applicant, the confirmation by two other students and the applicant's own acknowledgement that the applicant had slapped the victim, and all of the surrounding circumstances reviewed by the HRTO that discount that this was just a "play fight." Moreover, the HRTO found that by the time the officer took the victim's statement, she had formed reasonable and probable grounds to charge the applicant with assault, which constituted a rational, non-discriminatory explanation for the arrest that was credible on all the evidence (see paras 233, 234, 240–42, and 247).

65   *Ibid* at paras 162 and 191.

66   *Ibid* at paras 164, 166–69, 170, and 173.

for that year in its entirety.[67] Dr Osher found that one out of every 127.6 White students in the total school population was disciplined for fighting and/or bullying while one out of every 16.5 Black students was disciplined for the same offence. This meant that Black students were 7.7 times more likely to be disciplined for fighting and/or bullying in the 2007–08 school year. Dr Osher noted that this was a "huge disparity," which far exceeded the racial disparities that have been documented in other studies.[68]

The HRTO described the racial disparity as "so glaring as to cry out for further investigation and review" by the respondent school board. In the HRTO's view, it may point to an anomaly or "a deeper problem that needs to be identified and addressed." Thus, HRTO issued a non-binding recommendation to the school board to conduct a review, similar to Dr Osher's, that encompasses the three most recent school years and all offences for which students were suspended or expelled.[69] If the review resulted in a statistically significant disparity in suspension or expulsion rates between Black or racialized students and White students, then the HRTO recommended that the DCDSB "retain the services of an individual with expertise in anti-racism in the educational context to conduct further research to identify the causes of any such disparity, which may include interviews with affected students and school administrators, a review of how student discipline policies are being applied at the school, and an examination of the circumstances supporting the imposition of discipline in individual situations."[70]

H. ACCOMMODATION OF CREED IN SCHOOLS

Multani v Commission scolaire Marguerite-Bourgeoys[71] illustrates how racial profiling can occur when assessing health and safety risks associated with accommodating creed. A school board prohibited a Sikh student from wearing a kirpan because the board claimed, among other things, that the kirpan is a "symbol of violence" and that it sends the message that using force is the way to assert rights and resolve conflict. The Supreme Court of Canada found that the board's claim was contradicted by the evidence of the symbolic nature of the kirpan, was disrespectful to believers

---

67 *BC v Durham Catholic District School Board*, 2011 HRTO 2062.

68 *BC Final Decision*, above note 61 at paras 187 & 188.

69 *Ibid* at paras 251–53 and 255.

70 *Ibid* at para 254.

71 2006 SCC 6. A kirpan, a religious object, is a stylized representation of a sword (resembling a dagger) worn by Sikh men.

in the Sikh religion, and did not take into account Canadian values based on multiculturalism. Ultimately, the Supreme Court concluded that the risk of the student using the kirpan for violent purposes was low and prohibiting it violated the student's religious rights.[72]

I. CHILD WELFARE

There appear to be no decisions of the HRTO establishing that there was racial discrimination in an investigation conducted by a children's aid society. However, racial discrimination was considered by the Child and Family Services Review Board (CFSRB) in *DB v Children's Aid Society of Oxford County and Family and Children's Services of Guelph and Wellington County,*[73] albeit in an indirect manner given the mandate of the CFSRB. The CFSRB assessed, among other things, whether the applicant's rights under the *Child and Family Services Act*[74] to be heard and given reasons were respected by the Children's Aid Society of Oxford County (Oxford Society). In doing so, the CFSRB was mindful of *Code* principles and values and principles that apply to claims of racial discrimination.[75]

The applicant, an African Canadian woman, was concerned that racism was behind the investigations of the Oxford Society. The parties were advised by the CFSRB that it would apply the *Code* in its determination of whether the applicant was heard and/or provided with reasons for decisions under section 68.1 of the *CFSA*, but it did not have the same functions as the HRTO. The CFSRB stated that evidence of discrimination could be evidence that the applicant was not heard or given reasons. The CFSRB cited the Court of Appeal's decisions in *Parks* and *Pieters* when highlighting the subtle and pervasive nature of racial discrimination, in particular anti-Black racism. According to the CFSRB, prejudices can influence all stages of the investigative process.[76]

The applicant and her husband had been foster parents for several years. They had two daughters, aged sixteen and eight, and three foster children, a boy, aged nine, a girl, aged thirteen, and a boy aged seventeen. The youngest boy in foster care had many behavioural difficulties and the girl in foster care displayed several concerning behaviours. A worker

---

72   *Ibid* at para 71.

73   2013 CFSRB 41.

74   RSO 1990, c C.11 [*CFSA*].

75   Above note 73. It should be noted that employees from the Oxford Society did not testify in the proceeding.

76   *Ibid* at paras 7 and 28–33.

from the Oxford Society (the Oxford Worker) was assigned to the girl in foster care. The role entailed regular visits to the foster home.[77]

The facts were consistent with racial profiling. On one visit to the applicant's home, the Oxford Worker told the applicant that she was not familiar with Black people and that she had not seen Black people until she started watching MuchMusic. The Oxford Worker was then alleged to have said words to the effect of "your house is three times bigger than mine and I work." The CFSRB found that these comments engaged stereotypes about African Canadians as low-income individuals and as individuals who belong in the music industry. They reflected the historical disadvantage of African Canadians and suggested that "Black people have a certain place in society, in comparison to the place by the 'dominant' white society represented by the worker who 'works.'"[78]

The Oxford Worker subsequently initiated an investigation of the applicant's home, which focused on the applicant's children as assaulting the foster children. There was an allegation that the applicant and her husband egged on their children to beat the foster children. The applicant testified that she was advised by the female foster child and her mother that the Oxford Worker told the female foster child to make up the allegations. The Oxford's Worker's investigation scrutinized the condition of the applicant's home (no pillows, food locked away) and directly targeted her children as alleged perpetrators. The investigation resulted in the two youngest foster children being removed from the applicant's home.[79]

The CFSRB found that the Oxford Worker's conduct, including the racial comments, was evidence of her not having heard the applicant when making decisions about how to approach the information she received from her visit to the home and from the female foster child. The CFSRB determined that "[a]s a worker in a position of power, the Oxford Worker, in the context of her perceptions about African Canadians, shut the Applicant out of the decision-making process and made no attempts to communicate with her about the decision to investigate the condition of the home." Given her ongoing role with the applicant, it would have been appropriate for the Oxford Worker to hear the applicant before deciding to investigate locked food and pillows in the home since the youngest foster child was known to have issues with food and damaging property.[80]

---

77   *Ibid* at paras 12 and 35.
78   *Ibid* at para 37.
79   *Ibid* at paras 38 and 40.
80   *Ibid* at para 42.

An investigating officer from Oxford subsequently visited the applicant's home after conducting interviews with the removed foster children. The investigating officer was demeaning and rude towards the applicant, failed to engage with the applicant other than to make the rude comments, and did not ask the applicant clarifying questions. The CFSRB found that the investigating officer "spoke of her power over the applicant, who is an African Canadian: in effect, the power to put her in her place by removing her own children." As a result, the CFSRB concluded that the applicant was not heard or provided with reasons by the Oxford Society.[81]

J. EMPLOYMENT

Adams v Knoll North America Corp is an employment case that is consistent with racial profiling. The applicant, Colin Adams, was loud and rude during a dispute with his supervisor at work. The employer suspended Mr Adams for three days and required him to attend anger management counselling as a condition of his continued employment. Mr Adams accepted the suspension but denied that he had a problem with anger management and refused to agree to seek counselling. The HRTO found that the requirement that Mr Adams receive anger management counselling was influenced by the stereotype that Black men have a propensity towards violence and that the employer had discriminated against the applicant based on race.[82]

The employer brought an application for judicial review challenging the HRTO's decision. The Divisional Court determined that the HRTO's finding that Mr Adam's conduct was not in and of itself indicative of a propensity to violence was not irrational, especially since it was the first time that he had ever displayed such behaviour in his almost nine years of service. Furthermore, the decision to refer an employee to anger management counselling was highly discretionary, one that the employer rarely exercised. As a result, the HRTO was entitled to draw an inference that race and negative stereotyping played a role in the decision. It was an inference that recognized the subtle, pervasive, and unconscious nature of racism, and directly engaged the HRTO's specialized expertise. Thus, the Divisional Court concluded that the decision was reasonable and dismissed the application for judicial review.[83]

---

81   *Ibid* at paras 43–45.

82   2009 HRTO 1381.

83   *Knoll North America Corp v Adams*, 2010 ONSC 3005.

Yousufi v Toronto Police Services Board is another employment case that is consistent with racial profiling, but through harassment and a poisoned work environment. The complainant, Abdullah Yousufi, identified as a non-White person of Afghan descent. He was a civilian employee of the TPS who worked in the Planning Division of the Forensic Identification Service (FIS). On 12 September 2001, the day after the destruction of the World Trade Center in New York City, a co-worker of Mr Yousufi, Detective Bradshaw, left a voicemail message for another co-worker, Detective Constable Morrison. Mr Bradshaw informed Mr Morrison that Mr Yousufi had been taking airline pilot lessons at Buttonville Airport. Mr Bradshaw suggested that Mr Yousufi's locker should be searched for a flying manual in Arabic and stated that Yousufi was an "evil Islamic militant."[84] Mr Morrison reported the message, and it was promptly investigated. The call was traced back to Mr Bradshaw who admitted that he had left the message "as a joke" for Mr Morrison. Mr Yousufi was informed and interviewed. Mr Bradshaw immediately confessed and offered to apologize. His sick credits were docked by sixteen hours.[85]

The HRTO found that the manner in which TPS conducted its investigation was not discriminatory.[86] However, the HRTO found that Mr Bradshaw discriminated against Mr Yousufi contrary to section 5 of the *Code* on the basis of ethnic, origin, place of origin, and creed as a result of the message with "ugly stereotypes," which had a connection to the workplace. It had an accented voice, mimicked someone from the Middle East as speaking in broken English, and casted suspicions on the complainant as being involved in 9/11.[87]

The HRTO held that Mr Yousufi was subjected to a poisoned work environment because of office speculation that he was somehow connected to 9/11 and the TPS' failure to address the speculation. Mr Yousufi's witnesses and some of the respondents' witnesses confirmed that it was generally well known inside and outside FIS that Mr Yousifi had been named by someone in the TPS as being involved. The telephone message

---

84   2009 HRTO 351 at paras 1, 3, and 17.

85   *Ibid* at para 50.

86   The HRTO accepted an internal affairs officer's evidence that the questions put to Mr Yousufi about his country of origin and when he came to Canada were relevant to an explanation of why he might have been the target of the telephone message. The written notes of the investigation were consistent with the respondents' assertion that the only investigation taking place was about who left the message, not Mr Yousufi as a potential participant in 9/11 and a conspiracy to cover up a racially biased investigation (see paras 44–46).

87   *Ibid* at para 49.

was played freely around the unit and it was in keeping with the nature of office gossip that the rumour would spread. The TPS failed to address Mr Yousufi's legitimate concern that he was the subject of intolerable speculation. For example, a warning could have been issued that any harassment of Mr Yousufi over the incident would be severely dealt with.[88]

K. CONCLUSION

Much more needs to be done to challenge racial profiling. Policy change and accountability are needed in multiple sectors and at multiple levels of government. This will not be easy to achieve, of course. Developing substantive definitions of racial profiling that embody the values of the *Charter of Rights and Freedoms* and provincial human rights legislation, and are responsive to developments in the law and the reality on the ground, represents only one of the many challenges in the path ahead. However, in some respects, the opportunity to make change has never been timelier. We are in the middle of a national conversation about racial injustice. And we cannot let it go silent.

---

88   *Ibid* at paras 52–55.

CHAPTER 4

Applying the Racial Profiling Correspondence Test

DAVID M TANOVICH[*]

A. INTRODUCTION

In the landmark racial profiling case of *R v Brown*,[1] John Morden J, writing for a unanimous Ontario Court of Appeal, firmly recognized that racial profiling is a reality in policing in Canada that is "supported by significant social science research."[2] He acknowledged that racial profiling today is, at its core, largely about implicit bias — the reliance on learned stereotypes about race and crime, often subconsciously, in the decision-making process.[3] Following *Brown*, we can define racial profiling in policing as follows:

> Racial profiling occurs when race or racialized stereotypes about offending or dangerousness are used, consciously or unconsciously, to *any* degree in *suspect selection* or *suspect treatment*. The one exception to this is where race is used as part of a known suspect's physical description, the description

---

[*] Professor, faculty of law, University of Windsor; fellow, Royal Society of Canada. This article was written for the Law Society of Upper Canada, "The Six Minute Criminal Lawyer 2017," held in Toronto, 8 April 2017. Reproduced by permission of Thomson Reuters Canada Limited. I wish to thank my research assistant Natasha Donnelly (Windsor Law, 2017) for her outstanding editing.

1   (2003), 173 CCC (3d) 23 (Ont CA) [*Brown*].

2   *Ibid* at para 9. In *R v Grant*, 2009 SCC 32 at para 154, Binnie J similarly acknowledged that a "growing body of evidence and opinion suggests that visible minorities and marginalized individuals are at particular risk from unjustified 'low visibility' police interventions in their lives." See also *Peart v Peel Regional Police Services* (2006), 43 CR (6th) 175 at para 94 (Ont CA) [*Peart*], leave to appeal to SCC refused, 2017 SCCA No 10. In *Peart*, Doherty J noted that there is now "an acceptance by the courts that racial profiling occurs and is a day-to-day reality in the lives of those minorities affected by it."

3   *Brown*, above note 1 at paras 7–8 and 86.

is detailed and an individual is investigated because he or she reasonably matches that description.[4]

The central issue in *Brown* was whether the trial judge had conducted the proceedings in a fair and impartial manner. The Court of Appeal concluded that his insensitive and resistant approach to the issue — including suggesting that Brown apologize to the officer for having asserted that he was profiled[5] — raised a reasonable apprehension of bias.[6] In so holding, Morden J recognized that racial profiling cases must be conducted in a way that maintains public confidence in the justice system and fosters fair and unbiased adjudications.[7] Perhaps most significantly for the development of the law in this area, *Brown* established a *correspondence* test for proving racial profiling.[8]

This chapter aims to set out, in some detail, how and when the correspondence test can be applied. Section B sets out the test from *Brown*. Section C identifies the different manifestations of racial profiling. This is the first step in applying the correspondence test: understanding how racialized stereotypes can impact suspect selection and treatment. Section D examines the relevant indicators that can be used to meet the test. These indicators include context, pretext, and lessons learned. Section D also summarizes the carding/street check data that reveals the widespread nature of the disproportionate policing of Black and other racialized individuals in a number of cities in Ontario, as well as Montreal and Halifax. It is suggested that this evidence requires a reconsideration of the argument made by the African Canadian Legal Clinic in *Peart*, that in order to enhance adjudicative accuracy and fairness, there should be a rebuttable presumption of racial profiling in litigation.[9] Sections C and D

---

4   See *Peart*, above note 2 at paras 89–90; and *R v Lam*, 2014 ONSC 3538 at para 181. This definition was adopted by the Ottawa Police Service in its "Racial Profiling Policy" No 5.39 (27 June 2011). See, further, Ontario Human Rights Commission, *Paying the Price: The Human Cost of Racial Profiling* (Toronto: Ontario Human Rights Commission, 2003) at 6–8 [*Paying the Price*]; Michele Turenne, *Racial Profiling: Context and Definition* (Montreal: Commission des droits de la personne et des droits de la jeunesse, 2005). In this article, "racialized" refers to Black, Brown, and Aboriginal communities. This terminology is consistent with the Ontario Human Rights Commission that "describes communities facing racism as racialized." See Ontario Human Rights Commission, "Racial Discrimination (Brochure)," online: www.ohrc. on.ca/en/racial-discrimination-brochure.

5   Above note 1 at para 98.

6   *Ibid* at paras 84, 86–95, and 104–5.

7   *Ibid* at para 50.

8   *Ibid* at paras 44–45.

9   Above note 2 at paras 144–46.

are presented in a largely non-traditional format to enhance accessibility and appreciation of the nature and scope of the problem.[10]

The chapter concludes with a discussion of the relevance of the impact of racial profiling in assessing whether to exclude evidence found in breach of the *Charter* even where there is no finding of racial profiling in the particular case. This is an important contribution to our exclusionary rule jurisprudence and should be relied on in any case involving a racialized accused. Finally, Appendix A is included, which documents twenty-eight positive judicial and tribunal findings of racial profiling by police in the post-*Charter* era as of 8 April 2017. These cases provide a strong jurisprudential basis to assist in thinking about correspondence and how racial profiling can be effectively raised by lawyers in relevant cases.

B. THE CORRESPONDENCE TEST

As noted earlier, the relevant adjudicative standard for racial profiling cases comes from *Brown*, where Morden J, for the court, held:

> Where the evidence shows that the circumstances . . . *correspond* to the phenomenon of racial profiling . . . the record is then capable of supporting a finding that the stop was based on racial profiling.[11]

It is a test that relies on inductive reasoning — the engine that drives fact-finding where the evidence relied upon is largely circumstantial.[12] In

---

10   Many of the ideas set out here relating to the correspondence test are explored in more depth in my articles about racial profiling. See David M Tanovich, "Gendered and Racialized Violence, Strip Searches, Sexual Assault and Abuse of Prosecutorial Discretion" (2011) 79 *Criminal Reports* (6th) 132; David M Tanovich, "Rethinking the *Bona Fides* of Entrapment" (2011) 43 *University of British Columbia Law Review* 417; David M Tanovich, "A Powerful Blow against Police Use of Drug Courier Profiles" (2008) 55 *Criminal Reports* (6th) 379; David M Tanovich, "Moving Beyond 'Driving While Black in Canada': Race, Suspect Description and Selection" (2005) 36:2 *Ottawa Law Review* 315; David M Tanovich, "The Colourless World of Mann" (2004) 21 *Criminal Reports* (6th) 47; David M Tanovich, "E-Racing Racial Profiling" (2004) 41 *Alberta Law Review* 905; and David M Tanovich, "Using the *Charter* to Stop Racial Profiling: The Development of an Equality-Based Conception of Arbitrary Detention" (2002) 40:2 *Osgoode Hall Law Journal* 145.

11   Above note 1 at paras 44–46 [emphasis added].

12   Inductive reasoning is the process whereby we rely on logic, common sense, and human experience to fill in the inferential gap between a piece (or many pieces) of circumstantial evidence and a material fact. See David M Tanovich, "*Angelis*: Inductive Reasoning, Post-Offence Conduct and Intimate Femicide" (2013) 99 *Criminal Reports* (6th) 338 at 340–43. See, further, David M Tanovich, "Regulating Inductive Reasoning in Sexual Assault Cases" in Benjamin Berger, Emma Cunliffe, & James Stribopoulos, eds, *To Ensure That Justice Is Done: Essays in Memory of Marc Rosenberg* (Toronto: Thomson/Reuters Canada, 2017) 73.

thinking about how to apply the correspondence test, Doherty J observed in *Peart*:

> The courts, assisted by various studies, academic writings, and expert evidence have come to recognize a variety of factual *indicators* that can support the inference that the police conduct was racially motivated, *despite the existence of an apparent justification* for that conduct . . . .
>
> *The indicators of racial profiling* recognized in the literature by experts and in the caselaw can assist a trier of fact in deciding what inferences should or should not be drawn and what testimony should or should not be accepted in a particular case.[13]

C. THE VARIED MANIFESTATIONS OF RACIAL PROFILING

It is critical to understand how racial profiling manifests itself in order to understand the correspondence test. In this section, six different manifestations — from explicitly using race as part of a criminal profile, to negligently using race as part of a known suspect's physical description — are identified with cases and factual examples. Before detailing the manifestations, however, it is important to reflect on the voices of those impacted by profiling, some of whom shared their experiences with the Ontario Human Rights Commission in its investigation into the issue:[14]

- "My friends who are White are bewildered because their sons do not get stopped, and my friends with Black children are afraid, because they have already had their own teenaged sons stopped, or they have young sons coming up who they know will experience the same treatment . . . . [In the community] there is a chilling effect, a loss of trust, and fears for the safety of the children." (DW)

- "[Being stopped because I was driving a car registered to a union] tells me I'm not good enough to work for a union, because I am Black. And this made me feel less than a human being. And this shows that my contribution to Canadian society is not valued." (MW)

- "I have looked at the way I speak to them. I still ask when I'm pulled over . . . why are you stopping me. I have no tint on my car for the last 7 years. I am very polite. I say 'thank you'. I ask, 'How are you today officer?' My car is not the dream car anymore as I don't want to be branded as one of 'those.' My appearance appears to be more conservative." (NW)

---

13   Above note 2 at paras 95–96 [emphasis added].

14   *Paying the Price*, above note 4 at 24–25, 31, 34, 38, and 64 [additions in original].

- "A regular person would go in their car and they would drive about, not worrying about anything, if their papers are okay. But it got to a point where leaving my house, I would make sure I would check if all my lights were working, if everything is there, if my licence is there, because I know that somewhere down the line I am going to get pulled over." (RR)

- "[When the racial profiling occurred] I felt violated and ashamed to be Aboriginal . . . . I am not the person I was before the allegations. I am angry all the time and feel depressed most of the time."

The identified cases in this section (and in the rest of this chapter) are illustrative of cases where racial profiling was, or could have been, argued.[15] Their inclusion *does not* mean that there was a finding of racial profiling. A list of positive findings can be found in Appendix A.

1) Explicitly Using Race as Part of a "Criminal" Profile

a) Noting a Person Was "Middle-Eastern" and Linking It to "Security and Terrorism" in the Context of an Airport Search
- *R v Neyazi*, 2014 ONSC 6838 [paras 162 and 203–4]

b) Linking Asians to Marijuana Grow-Ops
- *R v Nguyen*, 2006 ONCJ 95 [paras 23–24]
- *R v Nguyen*, 2006 CanLII 1769 (Ont SCJ) [paras 7 and 25–26]
- *R v Mac*, 2005 CanLII 3392 (Ont SCJ) [paras 2–5] (Female)

c) Accused Targeted as a "Smuggler" Because He Was Asian
- *R v Chung* (1994), 23 WCB (2d) 579 (Ont Prov Ct) [para 17]

See further as an example this excerpt from a 2004 CISC report:

Across the country, Vietnamese-based groups remain extensively involved in multiple residential marihuana grow operations with distribution within Canada and to the U.S. These operations are widespread throughout the B.C. Lower Mainland, Alberta and southern Ontario and will continue to increase in Saskatchewan, Manitoba, Quebec and Atlantic Canada. Profits from marijuana cultivation are often reinvested in other criminal activities, such as in the importation of ecstasy and cocaine. Marihuana cultivation

---

15   To the best of my knowledge, the cases cited throughout this article involve Black, Brown, or Aboriginal individuals. If race was not referenced in the decision, confirmation was obtained from counsel or reliance on other indicia like name. Cases involving Aboriginals and women are specifically noted to assist in identifying these cases.

continues to affect Canadians' health and safety, often resulting in toxic moulds, condemned grow houses, fire hazards and chemical vapours from pesticides. Additionally, individuals involved in marihuana cultivation often experience violence through home invasions, assaults and booby-trap-related injuries.[16]

2)   Street Checks: Engaging in Heightened Surveillance of Racialized Individuals/Neighbourhoods Using General Investigative Powers

a)   Carding

- *Elmardy v Toronto Police Services Board*, 2017 ONSC 2074 (Div Ct)
- *R v Fountain*, 2015 ONCA 354
- *R v Daley*, 2015 ONSC 7164
- *R v K(A)*, 2014 ONCJ 374
- *R v Humphrey*, 2011 ONSC 3024
- *R v Allison*, 2011 ONSC 1459, aff'd 2013 ONCA 461
- *R v Buckley*, [2011] OJ No 2983 (Ct J)
- *R v Bramwell-Cole*, [2010] OJ No 5838 (SCJ) ("Officer Rendon [. . .] explained that he prepared a 208 for every person he stopped to talk with" [at para 30])
- *R v Davidson*, 2010 ONSC 1508
- *R v Ferdinand* (2004), 21 CR (6th) 65 (Ont SCJ)

b)   ID/Canadian Police Information Centre (CPIC) Checks

- *R c Gelin*, 2017 CanLII 41 (QCCM)
- *R v Charlie*, 2015 BCSC 1579 (Aboriginal)
- *R v Johnson*, 2013 ONCA 177 (Aboriginal)
- *R v Assiu*, 2012 ONCJ 327
- *R v Reid*, 2011 ONSC 6797
- *McKay v Toronto Police Services Board*, 2011 HRTO 499 (Aboriginal)
- *R v Banks*, 2010 ONCJ 553
- *R v Bruyere*, 2009 MBPC 24 (Aboriginal)
- *Willie v City of Vancouver*, 2007 BCPC 245 (Aboriginal Female)
- *R v Harris*, 2007 ONCA 574

---

16   Criminal Intelligence Service Canada (CISC), *Annual Report 2004* (Ottawa: Criminal Intelligence Service Canada, 2004) at 6. For a discussion of the CISC's annual reports and the link to racial profiling, see David M Tanovich, *The Colour of Justice: Policing Race in Canada* (Toronto: Irwin Law, 2006) at 15–18 and 91–94 [*The Colour of Justice*].

c) **Licence Plate Check**
- *Briggs v Durham Regional Police Services*, 2015 HRTO 1712

d) **Curfew/Recognizance Checks**
- *Elmardy v Toronto Police Services Board*, 2017 ONSC 2074 (Div Ct)
- *R v Trott*, 2012 BCPC 0174 (Aboriginal)
- *R v Davis-Harriot* (2007), 49 CR (6th) 265 (Ont SCJ), aff'd 2010 ONCA 161

e) **Conducting Opportunity Buys**
- *R v Sterling* (2004), 23 CR (6th) 54 (Ont SCJ) [paras 5–6] (in "area of Eglinton Avenue East between McCowan Road and Markham Road" and targeting young Black males in "baggy clothing")

3) **"Driving While Black": Using Highly Discretionary and Minor Statutory Powers to Justify Criminal Investigations Grounded in Racialized "Usual Offender" Stereotypes**

a) **Driver Not Wearing a Seat Belt**
- *R v Ohenhen*, 2016 ONSC 5782
- *R v Fortune*, 2016 ONSC 2186

b) **Not a Match with Registered Owner**
- *R v Ferguson-Cadore*, 2016 ONSC 4872

c) **Rear Seat Passenger Not Wearing Seat Belt**
- *R v Thompson* (2016), 28 CR (7th) 394 (Ont Ct J)

d) **Careless Driving for "Turning Too Quickly"**
- *R v Smith*, 2015 ONSC 3548

e) **Changing Lanes Without Signalling**
- *R v Carrington*, 2015 ONSC 7903
- *R v Alexander*, 2010 ONSC 2468

f) **Failing to Yield While Riding a Bike**
- *R v Graham*, 2014 ONSC 6880

g) **Failing to Stop Scooter at Stop Sign**
- *R v Gayle*, 2015 ONCJ 575

h) "Wellness Check" on Driver Asleep in Parked Car
- *R v Charles-Roberts*, 2014 ONSC 1261

i) Using Cellphone
- *R v Mattison*, 2012 ONSC 1795

j) Discarding a Cigarette
- *Longueuil (Ville de) c Debellefeuille*, 2012 QCCM 235

k) Swerving Vehicle
- *R v Huang*, 2010 BCPC 336

l) Concern of Tinted Windows
- *R v Yousofi*, 2011 ONSC 2298

m) Turning Left on a Red
- *R v Ahmed* (2009), 72 CR (6th) 187 (Ont SCJ)

n) Erratic Driving
- *R v Khan* (2004), 24 CR (6th) 48 (Ont SCJ)

4) "Spidey Sense": Interpreting Ambiguous Behaviour as Incriminatory When Applying the Investigative Detention Power from *R v Mann*

a) Hand or Body Movements
- *R v Fountain*, 2015 ONCA 354
- *R v Sterling-Debney*, 2013 ONSC 4584
- *R v Allison*, 2011 ONSC 1459, aff'd 2013 ONCA 461
- *R v Grant*, 2009 SCC 32
- *R v Yeh*, 2009 SKCA 112
- *R v Kang-Brown*, 2008 SCC 18
- *R v Digiacomo*, 2008 ONCJ 105
- *R v Campbell*, [2005] QJ No 394 (CQ)
- *R v Khan* (2004), 189 CCC (3d) 49 (Ont SCJ)

b) Apparent Nervousness
- *R v Neyazi*, 2014 ONSC 6838

c) "Looked Away"
- *R v Bruyere*, 2009 MBPC 24 (Aboriginal)

d) "Elongated Stare" or Failing to Make Eye Contact

- *R v Kang-Brown*, 2008 SCC 18
- *R v Grant*, 2009 SCC 32

e) Walking Away from Police

- *R v Darteh*, 2016 ONCA 141
- *R v Ferdinand* (2004), 21 CR (6th) 65 (Ont SCJ) (Officer testified re: his "Spidey sense" [para 23])

f) Flight

- *R v Atkins*, 2013 ONCA 586

g) Other "Evasive" Conduct

- *R v Glasgow*, 2012 ONCJ 311

h) Walking in a Group

- *R v FJ(RGT)*, 2013 MBPC 25 (Aboriginal Female)

i) Clothing

- "over-dressed for the weather": *R v Atkins*, 2013 ONCA 586 [para 3]
- "baggy clothing": *R v K(J)*, 2010 ONCJ 232
- "red bandana": *R v Flett*, [2002] MJ No 439 (Prov Ct) (Aboriginal)

j) Contents of Car

- *R v Calderon*, (2004), 188 CCC (3d) 481 (Ont CA)

5) "Any Negro Will Do"[17]: Unreasonably Using Race to Target an Individual Based on a Purported Match with the Physical Description of a Known Suspect

- *R v Jinje*, 2015 ONSC 2081 at para 47

    "There was nothing to connect Mr. Jinje to the robbery, other than the fact that the robbers were three black males and Mr. Jinje and his friends were also three black males."

---

17 See Fo Niemi & Gabrielle Michaud-Sauvageau, "Any Negro Will Do: Race and Suspect Description — The Slippery Slope towards Racial Profiling" (Montreal: Centre for Research-Action on Race Relations (CRARR), 2000). See also the discussion of this issue in *The Colour of Justice*, above note 16 at 151–69. This section could also be called "Any Aboriginal Will Do": see, for example, *R v Mann*, 2004 SCC 52; *Willie v City of Vancouver*, 2007 BCPC 245 at paras 26 and 55 (female); and, the 1988 shooting death of JJ Harper, online: www.ajic.mb.ca/volumeIII/chapter2.html.

- *R v Lam*, 2014 ONSC 3538 at para 207

[I]t is not difficult to understand Mr. Rusonik's submission regarding racial profiling. Whether the situation here can properly be described or not as, "All Asians look alike," or "any Asian will do," or "Even if we're wrong about him being the wanted party, the Asian passenger was likely up to no good," there was a recklessness on the part of the police respecting the applicant's s. 9 *Charter* right.

- *Maynard v Toronto Police Services Board*, 2012 HRTO 1220 at para 176

The problem is that Officer Baker cast his investigative net so wide that Mr. Maynard's race was the predominant factor that put him at risk of being investigated that day. I do not believe that if the suspect had been a Caucasian man in the same circumstances, with no other defining characteristics, particularly age, and with as little information available about the car and direction of travel, that Officer Baker would have chosen to investigate the first Caucasian man he saw driving the same car at the same intersection. It is consistent with a finding of racial profiling that all black men or all black men of a certain age, driving alone in the area in a black car were possible suspects at the moment that Officer Baker decided to commence his investigation of Mr. Maynard.

6) Overreaction: Intensifying the Investigation, for Example, with Unjustifiable Arrest, Searches, or Excessive Force, or Responding to Perceived Danger with Extreme Force

- *Elmardy v Toronto Police Services Board*, 2017 ONSC 2074 at paras 35–36 (Div Ct)

The Appellant was an innocent man who had fled his country looking for a society in which his rights would be respected. Instead ... he was subjected to humiliating, violent and oppressive behaviour from one of this city's police officers, all because of the colour of his skin .... For these reasons, there is a need for an award of damages that is significant enough to vindicate society's interest in having a police service comprised of officers who do not brutalize its citizens because of the colour of their skin ....

- *McKay v Toronto Police Services Board*, 2011 HRTO 499 at para 200 (Aboriginal)

I find that the repeated criminal records searches underscore my findings ... that despite releasing McKay at the scene, Fitkin remained suspicious of McKay and required McKay to provide proof of the bike receipt. It is reasonable to infer [. . .] that the suspicions of Aboriginal criminality, which permeated the encounter, continued even after McKay was released.

- *R v Nasogaluak*, 2010 SCC 6 at para 11 (Aboriginal)

Cst. Chornomydz yelled at Mr. Nasogaluak to stop resisting and gave him a third hard punch in the head. Mr. Nasogaluak was pinned face down on the pavement with Cst. Chornomydz straddling his back. When Mr. Nasogaluak refused to offer up his hands to be handcuffed, Cst. Dlin punched Mr. Nasogaluak in the back, twice. These blows were strong enough to break Mr. Nasogaluak's ribs, which later punctured one of his lungs. Cst. Olthof was kneeling on Mr. Nasogaluak's thigh throughout this brief struggle.

- *R v Bonds*, 2010 ONCJ 561 (Black female strip-searched by multiple officers, including a male officer who used scissors to cut off her bra, and left half-naked in a cell for over three hours following an arrest for public intoxication)

- *R v Banks*, 2010 ONCJ 553 at para 18

Lim's questioning of the defendant was solely a product of Hunt's instructions . . . . Indeed, even after removing the defendant from the car at gunpoint, no pat-down search of the defendant was conducted . . . — belying Lim's professed concern for officer safety.

- *Abbott v Toronto Police Services Board*, 2009 HRTO 1909 at para 46 (Female)

I find that Sergeant Ruffino's actions in this regard are consistent with a manifestation of racism whereby a White person in a position of authority has an expectation of docility and compliance from a racialized person, and imposes harsh consequences if that docility and compliance is not provided . . . .

- *R v Walcott* (2008), 57 CR (6th) 223 at paras 72, 108 (Ont SCJ)

. . . Officer Fonseca fired his taser almost two minutes after Officer Reimer had finished firing his, at a time when Mr. Walcott was lying on the ground, handcuffed, under control and compliant . . . . I find that Officer Fonseca's discharge of his taser on Mr. Walcott constituted 'cruel and unusual treatment' . . . .

D. THE INDICATORS

Having set out the different manifestations of racial profiling, the chapter turns to three indicators that can be used to prove racial profiling: (1) context, (2) pretext, and (3) lessons learned.

1) Policing in Contexts Vulnerable to Racial Profiling

RELEVANT INQUIRY: Did the police conduct take place in a context where experience has shown us that racial profiling manifests itself? These contexts include:

- Using race as part of a "criminal" profile
- Exercising "low visibility" powers
- Searching for suspects identified by race
- Carding and street checks
- Assessing behaviour for *R v Mann* power
- Exercising arrest/search powers and uses of force

As noted earlier, in *Peart*,[18] a civil racial profiling case, the African Canadian Legal Clinic (ACLC) argued that the burden of proof in racial profiling cases should fall on the police.[19] Justice Doherty responded to this argument as follows:

> [The ACLC] contends that the onus should fall on the police where the party who was subjected to detention or arrest is black. In effect, the ACLC submits that any arrest or detention of a black person by the police is as constitutionally suspect as a warrantless search and, therefore, merits the same rebuttable presumption of unconstitutionality.
>
> This contention is based on the argument that racial profiling is so common that where it is alleged, placing the burden on the police to disprove racial profiling is more likely to achieve an accurate result than is leaving the onus on the party alleging racial profiling. As *McCormick, supra*, indicates at 475–76:
>
> > Perhaps a more frequently significant consideration in the fixing of the burdens of proof is the judicial estimate of the probabilities of the situation. *The risk of failure of proof may be placed upon the party who contends that the more unusual event has occurred.* [Emphasis added.]
>
> The reality of racial profiling cannot be denied. There is no way of knowing how common the practice is in any given community. I am not prepared to accept that racial profiling is the rule rather than the exception where the police detain black men. I do not mean to suggest that I am satisfied that it is indeed the exception, but only that I do not know.[20]

Peart was decided in 2006. Since then, we have learned a lot more about the scope of disproportionate policing across Canada, particularly

---

18   Above note 2.

19   This is an argument that I also made in *The Colour of Justice*, above note 16 at 144–47.

20   Above note 2 at paras 144–46.

in southern Ontario. The following is a summary of the carding/street check and other data that has been released and publicized from 2010–17.

a) Toronto[21]

For black males, the ratio for most patrol zones ranges from about 4:1 to 8:1. For brown young men, most zones have a ratio of 2:1 to 8:1. For white young men, the typical range is between 1:1 and 2:1. For those designated as "other," most zones have a ratio of less than one to one.

Overall in Toronto, the number of carded young black men between 2008 and mid-2011 was 3.4 times higher than the young black male population. The ratio for young brown men was 1.8:1, and for white young men and those considered "other," the ratios dropped to 1:1 and 0.3 to one, respectively.

b) Peel[22]

The race-based data obtained Tuesday shows that in 2011, blacks were stopped in 5,830 street checks by Peel police out of 26,113 total checks, or 22 per cent of the times.

That year, blacks had three times the chance of being stopped, compared to whites, a number that remains consistent when using the street-check data from 2009-2014.

c) Waterloo[23]

Black people account for two percent of the regional population, but nine percent of all people stopped, seven percent of individuals carded just once, nine percent of individuals carded more than once and eight percent of all individuals carded.

---

21 See Jim Rankin & Patty Winsa, "Known to Police: Toronto Police Stop and Document Black and Brown People Far More Often Than Whites" *Toronto Star* (9 March 2012), online: www.thestar.com; Jim Rankin, Patty Winsa, Andrew Bailey, & Hidy Ng, "Carding Drops but Proportion of Blacks Stopped by Police Rises" *Toronto Star* (26 July, 2014), online: www.thestar.com [emphasis added].

22 See Sam Grewal, "Blacks Three Times More Likely To Be Carded by Peel Police Than Whites" *Toronto Star* (24 September 2015), online: www.thestar.com [emphasis added].

23 See Jeff Outhit, "Waterloo Regional Police 4 Times More Likely To Stop You If You Are Black" *The Record* (25 March 2016), online: www.therecord.com.

d) Hamilton[24]

In Hamilton, 11 to 14 percent of the police street checks were done on black people over the last five years. But only three percent of the population in Hamilton is black, according to the 2011 Census.

e) London[25]

Last year London police conducted about 8,400 street checks (far more than officers in other cities and at a rate triple of Hamilton and Ottawa). That included recording data of about 14,000. Of those, 7.7% of the people documented were black and 5.3% Indigenous. According to the 2011 census, only 2.5% of Londoners are black and 1.9% are Indigenous.

f) Ottawa (Street Checks)[26]

The police service's combined statistics from 2011 through 2014 show that 58 per cent of people they have street checked are white, 20 per cent are black and 14 per cent are middle eastern. Aboriginal, Asian, East Indian, Latin American and those whose race is unknown accounted for about seven per cent. The ethnicity of about 10 per cent of people street checked wasn't recorded.

But, according to the 2011 National Household Survey, black people account for just under 6 per cent of the population, while those classified as "Arab" make up less than 4 per cent of Ottawa's population.

g) Ottawa (Vehicle Stops)[27]

The disparities were more pronounced when looking just at young men. Middle Eastern men between the ages of 16 to 24 were 12 times more likely to be stopped, and young black men were 8.3 times more likely to be stopped. Young men police identified as white were stopped 1.7 times more than their population would suggest.

---

24   See Kelly Bennett, "Hamilton Police Disproportionately Stop and Question Black People" *CBC News Online* (23 July 2015), online: www.cbc.ca/1.3165182.

25   See Jennifer O'Brien, "Carding Stats Show Racial Bias on Police Force, Critics Say" *London Free Press* (14 October 2015), online: www.lfpress.com.

26   See Shaamini Yogaretnam, "Street Checks Data about Racialized Men Concerning to Civil Liberties Advocates" *Ottawa Citizen* (26 July 2015), online: www.ottawacitizen.com.

27   See "Ottawa Police Stopping Middle Eastern, Black Drivers at 'Disproportionate' Rate" *CBC News Online* (24 October 2016), online: www.cbc.ca/1.3816311.

h) Montreal[28]

The report suggests that the number of young black men stopped and questioned by police in Montreal's sensitive neighbourhoods is "much too high" and even amounts to "fishing expeditions."

Between 2001 and 2007, the report shows the frequency of police identification checks on individuals increased by 126 percent in the Montreal North borough and 91 percent in St-Michel.

This "alarming" increase "touched primarily blacks" such that *by 2006 and 2007 between 30 and 40 percent of young black men in these areas faced police identity checks, compared to 5 to 6 per cent of whites.*

Meanwhile, only about 5 percent of the checks yielded arrests or infractions. "A large proportion of these checks," study author Michel Charest concludes, "can be judged as arbitrary or malicious."

i) Halifax

New data shows that about 20 per cent of people stopped in police ("street checks") in Halifax are black, despite black people making up less than four per cent of the city's population.[29]

In a 10-year period between 2006 and 2016, there were 25,322 street checks done by police. Of that number, 2,981 were conducted on black people, 12 per cent of the total street checks . . . .

Data by RCMP also showed there were 1,246 street checks between January and October 2016. A total of 509 black people — 41 per cent — were checked with 475 checks being performed in Cole Harbour district, 93 per cent of the overall number of black people checked. In addition, 440 were in East and North Preston and the Cherrybrook area.[30]

Given what we (and by extension Doherty J) now know from the carding data about the extent of the disproportionate policing of racialized communities, it is time to reconsider the reverse onus/presumption argument put forward in *Peart*. At a minimum, this data should change where we start on the evidentiary scale for adjudication. I would argue that where the impugned police conduct takes place in a context vulnerable for racial profiling, judges should begin with the presumption that

---

28 Andrew Chung, "Racial Profiling 'Alarming' in Montreal" *Toronto Star* (9 August 2010), online: www.thestar.com [emphasis added].

29 Josh Dehaas, "Halifax Police Far More Likely To Stop Black People, Data Shows" *CTV News Online* (9 January 2017), online: http://ctv.news/ijFxMSf.

30 Sean Previl, "Halifax RCMP Conduct Street Checks on Black People More than Halifax Police" *Global News Online* (11 January 2017), online: www.globalnews.ca.

there is *some* evidence of the influence of racialized stereotypes in the exercise of discretion. The analysis would then turn to whether there is evidence of other indicators of profiling that would support a finding that racial profiling likely, or probably, occurred in the case, which is the required standard of proof in *Charter* cases. This would be ensuring what Doherty J referred to in *Peart* as "a sensitive appreciation of the relevant social context in which racial profiling claims must be assessed" in order to "[provide] further protection against the failure of meritorious claims as a result of the allocation of the burden of proof."[31] The chapter now examines two other indicators: pretext and lessons learned.

2) Using a Pretext

RELEVANT INQUIRY: Did the police purport to use a statutory or other investigative power or purpose as a pretext or ruse for a criminal investigation, leaving it open to conclude that what really drove the investigation was racialized stereotypes about crime?[32]

Proving that the exercise of authority was a pretext can be done on a "totality of circumstances" approach and relevant considerations include:[33]

Is the activity under investigation consistent with the normal duties of the officer?
e.g., Would not expect emergency task force officers to issue tickets for routine offences.

---

31   Above note 2 at para 147.

32   It is now well-accepted that using a pretext is an indicator of racial profiling. See *Brown*, above note 1 at para 48; *R v Ferguson-Cadore*, 2016 ONSC 4872 at paras 26–35; and *R v Smith*, 2015 ONSC 3548 at paras 168–83. In *Peart*, above note 2 at para 110, for example, Doherty J observed:

> Speeding can be a pretext for a racially motivated stop . . . . Whether it is a pretext will depend on the findings of fact in each case. For example, if as Mr. Peart testified he was travelling at ten to twenty kilometres over the speed limit at 3:30 in the morning when Officer Ceballo began to follow him, it would be open for a trial judge to find that Peart's excessive speed was a pretext for the officer following his vehicle.

See, further, David M Tanovich, "Operation Pipeline and Racial Profiling" (2002) 1 *Criminal Reports* (6th) 52.

33   See *The Colour of Justice*, above note 16 at 130–35.

How long did it take for the officer to stop the vehicle?
e.g., Would not expect an officer who claimed to be exercising their *HTA* power to refer to the violation having been committed *after* having followed the individual.

Did the officer have to go out of their way to make the stop?
e.g., Would not expect the police to make a U-turn in busy traffic or on the highway over a *possible* back seat passenger seat belt infraction.

Make of the vehicle.
Q: Was the individual driving an expensive car, thus potentially triggering the stereotype that he must be involved in criminal activity?

The location of the stop.
Q: Does it take place in an affluent neighbourhood, thus potentially triggering the "out of place" stereotype or so-called "high crime" area, triggering the "he could be up to 'no good'" stereotype?

Was there a call to dispatch or call for backup?
e.g., Would not expect the officer to only refer to possible criminal activity in the call if the intent was to enforce the *HTA* or request backup for a seat belt violation in the middle of the day on a busy street.

The nature of the questioning of the individual. Is it consistent with the purported reason for the stop or a criminal investigation? Are those with the driver or target questioned?
e.g., One would not expect the first questions to be about whether the driver or passenger is on bail or what they were doing in a particular area or during a set time frame.

3) Using Lessons Learned from Experience

RELEVANT INQUIRY: What have we learned from the jurisprudence (including human rights cases), the testimony of those profiled, human rights reports, academic studies, and commentary about the officers' conduct, and/or testimony consistent with racial profiling?

Some of the lessons learned include:

a) **Deciding to Investigate a Young Black Male Driving an Expensive Car**
- *R v Brown* (2003), 173 CCC (3d) 23 (Ont CA) [para 46]
- *R v Ohenhen*, 2016 ONSC 5782 [para 105]
- *R v Smith*, 2015 ONSC 3548 [para 183]
- *R v K(A)*, 2014 ONCJ 374 [paras 16, 45–46, and 54]
- *R v Khan* (2004), 189 CCC (3d) 49 (Ont SCJ) [para 68]

b) **Looking into the Car at Some Point Before Stopping the Vehicle**
- *R v Brown* (2003), 173 CCC (3d) 23 (Ont CA) [para 46]

c) **Inconsistent Evidence on When the Police Saw the Race of the Individual Under Investigation**
- *Peart v Peel Regional Police Services* (2006), 43 CR (6th) 175 (Ont CA) [para 114]
- *R v Thompson* (2016), 28 CR (7th) 394 (Ont Ct J) [para 10]

d) **Stopping the Person Where He or She Appears "Out of Place"**
- *R v Brown* (2003), 173 CCC (3d) 23 (Ont CA) [para 87]
- *Shaw v Phipps*, 2012 ONCA 155 [paras 2 and 35]
- *R v Ferguson-Cadore*, 2016 ONSC 4872 [paras 5–6]

e) **Lying About the Reason for the Stop**
- *R v Brown* (2003), 173 CCC (3d) 23 (Ont CA) [para 45]
- *Elmardy v Toronto Police Services Board*, 2017 ONSC 2074 (Div Ct) [para 22]

f) **Asking Questions About What the Person Is Doing in the Area, Whether They Are Subject to Bail Conditions, Have Any Outstanding Warrants, or Where They Are From**
- *Longueuil (Ville de) c Debellefeuille*, 2012 QCCM 235 [para 121]

g) **Purporting to Rely on a Racially Neutral "Criminal" Profile**
- *R v Chehil*, 2013 SCC 49 [paras 41–44]

h) **Failing to Investigate or Treating Differently Similarly Situated White Individuals**
- *Shaw v Phipps*, 2012 ONCA 155 [para 23]

i) **Discrepancies or Other Irregularities in the Officer's Notes or Testimony**
- *R v Brown* (2003), 173 CCC (3d) 23 (Ont CA) [para 46]
- *R v Thompson* (2016), 28 CR (7th) 394 (Ont Ct J) [paras 11–12]

j) **An Explanation for the Investigation That Lacks Credulity or Defies Common Sense**
- *Elmardy v Toronto Police Services Board*, 2017 ONSC 2074 (Div Ct) [paras 20 and 23]
- *Shaw v Phipps*, 2012 ONCA 155 [para 24]
- *Longueuil (Ville de) c Debellefeuille*, 2012 QCCM 235 [para 4]
- *R v Huang*, 2010 BCPC 336 [paras 13–16]
- *R v Khan* (2004), 189 CCC (3d) 49 (Ont SCJ) [para 65]

k) **Deviations from Standard Practice**
- *Johnson v Halifax (Regional Municipality) Police Service*, [2003] NSHR-BID No 2 [para 62]

l) **Where the Police Incite the Commission of an Offence Like Cause Disturbance, Mischief, or Resist Arrest to Justify Their Conduct**
- *R v Osbourne*, 2008 ONCJ 134
- *R v A(L)*, 2005 ONCJ 546

(It is unclear whether racial profiling was argued in these cases but it certainly could have been, given the facts.)

m) **In Suspect Descriptions Cases, There Are Clearly Distinguishing Features Between the Two Individuals; Or, the Officer Cannot Articulate What Other Parts of the Description He or She Was Relying on (e.g., Height, Weight, Age, Location, or Other Features)**
- *Maynard v Toronto Police Services Board*, 2012 HRTO 1220 [para 176]
- *Longueuil (Ville de) c Debellefeuille*, 2012 QCCM 235 [para 121]

E. CONCLUSION

One of the concerns I have written about over the years is the failure of lawyers to raise racial profiling in appropriate cases.[34] Given the paucity of judgments filed with databases like CanLII, Westlaw, or Quicklaw

---

34   See David M Tanovich, "The Charter of Whiteness: Twenty-Five Years of Maintaining Racial Injustice in the Canadian Criminal Justice System" (2008) 40 *Supreme Court Law Review* (2d) 655 and David M Tanovich, "The Further Erasure of Race in *Charter* cases" (2006) 38 *Criminal Reports* (6th) 84.

each year across Canada, this still appears to remain a problem. This chapter has attempted to facilitate the identification, litigation, and adjudication of racial profiling cases by setting out how the correspondence test can be applied, by identifying the many relevant factors and cases that can be relied upon, and by arguing for a presumptive "some evidence" starting point.

Even if after a considered decision to not raise racial profiling is made, or if it is raised and dismissed, a number of decisions have recognized that the experience of profiling by racialized communities remains a relevant consideration in assessing the seriousness of a *Charter* violation under section 24(2), if one is found. In *R v Harris*,[35] a case involving a check of a Black passenger during a vehicle stop, Doherty J observed that:

> The use of the broad powers associated with *Highway Traffic Act* stops to routinely investigate passengers who have nothing to do with the concerns justifying those stops must have a significant cumulative, long-term, negative impact on the personal freedom enjoyed by those who find themselves subject to this kind of police conduct. While for persons in some segments of the community, these stops may be infrequent, this record suggests that for others the stops are an all too familiar part of their day-to-day routine. Viewed from the perspective of those who are most likely to find themselves stopped and questioned by police, I think this form of interrogation is anything but trivial. It seems to me at some point it must become provocative.[36]

No racial profiling argument was advanced in *Harris*. In *R v Jinje*,[37] Nordheimer J held in excluding evidence of a gun under section 24(2):

> The impact on Mr. Jinje's *Charter* rights is significant . . . . The conduct of the police will . . . only serve to reinforce Mr. Jinje's perception of unequal treatment at the hands of the police. Mr. Jinje could hardly be faulted for having such a perception given the numerous times that Mr. Jinje has been stopped by the police, as outlined by him in his evidence. That evidence was confirmed, at least in part, by Officer Censoni who said that police records show twenty-seven instances of encounters between Mr. Jinje and the police. I should add, in that regard, that Mr. Jinje has no criminal record. He is employed and he goes to school. He deserves the same respect from the police as any other citizen of this city ought to receive.[38]

---

35   2007 ONCA 574.
36   *Ibid* at para 63.
37   2015 ONSC 2081.
38   *Ibid* at para 59.

And more recently, in *R v Athwal*,[39] Hill J observed in excluding gun and ammunition evidence under section 24(2) that:

> The arbitrary detention was not fleeting or technical given its duration and character. To repeat, the applicant was handcuffed and in custody without lawful authority for over 20 minutes.
>
> . . .
>
> While racial profiling has nothing to do with the actions of the police in this case, the courts, representing society, nevertheless cannot be seen as condoning the arbitrary detention of visible minority members of the community if we are to eliminate perceptions of racism on the part of the police within a community like Peel where 57% of the population are visible minority inhabitants. The impact of the arbitrary detention upon the applicant strongly favours exclusion of the statement evidence.[40]

These cases should also serve to support the raising of race-based *Charter* claims, leading to more racial profiling arguments being heard and recognized by the courts.

---

39   2017 ONSC 96.

40   *Ibid* at para 267.

APPENDIX A Positive Findings (1982–8 April 2017)

1982–2008 (11)	2009–13 (8)	2014–15 (4)	2016–17 (5)
CRIMINAL CASES (17)			
• R v Chung (1994), 23 WCB (2d) 579 (Ont Prov Ct)	• R v Ahmed (2009), 72 CR (6th) 187 (Ont SCJ)	• R v K(A), 2014 ONCJ 374	• R c Gelin, 2017 CanLII 41 (QCCM)
• R v Peck, [2001] OJ No 4581 (SCJ)	• R v Huang, 2010 BCPC 336	• R v Neyazi, 2014 ONSC 6838	• R v Ohenhen, 2016 ONSC 5782
• R v Khan (2004), 189 CCC (3d) 49 (Ont SCJ)		• R v Smith, 2015 ONSC 3548	• R v Ferguson-Cadore, 2016 ONSC 4872
• R v Safadi, 2005 ABQB 356			• R v Thompson (2016), 28 CR (7th) 394 (Ont Ct J)
• R v Campbell, [2005] QJ No 394 (CQ)			
• R v Mac, [2005] OJ No 527 (SCJ)			
• R v Nguyen, [2006] OJ No 272 (SCJ)			
• R v Nguyen, 2006 ONCJ 95			
HUMAN RIGHTS CASES/OTHER (11)			
• Johnson v Halifax (Regional Municipality) Police Service, [2003] NSHRBID No 2	• Abbott v TPSB, 2009 HRTO 1909	• Briggs v Durham Regional Police Services, 2015 HRTO 1712	• Elmardy v Toronto Police Services Board, 2017 ONSC 2074 (Div Ct)
• Nassiah v Peel (Regional Municipality) Services Board, 2007 HRTO 14	• Pelletier c Laberge, 2009 QCCS 729		
• Pelletier c Simard, 2007 QCCQ 9847	• McKay v TPSB, 2011 HRTO 499		
	• Shaw v Phipps, 2012 ONCA 155		
	• Maynard v TPSB, 2012 HRTO 1220		
	• Longueuil (Ville de) c Debellefeuille, 2012 QCCM 235		

PART II

Forms and Sector Analysis

CHAPTER 5

Bias-Neutral Policing

A Police Perspective on the Intersection of Racial Profiling with Modern-Day Policing and the Laws That Govern

GARY V MELANSON[*]

A. INTRODUCTION

This chapter provides a police perspective to and will examine how bias-neutral policing practices can guide police in their interactions with citizens and ground their stance on interactions with the public. The chapter will also review how, in law, racial profiling has intersected with policing in three key areas: the criminal law, the Ontario *Human Rights Code*, and police regulation (including during street checks) and police discipline. Finally, a discussion will also take place regarding possible avenues where solutions and/or progress may be found in the areas of police oversight, education, and data analysis.

B. OVERVIEW

How do the police approach bias-neutral policing?[1] The first step is a clear recognition and acceptance that it exists and that steps must be taken eliminate it, in order to properly serve our communities.

> The police are the public and the public are the police; the police being only members of the public who are paid to give full time attention to duties which are incumbent on every citizen in the interests of community welfare and existence — *Sir Robert Peel*[2]

---

[*]   Gary V Melanson is the senior director of Legal Services and Risk Management, Legal Services Branch, Waterloo Regional Police Service.

[1]   Sometimes referred to as "bias-free policing" or "impartial policing."

[2]   While attributed to Sir Robert Peel, this quote and his "Nine Principles of Policing," dating back to the 1820s, are likely a summary or paraphrasing of his speeches and

In order for our society to be a safe and vibrant place to live, we need to remember that community relations and their understanding of the role of the police are keys to that goal and a successful policing model. Sir Robert Peel's oft-quoted and -taught statement on policing by community consent has formed the backbone of Canadian policing philosophy. Several common law countries' policing models, including Canada, also rely upon Sir Robert Peel's "Nine Principles of Policing" that include the following:

> 5. To seek and preserve public favour, not by pandering to public opinion, *but by constantly demonstrating absolutely impartial service to law*, in complete independence of policy, and without regard to the justice or injustice of the substance of individual laws, by ready offering of individual service and friendship to all members of the public without regard to their wealth or social standing, by ready exercise of courtesy and friendly good humour; and by ready offering of individual sacrifice in protecting and preserving life.[3]

Without getting into the intricacies or implications of the above principle (as it relates to divorcing the role of the police from a policy or consequential analysis of the laws they are asked to maintain), the key concept that flows from this principle is the "absolute impartial service to law." This raises and leads directly into the concept of bias-neutral policing as an underlying edict to modern-day policing. However, the way this bias-neutral policing is practically employed is far from simple or free from confusion for the police or the public — especially when systemic pressures, both internal and external, come into play. With that confusion, or where the police stray away from those principles, is often where racial profiling (actual or perceived) will intersect with the law under which police operate: the criminal law, human rights law, and the *Police Services Act*. The tests and consequences of racial profiling are substantively and procedurally different under each of these areas of law but common threads include that, very often, findings of racial profiling are made indirectly, sometimes assumptively, and may arise out of "upstream"[4] systemic biases.

---

other communications (Susan A Lentz & Robert H Chaires, "The Invention of Peel's Principles: A Study of Policing 'Textbook' History" (2007) 35:1 *Journal of Criminal Justice* 69.

3   See "Principles of Good Policing," online: The Institute for the Study of Civil Society www.civitas.org.uk/research/crime/facts-comments/principles-of-good-policing/ [Emphasis added].

4   Systemic biases that originate in other areas of society or within the government system (e.g., poverty-based) that only become apparent or an issue through an interaction with police.

There are, however, potential areas where solutions and/or progress can be found. Some of this will only and naturally come to fruition if the problems can be better defined and police processes better explained. In addition, there is a need for better data collection and matrixes, with such aligning with better police oversight and accountability outside the court or hearing room. For prevention to take place, education, accountability, and transparency must be married up and form the foundation for public discourse. If the police wish to continue to police with the community's consent and approval, racial profiling must be weeded out from the decision-making processes (consciously or unconsciously) of individual police officers, the operational and policy decisions of those that oversee policing, and our society as a whole[5] — for equally, the police are the community and thus a product of broader systemic issues in society.

C. BIAS-NEUTRAL POLICING

Decades ago, many police services turned their policy-making attention to the issue of possible bias decision-making in policing. This was and remains a clear recognition by police leaders that racial profiling (by whatever name given) exists, is a serious issue, and must be addressed from within policing.

As a result, bias-neutral policies and/or procedures[6] were developed to govern and assist officers in their decision-making processes while investigating crimes and otherwise conducting their duties. Generally, these procedures (i.e., orders from the chief) demand that, as a provider of policing services, it is the service's practice to:

1) extend fair and equal treatment under the law to every individual without discrimination on the basis of age, ancestry, colour, race, citizenship, ethnic origin, place of origin, creed, disability, family status, marital status, gender identity, gender expression, record of offences (in employment only), sex and sexual orientation;[7] and

---

5   That is, are the police the tip of the iceberg of larger and more systemic biases and perceptions in our society?

6   Under the *Police Services Act* in Ontario, policies are made by the police services boards (as overreaching direction to the chief of police), while procedures are issued by the chief or commissioner of the OPP (as operational orders to all the members of a police service) — failure to abide by these policies and procedures can be the subject of misconduct proceedings.

7   Note that it is not restricted to race, age, or gender, but encompasses all of the grounds under the Ontario *Human Rights Code*, RSO 1990, c H.19.

2) maintain a respectful and co-operative relationship with the entire community while recognizing the importance of inclusion and the strength of diversity.[8]

These procedures will usually explicitly prohibit bias-based policing — that is, treating differently any person or persons on the basis of any of the prohibited grounds from the *Human Rights Code* — and, specifically, racial/biased profiling (the practice of linking a person or persons to an unlawful incident or incidents based primarily or predominantly on the grounds from the *Code*).

The procedure will also often provide that all of the police service members (uniform or civilian[9]) shall:

    a.   not use *racial/biased profiling*;

    b.   not use age, ancestry, colour, race, citizenship, ethnic origin, place of origin, creed, disability, family status, marital status, *gender identity*, *gender expression*, sex and sexual orientation as the primary or predominant reason for stopping a vehicle, issuing a provincial offence notice, making an arrest, conducting a field interview or search, investigative detention or the seizure of property;

    c.   articulate specific facts, circumstances, conclusions and legislative authority, if applicable, which support the decision resulting in actions such as an arrest, traffic stop or investigative detention;

    d.   treat all persons with courtesy and respect. Members shall not use language or display symbols or gestures that are commonly viewed as offensive to, or are indicative of a bias towards any group or person; and

    e.   upon request, identify themselves by rank, surname and badge number (sworn officers), unless providing this information would compromise officer or public safety, or would undermine an investigation.[10]

These procedures generally do allow members of the police service to take into account the reported age, ancestry, colour, race, citizenship,

---

8   Such standards are not uniform among all police services, and some have no such standards. To date, the government has not required such nor has it set out an adequacy standard. The majority of references to the contents of a bias-neutral procedure come from the example of Waterloo Regional Police Service's "Bias-Neutral Policing Procedure," one of, if not *the* first, police service in Ontario to formalize a chief's directive on bias-neutral policing.

9   With the increasing pressure to civilianize certain policing functions, such as crime analysis, it is key to include all members of a police service when establishing such policies or procedures.

10   Waterloo Regional Police Service's Bias-Neutral Policing Procedure [document in possession of the author].

ethnic origin, place of origin, creed, disability, family status, marital status, gender identity, gender expression, sex, and sexual orientation of a specific suspect or suspects in the same way they would use other descriptors such as age, height, or weight. However, the information must be trustworthy, current, and relevant, linking the suspect or suspects to a particular unlawful incident. This is associated with the permitted and necessary policing tool of *investigative profiling* which is defined to mean:

> a situation or presentation of facts or circumstances where a member has trustworthy and relevant information that forms reasonable suspicion or reasonable grounds linking a person or persons to a particular unlawful incident or incidents. Age, ancestry, colour, race, citizenship, ethnic origin, place of origin, creed, disability, family status, marital status, record of offences (in employment only), sex and sexual orientation can never be used as the primary or predominant basis for reasonable suspicion or reasonable grounds.[11]

As it relates to street check type interactions, there is (and was before the Ontario government passed their regulation[12]) also a clear prohibition as it relates to bias profiling, for example: "Members shall not engage in an interaction with a member of the public (e.g., an investigative detention or an interaction for the purposes of or that would lead to a street check), based on racial/biased profiling whether linked to an unlawful incident or not."[13]

Notwithstanding such, on the issue of carding (as it was known) or street checks, the policing community failed in dealing with this issue on many fronts (see below).

D. RACIAL PROFILING AND THE LAW

The concepts, ramifications, and judicial/quasi-judicial oversight and pronouncements on racial profiling and policing have primarily developed in three main areas of the law: criminal, human rights, and police regulation and discipline.[14] It is in these three areas that the police see and deal with

---

11 *Ibid.*

12 *Collection of Identifying Information in Certain Circumstances — Prohibition and Duties*, O Reg 58/16 [*COIICC*] under the *Police Services Act*, RSO 1990, c P.15.

13 Above note 10.

14 Civil actions could also be added to the list but the concepts merge with criminal law (especially when a criminal court has already made negative findings or the civil claims arise out of the same fact situation or allegations of *Charter* breaches — see, for

racial profiling — on both a professional and legal level with individuals and the community at large.

1) Criminal Law

> "A stop or search motivated by racial bias or racial profiling violates the Charter rights of the person stopped or searched."[15]

Police actions taken in the course of an investigation that led to charges, if found to involve racial profiling or in any way related to racial profiling, engage sections 8, 9, and 10 of the *Charter* and could result in the exclusion of evidence and/or a stay of proceedings.

The leading case on racial profiling is the Ontario Court of Appeal's decision in *R v Brown*.[16] The court summarized the law as follows:

> [7] . . . "Racial profiling involves the targeting of individual members of a particular racial group, on the basis of the supposed criminal propensity of the entire group." . . . Racial profiling is criminal profiling based on race. Racial or colour profiling refers to that phenomenon whereby certain criminal activity is attributed to an identified group in society on the basis of race or colour resulting in the targeting of individual members of that group. In this context, race is illegitimately used as a proxy for the criminality or general criminal propensity of an entire racial group.
>
> . . .
>
> [8] That attitude underlying racial profiling is one that may be consciously or subconsciously held. That is, the police officer need not be an overt racist. His or her conduct may be based on subconscious racial stereotyping . . . .

In most cases, the argument will centre around, as it did in *R v Brown*, whether the initial stop and detention was arbitrary. Therefore, in order to succeed with a Section 9 *Charter* application based on racial profiling, the accused must prove "that it was more probable than not that there was no articulable cause (to use the phrase commonly used before *R. v. Mann* (2004), 185 C.C.C. (3d) 308 (S.C.C.)) for the stop and that the real reason was the race of the defendant."[17]

---

example, *Elmardy v Toronto Police Services Board*, 2017 ONSC 2074 at paras 12 to 23 (Div Ct) [*Elmardy*]) and human rights litigation.

15   *R v Steele*, 2015 OJ No 1253 at para 24 (CA).

16   *R v Brown*, 2003 CanLII 52142 (Ont CA) [*Brown*].

17   *R v Khan*, 2016 ONCJ 739 at para 8.

The Court of Appeal in *R v Brown* went on to state, "where the evidence shows that the circumstances relating to a detention correspond to the phenomenon of racial profiling and provide a basis for the court to infer that the police officer is lying about why he or she singled out the accused person for attention."[18] As such, it is open for a court to infer that the stop was racially motivated. This is an essential part of the analysis within the criminal context because, except in the most outrageous of cases, racial profiling will not be overtly found on the evidence. It will, if found at all, be found based on reasonable inference.

Perhaps because of the absence of direct evidence of racial profiling, or perhaps due to the fact that courts tend to make decisions based on more objective evidence or standards (as opposed to the more presumptive, holistic approach and test used by human rights commissions — see below), there are, relatively speaking, very few reported cases where racial profiling has been found to have happened and/or been a factor in a detention or investigation.

Another factor that could influence this is the regime to obtain third-party records (*R v O'Connor*[19] and *R v McNeil*[20]). In order to build a body of inferential evidence, the accused will often seek employment records or other records that are non-fruits of the investigation (e.g., logs, traffic stops).[21] As Molloy J stated in *R v Khan*:[22]

> 22 . . . A mere allegation of racial profiling should not be sufficient to trigger a duty on the Crown to disclose documents not even in its physical possession and completely unrelated to the particular accused or particular offence charged.
>
> . . .
>
> 59 . . . The defence request for the documents is supported by nothing more than speculation and wishful thinking. This case falls squarely within the large body of case law prohibiting disclosure where the defence application is shown to be nothing more than a fishing expedition.

Those third-party applications are often done "in the dark," in the sense that the requesting party does not know what the records contain but must convince the trial judge of their predicted or anticipated "likely relevance." At the same time, those applications are often fishing exped-

---

18   *Brown*, above note 16 at para 45.
19   [1995] 4 SCR 411.
20   [2009] 1 SCR 66.
21   For example, see *R v McGann* (16 May 2014) (Ont SCJ), Glithero J.
22   [2004] OJ No 3811 at paras 22 and 59 (SCJ).

itions or, at the very least, are perceived to be such. In fact, when and if the application gets to the second stage of the *O'Connor* process and the records sought are viewed by the trial judge, not surprisingly, the records often provide little, if any, relevant information.

Practically, this may impact the overall strength or veracity of the accused's allegation of racial profiling. That is, where the accused has put forth an argument that third-party records will assist in making their case for bias *and* those records do not, the claim of bias is undermined, absent other and stronger evidence to allow the judge to infer racial profiling.

As time goes by — in particular, with the collection of data in other areas and the developing caselaw and trends in other forums (see the *Human Rights Code* below) that point to systemic-based racial profiling — it is more likely than not that the racial profiling-based *Charter* application will become more prevalent and/or will be more successful. As it becomes more known what kind of data is now collected/available and with public reporting of records that are data driven, it is even more likely that such will form the foundation for:

1) *O'Connor* applications;
2) expert/academic opinions filed in support of those applications; and
3) assertions of presumptive racial profiling.

Consequently, and building on such, there may be more arguable claims of racial profiling — whether that be of a more direct kind or, more likely, based on systemic profiling arising out of other social and/or economic factors that influence policing and crime.

Having said that, another reason that there are relatively few examples of successful claims of racial profiling may simply be due to the fact that it does not happen with great frequency. This does not take away from the gravity of the issue for an individual who was subjected to (or even perceived that they were subjected to) racial profiling.

An interesting aside that arises when a criminal court deals with racial profiling allegations against officers is that the forum does not afford the officer a venue or legal avenue to fully defend against the application/allegations. While the officer may have legal representation in a third-party application, the officer has no standing within an application in a criminal case based on their alleged racial profiling. The officer is not permitted to call evidence to the contrary to rebut any inferences, cross-examine the accused (or other witnesses), and, perhaps most importantly, make submissions in defence of their actions, factually or in law. That process puts the officer (and the service) at a disadvantage and can have a significant impact on related or consequential allegations of police misconduct or a breach of the *Human Rights Code*. It is an area where the law perhaps has to develop akin to judicially mandated third-party privacy protection-based processes — for example, *O'Connor* applications where the impacted third party is given proper notice of the application and the right to fully participate in the hearing.

2) *Human Rights* Code (Ontario)

Unlike criminal matters, human rights applications that allege racial profiling will almost always have the officer as a party or active participant in the matter.[23] As such and due to the different policy considerations that underlie human rights legislation and accountability, the process, test, and burdens are significantly different than the criminal context — save for and excepting the seriousness of the alleged violation of the *Code* and the need to often make inferential findings to support racial profiling.[24]

Similar to matters in the criminal court involving allegations of racial discrimination, there will seldom be instances where there is direct evidence that race was a factor in the officer's decision-making process or their actions. As such, the law has developed to recognize that the determination of whether a violation of the *Code* has occurred is based on "well-established principles applicable to circumstantial evidence cases."[25]

This does not mean that the police officer has the burden to disprove discrimination. It merely means that if the complainant has proved the *prima facie* existence of discrimination, that is,

1) That he or she is a member of a group protected by the *Code*;
2) That he or she was subjected to adverse treatment; and
3) That his or her gender, race, colour or ancestry was a factor in the alleged adverse treatment,[26]

---

23 While the trend in human rights litigation is to limit the responding party to the employer, where the allegations go to or arise out of the actions of an individual's racial profiling, that individual is usually named as and continues to be a party throughout the proceeding. While they may be jointly represented by the employer police service, they can have independent representation by choice or where their actions have created a conflict with the employer's legal position.

24 The same can be said for findings of liability in the civil law context (see, for example, *Elmardy*, above note 14, where *Charter* damages for racial profiling were awarded in the amount of $50,000 against the board plus an additional $25,000 for punitive damages against the board and the officer).

25 *Phipps v Toronto Police Services Board*, 2009 HRTO 877 at para 17 [*Phipps* HRTO], judicial review denied, 2010 ONSC 3884 (Div Ct), aff'd 2012 ONCA 155 [*Phipps* ONCA].

26 *Phipps* ONCA, *ibid* at para 14 (ONCA).

then the respondent officer (and police services board) must tender evidence, often based on a credibility assessment, that satisfies the tribunal that the inference of discrimination is *not* more probable from the evidence than the actual explanations offered by the respondent.[27]

Nevertheless and due to the nature of the allegations of racial profiling and the inferential analysis, the tribunal will explicitly be "mindful of the nature of racial discrimination as it is understood today and that it will often be the product of learned attitudes and biases and often operates on an unconscious level: *Nassiah v Peel (Regional Municipality) Services Board*, 2007 HRTO 14."[28]

As well and it must be pointed out that the *prima facie* burden of the applicant is limited to only showing that race was *a single factor* in the alleged adverse treatment and the respondent police officer can be found to have racially profiled if it was *but one* of the factors or considerations underlying a decision or action (it need not be a predominant or even conscious factor).

Even with that, there has not been an avalanche of decisions in the tribunal finding that the police have racially profiled.[29] This may be as a result of many factors including, but not limited to, the following:

1) Clear matters or matters that, on their face, have a high probability of negative findings are settled through mediation and/or before a hearing;

2) The process is now more "court-like" without commission involvement in investigations and with a lesser presence within hearings (except in limited circumstances where a broader question of law is at issue or a more general systemic remedy may be appropriate);

3) As such, often applicants are self-represented and may not fully appreciate the law or process at the tribunal and/or have a tendency to make general or wide-sweeping allegations of police misconduct rather than focusing on the single incident;

4) There may be a natural reluctance to effectively label a person as being discriminatory when the actions or decisions were based on so-

---

27 *Joshi v Regional Municipality of Peel (Regional Municipality) Police Services Board*, 2016 HRTO 1398 at paras 79–80.

28 *Phipps* HRTO, above note 25 at para 18.

29 Interestingly, as well, while the police have heard about the reluctance of individuals to bring a public compliant under the *Police Services Act* (based on a lack of trust of that system or fear), compared to the myriad of interactions with the public, there have been relatively few human rights complaints made (where trust and protection from reprisals are key elements of that system).

cietal biases/learned attitudes *when combined with* legitimate and law enforcement actions;

5) The stop of the individual may have been completely lawful and/or justified but subsequent conduct or treatment results in the suspicion of differential treatment; therefore, the matter may not be racial profiling but broader discrimination contrary to the *Code*;

6) In that regard, broader discrimination based on race does not always result in a finding or allegation of racial profiling;

7) On a pure evidentiary basis, it may be difficult to contradict and/or the evidence actually supports that the officer was not aware of the person's race when initiating the stop (in particular, vehicle stops) due to such factors as distance, window tinting, time of day;

8) General credibility considerations; and/or

9) The nature of circumstantial evidence.[30]

Having said that, it will be interesting to see if the regulation on street checks will impact findings at the tribunal. Will a violation of the regulation (substantive or technical) or even the recording of the *perceived* race of the individual "incorrectly" make it more likely to result in a finding of racial profiling? If that does happen, it will be an unfortunate consequence of a regulation that is difficult to explain, train, and/or follow.[31]

It is interesting to note that *discrimination* is not defined in the *Code*. However, as noted in *Maynard v Toronto Police Services Board*, "it has been consistently defined by the Tribunal and the Courts to mean adverse treatment, or a distinction which creates a disadvantage, on the basis of a prohibited ground."[32] In that regard, adverse treatment will often be the manner in which an individual is singled out for investigation (or now with street checks, in the attempt to collect information) *and* it "is irrelevant whether the conduct is ultimately found to be defensible."[33]

The commission's *Policy and Guidelines on Racism and Racial Discrimination* (June 2005) also provides an interesting insight into how discrimination may occur in "intersection" with other grounds of the *Code*;

---

30 Admittedly all of this is conjecture and may be something that should be the subject of academic study.

31 Police services across the province have struggled with the creation of practical training materials, extensive flowcharts, and computer programs in attempts to assist officers and the public.

32 2012 HRTO 1220 at para 149.

33 *Ibid* at para 152.

as well as a key consideration regarding an applicant's reaction to a police officer.[34] The commission opined the following:

> Finally, it is important to note that persons who reasonably believe they are being racially profiled can be expected to find the experience upsetting and might well react in an angry and verbally aggressive manner. A citizen who honestly and reasonably believes that he or she is being treated unjustly is entitled to protest vigorously, as long as there is no resort to threatening gestures to accompany the words. A Tribunal has stated that a person's use of abusive language in these circumstances requires reasonable tolerance and tact and cannot form the basis for further differential treatment.[35]

The Commission pointed out that other tribunals had already recognized this (in *Johnson v Halifax (Regional Municipality) Police Service*[36]). The Commission also noted that the Canadian Human Rights Tribunal recognized that the broader social and historical context that informed the complainant's feelings of concern, hurt, and resentment when he was pulled over and asked questions about his citizenship and place of birth are essential to consider.[37] Interestingly, a police officer is unlikely to have that social or historical context as it relates specifically to the complainant and, sometimes, a racialized or ethnic group. As such, the need for education and training of police officers in this regard combined with de-escalation techniques will be essential if positive developments are to be achieved (see below).

There are other areas where the law has developed uniquely within the Human Rights Tribunal.

Unlike in criminal matters, the issue of third-party records is generally not a hurdle for applicants. First of all, the records of the responding officer (general employment, training, or discipline) are not third-party records because the officer is a party and they are presumptively relevant.[38] In addition, the tribunal is much more willing to order produc-

---

34   On at least one occasion, the commission has asked the tribunal to consider that very concept in its analysis: *ibid* at para 154.

35   Ontario Human Rights Commission, *Policy and Guidelines on Racism and Racial Discrimination* (Toronto: Ontario Human Rights Commission, 2005) at 20.

36   (2003), 48 CHRR D/307 at paras 41 and 60 (NS Bd Inq).

37   *Hum v Royal Canadian Mounted Police* (1986), 8 CHRR D/3748 at paras 29696 & 29697 (CHRT).

38   *Nassiah v Peel Regional Police Services Board*, 2006 HRTO 18 [*Nassiah*]; *Washington v Toronto Police Services Board*, 2009 HRTO 217 [*Washington* HRTO], judicial review denied, 2010 ONSC 419 (Div Ct); and *King v Toronto Police Services Board*, 2009 HRTO 644; *Roberts v Toronto Police Services Board*, 2016 HRTO 1464.

tion of non-incident specific or data-related records under the production of potentially relevant material.[39]

Secondly, while expert testimony (1) on the phenomenon of racial profiling in police investigations based on empirical work and/or (2) providing an opinion about whether alleged facts provide indicia of racial profiling in a police investigation has been allowed,[40] the impact and necessity under the revised tribunal regime (post-commission direct involvement) is uncertain. The ultimate decision must be made by the tribunal. The development of commission policy and jurisprudence suggests that such expert evidence is unlikely to be allowed or significantly relied upon, as it might be within the criminal or civil court context. Arguably, expert evidence should be restricted to issues of systemic violations of the *Code* within policing and/or only when it is needed to assist the tribunal in crafting broader remedies.

In that regard and whether following a decision of the tribunal on the merits or by endorsed settlement involving the commission, the larger systemic issues that underlie individual experiences is an area that requires a much more sophisticated and independent expert assistance. Remedies that seek to address the broader or underlying issues — or even to attempt to understand or quantify those issues — will often require expert/academic assistance in how to frame the questions, methodology, and/or data collection/reporting remedies.[41] This is likely to be an area where the tribunal will focus great attention.

Finally, as a result of the law arising out of the Supreme Court of Canada's decision in *Penner v Niagara (Regional Police Services Board)*, 2013 SCC 19 and the Ontario Divisional Court's decision in *Ontario (Community Safety and Correctional Services) v De Lottinville*, 2015 ONSC 3085 (CanLII), the tribunal will no longer order a section 45.1 dismissal of an application because it was "appropriately dealt with" in a *Police Services Act* disciplinary hearing dealing with the same factual circumstances. However, there is a lack of clarity at the tribunal as to whether that law will have an impact on deferral applications pending the completion of that *Police Services Act* investigation and/or hearing or other related proceedings (criminal, provincial offences, etc.). It would seem to make sense and avoid depletion of limited tribunal resources and capacity to continue to defer applications pending the results of those related *Police*

---

39 For example, *McKay v Toronto Police Services Board*, 2009 HRTO 1220; *Washington HRTO*, above note 38.

40 *Nassiah*, above note 38.

41 See, for example, *Aiken v Ottawa Police Services Board*, 2015 ONSC 3793 (Div Ct).

Services Act investigations and/or hearings. There should always be deference to finding of facts made in related proceedings, but without still allowing for further evidence and information responsive to the function of the *Code* and the tribunal, and still applying the relevant human rights tests to those facts.

3) Police Discipline and Regulation

As it relates to police discipline, racial profiling is also dealt with under the *Police Services Act*, in particular, the public complaints system and the Act's regulation establishing a *Code of Conduct*[42] for officers. It is further but differently addressed, to some extent, under one of its other regulations dealing with "street checks," where specific discipline provisions were added dealing with compliance with that regulation.[43]

a) Regulation — That Is, Street Checks[44]

It seems uncontroversial that the police community failed to properly explain how and when a *proper* street check interaction occurs. In addition, there was very little public discourse or explanation given regarding the legitimate purposes for doing street checks, the successes that have led to increased public safety, and police leaders' commitment and steps taken to ensure their officers' engagement was and continues to be based on non-arbitrary, bias-free decisions.

Interestingly, from the police perspective above, the general community (including racialized groups) is not that far apart from the policing community, if at all, on the underlying matters. However, and concurrently, there has been a substantial failing in how these types of police operations have impacted those affected racialized groups or individuals. What police do need to deal with, and where they require community assistance, is proactively and reactively addressing incidents where these shared, laudable, and key pronouncements that form the basis of bias-neutral policing philosophy are not followed. No one should be subjected to racial profiling and, if they are, consequences must flow and change must occur with the community's assistance.

---

42   *Code of Conduct*, in *General*, O Reg 268/10, Schedule, under the *Police Services Act*, above note 12.

43   *Code of Conduct*, above note 42, s 2(1)(g), "unlawful or unnecessary exercise of authority."

44   As noted above, also known as "collection of identifying information in certain circumstances" or "carding," but for the purposes of this article, the general term of "street checks" will be used.

The ability to effect positive change and ensure accountability comes, in part, from a good relationship with community members and groups. Some of that also comes from viewing policing as a function and product of the community. Community policing models mean officers know members of the public and, as a result, the walls between them and the public will crumble or will not be as high . . . this is all based on a mutual trust and respect.

The problem with the conversation — sometimes debate, sometimes unproductive argument — on racial profiling (in particular, street checks) is the mistrust, lack of respect, and lack of understanding that can permeate the discussion.

There has been a dearth of actual and reliable data collection and analysis, all in the face of anecdotal stories that easily play out in the media. In fact, what is described as a street check is often confused with other police interactions (for example, a legitimate and lawful stop under the *Highway Traffic Act*, investigative detention) or for which there is no proof of the interaction.

The province clearly heard the concerns of individuals and community leaders and decided to act. While the issues tended to be primarily centred on only large urban communities, addressing the lack of clear direction (province-wide) resulted in a discussion on having enforceable guidelines. This was welcomed by police leaders, generally. The divergence came about in determining what the solution should be.

From a policing perspective, street checks[45] had historically always been the documentation of crime prevention or potentially relevant intelligence information garnered through an observation or interaction with members of the public. The most classic type of this information may be relating to gang or organized crime associations. This information could be garnered entirely *passively through an observation from a distance* (i.e., no interaction), as a *result of a lawful interaction where the information is given, or an observation made* (e.g., highway traffic stop, investigative detention, investigation or arrest regarding a specific offence and person. Once again, a classic example is to note that someone is wearing gang colours or white supremacist tattoos.)

---

45   It should be noted that before being regulated, the term "street check" was a generic term that described the documentation of the information in internal police records, not the interaction, and therefore included all the interactions that resulted in potential intelligence information inputted into police databases regardless of the source or type of interaction that spurned it.

But those are not the street checks that we are talking about as being the issue.

In its most simple terms, the contentious interaction involved the approaching of a person when there is only a suspicion of criminal activity or when there may be reason to believe that there could be relevant intelligence information to be acquired. This could include engaging with a passenger in a vehicle on a lawful traffic stop where the passenger is under no obligation to provide information (except in very limited circumstances) or in situations where the nature of a detention changes character. In these interactions, the person is under no obligation to provide information (including their name) but the interactions can and have been valuable in solving the most serious of crimes and protecting the community from gang/organized crime, drug trade, human trafficking, and the indiscriminate use of violent weapons (we never want to see another "Year of the Gun"). But at the same time, those interactions were seen as disrupting the liberties of the individuals and/or partially or wholly based on biases or stereotypes. Often repeated interactions with the same individuals only fuelled those issues.

Those types of interactions — despite being technically "voluntary" — are the only true street checks or carding that were seen as the issue and, if abused or misused, they not only undermine the relationship between the community and police but actually or potentially could undermine the usefulness of the information.

The province has attempted, through its regulatory power,[46] to address any real or perceived issues related to street checks and, by doing so, has created a separate regime that seeks to put limitations and preconditions on interactions and create a certain amount of accountability. Some might argue that street checks have gone from simply being ambiguous to being ambiguous and confusing; others would say the regulation has not gone far enough to limit the practice. Regardless, there are now limitations on when an officer can attempt to collect information from an individual within a racialized group:

Limitations on collection of certain information —

5. (1) A police officer shall not attempt to collect identifying information about an individual from the individual if,

    (a) any part of the reason for the attempted collection is that the officer perceives the individual to be within a particular racialized group unless,

---

46 *COIICC*, above note 12.

(i) the officer is seeking a particular individual,

(ii) being within the racialized group forms part of a description of the particular individual or is evident from a visual representation of the particular individual, and

(iii) the officer has additional information, in addition to information about the particular individual being in a racialized group, that may help to identify the individual or narrow the description of the individual; or

(b) the attempted collection is done in an arbitrary way.

(2) Without limiting what might constitute the additional information required under subclause (1) (a) (iii), such information may consist of information about,

(a) the appearance of the individual, including information about the individual's clothing, height, weight, eye colour, hair colour or hair style;

(b) the location where the individual might be found;

(c) the type of vehicle the individual might be found in;

(d) the associates the individual might be found with; or

(e) the behaviour of the individual.[47]

At first glance — especially the initial phrase in paragraph 5(1)(a), "[a] police officer shall not attempt to collect identifying information about an individual from the individual if . . . any part of the reason for the attempted collection is that the officer perceives the individual to be within a particular racialized group" — it would seem that the regulation goes beyond the restrictions imposed through bias-neutral policing directives.

It is actually the opposite.

The regulation goes on to allow interactions that are based on perception of race in specified circumstances (the "unless . . ." portions set out subparagraphs (i) to (iii)). Bias-neutral policing philosophy not only does not, as noted above, restrict itself to race but it also *only* allows prohibited grounds to be used pursuant to "investigative profiling." Again, that means that the information being relied upon must be trustworthy and relevant and form reasonable suspicion or reasonable grounds to link a person or persons to a particular unlawful incident or incidents. Furthermore, race can never be used as the primary or predominant basis for reasonable suspicion or reasonable grounds.

Recognizing that, for most police services, the regulated street checks only make up a small portion of the interactions police have and are certainly a minority of the intelligence data, some police services have

---

47   *Ibid.*

adopted procedures that also require the tracking of the non-regulated data collection — sometimes referred to as "intelligence notes" — where the data is gathered from passive observations without interaction or from another interaction that is lawful (e.g., a traffic stop) where the individual is required to provide certain information. In addition and to assist in future analysis and discourse, those police services are collecting the same data as required by the regulation. This may prove to be key to data integrity/analysis and explaining the reduction in the number of street checks, since historical data will include the interactions governed by the regulation and these (majority) non-regulated or intrusive matters.

In any event, it should be noted that the breadth of bias-neutral policing goes beyond street checks and applies equally to investigative detention[48] and formal detentions/arrests. Nevertheless, it should be understood, whether intentional or not, that the province of Ontario has created another formal category on the continuum of police/public interactions: street checks. Even before the regulation came into effect, there was and continues to be a substantial level of confusion as to when it applies: video postings online and social media only seem to reinforce the confusion. Legitimate arrest or lawful interactions based on investigative detention are met with demands for compliance with the regulation or, more concerning, a mistaken belief that a person does not have to follow an officer's lawful commands. As a result, there may be a perception of racial profiling that arises out of that confusion.

b) Police Discipline

The *Police Services Act* has specific misconducts under its *Code of Conduct* that deal with racial profiling:

> 2. (1) Any chief of police or other police officer commits misconduct if he or she engages in,
>
>   (a) Discreditable Conduct, in that he or she,
>
>   (i)   fails to treat or protect persons equally without discrimination with respect to police services because of race, ancestry, place of origin, colour, ethnic origin, citizenship, creed, sex, sexual orientation, age, marital status, family status or disability,
>
>   (ii) uses profane, abusive or insulting language that relates to a person's race, ancestry, place of origin, colour, ethnic origin,

---

48   A misnomer, as there is no actual detention (except and limited to when and if a pat-down for weapons is justified) — the person is free to go and not answer any questions — but rather it is a perceived detention based on the circumstances and reasonable assumption of a person stopped and questioned by a police officer about an offence.

citizenship, creed, sex, sexual orientation, age, marital status, family status or disability.[49]

In addition, an officer can be found guilty of general discreditable conduct for acting in a manner prejudicial to discipline or likely to bring discredit upon the reputation of the police force; a finding that racial profiling occurred will always result in bringing discredit upon the reputation of the police service. As well, a new misconduct was added when the province chose to regulate street checks: unlawful or unnecessary exercises of authority when collecting or attempting to collect identifying information about an individual under O Reg 58/16 ("Collection of Identifying Information In Certain Circumstances — Prohibition and Duties" — sometimes referred to as "COIICC"[50]).

An officer can also be insubordinate and/or neglectful in the exercise of their duties if their actions are found to be in contravention of a bias-neutral policing procedure because those procedures are deemed orders of the chief of police.

As a result, there is a multi-layered police misconduct regime designed to hold police officers accountable for their actions if they are bias- (race or otherwise) based. The police discipline system can be invoked by the chief of police (a "chief's complaint" or "internal complaint") or by a member of the public making a complaint about the conduct of an individual officer (a "public complaint").[51] As well, a member of the public can make a complaint about the overall services or policies of the service (a "service/policy complaint").[52] And, finally, the Office of the Independent Police Review Director, in addition to the power under "public complaints" to investigate, assign, review, and override decisions relating to whether misconduct has been substantiated or is serious or not (warranting a public hearing), has the independent and separate authority to conduct systemic investigations on a wide range of issues that includes racial profiling.[53]

As such and noted above, it seems prudent that the *Police Services Act* discipline process should precede a human rights matter (also awaiting the outcome of related criminal or provincial offence charges arising out of the interaction, if any).

---

49 *Code of Conduct*, above note 42, ss 2(1)(a)(i) & (ii).

50 *COIICC*, above note 12.

51 *Police Services Act*, above note 12, ss 58(1)(a), 60(6), and 76.

52 *Ibid*, s 58(1)(b).

53 *Ibid*, s 57.

As an aside, there is a compelling argument that a better system would be to treat all internal police misconduct matters as employment matters, still based on a code of conduct but with independent adjudication that removes any perceived biases built into the system (offset by the chief's inability to appeal an appointed hearing officer's decision). Police services could then move to a "college" or licensing model akin to other professions to deal with public complaints. All of this would be designed to ensure transparency and public accountability, as well as allowing racial discrimination and profiling victims to have a voice in the processes.[54]

E. POTENTIAL SOLUTIONS — OVERSIGHT, EDUCATION, AND/OR DATA ANALYSIS

1) Oversight

In policing there are a number of oversight/regulatory/disciplinary regimes that may come into play. In various degrees, the policing profession is gripped with oversight[55] — perhaps that is part of the problem. The oversight is divided, a patchwork, and often results in multiple proceedings relating to the same events but using different lenses, standards of proof, and even those with party status to the proceeding.

Experience has shown us both the criminal context and the police misconduct processes. You cannot discipline or enforce your way out of, or effect substantive change to, racial profiling. We have tried; in fact, many others have tried. We have tried and, relatively speaking, have all failed. That does not mean that discipline or negative consequences aris-

---

54 The Human Rights Tribunal, while imbued with wide remedial powers, does not have the authority to order the discipline or termination of an offending police officer.

55 Police officers are subject to *Police Services Act* discipline, either by a chief's complaint or a public complaint, *and* the Office of the Independent Police Review Director not only oversees that public complaints system, but it also has the ability and power to conduct systemic reviews. The Ontario Civilian Police Commission hears appeals of discipline decisions (although the chief does not have appeal rights, to balance the multiple delegated roles the chief has in the process) and has separate investigative, *systemic*, powers that include wide sweeping powers under section 25 of the Act. The Ombudsman now has an expanded mandate that allows for investigations and reports. The Ministry of Community Safety and Correctional Services has powers and oversight — including the power to establish adequacy standards and conduct audits. The Police Services Board can serve an important civilian oversight role. And, finally, the Human Rights Tribunal of Ontario and the courts (both criminal and civil) all play an important role in oversight and accountability.

ing from such do not serve an important role in addressing racial profiling in policing.

However, addressing only the consequences of racial profiling or taking an after-the-fact approach is both reactionary and myopic. While the principles of sentencing in police misconduct include general and specific deterrence and rehabilitation, they do not stand alone as the only factors and it must be remembered that *Police Service Act* complaints are still part of an employment discipline system.[56] Unless and until this system shifts to one that includes an independent licensing scheme and/or a "discipline and grieve later" employment model, it is unlikely that it will respond in a sufficient manner to address racial profiling on an individual basis (unless it is overt) or on a more general, systemic basis.

At the same time, one must never lose sight of the fact that an individual officer who has been accused of racial profiling should and must have the right to defend their actions and even their underlying decision-making processes. (Is the bias theirs or is it ours? Society's?) The criminal and quasi-criminal law[57] may need to develop better mechanisms to counterbalance the potential misuse of statutory, regulatory rights, and common-law powers to stop, detain, and/or demand identification.[58] There must be a distinction between having lawful authority and whether the exercise of that authority was lawful — that is, not motivated by improper considerations.[59]

2) Data Analysis

Data analysis and statistical analysis are going to be key to addressing these issues in the long term. However, they too are not the panacea.

We need to look at the issue, perhaps, through a different lens. The data analysis cannot be merely based on disproportionate representation of one or more racialized group as compared to baseline population statistics. As Steven D Levitt and Stephen J Dubner say in *Freakonomics*:

---

56 Paul Ceyssens & Scott Child, *Ontario Police Services Act, Fully Annotated*, 2017 ed (Salt Spring Island, BC: Earlscourt Legal Press, 2016) at 31–76.

57 In addition to considering the establishment of a process that allows officers against whom a claim of racial profiling has been made within a criminal proceeding to have notice of such allegations and the right to make submissions in their defence.

58 For example, *Highway Traffic Act* powers (ss 33 and 216, etc.), *COIICC*, above note 12, and investigative detention.

59 *R v Richards*, 1999 CanLII 1602 at para 34 (Ont CA).

Knowing what to measure and how to measure it makes a complicated work much less so. If you learn how to look at data in the right way, you can explain riddles that otherwise might have seemed impossible. Because there is nothing like the sheer power of numbers to scrub away layers of confusion and contradiction.[60]

Crime statistics and data regarding stops (whether that be traffic stops, investigative detention, and/or street checks) all provide important information: both baselining the issue to allow for measured change or trends and identifying areas where racial profiling *may* be occurring. However, they do not give us the whole picture or, in fact, prove or disprove racial profiling within policing. Better said, they do not provide direct evidence that racial profiling is occurring in policing independent of other factors or influence and/or are a product of those factors (the downstream or tip of the iceberg effect).

Crime does not, or those that commit crimes do not, abide by police jurisdictional boundaries, municipal lines, or even neighbourhood or area denotations. How large or small should the comparative population breakdown be? What about the fact that the place where the crime was committed can be a long way from where the person who committed the crime lives? Do the crime statistics generated from police create a self-fulfilling prophecy or vicious circle because they result in more police activity in those areas, which create higher crime statistics for those very same areas? If the neighbourhood is racialized, would this also generate an overrepresentation of that racialized group in the statistics?

While some contend or rely upon the axiom that an anecdote can be worth a thousand statistics, that too can be dangerous to the discourse and any possible solutions. Even if we find some assistance from statistical data collection and analysis, the lived experience of those who have or perceive that they have been subject to racial profiling is both compelling and has, at times, driven policy development or government action. So we need to first ensure that the facts underlying the anecdote are verified (to the extent possible) if we are going to act upon them and, most importantly, see if the data exists or enlightens us *before* developing policy. Secondly, we have to recognize that an individual's experience may be based on perceptions or biases — although having said that, the perception that a member or members of our community are subject to racial profiling by the police is, in itself, worrisome and needs to be addressed.

---

60   Steven D Levitt & Stephen J Dubner, *Freakonomics: A Rogue Economist Explores the Hidden Side of Everything*, 1st ed (New York: HarperColllins, 2005).

We have to recognize that anecdotal experiences and/or statistics may be symptoms of a greater societal or systemic race-based bias and/or the very perception that the police will racially profile undermines the relationship and confidence in the police by all or some of the community.

Therefore, one area that needs to be developed is the reduction or elimination (to the extent possible) of other upstream biases that may impact statistics and the analysis relating to police interactions and race. Should we be examining statistics that factor in or account for other societal influencers on crime (for example, poverty, education)? Or, is this merely an exercise that will result in self-fulfilling prophecies, the shifting of responsibility, and/or throwing our hands in the air because the problem of racial profiling is too big and owned by no one organization, institution, or community?

At the very least, it may be worth exploring statistics that tend to remove police influence vis-à-vis proactive crime initiatives (e.g., a particular neighbourhood that has a high crime rate will inevitably attract more enforcement initiatives). Looking at citizen-generated calls for service/complaints may be a better baseline approach. In addition, the conversation cannot be limited to just the police: the entire criminal justice system needs to be examined.

3) Education

An area that definitely needs to be expanded upon is police education: not just in content but in how and when that education is delivered. Canadian police services generally acknowledge that officers need to be better trained on what racial profiling is, the systemic drivers that influence it, and dealing with investigating and solving crimes, decision-making processes, and subconscious biases.[61] This requires training police officers a certain way, and exposing them to situations, to ensure that they are successful in solving crimes and dealing with exceptionally volatile situations. At the same time, they are expected to become aware of the patterns of thinking by which they have been molded.

Most importantly, police officers need to be educated in how others may perceive *them and their actions*. This should be done through a career-long program (starting as a prerequisite) that enlightens the police to their roles in historical, cultural, and socio/psychological incidents and

---

61   As part of *COIICC*, above note 12, mandatory training has been initiated as a prerequisite to doing a street check, but the training is only a start and needs significant broadening, refinements, and pedagogical review.

how they are perceived by different communities.[62] But at the same time, the training should provide positive examples of how these perceptions can be dealt with and/or overcome.

Police officers also need education on how to recognize and eliminate biases (racial or otherwise). There also needs to be a system in place for the community and officers to be able to freely bring forward observed contraventions of bias-neutral policing — whether they are individual or systemic, overt or subconscious.

Part of this is founded on a model of community policing. The importance of positive relationships with all racialized groups within the community cannot be underestimated. Stereotypes and biases are best challenged by open communication and building trust and relationships. One could argue that a majority of the problems surrounding street checks (carding) arose because the police were attempting to deal with serious criminal activities relating to guns and gangs in a reactive way, and officers who were tasked with this did not have a pre-existing or developing connection with the communities they were interacting with. "Success" was measured by frequency of contact and/or overall reduction of crime statistics.

And finally, the police and the community need to be educated on the importance of data collection, how to interpret and use it, as well as the traps and pitfalls of presumed cause and effect. The public and transparent accessibility of data will also assist greatly. But without considered and more global analysis of the data by an independent body or academics, we may simply create more questions than answers, more problems than solutions.

F. CONCLUSION

The oft-quoted and -relied upon quotation from Sir Robert Peel still forms the basis of modern day policing: "the police are the public and the public are the police."[63] But what does that truly mean?

It means the public needs to know that police leaders see racial profiling as a serious issue that must be dealt with. In the end, we are all responsible for ensuring our communities are safe and individual members — especially those who historically have been under advantaged or

---

62   Examples include how historically the police were used by governments to enforce what are now seen as bias-based laws, how police in other cultures are perceived or acting even to this day in oppressive manners, etc.

63   Above note 2.

lacked safety and security — are rightly protected by our laws that guard against injustice and discrimination. As Sir Robert Peel noted, a police officer is just the only one of us that signs up for that responsibility on a full-time basis and, as such, is given extraordinary powers. But if you ask any police officer, and it is not trite to say, they signed up for that role to serve their community, uphold the law, and protect the rights of *all* individuals. As such, they should and need to be the key players in dealing with and eliminating racial profiling. In order to do that, we, the public, need to assist them and at the same time hold them accountable when the principles of bias-neutral policing are not followed.

CHAPTER 6

"Singled Out"

Being a Black Youth in the Suburbs

CARL E JAMES[*]

A. INTRODUCTION

"The Longest Walk Ever"
by Dwight Campbell[1]

Blog Post, Wednesday, March 2, 2016

After a long Saturday evening of playing video games at my friend Lincoln's house, I decided enough was enough and headed home. It was a very cold night and although Lincoln's house couldn't possibly be more than a 7-minute walk to my house, due to the cold, those seven minutes felt like an eternity. Nonetheless I was almost home. I had just made the last and final turn onto my street and now was walking the homestretch. As I began my walk up the driveway a police cruiser driving by came to a stop and the officer proceeded to ask for my I.D. Young and under the assumption that this was my legal obligation, I handed it over without any hesitation. Moreover, since I had no criminal record and was unknown to the police, I thought there was no need to worry.

As the officer continued to run my identification, another cruiser pulled up, and a tall officer with an extremely muscular build appeared out of the car. He must have been at least 6 ft. 5 and 200 and 50 plus pounds. As he turned and glanced at me, the original officer still running my I.D. then said to his colleague: "Search him." The next thing I knew I was being slammed up against the back of the car and the police officer forcibly began searching me. As I was only fifteen years old, all I did was quiver in silence. While

---

[*]   Carl James is a professor and the Jean Augustine chair in education, community & diaspora, York University.
[1]   Used with permission through direct communication with Dwight Campbell.

this oversized cop continued to search me, he also emptied my pockets and threw my belongings into the snow. While this was happening, the other officer began to accuse me of peeking into other people's cars, and that I'm lucky that they caught me in front of my own house, otherwise they would have surely "F***ed me up." After confirming that my I.D. was clean the first policeman handed my identification papers over and told me to "Have a goodnight." I then picked my belongings out of the snow and went inside.

In the morning I told my parents and grandparents — who were visiting from Jamaica — of the encounter and they (my grandparents especially) scolded me about being out late, and all the dangers it comes with. I didn't really argue with them but I couldn't help but feel like they were wrong — as if there should be nothing wrong with a young Black fifteen year old walking home at approximately 10:30–11 p.m. on a Saturday night in Canada. Perhaps I was being naive. Unfortunately, this would not be the last encounter which I would have with Peel Police, but it was definitely one of the most memorable.

Dwight's encounter with police that Saturday night in his suburban neighbourhood is not atypical. In fact, "singled out" is how one young Black man described his experience living in a similar outer-suburban neighbourhood of the Greater Toronto Area. For these youth, and as Dwight's experience with police demonstrates, being stopped, scrutinized, searched, and beaten by police — even at the entrance to their homes — in part, are consequences of being singled out. Such consequences are seemingly what parents fear as they warn their children — especially their young sons — about "the dangers" of being out late at night. This fear is likely what prompted Dwight's parents and grandparents to "scold" him — even as they added to his abuse and false accusation by police while he "quivered in silence."[2]

More recently, the *Toronto Star* reported[3] on "charges of aggravated assault, assault with a weapon, and public mischief" brought against an off-duty Metro Toronto police officer, "allegedly" for beating a nineteen-year-old Black man in Whitby (a suburb east of Toronto) with a metal pipe, causing him "serious injuries." The officer, who was outside of his jurisdiction, is said, in December 2016, to have stopped the three youth and asked them "where they lived and what they were doing in the neigh-

---

2 Dwight demonstrates an understanding of his parents' actions — he "did not argue with them." But his assertion that "there should be nothing wrong with a young Black fifteen-year-old walking home at approximately 10:30–11 pm on a Saturday night in Canada" is quite appropriate for, like all other youth, he is entitled to freedom of movement.

3 Peter Goffin, "Alleged Victim's Family Speaks Out after Toronto Cop Charged with Assault" *Toronto Star* (18 July 2017), online: www.thestar.com/news/gta/2017/07/11/toronto-cop-charged-after-man-assaulted-in-whitby.html.

bourhood." When the youth continued to walk, "the officer chased them," and the one that was caught "was punched, kicked, and struck in the face repeatedly with a metal pipe." But in his account of the incident, the officer reportedly told the 911 operator (called by the youth, and from whom the officer took the phone) that he was beaten with a metal pipe by the youth whom he had arrested. Of the incident the youth's mother said: "I can't picture this happening to a group of white kids walking through a neighbourhood . . . . So I do think race played some part in it."

Therefore, the suburbs, to which many racialized parents have been migrating in the hopes of raising their children in "good" neighbourhoods, is proving not to be the safe, benign, and trouble-free places that they expected or wish for. In fact, as I have written elsewhere:[4] In Toronto many first- and second-generation families move from the "reception" areas of the city to the "outer suburbs" — often to new houses in newly established areas that for many of them represent the upward social mobility to which they aspire.[5] Also, these parents wish to escape the marginalized neighbourhoods, which — on the basis of low socio-economic conditions, high proportion of racialized and immigrant population, and schools with underachieving students — are stigmatized as "problem areas" and "dangerous" (because of illegal activities such as drug and gun use), and as a consequence, these neighbourhoods are "under the constant watch of surveillance agency personnel."[6]

The fact remains, for Black youth, life in the suburbs is not any safer or more socially favourable for them than it is for those living in the urban areas. In fact, the recent (July 2017) *Black Experience Project in the GTA*[7] report shows that there are no differences in experiences with racism among survey participants — including those from the four suburban areas of Toronto where nearly half (about 47 percent) of the Black population reside.[8] Specifically, the report shows that about one in two (52 percent) of the

---

4   See Chapter 8 of Carl E James, *"Colour Matters": Experiences, Education and Aspirations of Black Youth* (Toronto: University of Toronto Press) [forthcoming].

5   See also Robert A Murdie & Carlos Teixeira, "Towards a Comfortable Neighbourhood and Appropriate Housing: Immigrant Experiences in Toronto" in Paul Anisef & Michael Lanphier, eds, *The World in a City* (Toronto: University of Toronto Press, 2003) 132.

6   James, *"Colour Matters,"* above note 4 .

7   Environics Research Institute, *Black Experience Project in the GTA* (31 July 2017), online: www.environicsinstitute.org/projects/project-details/black-experience-project-in-the-gta.

8   Census data indicates that since 1981, there has been a consistent increase in the suburban Black population. The 2011 census shows that the Black population of Toronto is 53 percent, Peel 28 percent, York 6 percent, Durham 10 percent, and Halton 3 percent. *Ibid* at 27.

participants reported being "consciously aware of being Black in public spaces, including in their neighbourhood or at school, or when travelling or moving about . . . ."[9] Contributing to this consciousness is participants' experiences with racism such as "being observed or followed while in public places."[10] Young men (79 percent of twenty-five to forty-four year olds) reported "getting stopped in public places by police";[11] and "almost four in ten say they have been harassed or treated rudely by police."[12] Socio-economic status was found to have no bearing on these experiences. "Those with higher incomes and levels of education . . . are not noticeably less likely than average to have been stopped by the police in public, to have been harassed or treated rudely by the police, or to have had the police use force against them."[13]

The evidence indicates that Black youth are being singled out not only by police but by residents of the suburban communities who find their presence in the area to be unusual or "out of place" — hence the questions, suspicions, and treatment they receive from people who conceived of the suburbs as White middle-class spaces with long-time residents. This form of racial profiling is a process in which the youth's race and age intersect with place and space (i.e., the suburban neighbourhoods) to mediate the gaze, readings, surveillance, and containment of their Black bodies as they journey through the suburbs. In this chapter, I explore how being "singled out" as a form of racial profiling is experienced by Black youth in suburban spaces. Theories of race, space, and place are employed to offer insights into the role that space plays in their experiences — particularly in relation to the production of their sense of Black identification, their behaviours, and the ways in which they are differentiated and in turn interpret the world around them.[14]

---

9   *Ibid* at 42.

10   *Ibid* at 44.

11   *Ibid* at 47.

12   *Ibid* at 48.

13   *Ibid* at 49.

14   Simone Browne, *Dark Matters: On the Surveillance of Blackness* (Durham: Duke University Press, 2015); Ardavan Eizadirad, "Is It 'Bad' Kids or 'Bad' Places? Where Is All the Violence Originating from? Youth Violence in the City of Toronto" (2016) 38:2 *Review of Education, Pedagogy, and Cultural Studies* 162; Katherine McKittrick, "On Plantations, Prisons, and a Black Sense of Place" (2011) 12:8 *Social & Cultural Geography* 947; Rashad Shabazz, *Spatializing Blackness: Architectures of Confinement and Black Masculinity in Chicago* (Urbana: University of Illinois Press, 2015); Olúfẹ́mi Táíwò, "This Prison Called My Skin: On Being Black in America" in Jean Muteba Rahier & Percy Hintzen,

Following the theoretical discussion, using census data, I provide a concise demographic profile of the Black population in Toronto and its surrounding western suburban regions; then proceed to discuss the experiences, perceptions, and understandings of the young people who participated in studies I conducted in two suburban communities west of Toronto. In concluding, I contend that any discussion of racial profiling must give attention to the specificity of a racialized group taking into account how spatial contexts serve to mediate their socio-cultural situation, circumstances, and opportunities. For in operating to police, regulate, discipline, contain, and punish Black youth, racial profiling also serves to "cast a prison-like shadow"[15] over their movements, social situation, understanding of shared community, sense of social mobility, and possibilities in life.

B. RACE, SPACE, AND PLACE

In his book, *Spatializing Blackness*, about the relationship between people and place, and the "policing, surveillance, and architectures of confinement" that have been used to "spatialize blackness"[16] in Chicago, Shabazz writes that geography greatly influences our everyday existence: who we are, the habits we display, the conventions we follow, and things to which we might become susceptible. As such, "physical space and where one is located within it tell us much about [them]."[17] In essence, space does not simply play "a role in the production of identities," it is "fundamental to identity, and we depend on it to help construct meaning, to explain the world around us, and to highlight what is particular about us."[18] Therefore, how people identify with and come to be known in particular spaces are all structured by the social and political order of things. In this regard, space organizes social life and practices in particular ways "permitting certain actions and prohibiting others."[19] Essentially, space is not neutral; and as Shabazz states, it is "one of the most important and significant illustrators of uneven development, access, and social order.

---

eds, *Problematizing Blackness: Self-Ethnographies by Black Immigrants to the United States* (New York: Routledge, 2003) 35.

15 Shabazz, *Spatializing Blackness*, above note 14 at 118.

16 *Ibid* at 3.

17 *Ibid* at 1.

18 *Ibid* at 46.

19 Sherene Razack, "When Race Becomes Place" in Tania Das Gupta et al, eds, *Race and Racialization: Essential Readings* (Toronto: Canadian Scholars' Press, 2007) 77.

Its organization and how people are situated within it reflects social hier-archies."[20] Additionally, as Neely and Samura state, it "is often a more tangible manifestation of systemic racial inequalities."[21] Accordingly, Knowles contends:[22]

> Space is an active archive of the social processes and social relationships composing racial orders. Active because it is not just a monument, accumu-lated through a racial past and present — although it is also that — it is active in the sense that it interacts with people and their activities as an ongoing set of possibilities in which race is fabricated.

Any analysis of the role that geography or space plays in people's lives must necessarily be historicized in order to account for how institutions have contributed to the differentiated relationships among members in contemporary society.[23] In the case of Black people in the Americas, transatlantic slavery and plantation life as vestiges of colonialism remain salient features that today are reflected in practices of geographic sur-veillance, containment, and management that contribute to the difficult entanglements of racial encounters and the criminalization of Black bod-ies.[24] Black people's capacity to move about, live, and be seen in particular geographic spaces in the society is significantly connected to the struc-tural workings of racism as framed by Canada's colonial history. "Indeed, Blackness in the Americas," as McKittrick writes, "is deeply connected to sites of social and infrastructural decay and geographic surveillance."[25]

Understandably then, outside of this "bracketed geography,"[26] to quote Shabazz, they would be in violation of their de facto "assigned space" evidenced in their residential patterns. This has to do with the fact that based on their economic situation, Blacks are less likely to be home-owners, and a significant proportion of them tend to live in assisted hous-

---

20   Shabazz, *Spatializing Blackness*, above note 14 at 45.

21   Brooke Neely & Michelle Samura, "Social Geographies of Race: Connecting Race and Space" (2011) 34:11 *Ethnic and Racial Studies* 1933 at 1940.

22   Caroline Knowles, *Race and Social Analysis* (London: Sage, 2003) at 80.

23   Indeed, Razack argues that when studying White settler societies, connections must be made between racial and spatial processes, noting how Europeans installed themselves as legally "entitled to the land" since it was empty space they were able to inhabit. As such, they reproduced racial hierarchies through space. Razack, above note 19 at 74.

24   McKittrick, above note 14 at 955.

25   *Ibid* at 951.

26   Shabazz, *Spatializing Blackness*, above note 14 at 45.

ing.[27] This, in part, accounts for them residing in larger numbers in urban, as opposed to suburban or exurban, areas, in rental accommodation, and in low income areas. In the case of the Greater Toronto Area, findings indicate that slightly more than half of the Black population reside in urban Toronto, and they make up less than 40 percent, and in the majority of cases less than 20 percent, of any neighbourhood.[28] In addition to where they reside being described as "marginalized" neigbourhoods, they are also branded as "troubled"[29]and/or "stigmatized"[30] neighbourhoods, where, as Wacquant writes, social problems fester and "urban outcasts . . . , dishonest minorities, and disenfranchised immigrants" reside resulting in "disproportionately negative attention from the media, politicians and store managers."[31]

Cheryl Harris' discussion of "whiteness as property"[32] is relevant to this discussion, in that space — in this case, the suburbs — is taken to be the property of the many White long-time residents, hence must be policed and protected from outside intruders or "space invaders"[33] who, based on skin colour, may be coming from the stigmatized urban neighbourhoods. As Harris asserts, Whiteness conveys power, privilege, and agency that gives Whites a sense of belonging and entitlement to space, which they use to set lines of racial demarcation, exclude, and subjugate those less privileged.[34] Reflecting on Harris' contribution to the relational nature of race and space, Neely and Samura proffer that[35]

> The places whites control materially and symbolically require the unjust (dis)placement of people of colour — the reservation system and urban

---

27   See Carl E James, *Life at the Intersection: Community, Class and Schooling* (Halifax: Fernwood, 2012).

28   Environics Research Institute, above note 7. And even though the Black population might be less than one-quarter of the residents in a neighbourhood, as in Jane and Finch in Toronto, the area not only becomes known as a marginalized area, but also gets branded as a "Black area" (see *ibid*) — an area where, according to Eizadirad, above note 14 at 167, dominant narratives offer "simplistic explanations and overgeneralizations that blame residents of the neighbourhood for [its] social problems."

29   James, *Life at the Intersection*, above note 27.

30   Loïc Wacquant, *Urban Outcasts: A Comparative Sociology of Advanced Marginality* (Cambridge: Polity, 2008).

31   *Ibid* at 1.

32   Cheryl I Harris, "Whiteness as Property" (1993) 106:8 *Harvard Law Review* 1707.

33   Nirmal Puwar, *Space Invaders: Race, Gender, and Bodies Out of Place* (Oxford: Berg, 2004).

34   Harris, above note 32.

35   Neely & Samura, above note 21 at 1944.

ghettoization — are just two examples of this. Therefore, the maintenance of white property and the sense of entitlement that accompanies white identity cannot be divorced from the historically systemic exclusion of people of colour. From this perspective, white supremacy relies on (dis) placement, on both an abstract and a concrete level.

Referencing White supremacy, Puwar, writing of the workplace context, says that when Black bodies occupy "spaces they are not supposed to be in," they are considered "space invaders," and as such, they are "constantly challenged by a look which abnormalises their presence and locates them, through the workings of racialized framings, as belonging elsewhere." And the White gaze that is fixed on the Black body becomes "disoriented by the close proximity of these foreign bodies" whose presence as "equal members" of the community sets up a "different rhythm in the occupation of space" that challenges, disturbs, and disrupts the social order of things and the ways in which racialized bodies have been characterized and fixed.[36] Clearly, then, how Black youth, and Black people generally, come to see life in the suburbs is "a product of a dialectical relationship"[37] constitutive of the people with whom they have contact and interact. The fact that "many whites persist in seeing black individuality rather than the individuality of blacks unhinges this dialectic and makes the living, by blacks, of their individuality a rather arduous experience for them, especially those in the middle class."[38]

Contributing to the experiences of the youth is the "web of stereotypes"[39] by which they are judged. As I have written elsewhere, Black youth tend to be stereotyped as: *immigrants* (foreigners or newcomers who are "inassimilable" or still too "new" to the country to understand the rules), *fatherless* (children who have not had the needed insights, discipline, and other social and cultural capital from a male parent), *troublemakers* (being inassimilable and lacking the benefit of paternal discipline causes them to behave in "anti-social" ways), and *underachievers* (consistent with these interrelated stereotypes is the idea that they are intellectually deficient, academically lazy, and lacking in social and educational ambition).[40] These constructs of Black youth are taken to be antithetical to

---

36   Puwar, above note 33 at 42.

37   Táíwò, above note 14 at 43.

38   *Ibid.*

39   Tyrone C Howard, "Who Really Cares? The Disenfranchisement of African American Males in PreK–12 Schools: A Critical Race Theory Perspective" (2008) 110:5 *Teachers College Record* 954 at 966.

40   James, *Life at the Intersection*, above note 27.

the law-abiding, high-achieving, socially responsible "old stock Canadian" — to use former Prime Minister Stephen Harper's term[41] — suburban youth. Furthermore, these stereotypes consistently "overlap, intersect, and re-enforce each other" and reflexively serve to frame the perceptions and discourses of Black youth which in turn single them out.[42]

In the section that follows, I use census data to provide a demographic profile of the ethnic and racial group population in Toronto, as well as in Peel and Halton regions, noting the changes and the growth in the population over time, starting with 2011. Additionally, the average household income of the respective areas gives an indication of their socio-economic status.

C. DEMOGRAPHIC OVERVIEW OF THE BLACK COMMUNITY IN THE GTA, PEEL, AND HALTON REGIONS

Peel and Halton Regions are suburban communities west of the City of Toronto. Peel Region is comprised of three municipalities: the City of Brampton, the City of Mississauga, and the Town of Caledon. Halton Region is comprised of the City of Burlington, and the towns of Oakville, Milton, and Halton Hills. Peel and Halton Regions along with the City of Toronto and a number of other municipalities comprise part of the larger region referred to as the Toronto Census Metropolitan Area (CMA).

In 2011, the National Household Survey enumerated 397,175 Black people living in the Toronto CMA, representing 7.2 percent of the area's population. And as Table 6.1 shows, the Black population is not evenly distributed in the respective municipalities within the Toronto CMA. The largest number of Black people resides in the City of Toronto (218,160), representing 8.5 percent of the city's population. While the City of Brampton has less than half the Black population of the City of Toronto (70,290), the Black population represents 13.5 percent of the Brampton population. Conversely, Blacks represent only 2.7 percent of the population of the Town of Oakville.

---

41 Mark Gollom, "Stephen Harper's 'Old-Stock Canadians': Politics of Division or Simple Slip?" *CBC News* (19 September 2015), online: www.cbc.ca/1.3234386.

42 James, *Life at the Intersection*, above note 27.

TABLE 6.1   Growth in the Black Population, Peel Region, Halton Region, and the City of Toronto. 2001 to 2011.

MUNICIPALITY	POPULATION	2001 #	2001 % OF MUNICIPALITY	2006 #	2006 % OF MUNICIPALITY	2011 #	2011 % OF MUNICIPALITY	GROWTH RATE 2001–2011
Brampton	Black Pop	32,070	9.9%	53,340	12.3%	70,290	13.5%	119%
	Total Pop	325,428	—	433,806	—	521,315	—	60%
Caledon	Black Pop	770	1.5%	860	1.5%	1,205	2.0%	56%
	Total Pop	50,595	—	57,050	—	58,975	—	17%
Mississauga	Black Pop	37,850	6.2%	41,365	6.2%	44,775	6.3%	18%
	Total Pop	612,925	—	668,549	—	708,725	—	16%
Peel Region	Black Pop	70,695	7.1%	95,565	8.2%	116,265	9.0%	64%
	Total Pop	988,958	—	1,159,405	—	1,289,015	—	30%
Oakville	Black Pop	2,770	1.9%	3,535	2.1%	4,820	2.7%	74%
	Total Pop	144,738	—	165,613	—	180,430	—	25%
Halton Region	Black Pop	5,660	1.5%	8,100	1.8%	10,970	2.2%	94%
	Total Pop	375,229	—	439,256	—	495,440	—	32%
City of Toronto	Black Pop	204,075	8.2%	208,555	8.3%	218,160	8.5%	7%
	Total Pop	2,481,494	—	2,503,281	—	2,576,025	—	4%

Source: Statistics Canada, National Household Survey Profile, 2011.

While the Black population in the outer-suburban areas has grown at a faster rate than in the City of Toronto, the population remains relatively small. In fact, between 2001 and 2011, the Black population in Toronto grew by 7 percent, from 204,075 to 218,160 while its population in each of these suburban areas grew from a low of 18 percent in Mississauga (from 37,850 to 44,775) to a high of 119 percent in Brampton (from 32,070 to 70,290). This high rate of growth of the Black population in Brampton meant that the Black population went from being 9.9 percent of the city's population in 2001 to 13.5 percent of the population in 2011. And while the Black population in Oakville remains very small, it nevertheless grew at a higher rate than in Toronto — 7 percent in Toronto compared to 74 percent in Oakville between 2001 and 2011. That is, the Black population in Oakville increased by 74 percent from 2,770 to 4,820.

Compared to other racialized groups, Black people make up less than 10 percent of the population in Toronto CMA communities.[43] Halton Region (which includes Oakville), for instance, as Table 6.2 indicates, in 2011 had a population of 2.2 percent Black, 5.5 percent Asian, 6.4 percent South Asian, and 81.9 percent White. In Peel Region, Black people were 9 percent of the population, while they were 8.5 percent of the City of Toronto population. By contrast, Whites comprised less than half (43.2 percent) of Peel Region's population and just over half (50.9 percent) of the residents of the City of Toronto. South Asians were the largest racialized group (27.7 percent) in Peel Region while Asians were the largest racialized group in the City of Toronto[44] (19.7 percent).[45]

---

43   It is worth noting that while Canada accepts approximately 250,000 immigrants each year, the majority are arriving from Asian and South Asian countries. This accounts for the low proportion of Blacks compared to these other racialized groups. According to Murdie and Teixeira, "the inner city does not seem to have the same relevance as an immigrant reception area. Instead, most members of these [racialized] groups settle directly in outlying suburban areas, with their residential location determined by a combination of economic, cultural, and discriminatory factors." Murdie & Teixeira, above note 5 at 158.

44   Unlike Asians and South Asians, there is no area or neighbourhood in the suburbs where Black people reside in large numbers (see Murdie & Teixeira, *ibid*), and where the Black youth make up a large portion or majority of a school's student population.

45   See also Environics Research Institute, above note 7.

TABLE 6.2 Racialized Population, Peel Region, Halton Region, and the City of Toronto. 2011.

MUNICIPALITY	TOTAL POPULATION	WHITE		BLACK		ASIAN[1]		SOUTH ASIAN	
		#	% OF MUN.	#	% OF MUN.	#	% OF MUN.	#	% OF MUN.
Peel Region	1,289,015	556,210	43.2%	116,265	9.0%	150,935	11.7%	356,430	27.7%
Halton Region	495,440	405,590	81.9%	10,970	2.2%	27,150	5.5%	31,860	6.4%
City of Toronto	2,576,025	1,311,635	50.9%	218,160	8.5%	507,200	19.7%	317,100	12.3%

1 The Asian population includes the Statistics Canada "visible minority" categories of Chinese, Filipino, Southeast Asian, Korean, and Japanese.

Source: Statistics Canada, National Household Survey Profile, 2011.

TABLE 6.3 Median Household Total Income. 2010.

MUNICIPALITY	MEDIAN HOUSEHOLD TOTAL INCOME
Brampton	$77,787
Caledon	$98,502
Mississauga	$75,556
Peel Region	$77,588
Oakville	$101,713
Halton Region	$91,955
City of Toronto	$58,381

Source: Statistics Canada, National Household Survey Profile, 2011.

The differences in the distribution of the various racial groups in the Toronto CMA can be explained by a number of factors such as: parents' upward social mobility aspirations, as mentioned earlier, and their interest in living in a "good" neighbourhood with a "better" quality of life for their children, which is believed to be found in the suburbs;[46] and the cost of housing (suburban houses tend to be comparatively less expensive and are bigger). So as the cost of owning a home in the City of Toronto has increased over time, families from all racial backgrounds have sought affordable homes in the outer suburbs. And as Murdie and Teixeira point out, this movement of racialized people to the suburbs has precipitated "a Canadian version of 'white flight,' with some residents moving to more distant suburbs . . . leading ultimately to residential segregation in specific neighbourhoods."[47] Principally, the financial situation of various racial groups also plays a significant role in their residency patterns. As Murdie and Teixeira also mention, for African-Caribbeans (read Black), "low household income"[48] compounded by housing cost, cultural practices,[49] and discrimination operate as constraints to where they get to live.

Evidently, the household income of the residents of an area plays a significant role in determining the area's socio-economic level and, of course, affordability of housing. According to Statistics Canada, in 2010 the outer suburbs west of the City of Toronto had higher median household incomes than that of the city. As Table 6.3 shows, the median household income — i.e., the total combined income of all residents in the household fifteen years of age and over — in Peel and Halton regions were $77,588 and $91,955 respectively, while it was $58,381 in the City of Toronto.

The differences in the median income are reflective of the migration of households into, and out of, Toronto — with middle- and higher-income households migrating to the outer suburbs, while lower-income households

---

46   James, "*Colour Matters*," above note 4.

47   Murdie & Teixeira, above note 5 at 153.

48   *Ibid* at 157.

49   For instance, a Statistics Canada study found that one in ten households in Brampton is a multi-family dwelling; and since the 1990s, because of the demand for these homes, particularly by South Asian families (whose adult children are expected to take care of their elderly parents), homebuilders have begun to design houses with the multi-generational family in mind. Statistics Canada, *2011 Census of Population, Census in Brief: Canadian Households in 2011 — Type and Growth* (Catalogue No 98-312-X2011003, 2012); Dakshana Bascaramurty, "In Brampton, Three Generations, One House" *Globe and Mail* (31 May 2013), online: https://beta.theglobeandmail.com/news/national/in-brampton-three-generations-one-house/article12295651/?ref=http://www.theglobeandmail.com&.

remain in or migrate to the city.[50] The point is, the suburban areas are able to maintain their high socio-economic levels not merely because of the incomes of people who choose to reside there or the infrastructure (i.e., public transportation, roads, location of businesses and services) that enables easy access to jobs, schooling, recreation, and social services, but how the structures (put in place or maintained by policies and practices of local governments, developers, and real estate agencies) operate to keep unwanted "space invaders"[51] out of that area.

In the following section, I return to the notion of "singled out," noting how this process of racial profiling of Black youth who reside in the suburbs serves to remind them of their "outsider status." The stereotypes (especially as troublemakers or potential ones) to which they are subjected, along with the accompanying gaze that tells them they belong elsewhere,[52] operate to homogenize, categorize, essentialize, and disenfranchise them,[53] as well as undermine their sense of agency as they navigate and negotiate their suburban neighbourhoods. I reference data from studies conducted with Black youth in the Halton (specifically Oakville) and Peel regions to demonstrate how being "watched" by community members, underestimated or seen as "not smart" by teachers, and intimidated and falsely accused by police officers contribute to experiences of self-doubt and a sense of alienation among the Black youth who reside in these suburban areas.

D. THE EXPERIENCES OF BLACK YOUTH IN TORONTO'S OUTER SUBURBS — PEEL AND HALTON REGIONS

As mentioned earlier, for many parents the suburbs represent upward social mobility and a chance to provide their children with high-quality schooling opportunities, environments suited to the cultivation of "suitable" social networks, and safe neighbourhoods far from the "social ills" and violence of the city. This was the sentiment of most of the parents — mainly first- and second-generation Canadians — who migrated to the fairly affluent neighbourhoods of Halton Region seeking a "better" life

---

50   City of Toronto, "Profile Toronto: Perspectives on Household Income," online: Urban Development Services, Policy & Research (2004) online: www.toronto.ca/legdocs/2004/agendas/committees/plt/plt041004/it008.pdf.

51   Puwar, above note 33 at 42.

52   *Ibid.*

53   James, *Life at the Intersection*, above note 27.

for their children.[54] In the words of one parent: "Parents live here because it's safe; it's a nice place to raise kids . . . . It's quiet and away from the hectic life of Toronto." But well aware of the "stigma" that Black people face in the society, one parent went on to say "You think that by coming here you become less of that." This thought reflects the optimism that parents seem to cling to as justification of their choice of residence. They recognize that they too are, as one parent put it, "under the microscope." Hence, while they might have "decent jobs" and the money that they come by "honestly,"[55] still, as she continued: "Being Black means we have to resort to extraordinary means to keep quiet what others do openly — flaunt their wealth. The result is, we'll keep driving our present understated car in the hopes that we won't attract attention to ourselves."

However, despite their parents' optimism and the social appeal of the Halton suburb, the young people never felt welcomed. Hence, as one participant questioned, echoing many of her peers: "If I'm truly part of this community, why am I being singled out?" Being singled out by the constant gaze of community members, their peers, teachers, and police also meant that Black youth were treated differently because of their colour. They reported that as they journeyed through the neighbourhood, people would watch them in wonder. To quote one youth: "All of a sudden colour matters. People look at me. They do a double take, like: 'Is that a Black person?'" The youth took this reaction to mean that they were out of place and did not belong in that community as Black people.[56] They reported that sometimes, based on their actions, their White peers would consider them "ghetto": people from the stigmatized "inner city" who are to be feared. According to one male participant, "It was cold and I was

---

54   The parents — all of them Black and of Caribbean background — were part of the study, which was conducted with Maureen Brown. Twelve parents of the youths who participated in the study shared their experiences and aspirations for their children in a focus group that was exclusive to them. Twenty-eight young people between the ages of sixteen and twenty participated in three focus groups. The families had been living in the community for three to ten years with the majority of them living there an average of five years.

55   That it was important for this parent to use the word "honestly" is likely an indication of her attempt to counter prevailing questions about how they, as a Black family, have acquired their money — questions that seemingly are heightened in their affluent neighbourhood.

56   See also Audrey Kobayashi & Linda Peake, "Racism out of Place: Thoughts on Whiteness and Antiracist Geography in the New Millennium" (2000) 90:2 *Annals of the Association of American Geographers* 392.

walking out of the store with my hood on. Someone came up to me and said: 'Watch out gangster.'"

The youth related that teachers perceived of them to be academically limited — "you are not smart" — and hence likely to be educational failures. For this reason, one said: "You always have to show that you are not the stereotypical Black." Another suggested that "the first thing [the teacher] thinks is: 'this guy is going to fail; his marks are not going to be as high as the others.' . . . They don't think we are smart [because of] the way we dress or the way we act . . . . We just have to show we are smart." And there were the store owners and security guards whose surveillance the youth had to contend with. One youth recalled that he had to ask a corner-store owner, who demanded that he make his purchase and leave the store while others were allowed to browse, to leave him alone because he was "really a good kid."

Similarly, the youth in Peel Region[57] reported their life in the area was a constant struggle against the profile of them belonging to a group of people who are uninterested in education and more athletically talented, therefore more likely to be underachievers. According to one youth, "Schools don't take Black kids seriously. Teachers just think we are there to just chill and we are not serious." And in explaining the gendered ways in which they are stereotyped or profiled, one youth commented: "If males miss a day of school then [the stereotype is that] they're automatically not interested in having an education and are probably out looking for trouble . . . . [The stereotype is that] Black girls only come to school for friends and not to learn; . . . [and] only want certain jobs such as nursing or hairstyling." Invoking the metaphor of "battle" — insofar as they felt that they had to arm themselves to interact with their soldier teachers to get an education, one participant opined: "I think we have to fight an uphill battle in almost everything we do, especially school. I've had teachers tell me straight up that they don't believe my group of people could do certain things."

---

57   This study, "Fighting an Uphill Battle," commissioned in 2014 by FACES of Peel (Facilitating Access, Change and Equity in Systems), was conducted with Tana Turner. The collective made up of human service workers was particularly concerned with the situation of the marginalized young people of the community, particularly Black youth. Data on the youth's experiences with schooling, employment, social services, police, and recreation activities was gathered through an online survey of twenty-three Black youth, focus group interviews with thirty Black residents, interviews with thirty service providers, and twenty key informant interviews.

For the youth in both regions, racial profiling by police officers was considered to be a significant disadvantage to living in their communities. In Oakville, for instance, one young man talked of instances when he was unnecessarily stopped, "rudely" questioned, and threatened to be "beaten" by police. He said that he was asked to present his driver's licence although he was not driving; the two White females with whom he was travelling were never questioned. Another young man described an instance when he was walking home from work with his co-worker friend when two police cars stopped and the officers "interrogated" them, saying that they "fit the description of two Black youth who had robbed a convenience store earlier." Noting that they were wearing their fast-food restaurant uniforms when they were stopped, the youth indicated that he tried to reason with the officers, saying that their attire should be a signal that they were innocent of such offence; he also logically asked: "Why would I be walking towards the scene of the crime if I had robbed the store?" The officer, he said, responded saying, "That's a really good question" and let them go. But before reaching home, he was stopped again by police for the same reason. However, as he noted, except for race, the apprehended alleged robbers looked "nothing" like him and his friend.

Likewise, in Peel Region, the youth talked of being "targeted" by police — a practice which made them feel fearful and unsafe because of the possible criminalization and incarceration for "years for something I did not commit." Referencing the fact that they stand out in their community, one youth contended: "In Peel, you're already a target if you're Black. If you live in a certain area, or if you wear certain clothing you are a target of police. If something goes wrong you're automatically a suspect." Moreover, indicating how many Black youth are "targets everywhere they go" and not free to live like their White peers, one participant recalled an incident "at school where all kinds of kids were involved. I only saw the police handcuffing the Black students, and many of those students were not even involved. Anytime there is violence, it is assumed us Black youth have committed it." And in listing the stereotypes that make them "a target" in their communities and against which they struggled, one young man surmised:

> Law enforcement also stereotypes us and assumes because we are Black we all partake in drugs, etc. They also assume that all Black youth live in poverty and are struggling, which is not true. People in the stores assume I am going to steal, which is not true. I go out of my way to try not to look [like a] suspect. People are always staring at me, thinking I am a thief.

The narratives of these youth bring attention to the ways in which their lived race and gendered experiences of being "singled out" made them "targets" and "suspects" — much of which they attributed to their skin colour and the failure of community members, teachers, law enforcement agents, and even their peers to see them as "really good kids." In response, they appealed for "freedom" from the omnipresent stereotyping of them as misfits, failures, delinquents, and potential criminals.[58] They despair that they might fail at having people come to see them as law-abiding citizens and not threatening; hence there is no need for people to be suspicious of them.

E. CONCLUSION

In this chapter, I have made the case that racial profiling operates within a historical and contemporary framework of the entangled[59] relationship between race, space, and place and mediated by the economic, political, social, and cultural structures of society at the time. As such, the materiality of space and place cannot be overlooked or undervalued for they give meaning to the how, when, where, and why particular bodies are racialized. In the case of Black youth, their experiences with being "singled out," even as they tried to "fit in" — into the suburban communities which for their parents held the hope and promise of a good and productive life for their children — meant that it was their reality from which they were unable to escape. The fact is, the presence of Black young bodies in the suburbs serves to disrupt the often taken for granted mostly white middle-class homogeneous population, and as such Black youth are rendered "out of place." Faced with proving the legitimacy of their presence in such areas, Black youth, like their parents and other generations, are left to navigate the colonialist, racist, and classist systems and the discriminatory discourses that permeate suburban spaces.

Ultimately, for Black youth, life in the suburbs is understandably no different from that in urban areas. The gaze and treatments that make many of them feel unwanted and underrated are supported by an inequitable socio-political structure of the society that contributes to the preconceived ideas, social practices, educational procedures, and policing measures that

---

58 See also Carl E James et al, *Towards Race Equity in Education: The Schooling of Black Students in the Greater Toronto Area* (Toronto: The Jean Augustine Chair in Education, Community & Diaspora, Faculty of Education, York University, 2017).

59 I use entangled as opposed to interlocking or interrelated to convey the fact that these factors are inextricably linked or intertwined, that they are not independent of each other.

give rise to the "web of stereotypes" or racial profiling from which it is difficult for them to escape. What we need is a society in which everyone takes seriously and really puts into practice — especially those among us privileged by colour — the claim that we are a democratic, meritocratic, and multicultural society in which everyone, irrespective of colour and culture, has the right to live, learn, play, and work anywhere they wish. There is a need to acknowledge and repudiate the ways in which racial profiling and accompanying discriminatory practices resulting from surveillance by disciplinary agents are harmful to the well-being of otherwise law-abiding Black youth who reside in our communities.

CHAPTER 7

The Re-framing of Racial Profiling

Police Violence Against Black Women

ANDREA S ANDERSON[*]

A. INTRODUCTION

While the literature and research on racial profiling has grown substantially over the years, with strong evidence pointing towards systemic racism embedded within the police force and the criminal justice system, the experiences of women of colour, Black women in particular, have yet to be fully explored. Much of the academic scholarship in Canada on racial profiling focuses on the experiences of young Black men as the targets and victims of police violence and brutality. However, Black women have also been and continue to be subjected to racial profiling. An intersectional approach is required to conceptualize the experiences of Black women, as they are not only disadvantaged by their race but also their gender when they come in contact with the police. Relying on a number of incidences, this paper illustrates the ways in which Black women have been unjustly targeted and their rights violated by police officers.

. . .

Proactive policing investigations, such as racial profiling, have created a number of harms in communities of colour. These harms include disparities in experiences in treatment, fewer police protections, surveillance, stops, searches, excessive force, and police shootings. Attempts to explain these patterns have examined how young Black men have come to be the usual targets. However, few studies have considered how gender intersects with race in determining the negative effects of proactive policing

---

[*] Andrea S Anderson is a PhD candidate at Osgoode Hall Law School and a criminal defence lawyer.

practices on women. If the usual targets of racial profiling, for example, are Black men, what happens to the notions of crime and punishment when we shift the centre of focus on a group that has been seen as victims of racial profiling? Black women are far from exempt from harmful encounters with the police. Black women are victimized by the police and often in precisely the same ways as men: police stops, shootings, and racial profiling. In addition, they also experience police violence[1] in distinctly gender-specific ways, such as sexual harassment and sexual assault.[2] Unfortunately, such incidents have been overlooked in the national discussions and understandings of racism in policing and broader issues of police accountability. They also haven't drawn equal media attention or public outrage. Because of the unnamed police violence of Black women and girls, the discourse has been constructed around the idea that law enforcement profiling of women are isolated incidents. Lost in this discussion is the consideration of how Black women experience racial profiling due to racialized gender stereotypes.

The practice of racial profiling continues to be one of the most controversial topics in the criminal justice system and illustrates the ways in which dominant discourse on racial injustice can operate to exclude the narratives of women of colour. Racial profiling reinforces social hierarchies of race and gender identities. In challenging the common understanding that racial profiling is an act against men, this paper problematizes the practice of racial profiling by questioning the individuals whom it affects, and the ways in which it occurs. The paper begins, in Part B, by examining the meaning and implications of racial profiling on Black Canadians, specifically in Ontario. Part C briefly explores how racial profiling has been constructed as a male issue. Through examples of Black women's encounters with the police, in Part D, the paper examines how race and gendered stereotypes influence the policing of Black women and provides insight into how police violence remains patriarchal in focus, even when discussions centre on race. The paper concludes by discussing the importance of an intersectional approach in order to better understand the experiences of Black women and challenges the ways we have come to understand the practice and impact of racial profiling.

---

1   For the purposes of this paper, police violence includes physical and verbal abuse, false arrest, detention, illegal searches and seizures, and racial profiling.

2   Marcia Chatelain & Kaavya Asoka, "Women and Black Lives Matter" (Summer 2015) 63:3 *Dissent*, online: www.dissentmagazine.org/article/women-black-lives-matter-interview-marcia-chatelain.

B. THE ANATOMY OF RACIAL PROFILING: A BRIEF HISTORY

With respect to issues of racial bias within the justice system, racial pro-filing has been a diverse and polarizing issue. A number of writers and activists have documented the experiences of racial profiling and de-scribed its causes and consequences.[3] A critical mass of criminologists, social scientists, and legal scholars has emerged in the study of racial profiling.[4] The interest in racial profiling is likely related to continuing developments in the political and social context. Over the last decade, there has been an increase in newspaper stories, magazines articles, and judicial decisions on the phenomenon of racial profiling. With the prolif-eration of projects and organizations throughout the country dedicated to addressing anti-bias policing and other forms of systemic racism, the public has become familiar with claims of racial profiling. Ontario's Black communities have long argued that they are frequently the victims of racial profiling.[5] Indeed, the practice of racial profiling has become so pervasive in Black communities, for example, in the city of Toronto, that the phrase "DWB" (Driving While Black) is front and centre in the main-stream consciousness to describe the reason, at times, why people are pulled over by law enforcement officials.[6]

Racial bias in the criminal justice system and the overrepresentation of Black people in crime statistics can be considered a product of dis-criminatory decision making in the criminal justice system. For most in-dividuals, the police are the first point of contact in the criminal justice process. It is this first contact that often determines the direction the individual will take throughout the justice system. Questions relating to race and racism have reoccurred in debates around policing in Canada for three decades or more. Public discourse about police and racism has

3   See, for example, Desmond Cole, "The Skin I'm In: I've Been Interrogated by Police More Than 50 Times — All Because I'm Black" *Toronto Life* (21 April 2015) online: http://torontolife.com/city/life/skin-im-ive-interrogated-police-50-times-im-black/.

4   See, for example, Charles Smith, *Conflict, Crisis, and Accountability: Racial Profiling and Law Enforcement in Canada* (Ottawa: Canadian Centre for Policy Alternatives, 2007); David Tanovich, *The Colour of Justice: Policing Race in Canada* (Toronto, Irwin Law, 2006); Carol Tator & Frances Henry, *Racial Profiling in Canada: Challenging the Myth of a Few Bad Apples* (Toronto: University of Toronto Press, 2006).

5   Tator & Henry, *ibid* at 173.

6   See David Tanovich, "Using the *Charter* to Stop Racial Profiling: The Development of an Equality-Based Conception of Arbitrary Detention" (2002) 40 *Osgoode Hall Law Journal* 145 at 147 [Tanovich, "Using the *Charter*"]; Kenneth Meeks, *Driving While Black: Highways, Shopping Malls, Taxicabs, Sidewalks: How to Fight Back If You Are a Victim of Racial Profiling* (New York: Broadway Books, 2000) at 10.

revolved around narratives and media-driven exposés of police violence that has led to cycles of reactions, responses, and reforms. The impetus for the 1995 *Report of the Commission on Systemic Racism in the Ontario Criminal Justice System* ("Commission on Systemic Racism") was the growing sense of frustration in the increasingly vocal Black community about the racial bias in the justice system and, in particular, their vulnerability to police violence.

An overview of the race and crime dynamic in Ontario, for example, reveals that the over-criminalization of communities of colour is a heavily politicized issue in Canada. At the height of the racial tensions in the City of Toronto, Black communities continue to maintain that they are over- and under-policed, criminalized, and their culture portrayed as essentially deviant. The image of criminality as a peculiarity of the Black phenomenon has appeared not only in media discourse, but also through law enforcement practices. As early as the 1980s, perceptions of racism experienced by Black people in Ontario's criminal justice system extended first to more routine aspects of policing, such as police stops and arrest. Police violence is seen as part of a larger picture of systemic mistreatment of racial groups in the criminal justice system.[7] As the issue developed, so did the calls for adequate responses to what was seen as an abuse of power. Allegations that criminal justice was racially biased were continually dismissed by government officials as opinions of organizations and advocates.[8] Instead, government officials maintained that the vast majority of racialized citizens had "complete confidence in the police and criminal courts."[9] By the 1990s, racial tensions in Toronto mounted as private citizens, organizations, and advocates began to protest against the abuse of police powers.[10] In 1992, in response to the increasing calls for accountability and reforms to policing, particularly from those in Black

---

7   Toni Williams, "Racism in Justice: The Report of the Commission on Systemic Racism in the Ontario Criminal Justice System" in Susan Boyd, Dorothy Chunn, & Roberts Menzies, eds, *(Ab)using Power: The Canadian Experience* (Halifax: Fernwood, 2001) at 201 [Williams, "Racism in Justice"].

8   Scot Wortley & Andrea McCalla, "Racial Discrimination in the Ontario Justice System" in Julian V Roberts & Michelle G Grossman, eds, *Criminal Justice in Canada*, 3d ed (Toronto: Thomson Nelson, 2008) 187 at 188–90.

9   Wortley & McCalla, *ibid* at 188–90.

10 Between 1978 and 1992, Ontario police officers shot one Black woman and at least thirteen Black men, eight of whom were killed. Eleven of the fourteen shootings occurred in Toronto. Members of Toronto's Black communities reacted to these shootings by demanding change in the delivery of police services. See Williams, "Racism in Justice," above note 7.

communities, the provincial government established a Commission to examine and report on allegations of systemic racial bias in the Ontario Criminal Justice system. The final report was released in 1995 and is still one of the most comprehensive reports examining systemic racism in the criminal justice system.[11] One of the key findings of the 1995 Commission on Systemic Racism was the disproportionate use of police power against Black people to stop and search on the grounds of suspicion that they intended or had committed an offence. The Commission revealed, for example, that 28 percent of Black residents reported having been stopped in the previous two years, compared to 18 percent of White residents.[12]

1) Defining the Problem

There have been numerous attempts to formally define the practice of racial profiling, whether in reports, studies, and/or in judicial decisions. In their external report, *Paying the Price: The Human Cost of Racial Profiling*, the Ontario Human Rights Commission (OHRC) defines racial profiling as "any action undertaken for reasons for safety, security or public protection that relies on stereotypes about race, colour, ethnicity, ancestry, religion, or place of origin rather than on reasonable suspicion, to single out an individual for greater scrutiny or different treatment."[13] In its report, the OHRC made the following observation: "racial profiling is a form of racial stereotyping. As racial stereotype and discrimination exists in society, it also exists in institutions such as law enforcement agencies."[14] Racial profiling occurs when race, place of origin, religion, or stereotypes about offending or dangerousness associated with any of these characteristics are used, consciously or unconsciously, to any degree in suspect selection or treatment outside of the context of looking for a particular

---

11   Ontario, *Report of the Commission on Systemic Racism in the Ontario Criminal Justice System* (Toronto: Queen's Printer, 1995) [Commission on Systemic Racism Report].

12   The discrepancy further increased when the commission examined multiple stops and stops of Black males: 17 percent of Black residents reported having been stopped on two or more occasions over the previous two years, as compared to only 8 percent of White residents; and 43 percent of Black male residents reported having been stopped by the Toronto police in the previous two years, as opposed to only 25 percent of White male residents.

13   Ontario Human Rights Commission, *Paying the Price: The Human Cost of Racial Profiling* (Toronto: Ontario Human Rights Commission, 2003), online: www.ohrc.on.ca/sites/default/files/attachments/Paying_the_price%3A_The_human_cost_of_racial_profiling.pdf [OHRC, *Paying the Price*].

14   *Ibid.*

suspect who has committed an offence and who is identified, in part, by their race.[15] Judicial recognition of racial profiling has concluded that it exists and has greatly impacted racialized communities.[16] For example, in a leading case on racial profiling, *R v Brown* for the Court of Appeal, Morden J held:[17]

> I quote from the Report of the Commission on Systemic Racism in the Ontario Criminal Justice System . . . . The Commission's findings suggest that racialized characteristics, especially those of [B]lack people, in combination with other factors, provoke police suspicion, at least in Metro Toronto. Other factors that may attract police attention include sex (male), youth, make and condition of car (if any), location, dress, and perceived lifestyle. Black persons perceived to have many of these attributes are at high risk of being stopped. This explanation is consistent with our findings that, overall, [B]lack people are more likely than others to experience the unwelcome intrusion of being stopped by the police . . . .

In law enforcement literature, racial profiling is commonly defined using these specific determinants: (1) significant racial differences in police stop and search practices; (2) significant racial difference in customs search and interrogation practices; and (3) particular undercover or sting operations which target specific racial and/or ethnic communities.[18] In short, racial profiling exists when racial differences in law enforcement surveillance activities cannot be explained by individual differences in criminal or other illegal activity. While some police leaders, unions, and academics have questioned the validity of racial profiling and/or continue to deny the extent to which racial profiling actually occurs,[19] a large body of research maintains that communities of colour are more at risk than

---

15   See Ontario Human Rights Commission, "What Is Racial Profiling (Fact Sheet)," online: www.ohrc.on.ca/en/what-racial-profiling-fact-sheet; *R v Richards*, [1999] OJ No 1420 at para 24 (CA).

16   *R v S(RD)*, [1997] 3 SCR 484 at paras 46–47; *R v Campbell*, [2005] QJ No 394 at paras 30–33 (CQ); *R v Golden*, [2001] 3 SCR 679 at para 83; Commission on Systemic Racism Report, above note 11.

17   *R v Brown*, 2003 CanLII 52142 at para 9 (Ont CA).

18   See Scott Wortley & Julian Tanner, "Data, Denials and Controversy: The Racial Profiling Debate in Toronto" (2003) 45:3 *Journal of Criminology and Criminal Justice* 367 at 396; David A Harris, "Driving While Black and All Other Traffic Offenses: The Supreme Court and Pretextual Traffic Stops" (1997) 87 *Journal of Criminal Law and Criminology* 544.

19   See Thomas Gabor, "Inflammatory Rhetoric on Racial Profiling Can Undermine Police Services" (2004) 46 *Journal of Criminology and Criminal Justice* 457.

Whites of experiencing discriminatory police stops, searches, and/or being subjected to rude or hostile police treatment.[20]

2) The Dynamics of Racial Profiling

Racial profiling has been linked to racial oppression of groups who find "themselves under scrutiny in almost every aspect of their public and private lives."[21] As law professor David Tanovich suggests, the targeting of certain racial groups for security-related investigation is not simply the result of explicit racism.[22] Rather, racial profiling is another manifestation of systemic racism: "the day-to-day racial profiling that occurs in Canada today is preliminary about stereotyping rather than the expression of animus or overt racism."[23] The racialization of Blacks has a long history. This history includes almost two hundred years of enslavement and has profoundly shaped present-day realities and is deeply entrenched in Canadian institutions, such as policing. Thus, one cannot understand the disparate impact of this law enforcement practice without understanding the history of Black Canadians. The legacy of slavery remains: "racism, and in particular anti-black racism, is a part of our community's psyche. A significant segment of our community holds overtly racist views. A much larger segment subconsciously operates on the basis of negative racial stereotypes."[24] It is within this historical context that racial profiling must be understood.

Judicial acceptance has noted that racial profiling is also based on deep-seated stereotypes of criminality.[25] Through the criminalization of people of colour, the justice system has perpetuated the belief that certain races are deviant, which in turn justifies the targeting of particular communities for criminal prosecution. In this context, racial profiling "has criminalized many predominately black neighbourhoods in Toronto that are commonly referred to by police and media as 'high crime areas.'"[26]

---

20 Scot Wortley, "Racialized Risk: Police and Crown Discretion and the Overrepresentation of Black People in the Ontario Criminal Justice System" in Anthony Harriott, Farley Brathwaite, & Scot Wortley, eds, *Crime and Criminal Justice in the Caribbean* (Kingston, Jamaica: Arawak Publications, 2004) 173 at 176.

21 Smith, above note 4 at 13.

22 David Tanovich, "E-Racing Racial Profiling" (2003) 41 *Alberta Law Review* 905 [Tanovich, "E-Racing"].

23 Tanovich, *The Colour of Justice*, above note 4 at 13.

24 *Peart v Peel Regional Police Services Board*, 2006 CanLII 37566 (Ont CA).

25 Tanovich, "Using the *Charter*," above note 6 at 145.

26 *Ibid* at 163.

These perceptions of the racial identity of criminals are ingrained in the public consciousness so much so that "race does not even need to be specifically mentioned for a connection to be made between the two, because it seems that 'talking about crime is talking about race.'"[27] In short, this racialization of crime has contributed to the perception that there is a link between race and crime. In this way, racial profiling is the process of "social production of racial inequality in decisions about people and the treatment they receive."[28] It is a process that has created a disproportionately large class of racialized offenders and has shifted the racial alignment of the Canadian prison population in the last decade.

3) The Impact of Racial Profiling

A closer examination of the basis of racial profiling shows that it is based on flawed assumptions, is a practice that has a catastrophic effect on communities of colour, and, ultimately, contravenes the most basic and fundamental principles of equality. One of the most troubling aspects of racial profiling is the large number of Black individuals who have been stopped and harassed by police officers. Officers' justified interrogations have been described as humiliating, frightening, and degrading.[29] In this respect, it is not surprising that "blacks have been forced to alter the manner in which they go about an activity that so many of us take for granted,"[30] namely, travelling freely.

The effects of constant surveillance on communities of colour are well documented. In *Paying the Price*, the OHRC provides an extensive study of the impact racial profiling has on those who experience it. *Paying the Price* captures the range of emotions among victims of racial profiling, from physical and severe psychological harm, including fear, guilt, resentment, and breakdown of social networks, to isolation and lack of confidence in institutions. The report ultimately concluded:[31]

> It is impossible to quantify the cost to those individuals, their families, and friends, their communities and society overall of these psychological effects.

---

27 Kelly Welch, "Black Criminal Stereotypes and Racial Profiling" (2007) 23 *Journal of Contemporary Criminal Justice* 276.

28 Tanovich, "E-Racing," above note 22 at 912; Commission on Systemic Racism Report, above note 11 at 49.

29 Tanovich, "Using the *Charter*," above note 6 at 163.

30 *Ibid.*

31 OHRC, *Paying the Price*, above note 13 at 47.

Nevertheless, it is clear that the emotional and psychological damage inflicted by profiling is significant and we as a society cannot afford to ignore it.

C. THE USUAL SUSPECTS

When racial profiling first began to creep into the debate on race and policing in Canada, specifically in Ontario, most of those who made their concerns public were Black Canadians. While law enforcement agencies use racial profiling in a variety of ways, the most recognized incidents of racial profiling have been pretextual traffic stops.[32] The phrase "driving while Black" became the focus of racial profiling debate as it emphasizes that profiling is about race: "that one's blackness is the primary offence" leading to a stop.[33] In general, Black advocates have connected these practices with the other experiences of discrimination both inside and outside of the criminal justice system. Perhaps it is for these reasons that, at times, racial profiling has been framed as a Black issue — a concern of Black Canadians.[34] The labelling of racial profiling as a Black issue also has extended the idea that this is an issue that affects Black men. The perception that the face of crime is a person of colour has only further stigmatized the Black community. The heightened interrogations and searches by police officers that are based on race confirms to "all [B]lacks, rich or poor, that race still matters and that no matter how law abiding you are, your skin colour will always place you in a class of the usual suspects."[35] The stereotype of the "usual suspect" is the result of a "history of overt racism, a history that has made us far less likely to be critical of the suggestion that crime can be linked to certain racialized groups."[36]

While there has been greater recognition that racial profiling is a real and ongoing social and legal problem, the study of this issue is arguably still in its infancy. Although anti-racist law enforcement strategies have been politically useful to Black women, at some level, critiques of racial

---

32 See Sherri Sharma, "Beyond 'Driving While Black' and 'Flying While Brown': Using Intersectionality to Uncover the Gendered Aspects of Racial Profiling" (2003) 12:2 *Columbia Journal of Gender and Law* 275 at 278–79. Pretextual traffic stop refers to the practice of stopping drivers, particularly those of colour, for minor traffic violations, in order to search their cars for drugs, guns, and/or cash.

33 Sharma, above note 32 at 280.

34 David H Harris, *Profiles in Injustice: Why Racial Profiling Cannot Work* (New York: New York Press, 2002) at 129. Our understanding of racial profiling also includes the experiences of Indigenous and other communities of colour.

35 Tanovich, "Using the *Charter*," above note 6 at 164.

36 Tanovich, *The Colour of Justice*, above note 4.

profiling have also produced a discourse that has silenced their voices. To date, debates, litigation, and scholarship addressing policing and racism have been almost exclusively informed by a paradigm centring on the young Black heterosexual man as "the quintessential subject, victim, survivor of police brutality."[37] However, there is evidence that women of colour, particularly Black women, are also subject to racial profiling. For example, in *Paying the Price*, OHRC noted racialized women reported incidents of profiling "where they were assumed to be prostitutes because they were in a car with White men who were assumed to be customers."[38]

D. HOW BLACK WOMEN ARE RACIALLY PROFILED

The criminal justice system has had a tendency to treat race and gender as mutually exclusive categories.[39] The concept of intersecting identities that influence a person's experience and treatment in the criminal justice system "is often too complex for the dominant liberal ideology to fathom."[40] Usually only a single characteristic or aspect of a person's situation is taken into account when the law is used to address claims of injustice or discrimination.[41] Because of their intersectional identities as both women and people of colour, Black women are marginalized in both discourses.

Like many other justice concerns, the dominant discourse on police violence against communities of colour has yet to adopt an intersectional approach that puts women's experiences at the centre of its analysis. A consequence of centring only Black men's experiences when discussing racial profiling is a failure to acknowledge Black women as victims and, in turn, perpetuating the myth that Black women are immune from these forms of police practices. In the literature, women are often ignored in research on race and policing or the theoretical models used to explain discriminatory patterns of policing exhibit a "presumption of gender neu-

---

37   Andrea J Ritchie, "Law Enforcement Violence against Women of Color" in INCITE! Women of Colour against Violence, ed, *Color of Violence: The INCITE! Anthology* (Cambridge, MA: South End Press, 2006) at 139.

38   OHRC, *Paying the Price*, above note 13 at 45.

39   Kimberlé Crenshaw, "Demarginalizing the Intersection of Race and Sex: A Black Feminist Critique of Antidiscrimination Doctrine, Feminist Theory, and Antiracist Politics" (1989) 1 *University of Chicago Legal Forum* 139 at 143 [Crenshaw, "Demarginalizing"]. See also Joanne Belknap, *The Invisible Woman: Gender, Crime and Justice*, 3d ed (Belmont, CA: Thomson/Wadsworth, 2007) at 14.

40   Elena Marchetti, "Intersectional Race and Gender Analysis: Why Legal Processes Just Don't Get It" (2008) 17:2 *Social and Legal Studies* 155 at 156.

41   *Ibid.*

trality or uncritical focus on men."[42] Black women are subjected to police misconduct, yet as a consequence of this multiple marginality, Black women's experiences of police violence are perceived as isolated incidents.

Racial profiling data in Canada is rarely disaggregated by gender and race. This is not to say that Black women's narratives of law enforcement's practice of racial profiling have never been the subject of discourse or organizing. Research in the United States has shown that women and girls, particularly women of colour, are sexually assaulted, brutally strip-searched, shot, and killed by law enforcement officers. Thus, as lawyer Andrea Ritchie notes, women of colour are "experiencing many of the same forms of law enforcement violence as men of color, as well as gender-and-race specific forms of police misconduct and abuse."[43] Although a few studies have specifically compared how African-American women and men experience discretionary police practices, the research suggests this is an important area of inquiry. In general, younger Black women are significantly more likely to be arrested than White women or men.[44] Further, the increase of African-Canadian women who are incarcerated over the past two decades suggests a negative connection between proactive police strategies and women of colour.[45]

While there has been no conclusive list compiled accounting for Black women's incidents of violence at the hands of the police, there have been Canadian studies that analyze the experience of racially profiled women and reveal how women are profiled in gender-specific ways, for example, as suspected drug users, drug couriers, and sex workers.[46] The cases involving Black women and the police further illustrate that police violence is a reality for Black women and how racial and gender stereotypes can lead to police over-action.

---

42 Rod K Brunson & Jody Miller, "Gender, Race, and Urban Policing: The Experience of African American Youths" (2006) 20 *Gender & Society* 531 at 533.

43 Ritchie, above note 37 at 139.

44 Brunson & Miller, above note 42 at 534.

45 Government of Canada, The Correctional Investigator Canada, *A Case Study of Diversity in Corrections: The Black Inmate Experience in Federal Penitentiaries — Final Report* (Ottawa: Office of the Correctional Investigator, 2013) at para 18.

46 See Sonia Lawrence & Toni Williams, "Swallowed Up: Drug Couriers at the Borders of Canadian Sentencing" (2006) 56 *University of Toronto Law Journal* 285.

1) Audrey Smith

The 1993 incident involving Audrey Smith, a thirty-seven-year-old Jamaican tourist who was publicly stripped and searched in downtown Toronto, illustrates the ways Black women are victims of racial profiling. Audrey Smith's public strip search contributed to the heightened tensions between Black communities and Toronto police in the early 1990s.[47] In 1993, Smith was accused of having drugs in her possession and was immediately handcuffed and placed in a police cruiser. After being detained, her assertion of innocence ignored by the police officers, Smith thought her only option was consent to a search, presumably at the police station. Instead, Smith was publicly strip-searched on the busy streets of Parkdale. No drugs were found on her. In 1995, a three-person panel of inquiry cleared the three police officers (White) of the discreditable misconduct charged.[48]

2) Jacqueline Nassiah

Another example is the case of Jacqueline Nassiah. In 2007, the Human Rights Tribunal of Ontario ruled that a Black woman from Mississauga was the victim of racial profiling when she was subjected to an intense verbal interrogation even after evidence revealed she had been wrongly accused.[49] Nassiah was shopping for a bra at a Sears store in 2003 when she was stopped by a security guard and accused of stealing an item worth less than $10. The tribunal found that a Peel Regional police constable assumed Nassiah did not speak English, ignored the videotape evidence exonerating her, and called for a body search when he did not find the allegedly stolen items. After the second body search confirmed that she did not have the item, the investigation continued, lasting over two hours. The officer also subjected Nassiah to verbal abuse when he called her a "fucking foreigner" and threatened to take her to jail if she did not produce the item.[50]

---

47   Smith, above note 4 at 27.

48   *Ibid.*

49   "Peel Woman Wins Racial Profiling Case" *CBC News* (17 May 2007), online: www.cbc.ca/news/canada/toronto/peel-woman-wins-racial-profiling-case-1.660107.

50   See *Nassiah v Peel (Regional Municipality) Police Services Board*, 2007 HRTO 14. The Tribunal ordered Peel police and the officer to pay Nassiah $20,000 in damages. Peel Police were also ordered to address racial profiling with increased training for officers.

3) Stacy Bonds

In 2008, Stacy Bonds, a Black twenty-seven-year-old makeup artist with no criminal record, was questioned by two male officers (one White, the other Hispanic) on Rideau Street in Ottawa. One of the officers testified that he had seen Bonds with a beer bottle, speaking to occupants of a van. The officers saw her drink from the bottle and then throw the bottle into a garbage bin. After checking her name and date of birth, the officers released Bonds. Wanting to know more about why she was stopped, Bonds asked the officers why they had questioned her. They told her to go home. When Bonds insisted on an answer, one of the officers arrested her for public intoxication. The officer later testified that he could smell alcohol on her breath and she appeared to stagger when she walked away. After her street arrest and pat-down search, Bonds was taken into custody, where she was "forced to endure hours of gratuitous violence and humiliation, much of which was caught on videotape."[51]

Once in custody, Bonds was violently kneed twice in the back, had her hair pulled, and was forced to the floor with a plastic riot shield in the police department's booking room. She was then strip-searched in the presence of three male officers, a hand was shoved down her pants, and she had her shirt and bra cut off. After, she was left in a jail cell for a period of three hours, partially clad and having soiled her pants. These events were captured on police station videotape. The videotape showed that when Bonds was brought into the booking room, there was "no hint of violence and no hint of being aggressive."[52] Before she was searched, she was placed in a holding cell where she "was not aggressive and not belligerent [and] seemingly compliant."[53] Justice Lajoie of the Ontario Court of Justice found "no reasonable explanation" for the violent strip search of Bonds. In *R v Bonds*, the court held that the treatment of Bonds was "an indignity towards a human being" and "should be denounced."[54]

---

51 David Tanovich, "*Bonds*: Gendered and Racialized Violence, Strip Searches, Sexual Assault and Abuse of Prosecutorial Power" (2011) 79 *Criminal Reports* (6th) 132 at 133 [Tanovich, "*Bonds*"]. The *Ottawa Citizen* obtained a copy of the videotape and posted it, online: www.cbc.ca/news/canada/ottawa/ottawa-police-strip-search-video-re-leased-1.951045.

52 Tanovich, "*Bonds*," above note 51 at 133. *R v Bonds*, [2010] OJ No 5034 at para 11 (Ct J) [*Bonds*].

53 *Ibid* at paras 13–14. See Tanovich, "*Bonds*," above note 51 at 133.

54 *Bonds*, above note 52 at paras 24 and 26. The court stayed the charges against Bonds. See also "Ont. Judge Slams Ottawa Police Strip Search" *CBC News* (17 November 2010), online: www.cbc.ca/news/canada/ottawa/ont-judge-slams-ottawa-police-strip-

4) Sharon Abbott

In *Abbott v Toronto Police Services Board*,[55] the complainant, Sharon Abbott, a Black newspaper delivery woman, was out delivering newspapers to a west Toronto neighbourhood when her erratic driving caught the attention of a police officer. Abbott alleged that she was followed by a Toronto police sergeant who acted aggressively towards her, pinned her to a police car, handcuffed her, and held her for forty-five minutes before issuing seven tickets and releasing her.

Early one morning in 2007, Abbott was out on her route. At around 3:15 a.m., she parked her car by an apartment building on Glenlake Avenue in Toronto and went into the building to deliver papers. A Toronto police sergeant was out on patrol that morning and passed Abbott's car. The officer observed that the car was parked in a dimly lit, no parking area with its four-way flashers on. Because of the dimly lit conditions, the officer was unable to run the licence plate. He would proceed to where Abbott had parked her car. By this time, Abbott had exited the building and returned to her car. The officer took down the correct licence plate number and observed the complainant drive away. It was the officer's evidence that Abbott was not wearing her seat belt and did not signal when making a left turn.[56] The officer followed Abbott and was aware that Abbott was a newspaper delivery person. The officer got out of his car and indicated that he wanted to speak to Abbott. Abbott testified that, concerned that she might be the victim of an assault by someone impersonating a police officer, she started to call her husband. The officer repeatedly asked her for her driver's licence and insurance. She advised the officer that she would not speak to him until she had a witness on the phone. During this time, the officer attempted to place Abbott under arrest. A struggle commenced as he tried to handcuff her. According to the officer, they fell to the ground as they lost their balance. Crying out for help, Abbott maintained that the officer pinned her in order to handcuff her and that he grabbed her belt at her rear of her pants in order to get her back on her feet. During the struggle, both parties sustained minor injuries. Abbott sustained an abrasion over her left eye and cuts on the inside of her upper lip, as well as bruising from the handcuffs.[57] Abbott

---

search-1.889722. One of the officers in Bonds' case was charged with sexual assault by the Ontario Special Investigations Unit. In 2013, Sgt Steven Desjourdy was found not guilty in his sexual assault trial. See *R v Desjourdy*, 2013 ONCJ 170.

55   2009 HRTO 1909 [*Abbott*].

56   *Ibid* at para 7.

57   *Ibid* at para 22.

would be charged with seven offences under the *Highway Traffic Act*. She was acquitted of six of those charges.[58]

In *Abbott*, the Ontario Human Rights Commission concluded that her race and/or gender played a role in the sergeant's "failure to take steps to try to de-escalate the situation":[59]

> Racial discrimination, whether on its own or in combination with gender, involves the inappropriate exercise of power by a member of the dominant racial group over a member of what is perceived as a subordinate racial group. There is no doubt that the exercise of power is inherent in the inter-action between a police officer and any member of the public, given the powers that are granted to a police officer by statute. But this imbalance of power can be inappropriately exacerbated when it is layered on top of a racial and gender power dynamic.
>
> . . .
>
> In this case, I have tried to hypothesize a White woman out delivering papers in the early morning having fairly routine traffic matters escalate into an arrest. I have been unable to do so . . . . Most often racial discrimin-ation emanates from unconscious attitudes and belief systems. In a histor-ical context, some of these attitudes and belief systems include that Black persons (and other groups) are expected to "know their place" and that any Black person who talks back or refuses to comply is to be regarded as "uppity" and needs to be dealt with harshly. There is no evidence before me that [the officer] consciously subscribes to any such attitudes or beliefs. But these kinds of attitudes and belief systems are part of our historical and so-cial fabric, and are imbued in all of us through social interactions, the edu-cation system, the media and entertainment industries, and other means.
>
> . . .
>
> I find that [the officer's] actions in this regard are consistent with a manifestation of racism whereby a White person in a position of authority has an expectation of docility and compliance from a racialized person, and imposes harsh consequences if that docility and compliance is not provided.[60]

These cases raise questions about whether race and gender were fac-tors in the police officers' decisions to stop, detain, and ultimately arrest these women. For instance, what were the reasons that led to Bonds' in-itial stop? As Professor Tanovich asks, "[w]as she initially stopped, as a

---

58 There was no evidence before the tribunal concerning the seventh charge of not wear-ing a seat belt. Abbott was awarded $5,000.

59 *Abbott*, above note at 55 at para 42.

60 *Ibid* at paras 42 and 44–46.

result of her being profiled as a sex trade worker, given the time of night, location and the fact she is Black and was seen speaking to the occupants of a van?"[61] Bonds was not a real danger to the police officers. She was arrested for a minor provincial offence. When she was first approached by the officers she provided her information. As such, given what the officers knew at the time of arrest, including the fact that she did not have a criminal record, "their conduct had to be grounded in something else."[62]

Given what is known about racism in policing in Canada, it is reasonable to assume that gender and race were factors in each of these cases. These cases represent a persistent dilemma that confronts Black women's multiple identities. The gendered and racial stereotypes at play made these women more vulnerable to the police misconduct. While racial profiling and the use of force against women of colour take many of the same forms as they do with men of colour, "there are clearly gendered dynamics at play which require a more complicated analysis of racial profiling."[63] Racialized and gendered stereotypes led the police to overreact because they perceived the situation to be far more dangerous than it really was.[64] In each case gendered and racialized bias provide an explanation for why the conduct of the police departed from the minimal standard required by officers when interacting with the public.[65]

E. "GENDERING" RACIAL PROFILING: AN INTERSECTIONAL APPROACH

The construction of stereotypes affecting Black women in the criminal justice system is based on the history of Black enslavement. As Molly Schiffer notes, "due to the history of slavery and its implications, Black women are unable to fit within the 'good girl' or 'victim' stereotypes. While slavery applied to both genders, there are specific stereotypes that are solely pervasive in the experience of Black women [. . .] are pervasive enough to mold the subconscious of decision-makers in the criminal justice system."[66] Using an intersectional analysis, the discourse on racial profiling needs to be more inclusive of who is being profiled. Gender is

---

61   Tanovich, "*Bonds*," above note 51 at 136.

62   Ritchie, above note 37 at 149.

63   *Ibid.*

64   Tanovich, *The Colour of Justice*, above note 4 at 25.

65   Tanovich, "*Bonds*," above note 51 at 137.

66   Molly A Schiffer, "Women of Color and Crime: A Critical Race Theory Perspective to Address Disparate Prosecution" (2014) 56 *Arizona Law Review* 1203 at 1215.

not a separate issue from policing. Neither race nor gender discrimination alone can explain why these women were targets of police violence. It is the unique combination of Black women's intersectional identities that creates multiple oppressions. These examples illustrate the need for a centred-perspective of the experience of Black women's interactions with law enforcement.

The criminal justice system ostensibly operates within a set of race- and gender-neutral laws, policies, and discretions. Understanding intersecting oppressions is important because a theoretical framework rooted in this approach can help to explain why, with such neutral policies, there continues to be a disparate impact on Black women. Race-centred objectives and liberal notions have worked together inadvertently to erase the experiences of women of colour in the criminal justice system by making the narratives of the racial minority group, men, paramount. Formalistic notions of equality tend to treat all members of a racialized group as being equally positioned. This positioning, however, "tends to privilege [the] male experience."[67] In turn, the criminal justice process has tended to highlight the colonial harm done to men without regard to the damage done to women. This process does not see beyond the patriarchal and cultural values of the hegemonic state.[68] Thus it is not surprising that, in the course of the debates on racial profiling that centre exclusively on race, women's experiences are secondary. Black women have been excluded from the analysis, which ultimately reveals only fragments of their experiences, not the totality. The impact of police violence and abuse in Black women's lives cannot be fully captured by separating the race and sex dimensions of these experiences.

The analytical frameworks that have traditionally formed both anti-racist and feminist agendas tend to focus on only one identity.[69] Thus, those agendas have been incapable of developing solutions to address the marginalization of Black women as victims of racial profiling. Black women fall into "the void between concerns about women's issues and concerns about racism."[70] In 1989, Kimberlé Crenshaw coined the term intersectionality to recognize "that people live multi-dimensional identities

---

67   Marchetti, above note 40 at 169.

68   Emma LaRocque, "Re-examining Culturally-Appropriate Models in Criminal Justice Applications" in Michael Asch, ed, *Aboriginal and Treaty Rights in Canada: Essays on Law, Equality and Respect for Difference* (Vancouver: UBC Press, 1997) 75 at 89.

69   See Kimberlé Crenshaw, "Mapping the Margins: Intersectionality, Identity Politics, and Violence against Women of Color" (1991) 43:6 *Stanford Law Review* 1241.

70   *Ibid* at 1281.

— specifically race, class and gender — due to interlocking systems of oppression."[71] One commonly noted aspect of this theory is that Black women are double burdened, "subject in some ways to the dominating practices of both a sexual hierarchy and a racial one."[72] As a result, Black women's burdens "are suppressed as the terms of racial and gender discrimination" that require that Black women mold their "experiences into that of either white women or black men in order to be legally recognized."[73] These intersecting structural positions result in inequality. As Crenshaw points out:

> Black women sometimes experience discrimination in ways similar to [W]hite women's experiences; sometimes they share very similar experience with Black men. Yet often they experience double discrimination — the combined effort of practices which discriminate on the basis of race, and on the basis of sex. And sometimes, they experience discrimination as Black women — not the sum of race and sex discrimination, but as Black women.[74]

The heightened police interaction mentioned in the above Canadian cases is not only because they are Black, but also because they are women. By not addressing the specific racialized and gendered nature of their experiences, the practice of racial profiling against women is not fully understood. As Professor Tanovich points out, "the issue of gendered violence against racialized and Aboriginal women by police officers is an under-studied and litigated area in Canada."[75] With respect to racial profiling of Black women, the race and gender dynamic is vaguely understood; the incidents of police violence and misconduct against Black women that have received public attention should not be viewed as isolated incidents or as a deviation from the policing norm. Rather, the lack of understanding on law enforcements' misconduct against Black women

---

71   Nnennaya Amuchie, "'The Forgotten Victims': How Racialized Gender Stereotypes Lead to Police Violence against Black Women and Girls: Incorporating an Analysis of Police Violence into Feminist Jurisprudence and Community Activism" (2016) 14:3 *Seattle Journal for Social Science* 617 at 622. See also Crenshaw, "Demarginalizing," above note 39 at 140.

72   Kimberlé Crenshaw, "Whose Story Is It Anyway? Feminist and Antiracist Appropriations of Anita Hill" in Toni Morrison, ed, *Race-ing Justice, En-gendering Power: Essays on Anita Hill, Clarence Thomas, and the Construction of Social Reality of Race* (New York: Pantheon Books 1992) 402 at 404.

73   *Ibid* at 404.

74   Crenshaw, "Demarginalizing," above note 39 at 149.

75   Tanovich, *"Bonds,"* above note 51 at 149.

is "another manifestation of the ongoing sublimation of women of color's experiences to those of men in struggles for racial justice."[76] The case of Majiza Philip, a Black woman who alleged her arm was broken by Montreal police in 2014;[77] the most recent death of Ethiopia native, Amleset Haile,[78] who died from injuries following an interaction with Toronto police; and the 2016 Edmonton Report[79] that revealed Black and Indigenous people, particularly women, were stopped at higher rates than their counterparts illustrate what are at risk when we ignore the marginalized voices in this national debate concerning police violence. Not only do we miss half of the narrative, but we also fail to grasp how laws, policies, and culture are rooted in intersectional levels of oppression and inequality that reinforce police practices such as racial profiling and other forms of anti-Blackness within policing. To understand the deeper implications of racial profiling and begin to reconceptualize the study of race, gender, and the criminal justice system, it is important to rethink the current assumptions about, approaches to, and consequences of, the practice of racial profiling in Canada.

F. CONCLUSION

The dominant paradigm of racial profiling fails to adequately address the experiences of Black women. It has been taken for granted that men aren't the only targets of police violence. We must challenge the intersections of race, class, gender, and sexuality that structure women's experiences in the criminal justice system, "rather than viewing women's bodies solely as gendered, we need to recognize that gender is always racialized and classed."[80] Until mainstream discourse on racial profiling integrates the

---

76   Ritchie, above note 37 at 141.

77   Nathalie Laflamme, "Woman Says Arrest and Charges Were Racial Discrimination" *Montreal Gazette* (5 April 2015), online: http://montrealgazette.com/news/local-news/woman-says-arrest-and-charges-were-racial-discrimination.

78   Wendy Gills, "Friends Seek Answers as SIU Probes Death of 60-Year-Old Toronto Woman" *Toronto Star* (2017 February 20), online: www.thestar.com/news/gta/2017/02/20/friends-seek-answers-as-siu-probes-death-of-60-year-old-toronto-woman.html. This case illustrates the intersections between race, gender, and mental health.

79   Jonny Wakefield, "Black People, Aboriginal Women Over-represented in 'Carding' Police Stops" *Edmonton Journal* (27 June 2017), online: http://edmontonsun.com/2017/06/26/black-people-aboriginal-women-over-represented-in-carding-police-stops/wcm/1082a4fb-4b7a-40fd-ado2-6c8df3a1677a.

80   Julia Sudbury, *Global Lockdown: Race, Gender, and the Prison-Industrial Complex* (New York: Routledge, 2005) at xv.

realities of Black women's interaction with law enforcement, the voices of the most marginalized will continue to be silenced. We cannot fully understand the impact of racial profiling on women through the lens of racism alone. Ultimately, an emphasis on intersections of race and gender is necessary to account for multiple grounds of oppression and marginality when considering how police interact with Black women.

Addressing the struggles of Black women against police misconduct based on gender and race, as well as other structural oppressions such as class, gender identity, and expressions, is required. Absent the adoption of an intersectional approach, there is little chance for the criminal justice system to be more inclusive. Arguably, these cases of Black women can bring "greater recognition and understanding of gendered and racialized violence in policing and attempts by academic and lawyers to develop legal strategies to address the problems."[81] A conscious effort would also require the process to include a number of "narratives and stories, accounts of the particular, different, and the hitherto silenced."[82] Different dimensions of power, as it exists in the lives of both women and men of colour, need to be made explicit in the position of those most vulnerable. As Kimberlé Crenshaw points out, the problems of exclusion cannot be solved by simply including Black women within an already established analytical structure. Rather, efforts of combating racial profiling must recognize and reflect that Black women "have been and continue to be subject to racial profiling and use of force on the streets and highways" across Canada.[83] The reframing of our understanding of racial profiling calls for an intersectional, feminist perspective that includes Black people in every category, such as race, gender, gender identity, and sexual orientation. Such accounts need to be actively sought by inquires, litigated in the courtrooms, and documented in statistics. In order to achieve this, the process used to obtain different narratives must be informed by cultural and appropriate practices.

---

81   Tanovich, "*Bonds*," above note 51 at 150.
82   See Marchetti, above note 40 at 170.
83   Ritchie, above note 37 at 146.

CHAPTER 8

Damaged Goods

A Critical Perspective on Consumer Racial Profiling in Ontario's Retail Environment

TOMEE ELIZABETH SOJOURNER-CAMPBELL[*]

A. INTRODUCTION

Until recently in Ontario, the public discourse about racial profiling had focused primarily on police services and their officers' conduct towards members of Black and Indigenous communities, namely youth, adult men, and some women.[1] The racial profiling in these situations has included unlawful stops and detentions, completion of contact cards (i.e., "carding"), and street stops, also referred to as "driving while Black."[2] These incidents have been documented in Ontario's caselaw, in media reports, and in the Ontario Human Rights Commission's report on racial profiling.[3]

However, there has been growing public interest in another form of racial profiling: racial profiling in Ontario's retail environments, also

---

[*] Tomee Elizabeth Sojourner-Campbell is a mediator, diversity and inclusion consultant, and interdisciplinary legal researcher. The author wishes to thank her copy editor, Saada Branker, and her wife, Njeri Damali Sojourner-Campbell, for reviewing and commenting on drafts of this chapter.

1 Andrea S Anderson, "Seeing Gender Differently in Racial Profiling" (2017) 14:1 *Canadian Diversity* 22; Jim Rankin, "Police Target Black Drivers, Star Analysis of Traffic Data Suggests Racial Profiling" *Toronto Star* (20 October 2002); David M Tanovich, "E-Racing Racial Profiling" (2004) 41 *Alberta Law Review* 905 at 907 [Tanovich, "E-Racing"].

2 Ontario Human Rights Commission, *Under Suspicion: Research and Consultation Report on Racial Profiling in Ontario* (Toronto: Ontario Human Rights Commission, April 2017) at 10. [OHRC, *Under Suspicion*]; Tanovich, "E-Racing," above note 1 at 929.

3 *R v Brown*, 2003 CanLII 52142 at para 7 (Ont CA); *D'Mello v Law Society of Upper Canada*, 2013 HRTO 1245; *Phipps v Toronto Police Services Board*, 2009 HRTO 877; *Sinclair v London (City)*, 2008 HRTO 48; OHRC, *Under Suspicion*, above note 2 at 31–45.

referred to as consumer racial profiling.[4] It is a practice of targeting a consumer for discriminatory treatment (e.g., arbitrary bag searches, unsubstantiated accusations of shoplifting, physical body "strip" searches) based on an arbiter's unconscious or conscious biases and stereotypes about a consumer's race, skin colour, ethnicity, appearance, gender/sex, and ability to pay or an intersection of these perceived identities.[5] These arbiters include loss prevention employees, security guards, front-line employees, and management.[6] Further, consumer racial profiling is often practiced in the context of loss prevention, however, it also includes denial or degradation of services, goods, and products.[7]

For the most part, consumer racial profiling from a legal academic perspective has been under-researched. As legal practitioners, human rights advocates, community members, and consumers, the matter of consumer racial profiling should be top of mind when we consider three factors. The first factor is that many Ontarians are consumers of household and personal products, goods, and services.[8] They rely on retail businesses as the primary source of these everyday items.[9] Moreover, many

---

4   Tomee Elizabeth Sojourner, "'Can I Help You?' Taking Seriously Consumer Racial Profiling in Ontario's Retail Sector" (2017) 14:1 *Canadian Diversity* 29. [Sojourner, "Can I Help You?"]. As a point of clarification, I recognize that consumer racial profiling practices are not unique to the retail sector and cut across all types of private and public sector consumer services (e.g., banks, hotels, restaurants, insurance, health care, security, travel, and education) (*ibid* at 30).

5   Nova Scotia Human Rights Commission, *Working Together To Better Serve All Nova Scotians: A Report on Consumer Racial Profiling in Nova Scotia* (Halifax: Nova Scotia Human Rights Commission, 2013) at 81 and 100. [NSHRC, *CRP Report*]; *Gilpin v Halifax Alehouse Limited*, 2013 NSHRC 43798 at para 22 [*Gilpin*]. I am using the concept of intersectionality in the manner contemplated by the Ontario Human Rights Commission in Ontario Human Rights Commission, *An Intersectional Approach to Discrimination: Addressing Multiple Grounds in Human Rights Claims* (Toronto: Ontario Human Rights Commission, 2001) at 3.

6   Recent human rights consumer racial profiling and racial profiling case examples include: *Danielson v Dollar Giant Store and another*, 2013 BCHRT 108; *Gilpin*, above note 5; *Rai v Shark Club of Langley, Limited Partnership*, 2013 BCHRT 204; *Nassiah v Peel (Regional Municipality) Police Services Board*, 2007 HRTO 14 [*Nassiah*].

7   Anne-Marie G Harris, Geraldine R Henderson, & Jerome D Williams, "Courting Customers: Assessing Consumer Racial Profiling and Other Marketplace Discrimination" (2005) 24:1 *Journal of Public Policy & Marketing* 163 at 163 [Harris et al, "Courting Customers"].

8   OHRC, *Under Suspicion*, above note 2 at 70.

9   "Most expenditures by consumers for goods and services occur through retail transactions. This retail spending accounts for between 50 and 55 percent of Canadian

retail businesses operating in Ontario have made public commitments to embrace diversity and inclusion values as part of their corporate social responsibility mandates, in particular large-size corporations (e.g., Shoppers Drug Mart and Sobeys).[10]

These businesses also employ approximately 48 percent of the total diverse labour force in Canada's private sector.[11] Their combined power and influence on Ontario's society is considerable. It is for these reasons that the role of retail businesses and their representatives becomes pivotal for legal scholars and human rights practitioners to think about as they work on consumer racial profiling as an access to justice matter.

The second factor is that retail businesses and their representatives (e.g., employees and private licensed security guards)[12] have the legal power to determine who has access to their premises, the types of behaviours from members of the public and their customers that they deem acceptable, how much "freedom" each person has while on the premises, who is targeted for "stop and search" procedures, and who can be asked to leave.[13] These businesses take their statutory power from legal authorities, including the *Trespass to Property Act* (*Trespass Act*), section 494 of the *Criminal Code*, the Ontario *Human Rights Code* (*Code*), as well as other statutes, regulations, policies, and municipal bylaws.[14] These authorities

---

households' consumption": Industry Canada, Office of Consumer Affairs, "Consumer Trends Report" (Ottawa: Industry Canada, 2005) at 38, online: www.ic.gc.ca/eic/site/oca-bc.nsf/vwapj/EN_CTR.pdf/$FILE/EN_CTR.pdf.

10 In *David v Sobeys Group Inc*, [2016] NSHRBID No 2 at paras 23 and 25 [*David*], the Board of Inquiry chair notes that Sobeys has a commitment "to diversity and equality, as an objective within the realm of their own policy and procedures." The Shoppers Drug Mart (SDM), "Our Culture" page contains their diversity commitment to customers, online: http://careers.shoppersdrugmart.ca/our-culture [SDM, "Our Culture"].

11 Retail businesses employ "nearly five million Canadians or 48 percent of the total labour force in the private sector": Industry Canada, Office of Consumer Affairs, "Consumer Trends Update" (2013) at 7, online: www.ic.gc.ca/eic/site/oca-bc.nsf/eng/ca02852.html.

12 As of 1 May 2018, Ontario has 74,399 licensed security guards. (Interview of Paul Obara, manager, program development, Public Safety Division, Ministry of Community Safety and Correctional Services, Private Security & Investigative Services Branch, by Tomee Elizabeth Sojourner (20 April 2016) Toronto).

13 George Rigakos, *In Search of Security: The Roles of Public Police and Private Agencies*, Law Commission of Canada Discussion Paper (Toronto: Law Commission of Canada, 2002) 1 at 11 [Rigakos, *In Search of Security*].

14 *Trespass to Property Act*, RSO 1990, c T.21 [*Trespass Act*]; *Criminal Code*, RSC 1985, c C-46, s 494; Ontario *Human Rights Code*, RSO 1990, c H.19, s 1 [*Code*].

are used in the development, implementation, and enforcement of their loss prevention policies (e.g., bag policy, Sears' shop theft policy).[15]

Despite the legal obligation for retail businesses to comply with section 1 of the *Code* that states "[e]very person has a right to equal treatment with respect to services, goods and facilities, without discrimination because of race, ancestry, place of origin, colour, ethnic origin, citizenship, creed, sex, sexual orientation, gender identity, gender expression, age, marital status, family status or disability,"[16] it is the arbitrary application of loss prevention policies directed at racialized and Indigenous customers that leads to allegations of consumer racial profiling.[17]

The third factor is that Ontario has the largest visible minority and Indigenous populations in the country, with over 3,279,600 people who identify as visible minorities, and 301,425 who identify as Indigenous.[18] Armed with this demographic information, it is imperative that legal practitioners and human rights advocates develop, and use, an intersectional lens to gain deeper knowledge about the ways consumer racial profiling impacts the "dignity and worth"[19] of racialized, specifically Black and Indigenous, consumers (e.g., Black women, racialized gender non-conforming individuals). In addition, Canadian and American researchers have found that racialized, in particular Black and Indigenous, consumers are disproportionately targeted for this practice.[20]

It is with these factors and the increased public discourse about consumer racial profiling that this chapter provides a critical perspective on this phenomenon in Ontario's retail environments. To do this, the chapter is divided into three sections. The first section will define consumer racial profiling and provide an argument in support of broadening its

---

15   *Nassiah*, above note 6 at para 86.

16   *Code*, above note 15, s 1.

17   Rigakos, *In Search of Security*, above note 14 at 40; NSHRC, *CRP Report*, above note 5 at 10 and 78; Harris et al, "Courting Customers," above note 7 at 166; Shaun L Gabbidon et al, "The Consumer Racial Profiling Experiences of Black Students at Historically Black Colleges and Universities: An Exploratory Study" (2008) 36:4 *Journal of Criminal Justice* 354.

18   Statistics Canada, *National Household Survey 2011: Immigration and Ethnocultural Diversity in Canada Analytical Document* (Ottawa: Statistics Canada, 2013) at 15; Statistics Canada, *National Household Survey 2011: Aboriginal Peoples in Canada: First Nations People, Métis and Inuit Analytical Document* (Ottawa: Statistics Canada, 2013) at 8.

19   Harris et al, "Courting Customers," above note 7; *Code*, above note 15, preamble.

20   NSHRC, *CRP Report*, above note 5 at 15; see OHRC, *Under Suspicion*, above note 2 at 15. In this chapter, I use the term "Indigenous" to refer to members of First Nations, Métis, and Inuit communities (see OHRC, *Under Suspicion*, above note 2 at 15).

definition. The second section will draw on the Human Rights Tribunal of Ontario cases of *Nassiah v Peel (Regional Municipality) Police Services Board* and *McCarthy v Kenny Tan Pharmacy Inc* to provide examples of some of the ways consumer racial profiling manifests in Ontario's retail environments.[21] The last section will offer a few recommendations to address these phenomena in Ontario's retail environments.

1) Defining Consumer Racial Profiling

Consumer racial profiling is generally defined as a racialized or Indigenous customer being targeted for discriminatory treatment by an employee or a loss prevention professional. American Marketplace scholar Anne-Marie Harris expands the definition to include "any type of treatment of consumers in the marketplace based on race or ethnicity that constitutes a denial or degradation in the product or service offered to the consumer."[22] However, it is my view that the definition of consumer racial profiling should be broadened to further recognize the differential impact of this phenomenon on consumers depending on the intersections of their identities, including but not limited to their race, skin colour, indigeneity, socio-economic status, geographical location, religion, gender expression, gender, (dis)abilities, ethnicity, and language.[23]

2) Different Forms of Consumer Racial Profiling

The jurisprudence on consumer racial profiling in Ontario's retail environments is limited. The next section provides a brief summary of *Nassiah v Peel (Regional Municipality) Police Services Board* and *McCarthy v Kenny Tan Pharmacy Inc*, followed by a brief discussion about two insights from each case.[24]

---

21   *Nassiah*, above note 6; *McCarthy v Kenny Tan Pharmacy Inc*, 2015 HRTO 1303 [*McCarthy*].

22   Anne-Marie Harris, "Shopping While Black: Applying 42 U.S.C. § 1981 to Case of Consumer Racial Profiling" (2003) 23:1 *Boston College Third World Law Journal* 1 at 4.

23   This point is supported by recent survey information shared during the Ontario Human Rights Commission's racial profiling dialogue that Black women respondents experienced the highest incidences of racial profiling in the retail sector. See Remi Warner, "Racial Profiling: A View from the OHRC Survey and Review of HRTO Applications" (Presentation to the Ontario Human Rights Commission Racial Profiling Policy Dialogue, Toronto, 16 February 2016) [unpublished].

24   *Nassiah*, above note 6; *McCarthy*, above note 23.

3) Summary of *Nassiah*

Nassiah[25] is an example of one form of consumer racial profiling that occurs when the profiled subject is a racialized person in a retail environment, and the profiler or profilers are members of dominant groups, specifically White men of European descent, in decision-making positions; in this case, a police officer and a licensed private security guard with power and legal authority.[26] In *Nassiah*, the complainant, Ms Jacqueline Nassiah was a thirty-six-year-old Black Trinidadian-Canadian woman, and a single mother with a small child, who was subjected to consumer racial profiling at the Sears outlet store in Dixie Mall, Mississauga.[27] Ms Nassiah alleged that on 18 February 2003, Officer Richard Elkington[28] of the Peel Regional Police Services, a thirty-five-year-old White British male, and the Peel Regional Police Services Board ("Peel") "discriminated against her in the provision of a service in the manner [Officer Elkington] conducted his police investigation into the allegation that she had stolen a bra from [the] Sears store."[29] The incident also involved Sears security guard John Nevers, identified in the HRTO decision as a White male.[30]

On 11 May 2007, the tribunal rendered its decision stating that Ms Nassiah had been discriminated against on the basis of race by Officer Elkington in the provision of service because "she was subject to a more intensive, suspicious and prolonged investigation."[31] In support of its decision, the tribunal found the following facts of Ms Nassiah's allegations to be credible. First, the tribunal opined it was more probable than not that, despite his consistent denials, Officer Elkington became more abu-

---

25   Note that *Nassiah* was litigated under the previous human rights enforcement system in Ontario: see Andrew Pinto, *Report of the Ontario Human Rights Review 2012* (Toronto: Ministry of the Attorney General, 2012) 1 at 7–10) [Pinto, *Report*].

26   Ontario Ministry of Finance, "2016 Census Highlights: Factsheet 9: Ethnic Origin and Visible Minorities," online: www.fin.gov.on.ca/en/economy/demographics/census/cenhi16-9.html.

27   Based on the *Toronto Star* article, Ms Nassiah was forty years old when the tribunal published its decision in 2007. I calculated her age to be thirty-six at the time of the incident (Christian Cotroneo, "A Victim of Racial Profiling" *Toronto Star* (18 May 2007), online: www.thestar.com/news/2007/05/18/a_victim_of_racial_profiling.html).

28   Officer Elkington was identified as a forty-three-year-old man. I used his age in the story to calculate approximately how old he would have been at the time of 18 February 2003 incident (News Local Police Briefs, "Former Cop Faces Drunk Driving Charges" *The Sudbury Star* (29 July 2011), online: www.thesudburystar.com/2011/07/29/local-police-briefs).

29   *Nassiah*, above note 6 at para 1.

30   *Ibid* at para 39.

31   *Ibid* at para 172.

sive, and did refer to Ms Nassiah as a "fucking foreigner,"[32] when he could not locate the bra; as well, he threatened to take her to jail if she did not produce the bra.[33] The tribunal concluded that Officer Elkington had drawn on derogatory anti-Black stereotypes to determine that Ms Nassiah was "likely a foreigner because she [was] Black."[34]

Second, the tribunal found Officer Elkington had subjected Ms Nassiah to verbal abuse by repeatedly asking her in a "hostile tone": "Where's the bra?"[35] Third, the tribunal concluded Officer Elkington "stereotypically assumed a Black suspect may not speak English well"[36] and it is for this reason that he asked Mr Nevers after seeing that Ms Nassiah was Black "if she spoke English."[37]

Lastly, the tribunal opined that, despite video evidence clearing Ms Nassiah of wrongdoing and Officer Elkington being informed by Ms Nassiah and Mr Nevers that Ms Nassiah had been physically searched before his arrival where no bra was found, he subjected her to a second strip search.[38]

In its determination of appropriate individual remedy, the tribunal found Peel and Officer Elkington jointly liable and ordered them to pay Ms Nassiah $20,000 for general damages and for mental anguish.[39] However, the tribunal also took into account that "Ms Nassiah's reaction to February 18, 2003 was due in part to the unlawful detention by Mr Nevers and his treatment of her."[40]

In regards to a systemic remedy, the tribunal ordered Peel to implement several measures, including: hire an external consultant with subject-matter expertise to work with them to prepare training materials on racial profiling for new recruits, current officers, and supervisors; develop a directive prohibiting racial profiling compliant with the *Code*; and

---

32 *Ibid* at para 75.

33 *Ibid.*

34 *Ibid* at paras 52 and 107.

35 *Ibid* at paras 11–13.

36 *Ibid* at para 166.

37 *Ibid* at paras 2, 9, 70, 100, 102, 104–6, 166, and 184.

38 *Ibid* at paras 62, 64–65, and 83–84.

39 *Ibid* at para 184. The tribunal also ordered the respondents to pay pre- and post-judgment interest in accordance with section 127 of the *Courts of Justice Act*, RSO 1990, c C.43 (*Nassiah*, above note 6 at para 212(9)); the tribunal found that Ms Nassiah did suffer from a degree of emotional distress caused by the events, and by Officer Elkington's "wilful" derogatory comments, which met the threshold for mental anguish under the *Code* and justified an award for mental anguish (*Nassiah, ibid* at para 182).

40 *Ibid* at para 183.

within one year train all employees, including Officer Elkington, on this topic, in a session no less than two hours long.[41] The tribunal stated that these orders were made with the intent to train officers on what steps and actions may lead to a "racially biased investigation" and to prevent future discrimination similar to Ms Nassiah's complaint.[42]

B. INSIGHTS DRAWN FROM *NASSIAH*

In considering the form of consumer racial profiling Ms Nassiah experienced and its impact on her, this section focuses on insights gleaned from the tribunal's findings, Ms Nassiah's witness testimony, and my critical reflections.

1) Security-Guard Power: Securing the Aisles by Any Means Necessary

Ms Nassiah testified that during her detention, between 5:40 p.m. (when she was detained) and 7:16 p.m. (when she was free to go), she had expressed discomfort with being left alone in the Sears security office with a man, specifically Mr Nevers, thus she requested a female employee be present.[43] Ms Nassiah also noted that prior to Officer Elkington's arrival at 6:14 p.m., she was very upset, crying, and repeatedly asked Mr Nevers to "look in [her Sears] bag."[44]

Despite her requests, the tribunal found that throughout Ms Nassiah's detention she was left alone with Mr Nevers, and at different times with Officer Elkington.[45] The tribunal noted that the denial of Ms Nassiah's request was a direct violation of Sears's store policy as per the evidence submitted.[46] The policy stipulated that a female employee had to be present in the security office if a female suspect had been detained.[47] The fear expressed by Ms Nassiah based on the psychological violence

---

41   *Ibid* at para 212; under section 41(1)(a) of the *Code*, an adjudicator who finds that a person's rights have been infringed under the *Code* can direct a party to "do anything that, in [her] opinion, ought to [be done] to achieve compliance with this Act, both in respect to the complaint and . . . future practices" (*ibid* at paras 187 & 188).

42   *Ibid* at paras 201 and 209.

43   *Ibid* at paras 6 and 89.

44   *Ibid* at paras 5, 7, 24, and 34.

45   *Ibid* at paras 6, 46, and 89.

46   *Ibid* at paras 20, 42, 55, and 89.

47   *Ibid* at para 42.

she experienced at the hands of Mr Nevers is an example of racialized gender-based violence.[48]

Arguably, another example of racialized gender-based violence that Ms Nassiah experienced was when, as she testified, Mr Nevers subjected her to a strip search by a female employee where no bra was found.[49] However, he continued with his investigation with no evidence that she had stolen a bra.[50] Ms Nassiah noted that when she asked Mr Nevers' permission to call her babysitter in order to explain her delay, he informed her that she could only call her lawyer.[51] She also recalled that when she asked to view the surveillance footage, he denied her access to it, and at some point during her detention, she alleged that he told her to "shut up."[52]

Mr Nevers repeatedly ignored the Sears shop theft policy[53] in his dealing with Ms Nassiah, as well, his "unlawful detention . . . and his treatment of [Ms Nassiah]" requires further discussion given the legal authority and power he had under *Trespass Act* and section 494 of the *Criminal Code*.[54] For example, under section 1(b) of the Act, as a security guard, Mr Nevers had a "responsibility for and control over . . . the activities there carried on, or control over persons allowed to enter the premises."[55] In addition, under subsection 2(1)(a)(ii) of *Trespass Act*, Mr Nevers was empowered to instruct any person engaging in activity prohibited under the Act that they were subject to a trespass notice.[56] Lastly, under subsections 9(1) and 9(2), he was authorized to arrest without warrant

---

48   Although Nnennaya Amuchie's article does not address Black women's experiences of racialized gender-based violence at the hands of private security guards, I drew inferences from her arguments about the devaluation of Black women and applied it to how gendered forms of anti-Black racism play a role in consumer racial profiling practised against Black women. I also drew inferences from her call for the use of an intersectional lens and approach when analyzing cases involving Black women and police violence. In this chapter, I make a similar call to legal practitioners to use intersectional and critical race feminist approaches. See Nnennaya Amuchie, "'The Forgotten Victims': How Racialized Gender Stereotypes Lead to Police Violence against Black Women and Girls: Incorporating an Analysis of Police Violence into Feminist Jurisprudence and Community Activism" (2016) 14:3 *Seattle Journal of Justice* 617 at 619–21.

49   *Nassiah*, above note 6 at paras 6, 8, 39, 49, and 57.

50   *Ibid* at para 43.

51   *Ibid* at para 8.

52   *Ibid*.

53   *Ibid* at para 86.

54   *Trespass Act*, above note 15; *Criminal Code*, above note 15.

55   *Trespass Act*, above note 15, s 1.

56   *Ibid*, ss 2, 9(1), & 9(2).

any person he believed on reasonable and probable grounds to be violating section 2, and then deliver them to the police.[57]

The legal authority of Mr Nevers is raised to highlight that licensed private security guards are given a broad set of legal powers that require a critical review, especially in light of their role in retail environments. This point was raised by a former security guard in *Under Suspicion*. They stated that it is "concerning that security guards can use the [*Trespass to Property Act*] to ban people from the premises, without the need to prove that they engaged in problematic behaviour. The decision to ban someone may be open to the influence of unconscious or conscious racial bias."[58]

I suggest that legal practitioners and human rights advocates working with clients alleging consumer racial profiling by a security guard should use a critical race feminist approach when reviewing their clients' facts. In addition, as legal practitioners review the facts with their client, they may consider naming individual security guards or security firms as respondents. For example, in *Nassiah*, Mr Nevers and Sears were not named as respondents, however, as the tribunal noted, his actions played a role in Ms Nassiah's experience of the incident.[59]

2) Making the Case That Consumer Racial Profiling Is Part of Racialized Gender-Based Violence

In regard to Officer Elkington's subjecting Ms Nassiah to a second strip search, where she had to again reveal that she had not concealed the bra under her clothes, inside the waist of her pants, inside her boots, and in the pockets of her coat, I argue it was not only an act of consumer racial profiling, it was also a form of racialized gender-based violence. Officer Elkington's actions are an example of what legal scholar Jennifer C Nash describes in "From Lavender to Purple: Privacy, Black Women, and Feminist Legal Theory": that Black women's bodies are "always public, a site of . . . scrutiny, because of [their] perceived links to 'social ills' including crime . . . [leaving them] subject to particular forms of cultural and legal hyper-surveillance."[60] It is therefore reasonable to assert that retail environments are where Black women were, and are, subjected to layers of

---

57   *Ibid*, ss 2 and 9.

58   OHRC, *Under Suspicion*, above note 2 at 72.

59   *Nassiah*, above note 6 at para 183.

60   Jennifer C Nash, "From Lavender to Purple: Privacy, Black Women, and Feminist Legal Theory" (2004–2005) 11 *Cardozo Women's Law Journal* 303 at 320.

scrutiny, increased vulnerability to discriminatory practices, and harm in these settings.[61]

Lastly, the type of racialized gender-based violence Ms Nassiah was subjected to by Officer Elkington, in particular, and Mr Nevers has emotional costs. Moreover, the trauma and the psychological violence experienced by Ms Nassiah are not unlike the trauma of rage and humiliation that African-American legal scholar Patricia J Williams shares in her book, *The Alchemy of Race and Rights*, in which she describes being racially profiled in 1986 by a young White male Benetton employee who denied her entry into the store at 1 p.m. while several White shoppers were in the store.[62] According to African-American legal scholar Katheryn Russell-Brown, "there are personal costs associated with profiling. Those who have been subjected to profiling tell stories of fear, alienation, and self-doubt."[63]

3) An Observation for Human Rights Practitioners

Human rights practitioners who assist clients in preparing their HRTO applications and represent these clients in the process, including at HRTO hearings, must understand the psychological trauma Ms Nassiah experienced during this consumer racial profiling incident in order to assess and advocate for general damage awards that fully address the harm caused by profiling.

4) Using Critical Race Feminist and Intersectional Approaches

Using a critical race feminist lens, Kimberlé Crenshaw, in her TED Women 2016 presentation, "The Urgency of Intersectionality," emphasized that Black women as a group experience racial profiling and police violence in gendered and intersectional ways.[64] Moreover, Crenshaw argued that

---

61　Erica Lawson, "Images in Black: Black Women, Media and the Mythology of an Orderly Society" in Njoki Nathani Wane, Katerina Deliovsky, & Erica Lawson, *Back to the Drawing Board: African Canadian Feminisms* (Toronto: Sumach Press, 2002) 199 at 199, 200, and 209; Patricia J Williams, *The Alchemy of Race and Rights* (Cambridge: Harvard University Press, 1991) at 44–51.

62　Williams, *ibid* at 44–48.

63　Katheryn Russell-Brown, *Underground Codes: Race, Crime, and Related Fires* (New York: New York University Press, 2004) at 116.

64　Kimberlé Crenshaw, "The Urgency of Intersectionality" (2016), online: TED Conferences www.ted.com/talks/kimberle_crenshaw_the_urgency_of_intersectionality. See

Black women's experiences cannot be examined and understood from a single-axis frame, whether it is a "race" or "sex" lens, because "this is a trickle-down approach to social justice, and many times it just doesn't work. Without frames that allow us to see how social problems impact all the members of a targeted group, many will fall through the cracks."[65]

Similarly, Nigerian feminist lawyer Nnennaya Amuchie states that racialized gender stereotypes influence police violence against Black women, and they need to be understood within the context of "how hegemonic structures intersect to oppress groups of people based on their identity."[66] Moreover, Amuchie argues that Black women's lives continue to be negatively impacted by colonial social hierarchies established by White people in positions of power, leading to the "devaluation of Black women [which] has normalized violence against Black women."[67] Amuchie provides examples of the different forms of police violence Black women are exposed to including "verbal abuse, . . . psychological intimidation, emotional violence, false arrest, and racial profiling."[68] I drew inferences from Amuchie's research to inform my understanding of this type of violence. So far in my research, I have been unable to locate a Canadian study on the topic of Black women's experiences of consumer racial profiling by security guards, and the impact of racialized gender-based violence in these cases. Further research on this topic is required.

In order to competently represent racialized women in consumer racial profiling cases, legal practitioners must look at similar evidence presented by the client and consider how the intersection of race, sex, colour, and other *Code*-based grounds may have factored into the ways their client was impacted by consumer racial profiling. This information may allow practitioners to include requests for subject matter experts who have research and scholarship in the areas of critical race feminism and racial profiling in retail environments. This approach would be similar to the one taken by the commission in *Nassiah* when it sought to

---

Crenshaw's reference to the audience that the only difference between the names on two lists she read out was gender (see the 2:16–2:17 minute point in 13:45 minute clip); see segment 2:42–2:56 for Crenshaw's argument that "everywhere, the awareness of the level of police violence that [B]lack women experience is exceedingly low."

65   *Ibid* at the 4:07 minute point in clip; also see Kimberlé Crenshaw, "Demarginalizing the Intersection of Race and Sex: A Black Feminist Critique of Antidiscrimination Doctrine, Feminist Theory and Antiracist Politics" (1989) 1989:1 *University of Chicago Legal Forum* 139 at 140–44 and 147.

66   Amuchie, above note 48 at 619 and 621.

67   *Ibid* at 620.

68   *Ibid* at 621, 663, and 668.

include the expert evidence of Scot Wortley, a subject matter expert in racial profiling and police.

5) Store Loss Prevention Policy Consideration: What If the Suspect Has a Small Child?

At the time of the incident, Ms Nassiah was a parent with a small child in the care of a babysitter. According to Mr Nevers' testimony, Ms Nassiah was informed that, under Sears shop theft policy, as a suspect she was only able to phone a lawyer.[69] This "neutral policy" had an adverse impact on Ms Nassiah as a single mother who was denied access to her child and his caregiver. If her legal counsel or the commission at the time had applied an intersectional lens or a critical race feminist lens to her complaint, they may have considered the relevance of her sex, as well as her family status, in how she experienced the consumer racial profiling incident. Drawing on this example, I suggest that legal practitioners working with retail clients to develop loss prevention policies take the time to consider the potential adverse impact and potential *Code* violations of these policies.

6) *McCarthy*: The Case of Consumer Racial Profiling in the Oral Care Aisle of Kenny Tan Pharmacy

McCarthy is an example of one form of consumer racial profiling that takes place in a retail environment where the profiled is a racialized customer, and the profiler is a racialized store employee with the legal authority to stop, search, and detain a customer they suspect is committing an illegal activity, including theft of merchandise.[70] This brief summary will provide a few of the tribunal's findings and reference aspects of Ms Mary McCarthy's testimony and the respondent's witnesses testimonies to give the reader an overview of the case.

At the time of the alleged consumer racial profiling incident, Ms McCarthy was a fifty-five-year-old Black woman and PhD student from New Brunswick. She lived in a University of Toronto student residence near Shoppers Drug Mart franchise, Kenny Tan Pharmacy Inc.[71] She was also a

---

69 *Nassiah*, above note 6 at paras 18, 45, and 70.

70 *McCarthy* was litigated in the current Human Rights Tribunal of Ontario (HRTO) process that came into effect on 30 June 2008 with the full implementation of the *Human Rights Code Amendment Act, 2006*, SO 2006, c 30 (see Pinto, *Report*, above note 25 at 1).

71 *McCarthy*, above note 23 at paras 1, 2, 16, 46, & 47.

regular customer at Shoppers Drug Mart stores, as well as the pharmacy, between September 2010 and May 2011.[72] The respondent store's main witness and subject of Ms McCarthy's allegations was night supervisor, Ms Ujjaijini "Jenny" Balachandra, a South-Asian woman employed five years at the respondent store.[73]

On 22 May 2011, between 10:10 p.m. and 10:29 p.m., Ms McCarthy was in the respondent store's oral care aisle closing up her backpack after taking her wallet out to retrieve information about a mouthwash product she wanted to purchase.[74] Ms McCarthy testified that as she was zipping up her backpack she was confronted by Ms Balachandra who did not identify herself as a store employee and, in two separate requests, demanded in an "elevated tone" to search her backpack.[75] Ms McCarthy recalled refusing Ms Balachandra's request and stating that she had "done nothing wrong."[76] She also stated Ms Balachandra informed her that she had the right to look inside the backpack.[77] Ms McCarthy testified that she placed her backpack on the ground in front of Ms Balachandra who proceeded to look inside and then walked away without apologizing.[78] Ms McCarthy recalled "she felt demoralized by being called a common thief" in front of two or three customers who had witnessed the incident in the oral care aisle.[79] As a result of this incident, on 22 May 2012, Ms McCarthy filed an application under section 34 of the *Code* alleging that the respondent store had racially profiled and discriminated against her because of her race and colour and infringed on her rights under section 1 of the *Code* with respect to services and facilities.[80]

The following excerpts from Vice-Chair Bhattecharjee's findings assist in my understanding of his decisions as it related to the respondent. They also help in the development of two observations gleaned from the case. In the first excerpt, the vice-chair found that he did not believe

---

72   According to transactional records submitted by the respondent at the hearing, between 2007 and 2014, Ms McCarthy had spent money at various Shoppers Drug Mart stores over 400 times, "and purchased approximately 2,000 items" (*McCarthy, ibid* at paras 1 and 23).

73   *Ibid* at paras 19, 85, 88, and 90.

74   *Ibid* at paras 5, 9, 12, 24, 72, and 78.

75   *Ibid* at paras 5 and 25.

76   *Ibid* at para 25.

77   *Ibid* at paras 24 & 25.

78   *Ibid* at paras 25 and 31.

79   *Ibid* at para 26.

80   *McCarthy v Kenny Tan Pharmacy Inc*, 2013 HRTO 159 at para 2 (interim decision); *McCarthy*, above note 23 at para 6.

Ms Balachandra's testimony about the incident occurring after midnight when the store had closed.[81] He pointed out that prior to the hearing, neither the respondent nor Ms Balachandra disputed Ms McCarthy's position that the incident occurred between 10:10 p.m. and 10:29 p.m. on 22 May 2011.[82] To resolve this factual dispute, the applicant provided evidence that she received a receipt from the cashier prior to leaving the store at 10:29 p.m.[83]

In the second excerpt, the vice-chair did not accept Ms Balachandra's testimony that she asked the applicant to open her bag and searched it because theft was higher when the store was closing.[84] He stated "in my view, Ms. Balachandra concocted this allegation at the last minute in an attempt to protect herself and bolster the respondent store's case."[85] However, the vice-chair asserted that it was not "unreasonable or discriminatory for a store employee to have her suspicion raised by an individual who is crouched on the ground in an aisle and zipping up her bag."[86]

In the third excerpt, the vice-chair did not accept Ms Balachandra's claim that she did not notice Ms McCarthy was Black; he thought it was "simply an attempt to evade the allegation of racial profiling and discrimination."[87] He also found that in cross-examination Ms Balachandra testified "she was 'confident' and 'pretty sure' that the applicant had stolen something,"[88] although she did not witness Ms McCarthy place store merchandise in her bag.[89] He stated that "the illogical nature of Ms. Balachandra's strong belief, coupled with the fact that the applicant is a Black woman, is indicative that Ms. Balachandra was being influenced, consciously or unconsciously, by the stereotype that Black people are thieves."[90] He also noted that when Ms Balachandra was asked if she had treated White and non-Black customers in a similar manner, she was not able to provide an example despite testifying that for five years she had dealt with shoplifting incidents on most of her shifts.[91]

---

81   *Ibid* at paras 72 & 73.
82   *Ibid.*
83   *Ibid* at paras 28, 37, & 38.
84   *Ibid* at para 73.
85   *Ibid.*
86   *Ibid* at para 81.
87   *Ibid* at para 80.
88   *Ibid* at para 82.
89   *Ibid.*
90   *Ibid.*
91   *Ibid* at para 85.

The last excerpt relates to the respondent store's loss prevention policy detailed in Shoppers Drug Mart's November 2015 Employee Handbook.[92] It stipulated that store employees were not supposed to approach or follow customers they thought were acting suspiciously.[93] In addition, the respondent store owner, Mr Kenny Tan, testified that he instructed his employees not to follow a customer out of the store who they suspect may have shoplifted.[94] The respondent store also had an informal (unwritten) loss prevention policy and procedures created by the retail manager, Mr Ira Abroms, and followed by Ms Balachandra.[95]

In contrast to Mr Tan's instructions, Mr Abroms testified he directed employees, if they were comfortable, to wait until the suspect had left the store and then approach the individual requesting they return to the store.[96] However, he stated if the store was closed then he informed his employees to approach customers they suspected of shoplifting.[97] Moreover, in cross-examination, he admitted he had told employees to approach customers in the store at any time because the store had high merchandise loss, even though these instructions contravened formal Shoppers Drug Mart policies.[98] Similarly, the vice-chair found that Ms Balachandra tried to rationalize her interactions with Ms McCarthy by also claiming the respondent store had higher losses at closing time, which led to her violating the respondent store and Shoppers Drug Mart policy.[99]

On 1 October 2015, Vice-Chair Bhattacharjee found, based on the testimonies and evidence submitted, that Ms McCarthy had been subject to racial profiling and discrimination by the respondent's witness, Ms Balachandra, because she was Black, and he had "no doubt that she w[ould] feel the negative effects of it for the rest of her life."[100] In concluding that Ms McCarthy had proved on a balance of probabilities that her race and colour were factors in the adverse treatment she received from

---

92 Reviewed copy of Shoppers Drug Mart's Employee Handbook (November 2015) as part of LLM thesis research (Tomee Sojourner, *Researcher Notes* at 1 and 2).

93 *McCarthy*, above note 23 at paras 21 and 85; see Shoppers Drug Mart Employee Handbook, above note 92 at 38.

94 *McCarthy*, above note 23 at para 21.

95 *Ibid.*

96 *Ibid.*

97 *Ibid* at para 42.

98 *Ibid.*

99 *Ibid* at paras 73 and 85.

100 *Ibid* at para 97.

the respondent store employee, the vice-chair found the respondent store liable for Ms Balachandra's actions under section 46.3 (1) of the *Code*.[101]

The vice-chair applied the tribunal's remedial powers under section 45.2 of the *Code*, which allowed it to order "the party who infringed the right to pay monetary compensation to the party whose right was infringed . . . for injury to dignity, feelings and self-respect."[102] In considering the quantum of damages for this loss and Ms McCarthy's request for an award of $8,000 for injury to her dignity, feelings, and self-respect, the vice-chair referred to *ADGA Group Consultants Inc v Lane* and *Arunachalam v Best Buy Canada Ltd*.[103] He also took into account that the incident was a serious violation of the *Code*; however, it "only lasted a few minutes" and the applicant did not submit evidence that she sought medical treatment.[104]

McCarthy offers several insights into the practice of consumer racial profiling that takes place between a racialized arbiter and a racialized, specifically Black, customer. For the purpose of this chapter, the following section will focus on two key insights from *McCarthy*.

7) It Is Not Racial Profiling Because Both Parties Are Racialized: Centring Inter-group Racism

The respondent store owner, Mr Tan, argued that it was not possible for Ms McCarthy, a fifty-five-year-old Black woman, to have been racially profiled by Ms Balachandra, a South-Asian woman, because she too was a "visible minority."[105] This form of racism is often referred to as inter-group racism, where an alleged profiler's racial and/or ethnic group mem-

---

101 *Ibid at* para 91.

102 *Ibid at* para 92.

103 *ADGA Group Consultants Inc v Lane*, 2008 CanLII 39605 at para 153 (Ont Div Ct) (referred to in *McCarthy*, above note 23 at para 94); *Arunachalam v Best Buy Canada Ltd*, 2010 HRTO 1880 at paras 52, 53, & 54 (referred to in *McCarthy*, above note 23 at para 96). The vice-chair considered that the following cases contained the relevant quantum of damages for the injury to an applicant's dignity, self-respect, and feelings: *Pieters v Peel Law Association*, 2010 HRTO 2411; *Simpson v Oil City Hospitality Inc*, 2012 AHRC 8; and *Direk v Coffee Time Donuts*, 2009 HRTO 1887 (all referred to in *McCarthy*, above note 23 at para 98).

104 *McCarthy, ibid* at para 97.

105 *Ibid* at paras 36, 80, and 88.

bership appears to be different from the profiled individual.[106] Vice-chair Bhattacharjee addressed this issue directly by stating:

> In my view, it is not in dispute among well-informed, reasonable persons that racial stereotypes about persons of Black African descent exist in South Asian communities in both South Asia and Canada . . . undoubtedly [South Asian individuals in positions of power] have the capacity to discriminate against Black individuals.[107]

However, the vice-chair was clear that he was not suggesting that the existence of anti-Black racism in South-Asian communities made it more likely that Ms Balachandra discriminated against the applicant.[108] The vice-chair also clarified that he did not accept that because she was South Asian it was impossible or less likely she would discriminate against Ms McCarthy.[109] He noted he had addressed similar issues in *Armstrong v Anna's Hair & Spa Inc* and *Bageya v Dyadem International Ltd*.[110]

Drawing on the vice-chair's observations on this issue necessitates that legal practitioners with racialized clients alleging similar facts to *McCarthy* turn their minds to the possibility that inter-group racism may be a factor in the treatment of their client; especially as Ontario's urban, rural, and suburban communities continue to experience demographic changes, including increases in racially and ethnically diverse populations.[111] Similarly, legal practitioners advocating on behalf of respondents need to be mindful that if their client's employee or representative is a racialized or Indigenous person, then their defence against allegations of consumer racial profiling should consider what, if any, role inter-group racism may have played in the interaction.

---

106 Elizabeth Brondolo et al, "The Perceived Ethnic Discrimination Questionnaire: Development and Preliminary Validation of a Community Version" (2005) 35:2 *Journal of Applied Social Psychology* 335 at 346.

107 *McCarthy*, above note 23 at para 88.

108 *Ibid*.

109 *Ibid*.

110 *Ibid*; *Armstrong v Anna's Hair & Spa Inc*, 2010 HRTO 1751 at paras 55, 53, 54, & 55; *Bageya v Dyadem International Ltd*, 2010 HRTO 1589 at para 136.

111 Statistics Canada, *Insights on Canadian Society: Recent Changes in Demographic Trends in Canada*, by Laurent Martel (Ottawa: Statistics Canada, 2015) at 1.

8) Kenny Tan Pharmacy Inc's Formal and Informal Loss Prevention Policies: Arbitrary Treatment and Who Loses

The respondent store's witnesses, Mr Tan, Mr Abroms, and Ms Balachandra, testified that the pharmacy was a high-crime store, due in part to its location in a diverse, urban, densely populated neighbourhood with close proximity to a busy subway station.[112] This point was made as a rationale for the arbitrary application of the respondent store's verbal loss prevention policy and Shoppers Drug Mart's formal loss prevention policy. For example, Mr Tan testified to the use of security measures, including "having employees make contact with customers to create a presence, paging 'security scan all aisles,' tagging high value items with an alarm trigger, and having patrols by plain clothes security officers."[113]

Having worked in retail and as a security guard in the retail sector, I think that a retail business has the right to enforce policies that protect everyone who accesses their premises and to assist in minimizing loss of goods. However, I believe these businesses and their employees have a fundamental obligation to respectfully and transparently — with an openness to the realities of consumer racial profiling in their industry — take seriously allegations made by racialized and Indigenous customers.

I make these observations knowing that retail businesses and their representatives have legal authority under different statutes to control which individuals or groups they allow on their premises and access to their goods and services. For example, under the *Trespass to Property Act*, section 1(1)(b), business owners, employees, and private security guards have "responsibility for and control over . . . the activities . . . carried on, or control over persons allowed to enter the premises."[114] Under subsection 2(1) of this Act, employees also have the legal authority to ask a person to leave the premises.[115] In addition, under section 494(2) of the *Criminal Code* of Canada, employees "may arrest a person without a warrant"[116] if they have reasonable suspicion that the individual has committed a criminal offence, and then deliver the person to a police officer.[117]

As the commission noted in *Under Suspicion*, members of racialized, specifically Black and Indigenous, communities are adversely affected by

---

112   *McCarthy*, above note 23 at paras 17, 18, and 60.
113   *Ibid* at para 61.
114   *Trespass Act*, above note 15.
115   *Ibid*, s 2.
116   *Criminal Code*, above note 15, s 494.
117   *Ibid*, s 494(3).

consumer racial profiling practices.[118] It is for this reason that I suggest legal practitioners and human rights advocates working with clients, both applicants and respondents, on matters related to allegations of consumer racial profiling consider applying a critical race feminist lens to review loss prevention policies and procedures. Applying this lens may assist legal practitioners to develop a deeper understanding about the degradation in services, emotional and physical stresses racialized and Indigenous customers experience, and the consequences they face being labelled a suspected shoplifter (e.g., contact with the criminal justice system after being falsely charged with an offence, arrested by a police officer, and/or issued a trespass notice with no recourse under the *Trespass Act*).[119]

C. RECOMMENDATIONS

It is part of Ontario's public policy to:

> recognize the dignity and worth of every person and to provide for equal rights and opportunities without discrimination . . . so that each person feels a part of the community and able to contribute fully to the development and well-being of the community and the Province.[120]

However, many racialized, in particular Black and Indigenous, consumers are not afforded these rights when they are subjected to consumer racial profiling.[121] Simply put, this matter is an access to justice issue.

Legal practitioners, human rights advocates, consumer advocates, and private arbiters can generate new opportunities for those seeking access to justice who have been harmed by consumer racial profiling. They can achieve this by using legal instruments, public policies, and tools. I offer the following recommendations to assist in the creation of these new opportunities. These recommendations draw on the lessons I gleaned from analyzing *Nassiah* and *McCarthy*, as well as reflections on insights relayed by consumers who have contacted Prevent CRP (Consumer Racial Profiling), and lastly, the stories shared by participants in the commission's racial profiling survey reported in *Under Suspicion*.

---

118   OHRC, *Under Suspicion*, above note 2 at 70.

119   *Ibid* at 28, 29, 30, 68, and 70.

120   *Code*, above note 15, preamble.

121   OHRC, *Under Suspicion*, above note 2 at 30.

1) Recommendations to Assist Private Security Guards: Learning and Development

Subsection 10(1)(b)(iii) of the *Private Security and Investigative Services Act* (*PSIS Act*) stipulates that a person applying to be a security guard has to successfully complete "all prescribed training and testing."[122] The Ministry of Community Safety and Correctional Services regulates Ontario's private security sector, and it has developed a syllabus that requires security guards to complete a minimum of forty training hours, including first aid and CPR certification, and to pass a written test in order to obtain a licence, which is renewable every two years.[123] I encourage the ministry to review the syllabus and consider amending the following sections. In section two, security guards are taught the *PSIS Act* and the *Code of Conduct*.[124] They are required to understand the consequences for not complying with the statute and regulations, including the public complaints provision.[125] I suggest adding a requirement that each security guard participate in an annual mandatory retraining on the *Code of Conduct*. The session should be facilitated by a subject matter expert on consumer racial profiling in Ontario's retail environments.

In section three of the syllabus, security guards are taught basic security procedures: how to respond to changes in their environments, including decision making, and situational awareness.[126] Given the rapidly changing demographics in Ontario, I suggest the ministry work with a subject matter expert to develop a module on practical ways to apply a critical race feminist and intersectional analysis to security procedures.[127]

The second recommendation relates to the *PSIS Act*, and section 2 (d) of the *Code of Conduct*, which states that each licensee must "treat all persons equally, without discrimination based on a person's race, ancestry, place of origin, colour, ethnic origin, citizenship, creed, sex, sexual orientation, age, marital status, family status or disability."[128] If they contravene this regulation, then as per section 1, they are in breach of

---

122 *Private Security and Investigative Services Act*, SO 2005, c 34, s 10 (1) [*PSIS Act*].

123 *Training and Testing*, O Reg 26/10, s 10(1)(b)(iii); see Ministry of Community Safety and Correctional Services, *Training Syllabus for Security Guards* (Toronto: Queen's Printer for Ontario, 2015), online: www.mcscs.jus.gov.on.ca/sites/default/files/content/mcscs/docs/ec168325.pdf [*Training Syllabus*].

124 *Ibid*; *Code of Conduct*, O Reg 363/07.

125 *Code of Conduct*, *ibid*, s 19.

126 *Training Syllabus*, above note 123 at 7–10.

127 *Ibid* at 8–9.

128 *Code of Conduct*, above note 124, ss 1 and 2(1)(d).

the *Code of Conduct*.[129] I suggest a review of this *Code* using a critical race feminist lens to identify areas to improve its effectiveness in addressing allegations of consumer racial profiling. In addition to these suggested amendments, the ministry through its policy-making function could create a provision mandating all security guards to file a daily contact report in the course of their loss prevention duties. This report would be completed when a security guard interacts with a person they perceive to be racialized and/or Indigenous. This report would document the reasons for the stop in accordance with privacy provisions of *PIPEDA*,[130] and a copy of the report would be given to the individual customer and/or their representative.

2)   Recommendations to Assist Businesses and Employees in Retail Environments: Learning and Development

As previously mentioned in the introduction section, retail is the second largest industry in Ontario, and retail businesses with storefronts make up "97% of employment in the sector."[131] Some large retail businesses (e.g., Shoppers Drug Mart and Sobeys) have publicly declared corporate commitments to diversity and inclusion as part of their corporate social responsibility.[132]

For example, Shoppers Drug Mart franchisee Kenny Tan Pharmacy Inc, the respondent in *McCarthy*, had organizational policies instructing employees to treat customers with respect and abide by anti-discrimination values.[133] From corporate Shoppers Drug Mart, their store standard for diversity was, and is, to "[provide] excellent customer service to all segments of the public, without discrimination."[134] There are disciplinary steps for "anyone found engaging in discriminatory or harassing behaviours against co-workers, customers or members of the public."[135] They also expect their employees to "[a]bide by the values of equal opportunity and non-discrimination and with Human Rights Codes and legislation

---

129   *Ibid*, s 1.

130   *Personal Information Protection and Electronic Documents Act*, SC 2000, c 5 [*PIPEDA*].

131   Government of Canada, Labour Market and Socio-economic Information Directorate, "Sectoral Profile Retail Trade Ontario 2015–2017" at 1, online: www.jobbank.gc.ca/content_pieces-eng.do?cid=9983&lang=eng.

132   *David*, above note 11 at paras 23 and 25; SDM, "Our Culture," above note 11.

133   *McCarthy*, above note 23 at para 22.

134   SDM, "Our Culture," above note 11.

135   *Ibid*.

. . . [and employees are encouraged to] promptly report any instance of discrimination or harassment that is inconsistent with the law or store policies outlined in *Equitable* the employee handbook."[136]

Shoppers Drug Mart is used as an example for one reason. In *McCarthy*, the vice-chair found under section 46.3(1) of the *Code* that Kenny Tan Pharmacy Inc was vicariously liable for the conduct of its employee, Ms Balachandra.[137] It is because of the risk of vicarious liability, I suggest that Ontario's retail businesses use a critical race feminist approach to conduct thorough reviews of their loss prevention policies and procedures to address allegations of consumer racial profiling.[138] I also recommend that these measures move beyond the corporate framing of diversity, inclusion, and equality, and move towards an integrated framework that directly addresses anti-Black racism and other discriminatory practices.[139]

3) A Recommendation for the Ontario Human Rights Commission

Lastly, in addition to the above recommendations, I call on the Commission, as part of its upcoming public policy on racial profiling, and as part of its statutory commitment under section 29(f) of the *Code*, to develop a mandatory and comprehensive consumer racial profiling awareness training program for all retail businesses and their representatives operating in Ontario.[140] This program should be developed with legal scholars, human rights practitioners, retail businesses, and members of racialized and Indigenous communities.

D. CONCLUSION

In closing, this chapter has focused on increasing the visibility of consumer racial profiling. First, by defining consumer racial profiling and showing how its meaning has changed within the context of different academic disciplines (e.g., marketplace discrimination) and over time. Second, by placing the HRTO cases of *Nassiah* and *McCarthy* at the centre, this chapter has provided critical observations about two forms of consumer racial profiling that exist within retail environments. It also situated Ms Nassiah

---

136 *Ibid.*
137 *McCarthy*, above note 23 at paras 90 & 91.
138 *Ibid* at para 91.
139 Sojourner, "Can I Help You?," above note 4 at 30.
140 *Code*, above note 15, s 29(f).

and Ms McCarthy's respective stories as examples of the types of harms and traumas (e.g., racialized gender-based violence) some Black women face in their everyday lives as consumers. In addition, the role of arbiters and some of their consumer racial practices were raised. Third, the recommendations were offered as a starting point for future research, policy, and learning development.

The marginalizing effects of consumer racial profiling go against the promises made in section 1 the *Code*. It is clear from the observations made in this chapter that the mere existence of this provision does not prevent racialized and Indigenous consumers from being adversely impacted by the discretionary practices of arbiters in policing, security, and retail businesses. It is therefore essential for legal practitioners and human rights advocates to develop a critical race feminist and intersectional lens through which they can gain a deeper understanding about the complexities and multi-faceted ways members of racialized and Indigenous communities have been, and continue to be, disproportionately impacted by different forms of consumer racial profiling.

CHAPTER 9

Racial Profiling of Women in Canada

Beyond a "Gender-Free" Lens

TAMMY LANDAU[*]

A. INTRODUCTION

It might well be argued that narratives with respect to racial profiling in Canada have had, to date, two overlapping histories. The first, which generally emerged after the shooting by the Toronto Police of a number of unarmed Black men, can be dated from the 1970s until the early 1990s. The term "racial profiling" was typically not in use; however, the discourses linking race and crime clearly reflect that as an underlying narrative. While there was clear evidence to support the allegations of racialized policing, there was little official response to the incidents beyond the commissioning of reports on "police-minority relations."[1] This period was followed by two decades of extensive community and scholarly work that documented the nature, extent, and, to a lesser degree, community experiences of racial profiling.[2] While the issue still met

---

[*] Tammy Landau is chair and associate professor in the Department of Criminology, Ryerson University. I would like to extend a special thanks to Sumaio Ugas, the African-Canadian Legal Clinic, the Department of Criminology, Ryerson University, Susan Gomez Baez, and Rolando Gomez Baez. I would especially like to acknowledge and express my gratitude to the women who shared their stories with me, often with great emotion, always with complete dignity.

1   Ontario Ministry of the Solicitor General, *Policing in Ontario for the Eighties: Perceptions and Reflections: Report of the Task Force on the Racial and Ethnic Implications of Police Hiring, Training, Promotion and Career Development*, by Reva Gerstein (Toronto: Ministry of Government Services, 1980). Ontario, *The Report of the Race Relations and Policing Task Force*, by Clare Lewis (Toronto: Task Force, 1989).

2   Maureen Brown, "In Their Own Voices: African Canadians in Toronto Share Experiences of Racial Profiling" in Carol Tator & Frances Henry, eds, *Racial Profiling in Canada:*

with considerable resistance from the police and political ranks, there was nevertheless important work that focused on the institutional, legal, and political contexts, which enable and sustain such practices.[3] Since the events of 9/11, the "browning" of racial profiling has become a part of that narrative, and with it a broader consideration of geographic and social spaces in which these practices occur.[4]

While these histories have provided important frameworks for analysis, they have, at the same time, limited our full consideration of the nature and impact of the profiling practices. In particular, embedded in these histories is the assumption that the targets of racial profiling are exclusively men, and the agents of racial profiling are primarily state security workers. In this paper I will present data on women's experiences of racial profiling in a variety of arenas that clearly challenge both of those assumptions. I argue that discourses on racial profiling are typically "gender-free," as distinct from gender neutral. That is, they rarely address gender at all, implying that gender does not matter when, in fact, it profoundly affects where and how the practices occur. Through an analysis of women's experiences, we will see that the contexts in which women are racially profiled are not largely limited to state security apparatus. Indeed, they spill over into the everyday activities of women's lives and can be characterized as yet additional mechanisms of regulating women, specifically racialized women, who are, at times, distinct from the social, political, and geographic regulation of racialized men.

Challenging the Myth of "A Few Bad Apples" (Toronto: University of Toronto Press, 2006) 151 [Tator & Henry, eds, *"A Few Bad Apples"*]; Gabe Mythen, Sandra Walklate, & Fatima Khan, "I'm a Muslim, but I'm Not a Terrorist: Victimization, Risky Identities and the Performance of Safety" (2009) 49 *British Journal of Criminology* 736 [Mythen et al]; Jim Rankin et al, "Singled Out" *Toronto Star* (19 October, 2002), online: www.thestar.com/news/gta/known-topolice/2002/10/19/singled-out.html; Charles Smith, *The Dirty War: The Making of the Myth of Black Dangerousness* (Ottawa: Canadian Centre for Policy Alternatives, 2014).

3   Commission on Systemic Racism in the Ontario Criminal Justice System, *Report of the Commission on Systemic Racism in the Ontario Criminal Justice System*, by David Cole & Margaret Gittens (Toronto: Government of Ontario, 1994); Frances Henry & Carol Tator, *Racial Profiling in Toronto: Discourses of Domination, Mediation, and Opposition* (Toronto: Canadian Race Relations Foundation, 2005); David M Tanovich, *The Colour of Justice: Policing Race in Canada* (Toronto: Irwin Law, 2006).

4   Charu A Chandrasekhart, "Flying While Brown: Federal Civil Rights Remedies to Post-9/11 Airline Racial Profiling of South Asians" (2003) 10:2 *Asian Law Journal* 215; Karim Ismaili, "Surveying the Many Fronts of the War on Immigrants in Post-9/11 U.S. Society" (2010) 13:1 *Contemporary Justice Review* 71; Sherri Sharma, "Beyond 'Driving While Black' and 'Flying While Brown': Using Intersectionality to Uncover the Gendered Aspects of Racial Profiling" (2003) 12 *Columbia Journal of Gender & Law* 275.

B. HISTORY 1: SEE NO EVIL

The social and political context for examining problematic police practices in Ontario was set almost half a century ago by allegations of police misconduct within the Metropolitan Toronto Police Force. While concerns were raised in the 1970s in the context of allegations of extreme police brutality,[5] they were followed by the separate police shootings of a number of unarmed Black men in the 1980s and a complete lack of political or police action.[6] The crisis of legitimacy[7] that arose was met with largely lackluster reports on "police-minority relations" and an unwillingness to admit that policing in Toronto was increasingly contentious for policed communities.[8]

The primary response of the Government of Ontario was to implement a largely ineffective mechanism for handling public complaints against the police in which the police continued to investigate themselves and "no further action" was taken in the vast majority of cases. This left both complainants and the community at large with very little confidence in the system.[9] Broadly based as it was (it handled complaints dealing with everything from "incivility" to police violence) and focusing more on retaining power and control of police oversight within police management, this process could not directly address the extent to which policing in Toronto had become racialized.

The narrative was dramatically changed in 1992 when the sleepy streets of Toronto erupted, as they did in many communities across

---

5   Municipality of Metropolitan Toronto, *Report to the Civic Authorities of Metropolitan Toronto and Its Citizens*, by Cardinal Gerald E Carter (Toronto: Archdiocese of Toronto, 1979); Ontario, *The Royal Commission into Metropolitan Toronto Police Practices*, by Donald Morand (Toronto: The Royal Commission, 1976).

6   David Cole, "Let's Face It: Toronto Police Have a Racism Problem" *Toronto Star* (15 July 2015), online: www.thestar.com/opinion/commentary/2015/07/15/lets face it toronto police has a racism problem.html; Tammy Landau, *Public Complaints against the Police: A View from Complainants* (Toronto: Centre of Criminology, University of Toronto, 1994); Maeve McMahon & Richard V Ericson, *Policing Reform: A Study of the Reform Process and Police Institution in Toronto* (Toronto: Centre of Criminology, University of Toronto, 1984).

7   McMahon & Ericson, *ibid.*

8   Metropolitan Toronto Police Force, *Review of Race Relations Practices of the Metropolitan Toronto Police Force*, by Allan Andrews (Toronto: Metropolitan Toronto Police Force, 1992); *The Report of the Race Relations and Policing Task Force*, above note 1; Ontario, Metropolitan Board of Commissioners of Police, *Report to the Metropolitan Board of Commissioners of Police*, by Arthur Maloney (Toronto: publisher unknown, 1975).

9   Landau, above note 6.

North America, upon the acquittal of the Los Angeles police officers who were caught on videotape brutally assaulting Rodney King. Mobilized more out of fear of a repeat of such incidents than acknowledgment that the police across North America, including Toronto, were racist, the premier of Ontario asked for yet another report. This time, however, both the focus and the urgency of the report were clear: it was to have racism in Ontario as its primary focus and it was to report back in thirty days. *The Report of the Advisor on Race Relations to the Premier on Racism in Ontario,*[10] written in the form of a letter to Premier Bob Rae, could not have been clearer or more dramatic. "[W]hat we are dealing with, at root, and fundamentally, is anti-Black racism."[11]

The most significant outcome from the Lewis Report was the creation of the *Commission on Systemic Racism in the Ontario Criminal Justice System,*[12] which, as its title suggests, had systemic racism as its guiding framework. While the commission's terms of reference spanned the entire criminal justice system, including pretrial detention, the experiences of racialized communities with policing could not help but set the tone. Indeed, racial profiling is singled out as "a police practice that has probably done more than any other to exacerbate tensions and fuel mistrust" between the public police and racialized communities.[13]

The commission's analysis and recommendations were extensive, aimed at rooting out systemic forms of racism, particularly as it related to the Black community in Ontario. Unfortunately, the commission's report was released after the fall of the Bob Rae government that struck it, leaving many of its valuable recommendations unanswered.

Allegations and concerns about racial profiling continued to dog public policing organizations and finally came to a head with a series of articles by the *Toronto Star* that looked at discretionary police actions in two contexts: processing for minor drug offences and traffic stops.[14] Not surprisingly, and perhaps predictably, they found dramatic differences in the processing of Black citizens when compared to White citizens. For example, Blacks charged with simple possession of drugs were more than twice as likely to be taken to the police station as were White suspects, and were held in detention overnight to await a bail hearing at twice the

---

10   Ontario, *The Report of the Advisor on Race Relations to the Premier of Ontario, Bob Rae*, by Stephen Lewis (Toronto: Ontario Advisor on Race Relations, 1992).

11   *Ibid* at 2.

12   Commission on Systemic Racism in the Ontario Criminal Justice System, above note 3.

13   *Ibid* at 337.

14   Rankin et al, above note 2.

rate as Whites. They also demonstrated empirically, perhaps for the first time in Canada, that "driving while Black" attracted a disproportionate amount of police attention, resulting in higher rates for ticketing of Black drivers for moving violations, generally used as a pretext for other charges, than Whites.

The findings, despite being based on data from the Toronto police, were met with more than simple denial, although that was the routine response. Then Metropolitan Toronto Police Chief Julian Fantino, who opposed the release of the data and that took seven years to access, told the *Toronto Star*: "We're not perfect people but you're barking up the wrong tree. There's no racism . . . we don't do profiling."[15] More dramatic was the response of the police union, which attempted, unsuccessfully, to launch a lawsuit against the paper.[16] Some academics, too, gave voice to the resistance; they either qualified the significance of the findings in some way[17] or dismissed the findings altogether as "junk science."[18]

C. HISTORY 2: NO LONGER A BLACK AND WHITE ISSUE

By the mid-2000s, most of the literature and community work had abandoned trying to "prove" what African Canadians and other racialized communities already knew — that racial profiling was a routine practice of police forces across Canada. Instead, the focus shifted to documenting the nature and extent of the practices and, to a more limited extent, how they were experienced by many in the community. At this point, there was considerable acknowledgment that Black males were generally over-scrutinized and routinely stopped by the police.[19]

---

15 *Ibid.*

16 Peter Small, "Police Union Sues Star over Race Crime Series" *Toronto Star* (18 January 2003) A6.

17 Ron Melchers, "Do Toronto Police Engage in Racial Profiling?" (2003) 45:3 *Canadian Journal of Criminology and Criminal Justice* 347.

18 Toronto Police Service, *An Independent Review of the Toronto Star Analysis of Criminal Information Processing System (CIPS) Data Provided by the Toronto Police Services*, by Edward B Harvey with the assistance of Richard Liu (Toronto: Toronto Police Service, March 2003).

19 Brown, above note 2; Henry & Tator, above note 3. Charles C Smith, "Racial Profiling in Canada, the United States, and the United Kingdom" in Tator & Henry, eds, *"A Few Bad Apples,"* above note 2 at 55.

To assert that the impact of the events of 9/11 on racialized communities has been profound would be a gross understatement.[20] During the last fifteen years, we have seen an expansion of both the subjects and the contexts of racial profiling to include "brown bodies,"[21] i.e., individuals who are, or appear to be, Muslim or Middle Eastern. Patel notes that "what is actually occurring in a post-9/11 environment, is that a growing allocation of 'brown' labels has created fear and insecurity — what they call the 'browning of terror'."[22] In addition, however, we can see the expansion of the boundaries and contexts in which these practices occur. Initially understood or concretized as traffic stops (driving while Black), the multiplicity of national borders and points of entry between Canada and the United States has evolved the practices into "flying while Brown."[23] In most cases, the framework for analysis has stopped there.

D. HISTORY 3: FROM "GENDER-FREE" TO GENDER-SPECIFIC NARRATIVES ON RACIAL PROFILING

Sharma[24] has noted the "under-inclusivity" of most narratives of racial profiling.

> Because "Driving While Black" has come to symbolize the problem of racial profiling, it not only reflects the way racial profiling has been constructed as a *state* act that primarily affects *men*, it furthers this construction. The focus on racial profiling as a male-state relationship is problematic because it simplifies the practice of profiling, the individuals whom it affects, and the ways in which it occurs.

---

20   Susan M Akram & Maritza Karmely, "Immigration and Constitutional Consequences of Post 9/11 Policies Involving Arabs and Muslims in the United States: Is Alienage a Distinction without a Difference?" (2004) 38 *UC Davis Law Review* 609; Louise Caincar, "Post 9/11 Domestic Policies Affecting U.S. Arabs and Muslims: A Brief Overview" (2004) 24:1 *Comparative Studies of South Asia Africa and the Middle East* 245; Ismaili, above note 4; Deborah Ramirez, Jennifer Hoopes, & Tara Lai Quinlan, "Defining Racial Profiling in a Post-September 11 World" (2003) 40 *American Criminal Law Review* 1195.

21   Tina G Patel, "Surveillance, Suspicion and Stigma: Brown Bodies in a Terror-Panic Climate" (2012) 10:3/4 *Surveillance and Society* 215 at 218.

22   *Ibid.*

23   Chandrasekhart, above note 4; Anna Pratt & Sara K Thompson, "Chivalry, Race and Discretion" (2008) 48 *British Journal of Criminology* 620; Sharma, above note 4; Deborah Wilkins Newman & Nikki-Qui D Brown, "Historical Overview and Perceptions of Racial and Terrorist Profiling in an Era of Homeland Security: A Research Note" (2009) 20:3 *Criminal Justice Policy Review* 359.

24   Sharma, above note 4 at 299.

She argues that racial profiling also occurs where race and gender identities intersect and, as a result, has an adverse impact on women of colour. Indeed, she notes the higher incidence of both stops and strips searches of Black women at border crossings, compared to both White women and Black men. "[T]he female victims of profiling are rendered invisible, and their experiences remain unaccounted for, unexplained, and unchallenged."[25]

There has, indeed, been minimal recognition that women experience high degrees of racial profiling, which spans geographic and social spaces.[26]

> Black women who are profiled, beaten, sexually assaulted, and killed by law enforcement officials are conspicuously absent from this frame even when their experiences are identical. When their experiences with police violence are distinct — uniquely informed by race, gender, gender identity, and sexual orientation — Black women remain invisible.

For example, in 2003, the Ontario Human Rights Commission conducted a study on the social impact of racial profiling on individuals and communities. The OHRC noted that, while its own definition of racial profiling referred (at that time, at least) only to prejudicial behaviour based on "race, colour, ethnicity, ancestry, religion, or place of origin," both age and/or gender could also be factors in profiling.[27] However, it did not include any gender-specific analyses in its report. Tanovich[28] notes that African-Canadian women are often profiled as drug mules but provides little engagement with the issue. Mythen et al conducted focus groups with Pakistani Muslim men and women in the UK with respect to images of Islam and participants' experiences with UK security measures.[29] While women constituted half of the sample, their responses were integrated and no gender-specific issues were included. Even the reports of the *Toronto Star*, which documented quite powerfully the nature and extent of police profiling practices, first in 2002 and then again in 2010, failed to give any space to the practices as they apply to women.

---

25 *Ibid.*

26 Kimberlé W Crenshaw & Andrea Ritchie, *Say Her Name: Resisting Police Brutality against Black Women* (New York: Centre for Intersectionality and Social Policy Studies, African American Policy Forum, 2015) at 3; Andrea J Ritchie & Joey L Mogul, "In the Shadows of the War on Terror: Persistent Police Brutality and Abuse of People of Color in the United States" (2008) 1 *DePaul Journal for Social Justice* 175.

27 Ontario, *Paying the Price: The Human Cost of Racial Profiling* (Toronto: Ontario Human Rights Commission, 2003).

28 Tanovich, above note 3.

29 Mythen et al, above note 2.

We know little of this empirically, not because the experiences are rare, but because the analysis has typically been "gender free," presumed to be either only relevant to men (regardless of whether they are Black, Brown, Muslim, or Asian), or the same for women, or simply not significant. "In the course of the debates on racial profiling, which contains concerns about race, gender has become invisible."[30] Indeed, Anderson[31] has noted that "the discrimination racialized communities face has been grouped into one category. The narratives of the usual offenders in racial profiling are racialized men." She goes on to provide an incisive analysis of the racial profiling of African-Canadian women by the public police.

Equally problematic, however, is the narrow focus on state security apparatus such as the public police and border controls. We must acknowledge in this context, as in others, that the regulation and surveillance of women occurs in a range of public and private spheres and cannot be adequately captured through such a narrow lens. In the context of racially marginalized women, mass incarceration, and punishment, Crenshaw states: "social control is not only a function of the criminal justice system but a function of the welfare state and of private social ordering as well. That is to say, women of color experience punishment across a range of state apparati and formally private systems."[32]

Indeed, in a small study of women in Toronto, all of whom wore clothing that identified them as practicing Muslims, Ugas and Landau found that half experienced racial profiling at the airport.[33] Other contexts in which women reported being racially profiled included educational settings, banks, the workplace, on public transit, and at the grocery store.

Breaking out of the traditional, restrictive narratives that have been particularly prejudicial to women and have erased their experiences in both the literatures and public narratives on the practices is critical. This project attempts to do this by presenting qualitative data on women's

---

30   Andrea Anderson, *Voices Unheard: The Invisibility of Women in Policing Race in Canada* (Paper presented to Accessing Justice & Accountability in Policing, Faculty of Law, University of Windsor, 2011) [unpublished] at 27. Also see: Kimberlé W Crenshaw, "From Private Violence to Mass Incarceration: Thinking Intersectionally about Women, Race and Social Control" (2012) 59 *UCLA Law Review* 1418; Crenshaw & Ritchie, above note 26.

31   Anderson, above note 30 at 18.

32   Crenshaw, above note 30 at 1428.

33   Sumaio Ugas & Tammy Landau, "Racial Profiling of Muslim Women in the Community: A Pilot Project" (Poster presented at the American Society of Criminology, Washington, DC, 14–17 November 2012).

experiences with racial profiling across a variety of contexts, engagement of which is not constrained in the ways described above.

E. THE CURRENT STUDY

This research was conducted in collaboration with the African Canadian Legal Clinic (ACLC), a provincially funded legal clinic with the mandate to address anti-Black racism in Canada.[34] The content of the interview schedule was devised in conjunction with the ACLC, and the poster to recruit potential participants was widely distributed to their community network. Women who self-identified as racialized and who had experienced racial profiling were asked to contact the principal investigator in order to participate in a confidential, private, face-to-face interview. The recruitment flyer indicated that women would receive $20 and two transit tokens for participating in the study. For the purposes of this study, racial profiling was defined as "being subject to additional scrutiny or surveillance or closer examination *because* you are a racialized woman."

This is a qualitative study in which women's own words, based on their experiences, form the basis of the data and thematic analyses. Women were asked about their experiences with racial profiling across a variety of contexts — by public police; at border crossings; by private security; by social, income support, and child welfare workers; in the education system; and any other context in which it may have occurred in their lives. Women were also asked about how they responded in each specific situation and the impact of racial profiling on them individually as well as on their community more broadly. Finally, women were asked about strategies for moving forward and dealing with the realities of racial profiling.

1) The Sample

Twenty-three self-identified racialized women were interviewed for this study. They ranged in age from sixteen to sixty-two years old, with an average age of thirty-three. All were residents of Toronto or a community nearby. Seventy percent of the women had children and a third of the women had a spouse. Seventy-four percent had some college or university, and 9 percent went to graduate school. Seventy percent of the women were working either full-time or part-time at the time the

---

34   African Canadian Legal Clinic, online: www.aclc.net.

interview took place. Three were receiving disability benefits and two were receiving general social benefits. All of the women were Canadian citizens or permanent residents; indeed, two-thirds were Canadian born. Fifteen women self-identified as African Canadian, Afro-Canadian, Black, Afro-Caribbean, or of Caribbean descent. One women self-identified as Japanese Canadian, one woman self-identified as South Asian, one woman as "mixed Arab and White," one as Chinese, and one as "mixed." The other three identified as East-Asian, Armenian and Iraqi, and Black queer.

F.   EXPERIENCES WITH RACIAL PROFILING

One challenge in carrying out this research was conveying the distinction, often arbitrary and certainly, in other contexts, irrelevant, between outright racism and racial profiling practices specifically. Clearly women had no shortage of racist experiences in all of the contexts raised. They were the targets of racist comments and actions by shopkeepers, police officers ("Shut up, you Black bitch"), border security officers, and teachers. To maintain the research focus on racial profiling specifically, participants were regularly reminded of the definition presented above. It is those experiences that are discussed below.

Looking at the data thematically, we can see that the "security umbrella," which often provides the pretext for hyper-scrutiny of racialized men, is inadequate for capturing the range of women's experiences. To be sure, such experiences were not uncommon among the women interviewed, and the presence of men may have triggered the incident. However, many women experienced racial profiling in contexts that underline how the social ordering and policing of women's lives extend to the private sector and to the social, economic, and educational arenas.

1)   Policing Mobility — Racial Profiling on Streets, Cars, and at International Borders

Four women recounted experiences of being racially profiled by the public police while driving.

> Yeah, with police. Absolutely, absolutely. There are certain cases where I was driving and they kind of stopped me. I was going at the speed limit, my license was good, my insurance was on point and they just stopped me for a basic, routine check. And I would just ask, "Is there anything I did?" And they kind of not really answered me, and I know that it is a right for them to answer me. And I'm like "Well, I can't give you anything until you tell me

what I did." They're like "if you don't give it to us, that's also a violation." So I have no choice but to do it. And then they just say "OK, well, you're free to go."

When I was driving I would call it — it was a nice vehicle but it wasn't expensive — I wasn't getting pulled over at all, wasn't even looked at. When I purchased a new truck after working so hard for it I was pulled over every time I came into the city.

In one instance, a woman and her young male cousin were leaving a fast-food restaurant and on their way home when they were pulled over by six police cars.

And they pulled us over and told us to get out of the car. We kept asking "What did we do? What did we do?" They surrounded us, they dragged my cousin out of the car, threw him down on the ground. He was crying, I was like "What's going on?" I put my hands up in the air. I had my key chain in my hand so they thought it was a weapon, threw me to the ground, and said that we fit the profile of somebody who just robbed somewhere. I'm like "Who? What profile is that?" Whatever, they got a profile on their car and they said it was a White male who had robbed the store. So I heard that and I'm thinking how did we fit the profile? My cousin is face down on the asphalt. I'm over the hood of the car. And we're just both traumatized. They didn't say sorry. They just left us.

In addition, six women spoke of being racially profiled, which they attributed to the neighbourhood they were either walking in or living in at the time.

They kind of stopped us, they stopped me, asked if I knew so-and-so when I'm totally not a part of that, you know. So for me, I was totally racially profiled for the mere fact that I'm a Black woman living in a particularly geographical location and so forth. And because of that, they also additionally illegally searched our home as well, too.

[The police said to us] . . . "Why are you here in this area, do you know which area you are in?"

One woman encountered racial profiling by the Toronto Transit Commission, when the bus driver accused her of not paying her fare when she clearly had. The bus was taken out of service while the public police were called in. The incident did not escalate further than that, although it consumed most of her afternoon. Another woman reported that she experiences racial profiling approximately three times each month, most recently on the day of the interview when she was stopped by police while riding her bike. They asked her for identification and demanded to look inside her bag.

Ten women recounted experiences of being racially profiled while trying to cross the border, either at the airport or at a land crossing.

> Recently, I was travelling to New York on the bus and everybody, of course, has to get off, and go through customs just like everyone else, and it's hard at the border because they are so . . . it's so discretionary, there's really no rules, you really have no idea what they can or can't do. You don't know what they're gonna do.
>
> I mean I was alone, and I'm a young Black female travelling from Toronto. And so there were just a lot, a lot, a lot of questions about where am I going, who am I staying with, how long will I be there, do I work, where do I live, what do I do, can I see your, your itinerary . . . "I wanna see your return flight."

Women recounted having their children's diaper checked when trying to enter Jamaica, being pulled aside at the border because the family has a very traditional Middle Eastern name, and being pulled over at the border because she and her boyfriend both had dreadlocks.

> Driving at Buffalo by Niagara Falls. They just pulled us over, they checked to see if we have weed. One of the border patrol told us, it's because you have locks, it's because you have dread locks. You guys look like Bob Marley, we know Bob Marley smokes a lot of weed.

Three women were not allowed into the United States because they were deemed to not have sufficient cash with them.

G.   RACIAL PROFILING AND PRIVATE SECURITY

Women's experiences, as recounted here, highlight the case for why we need to reach beyond narrow conceptions of state "security" (i.e., national security or violent crime) and public or state-security organizations. Indeed, women reported the most pervasive and most frequent forms of surveillance by private security workers. These experiences are rarely about violence, disorder, or threats to public safety and more about a general suspicion toward racialized bodies, in particular, racialized women's bodies.[35]

---

35   William Rose, "Crimes of Color" (2002) 16:2 *International Journal of Politics, Culture, and Society* 179.

Over half of the women interviewed are regularly racially profiled in retail stores. Indeed, for racialized women, these experiences are routine, even routinized.

> It's just a part of life, I guess. It's like . . . not disappointed, not surprised, not really upset.
>
> And that's kind of just been part of my life, ever since I was a kid, with my mother, I remember people following us.
>
> I expect it. I'm surprised when I don't get it.

Whether women are directly approached under the guise of "helping" them or closely monitored from the minute they enter an establishment, they know that their racialized status means they are inherently suspect.

> I've gone into stores in (a certain neighbourhood) and I will be dogged the entire time. There will be at least one or two people following me the whole time. So what I end up doing is saying, "If you're going to follow me, could you hold on to these things for me? I'll be over here now."
>
> But I always experience it when I walk into a store, and, especially if I'm one of the only Black people in the store, they'll always try to follow me and see if I'm stealing something. It actually just happened to me the other day.

Some women who participated in the study were themselves trained security workers and verified that racialized women, particularly African Canadian women, are flagged to receive heightened surveillance.

> They say this to me as an employee. And they'll be like "look after her." There's a certain — it's not just like all Black — there's a certain look that they're also looking for . . . . So in those situations, I have to additionally prove to myself that it's not just Black women . . . . so what I have to do is search, like really look at everybody else. And the result was I have found other colours, [and] not just women, too. Men steal as well, children steal for their parents as well, too. So I had to really prove to them that it's not just a particular group and I felt like I don't have to do that. It is a part of my job to prevent . . . loss prevention . . . but I don't have to prove that a group does it. It's just, anybody can do it.
>
> [During training] I had one of the guys say "look out for the coloured people." Well, he didn't use the word coloured, but I'm going to use the word coloured. I guess he said Black people. Yeah. Black people would steal. Because the community was Black, Spanish and Portuguese. But I mean, surprisingly, the people he was telling me to look out for, that was not the people we caught stealing.

H. POLICING THE PERSONAL — RACIAL PROFILING IN INCOME SUPPORT, CHILD WELFARE, AND EDUCATION

By expanding the definition of racial profiling and the contexts in which it occurs, we can more adequately capture women's daily experiences. Many, if not most, incidents of racial profiling don't involve men and occur in the publicly regulated private spheres of child welfare and income support. In these contexts, too, racialized women are generally suspect, over-surveilled, and generally disbelieved.

Three women reported being racially profiled by income support workers. That is, when making an application to receive social benefits or when checking in with their benefits worker, they were not seen as being truthful about their financial need or their educational achievements.

> I feel like when you talk to a White person, they assume that you're coming from a position of dishonesty. You're trying to cheat them, especially if you're a degreed person.
>
> I think my mom has more of a difficulty dealing with income and welfare programs because she's a single parent with so many kids and my dad's out of the picture so they may just see her situation as something that they can't really help, comes with some preconceived notions because of how many kids she has, and how she doesn't have a man to support her so some of those assumptions come into play when my mom tries to seek assistance.
>
> I feel like being a Black woman, and being a woman (especially for my mom) that's on social assistance, because it's so common for them, I feel like it's a war against us. It's like "well, we already gave it to you, now you can't meet up to the expectations, like c'mon, now."
>
> A number of years ago when I had finished university and I was in (another town) and I had fallen between two jobs. So I had a period before my next job started and I had no savings, so I had to apply for what was called welfare at that time. And I got a worker who took a look at — did this head-to-toe thing — and said, "You couldn't possibly have a university degree."

One of the women was racially profiled by child welfare authorities, whom she believed acted hastily and without proper grounds when they permanently removed her son from her home. In her experience, this is a frequent occurrence. She believes there is a general bias on the part of the workers who have extraordinary power over women's custody of their children.

> They have lots of young, Black women [on their caseloads]. They had their kids taken away and they had not done anything wrong. And I think that's a racial profiling. It's the workers.

Women had experiences with racist practices and racial profiling in the education system, both when they were children and adult learners, as well as with respect to their own children. In some cases, the profiling was linked to presumed limited abilities of racialized children.

Often, when incidents happen, it's similar to my experience when I was growing up. You know, people will tell them that their child is not smart. They need to be in ESL or some sort of — I shouldn't say ESL — like a specialized class. When as a parent you're trying to say, "Well, you know, my child is up to standard. They do x, y, and z. I think there's something else." Perhaps the teachers are not looking, or not wanting to look at other ways to deal with it. They just think it's just an issue with not understanding material instead of thinking of other ways to help the child.

One woman, currently in a graduate program, reported being discouraged from going to university.

"You know, maybe you should try being secretarial or going into a trade or just looking for work." I said, "Why can't I go to university?" "Maybe university is not for you."

Also recounted were experiences where racialized children, particularly Black children, were regularly treated as though their behaviour was disruptive.

And it was only the Black and the brown kids who were always getting sent to detention, always getting sent to the special education class, always far removed from the so-called fun activities or being in a normal class environment.

Over-monitoring, being lumped in with the group that I am not a part of, as a problem child or something like that. Even teachers taking fewer opportunities to provide positive reinforcement. Assumptions being made really, really quickly, about what group I was with, or where I was if I was there. Yeah, almost as if — I was a pretty good kid in school — but if any little thing, if there is any little slip-up then suddenly there is like a huge . . . a problem.

I. IMPACTS OF RACIAL PROFILING ON WOMEN

While experiences of being racially profiled may be routine and routinized for many women, the impact on them is profound. Not surprisingly, some women became quite emotional when recounting experiences, even those that occurred many years ago. Single incidents, alongside repeated incidents, have widespread, long-term personal effects on racialized women.

Women identified how racial profiling negatively shapes their self-esteem.

> It hurts the way you feel about yourself, because you're still human right but sometimes people don't see you as human just because of your colour.
>
> I think the effect is that it damages self-esteem in different ways. It damages self-esteem in the sense that in an academic world, you want to come in, you want to bring in your ideas, you want to feel appreciated by your peers, and know that your peers are hearing what you have to say. If you feel that people are looking at you and basing everything you have to say on the colour of your skin, you don't feel confident enough to present your ideas.
>
> It's very demeaning, obviously. It affects your spirit and your sense of self-worth probably much more than we realize. I mean, just logically, stepping out of it and sort of viewing it logically for a second, to kind of walk through life feeling lesser than or feeling that somebody would treat you lesser than, it's sort of — it is just that. You start to accept a lower standard of living than you should.

Some women did not feel like they could be themselves, or had to negotiate a public persona, in order to manage the inevitability of being racially profiled, and to negotiate entrenched stereotypes of racialized women.

> [Racialized women] can't be free. Everything that they do they have to think consciously "how would others see me if I'm doing something right now?"
>
> But I think that emotionally it's always a role that the way you portray yourself, you have to be extra guarded that you don't want to be a stereotypical . . . you don't want to strengthen the stereotype that people might have against South Asian women, or racialized women.
>
> I think you get caught up in the two. You get really upset. You get really angry. What's the word I'm looking for? You try to counter it. "Listen, I'm still gonna do me. You have to take the time out to get to know me." Or you try the other approach, where you try to be a chameleon and try to fit into both worlds . . . . But I think for a lot of young women, until you get to that point of realizing that you need to be able to be seamless and walk through it, you get the angry Black woman. Or you get the woman who's just trying to do her and no matter what you do, you're perceived as the angry Black woman.

Women spoke of how repeated experiences marginalized them, "othered" them, and made it difficult for them to feel fully engaged in society, as individuals, on their own terms.

I'm feeling uncomfortable. And going home just to think about these things happen on day time and I'm feeling very, very uncomfortable. I moved immigrant to Canada. I thought Canada is very beautiful country. Everybody should be very nice. But this changed me. It's totally different. It's totally different. What should I do? What happened to this country? But you have the immigrant system. The policy. You will have immigrant coming from all over the world. Sounds like they don't like immigrants. It sounds like "why you come here? You should go back to your country."

It's demoralizing, and there's a sense of helplessness, I find. I know there is a couple of women in my building alone . . . in my building, it's mostly racialized women that are there . . . and it makes them afraid to say anything or go anywhere, certain areas, certain places because they know. So I think it really, really negatively impacts them, especially when people keep saying, "Don't complain. Don't say anything about it." They internalize it and then it affects their family, their children. It's bigger than just one incident and just brush it off. It really impacts who you are, where you go, how you conduct your business in the community.

I think you internalize this notion of being an "other," is really how I think of it. I think you really sort of start to take on this idea that you are out of place in some way. If I think of my own experiences and I try to imagine other women, you start to just accept this notion that you need extra screening, you need extra surveillance because you're part of this group that is threat and you're seen as a threat. And you're not, if you think about Canada, you're not considered native to Canada, so you're considered a threat. You're coming from the outside, you have to be screened for the potential of being different.

There's a sense of . . . growing up you sort of get taught how to behave as a Black person. My mother taught me, you know, "If there's a problem, make sure you are not anywhere near it because you will be blamed" and things like that. So that's just how I grew up. So I sort of make common sense decisions all the time. So I sort of do live in that perpetual state of being aware that I'm not like everyone else.

So essentially, that "othering," that sense of not belonging that I think the racial profiling makes me feel and perhaps it makes other people feel. If you don't fight it, whether you decide to or you don't decide to, then I think you kind of placate and start to do that in your everyday life and just try to pass through and be unnoticed and not disturb.

Perhaps most troubling is that some women do not themselves feel protected by those very agencies that suspect and mistreat them. Such routine and negative experiences undermine their confidence that they could turn to policing authorities, either public or private, when in need.

> Sometimes I feel like — "Can I trust them?" kind of thing. I look at it like, what if something was happening to me in the mall or in the store, and you guys are here watching me to see if I steal anything but say, how quick would you be to call an ambulance or something like that, you know? That's how I look at it, so yeah, I can't really say I can trust them, but, yeah . . . I can't really trust them . . . .
>
> So, you know, I would hesitate to get support from certain authorities because of how it may be perceived. Sometimes I feel there may be a bias depending on what the other side may be. If that were someone else who was racially profiled, they would be hesitant to seek support.
>
> But (campus security) . . . they don't really address other communities. So for me, I don't feel safe as well, too, on campus. So when I do ask for assistance to, you know, walk because the buses are no longer available. I actually had — unfortunately, one time, a [campus security guard] was like "You don't need to be protected, like, they're not going to go after *you*."
>
> The effect that it has, at least for racialized women like myself, at least from my experiences, is that you don't feel safe anymore. I know that I felt in that sort of mall — I didn't feel that I was being protected.

J. IMPACTS ON THE COMMUNITY

When women were asked about the impact that racial profiling has on the community more broadly, their responses mirrored, to some extent, the impact on individual women: repeated experiences of racial profiling were undermining, limiting, disempowering, and disengaging on so many very basic dimensions.

> I feel that it limits us from growth, as a stronger community and unite together . . . . Just being raised and born (outside Toronto) I feel that if people of all different races, weren't judging by colour or someone's disability we would be a stronger community . . . I just feel like it's limiting us as a whole.
>
> I feel like we stay in violent situations because we know that in this world that if we went to a police officer, going to ask for assistance, or going to ask for help in that very violent situation, we're going to be wait-listed or we're going to be dismissed.

In terms of my community and in terms of women, I think it takes away some power away from people. I feel like I have a voice. I feel most people probably who are profiled probably don't feel as much as they have a voice and then you just become . . . you're already marginalized, and then the community becomes even more marginalized.

Well, it diminishes our opportunities. It closes doors to us and it colours our whole world. It colours our world perception. It colours the choices that we make. Every day decisions are a thousand considerations before we act because we have to anticipate this, and this, and this and this.

K. RESPONDING TO RACIAL PROFILING

Women offered a range of strategies to confront racial profiling both in the moment, as well as a general approach to challenging the practices. Of course, their strategies are somewhat context-dependent, often constrained by the gravity of the situation (such as those at the border or involving armed police). At other times, however, their strategies reflect approaches to the surveillance of everyday life.

Clearly, encounters at the border (land or air) are often going to be those in which compliance is an important, pragmatic strategy:

Resistance is a nice idea, but nowadays, it can be very dangerous, especially for males because it tends to be interactions with officers. But I guess for me I feel like I can resist when there's less power, so borders, I'm not going to . . . I'm just going to go along with it kind of thing.

. . . I know that if I challenge them it's going to end up in big trouble. We just wanted to go to our vacation. We don't want to cause any trouble.

Especially at the border, no. 'Cause to me that would just create more problems. Yeah, and potentially they're looking for push back, which would create a reason to separate or isolate me, so no. I would never . . . . Not at this point.

That said, some women indicated that compliance was a general strategy for them and for others in their community.

But my mom comes from the old school mentality, the teacher is always right, try not to cause any trouble, because I wanted to complain about it but she said don't, you don't want to make trouble.

I don't believe anyone who's racialized needs to be scrutinized excessively because they are of a particular race but I start to accept that that's the position I'm in and I try to placate and just make myself as acceptable and as non-threatening as possible, in any way that you can. Just sort of go through the motions, I don't object, I smile, I be nice. I do as they say.

I've learned not to be abrasive. There's a Jamaican saying that they used to tell us: they have the handle and I have the blade. So if I'm going to continue to aggravate the situation, the only person I'm hurting is myself.

While the context of being racially profiled by private security is the most common experience for the women in this study, it is also, in some ways, the situation in which the women expressed feeling the most freedom to resist, often by taking their business elsewhere.

Sometimes, with me, if certain stores I go into are racial profiling me, I will not want to go in those stores. So it makes me not want to shop in the store and not want to buy any of your products even though I will like it, I won't buy it or I'll ask somebody else to buy it. Just because I don't want to feel like I'm being watched more than anybody else.

But if it's a building or a mall, the Eaton Centre or something like that, I feel like that is something that I can identify who the owner of the store is, who the owner of the mall is, I can tweet about it, I can blog about it, I could talk to other people about it. So I guess I feel that I could file a complaint if I wanted. So yeah, resistance is kind of tricky because it could lead to more problems.

I would have to (speak up), and I don't do it aggressively. I do it in an assertive, positive and uplifting way. I'm trying to make them see my point of view. Stop looking through with that narrow tunnel you're looking through and look through my view. Imagine if you're in my shoes and I was doing that to you — I wouldn't do that to someone. But I'm trying to open your eyes too, to let them know we are human beings too.

I find that usually if I can get to a place, just calm myself down, maybe count to 5, and really assess and say, "You know what? You're wrong. You are not allowed to speak to me this way. You're also not allowed to come and do what you're doing. You know this is racial profiling?" And I would advise you to call people out because I find when people hear those words or you call them out, just say, pinpoint it, they get scared. They say, "Oh no. I'm not doing that." And you say, "Oh yeah. I can report you to someone." And usually they back off and they run away scared because they don't want to be put into that category even though that's where they've decided to go.

A number of women suggested general strategies for responding to racial profiling practices, regardless of the context. Action, organizing, and educating future generations were seen as some of the more hopeful courses of action.

But then, also, there's agencies within the community that deal with oppression and discrimination. Definitely getting in contact with that. For example, if it's police profiling, make a complaint. You have a voice. Use your voice. So connecting with agencies that can help them, or individuals that can help them facilitate that complaint. And even coming together as a group of women to talk about their experiences have been and how it's impacted them. So having . . . group sessions can be cathartic.

Well, first, you have to identify it. I think that's the hardest part. And for me, I can identify it. It's identifying when things happen that this is an issue. It's not just a one-off thing. You have to identify it, recognize it and then speak about it . . . if it's something like teachers, or police, or institutions, I think it's good for us to write about it. Or whatever medium is actually best for you — some people are better at writing, some people are better at speaking. But kind of putting it out there and sharing with other people: this is what's happened to me.

I think these things need to be talked about in school: what is racial profiling and what is your right as a human being from the authorities. Because if they don't teach us in school, we're not going to know. It will happen throughout our whole life, and when we finally realize, we're like, "Wow, I could've stepped up but I didn't know."

I was brought up right; I was brought up to not be racist, that we are all one type of thing. But not everyone is brought up like that, a lot of people are brought up to hate Black people, or hate Chinese, or hate White people, or something like that, you know? There's even a lot of Blacks I know who hate White people, that's just because of how they were brought up. So it's just breaking the cycle for the future generation and the kids, we just have to teach them that racism doesn't exist, skin colour doesn't exist, we are literally all one.

L. CONCLUSIONS

There are a number of limitations to this study. The data from this research are based on experiences of women who have self-identified as having experienced profiling across a range of contexts. This is designed to be a targeted, self-selected sample of women and is not designed to give an indication of the statistical likelihood of its occurrence. It is possible that the offer of $20 for participation may have influenced the sample in some way, but it does not seem likely, given the fact that most women were gainfully employed at the time of the interview and none seemed terribly focused on the payment. Finally, it is likely that racialized women experience profiling in additional contexts not included in the questionnaire used here.

The data are powerful, nevertheless, in that they give voice to women's experiences and confirm that these experiences are embedded in women's everyday lives in routine ways. As was indicated, in some instances, racial profiling occurred while in the presence of men, typically with respect to border patrol or the uniformed public police. But the vast majority of experiences recounted here occurred separate from those and are likely *more* common for women. The primacy given to men's experiences, or assuming that profiling occurs largely in the same social and geographic spaces as it does for men, quickly breaks down. Quite simply, racial profiling is neither gender-neutral nor gender-free.

The profoundly negative impact of the racial profiling experience also rings loud and clear. This sample of women is fully engaged in the community — virtually all had post-secondary education, most worked, and many volunteered in various capacities in the community. Yet they feel excluded from civic life, "othered" by everyday encounters with both state and non-state authorities, and are often not confident that they would be protected in a time of need. As confident as they are that the source of the problem is elsewhere, they were, at the same time, profoundly aware of the consequences of resisting or challenging in the moment. While they acknowledge an arsenal of strategies, experience tempers them. They are, as Mythen et al note, "performing safeness" in virtually all public interactions; a gendered burden to be sure.[36]

---

36   Mythen et al, above note 2 at 749.

PART III

Preventing and Responding to Racial Profiling

CHAPTER 10

The Importance of Collecting Race Data

Preventing Racial Profiling and Promoting Inclusive Citizenship

LORNE FOSTER & LESLEY JACOBS[*]

A. INTRODUCTION

Over the past two decades, issues of racial profiling as part of police practices in Canada have come to the forefront of public attention. Complaints about racial profiling and racial bias are increasingly being brought to Canadian courts and human rights tribunals. Allegations of "driving while Black" have become commonplace. In fact, the problem is now frequently characterized as a systemic one for Canadian police services. Indeed, complaints about racial profiling are generally framed as systemic when they are heard by Canadian courts and human rights tribunals. Often, however, concerns about racial profiling are dismissed by defenders of the police as anecdotal and an indicator of an occasional bad apple, and in no sense a part of everyday policing in Canada.

Relations between Canadian police and the members of racialized minority groups have been the object of several official inquiries over the past three decades.[1] In almost every region of the country, the relations between police and minority groups have undergone close examination, and much of this attention has been prompted by police action that resulted in the

---

*   Lorne Foster is a professor of public policy and equity studies, as well as co-chair, Race, Inclusion and Supportive Environments, York University. Lesley Jacobs is a professor of law & society and political science, as well as the director of the Institute for Social Research, York University.

1   For a review, see Scot Wortley, "Police Use of Force in Ontario: An Examination of Data from the Special Investigations Unit Preliminary Report" (2007), a research project conducted on behalf of the African Canadian Legal Clinic for submission to the Ipperwash Inquiry.

death or serious injury of members of minority groups. With the increasing focus of attention and debate about law enforcement's relationship with people of colour and police "use of force doctrine," accompanied by hundreds of demonstrations in various jurisdictions, efforts to more fully understand police-community relations have placed a premium on systematic collection of statistics and information regarding law enforcement activity.

Yet, unlike in, for example, the United States or the United Kingdom, Canadian police services have no history of collecting racial data about who they serve or stop or why. Without this data, it is difficult, if not impossible, to evaluate seriously the extent, if at all, to which racial profiling is a systemic problem among Canadian police services. In other human rights areas, such as employment discrimination and housing discrimination, Canada has been a pioneer in gathering publicly accessible relevant data to assess allegations of systemic bias. In this chapter, we argue that an important step forward to address concerns about racial profiling and racial bias is to also gather racial data regarding police practices.

Contemporary police-minority relations are often complicated, choleric, and hard to grasp. The dearth of racial data frustrates rational, informed debate, and leaves a vacuum to be filled with innuendo, suspicion, and repressed hostility. The resulting tension and social inertia make it hard to stand back from issues and to fashion an encompassing picture of what is going on. This chapter argues that the complexity of racial disparities has made data collection a required tool. Systematic and carefully crafted race-data collection and analysis can be a major device for unpacking, addressing, and preventing police-community problems, while promoting bias-neutral policing and inclusive citizenship. The chapter concludes with a discussion of seven major uses of data collection for the purposes of racial equality, anti-racism, and inclusion. These include: (1) Documenting the extent and nature of ethno-racial disparity; (2) Identifying the causes of ethno-racial disparity; (3) The development of evidence-based policies and programs; (4) The evaluation of anti-racism policies and equity strategies; (5) Increased system accountability; (6) Increased transparency and perceived system legitimacy; and (7) Improved public education and increased knowledge with respect to systemic racism and its consequences.

B. POLICE-MINORITY RELATIONS IN CANADIAN SOCIAL CONTEXT

Contemporary public policing has been profoundly influenced by the pace and nature of social change in the context of globalization.[2] As society has developed and become more complex in its demographic landscape, the multicultural reality helped transform the traditional paramilitary policing model, shaping a new professionalism. The role expectations for the modern police officer demand both a "crime fighter" and a "public servant," whose duties are to "protect and serve" multiple publics.[3] Blending the traditional crime control function with modern public service values — such as respect for diversity, democracy, and professional integrity[4] — requires police agencies to come to grips with the difficult task of maintaining law and order in increasingly vibrant and mixed communities who often contest the boundaries of the status quo.[5] The magnitude of this challenge to both protect and serve in a diverse society are reflected in the growing frequency of newspaper and media accounts of confrontations in multiple jurisdictions over the "use of force" doctrines, "stop and search" protocols, and racial profiling. Television news programs and social media campaigns sometimes provide dramatic supporting videos, graphically depicting the visible tensions between the police and racialized minority communities.

The current rise in the public temperature and debate about police-minority relations has been amplified full throttle across the continent and abroad. Sparked by the unrest in Ferguson and New York, a vigorous dispute about law enforcement's relationship with people of African descent and police "use of force doctrine" has gone global. The events surrounding the deaths of Black teen Michael Brown in Ferguson, Missouri, and New York's Eric Garner launched public protests and rallies against police brutality, highlighted in the United States by the "Hands Up, Don't

---

2   Maurice A Martin, *Urban Policing in Canada: Anatomy of an Aging Craft* (Montreal: McGill-Queen's University Press, 1995); Graham Ellison & Nathan W Pino, *Globalization, Police Reform and Development: Doing It the Western Way?* (New York: Palgrave Macmillan, 2012).

3   Norm Stamper, *To Protect and Serve: How to Fix America's Police* (New York: Nation Books, 2016).

4   Colin Hicks, "A Case for Public Sector Ethics" (2007) 3:3 *Policy Quarterly* 11.

5   Lorne Foster & Lesley Jacobs, "Human Rights Evaluation Report: Windsor Police Service Human Rights Project" (2015) at 57, a report for the Windsor Police Service, online: www.police.windsor.on.ca/about/human-rights/Documents/Final%20REPORT_Foster_Jacobs%20January%202016.1.pdf [Windsor Report].

Shoot" and "I Can't Breathe" campaigns. Thousands of racialized Canadians and allies gathered in major cities across Canada and participated in symbolic public "die-ins" to show their solidarity with protesters south of the border, and to underline the deadly confrontations between African Canadians and the police, sparked by the shooting of Jermaine Carby, purported to be gunned-down during a routine traffic stop in Brampton, Ontario. The collective action eventually routinized into a common cause through the launch of the twenty-first-century Black Lives Matter movement.[6]

1)   Race Socialization Processes

Police-minority tension has had an impact on socialization processes as well. Studies have shown that by ten years of age, most children are aware of cultural stereotypes of different groups in diverse societies, and children who are members of stigmatized groups are aware of cultural types at an even younger age.[7] Research in the United States and Canada has consistently found that the reputation of Blacks has been besieged by beliefs about predispositions toward criminality[8] that can be traced back to the Atlantic slave trade.[9] The prevailing modern myth of the "criminal Black man" has been identified as a composite of White fears of Black men's inclinations towards criminality and deviance. Stereotyping of Blacks as criminals is now so pervasive that "criminal predator" is used as a euphemism for "young Black male."[10] On the other hand, there is also some evidence of a pushback from Black mothers who regularly engage in attempts to resist this negative stereotyping by "race proofing" their children, particularly young males.[11] A typical strategy is attempting to build "cultural capital" assets through an emphasis on Black-focused edu-

---

6   See Herbert G Ruffin II, "Black Lives Matter: The Growth of a New Social Justice Movement" (2016), online: BlackPast.org www.blackpast.org/perspectives/black-lives-matter-growth-new-social-justice-movement.

7   Brenda Major & Laurie T O'Brien, "The Social Psychology of Stigma" (2005) 56:1 *Annual Review of Psychology* 393.

8   Randall Kennedy, *Race, Crime, and the Law* (New York: Vintage Books, 1998).

9   Scot Wortley & Akwasi Owusu-Bempah, "The Usual Suspects: Police Stop and Search Practices in Canada" (2011) 21:4 *Policing and Society* 395.

10   Kelly Welch, "Black Criminal Stereotypes and Racial Profiling" (2007) 23:3 *Journal of Contemporary Criminal Justice* 276.

11   Tamari Kitossa & Katerina Deliovsky, "Interracial Unions with White Partners and Racial Profiling: Experiences and Perspectives" (2010) 3:2 *International Journal of Criminology and Sociological Theory* 512.

cation and curriculum — recognizing Black history and art, and leaders and heroes, in an attempt to give Black youth the advantage of higher expectations.[12] This also can involve cautiously home schooling Black youth in the "racialization of crime" by the police and criminal justice system and its pernicious effects. The curriculum of the street is as important to many Black mothers as the curriculum in schools. The precarious hyper-policing of Black youth is not lost on the mothers whose constant message to their children in word and deed is to "keep your antenna up and your head under the radar." Race proofing is a socialization tool in the Black family meant to transmit some survival skills for the effective management of stigma and to reinforce the self-esteem of Black children. To date it has had an uneven success.

2) Microaggressions and Macroaggressions of Race

Concerns about racism by police have expanded in recent years beyond flagrant patterns of police brutality, harassment, and excessive use of force to include more subtle racial profiling practices like "out-of-sight" traffic violations, "driving the wrong car" syndrome, "driving in the wrong neighbourhood" syndrome, and other "pretext stops."[13] Complaints about the police by members of racialized groups now range from macroaggressions (premeditated and open depravations) to microaggressions (more casual and hidden degradations).[14] Indeed, the majority of racialized minority concerns that once related to traditional overt forms of discrimination are giving way to concerns related to more subtle and systemic issues. These include, among other things, the use of non-excessive force by police to stop, question, and search people in public places; "blaming the victim" of crime when the victim is a member of a minority group; over-policing of the communities in which they live; and under-representation of minorities among the members of police organizations. It is also observed that while monitoring and controlling minority populations has always been a feature of police work, new fears, new "suspect populations," and new powers intended to control them have arisen in the face of instability

---

12   Pierre Bourdieu, "The Forms of Capital" in John G Richardson, ed, *Handbook of Theory and Research for Sociology of Education* (New York: Greenwood Press, 1986) 241.

13   Windsor Report, above note 5 at 59.

14   Derald Wing Sue, Christina M Capodilupo, & Aisha MB Holder, "Racial Microaggressions in the Life Experience of Black Americans" (2008) 39:3 *Professional Psychology: Research and Practice* 329.

associated with rapid global change and local expressions of geopolitics.[15] These emerging conditions have increased the propensity for police-minority contentions and are a key issue for policing scholarship and the courts, and for public debate about liberty and security, more generally.[16]

C. POLICE-MINORITY RELATIONS IN A DIVERSE SOCIETY

The traditional diversity paradigm in Canadian society has generally assumed that patterns of discriminatory behaviour in organizations are conscious; that people who know better do the right thing, and those who do not cause bias. As a result, we have developed a "good person/bad person" paradigm of diversity: a belief that good people are not biased, but inclusive, and that bad people are the biased ones.[17] Usually this is based on the notion that people make choices to discriminate due to underlying negative feelings towards some groups or feelings of superiority about their own. There is no doubt that this is often true. As it turns out, however, there is an impressive body of research spanning decades revealing that unconscious or "implicit biases" are linked to discriminatory outcomes across social sectors and major institutions in society including policing.[18] Contemporary forms of prejudice may be less conscious and more imperceptible than overt traditional forms, while having the same potential for adverse impacts on its victims. Racial bias and racial discrimination can occur even when people have good intentions.[19]

There are some uncomfortable implications of the science of bias for policing. The ill-intentioned or "bad apple" cop who produces biased policing and the well-intentioned police officer or "good cop" who aspires to be fair and impartial can both be wittingly or unwittingly complicit in the perpetuation of discrimination. Ugly pockets of conscious bigotry exist in policing and are often called to task. The urge for citizens and police

---

15   Leanne Weber & Ben Bowling, *Stop and Search: Police Power in Global Context* (New York: Routledge, 2012).

16   *Ibid.*

17   Howard Ross, "Exploring Unconscious Bias: Proven Strategies for Addressing Unconscious Bias in the Workplace" (2008) 2:5 *CDO Insights* 1.

18   Nilanjana Dasgupta, "Implicit Attitudes and Beliefs Adapt to Situations: A Decade of Research on the Malleability of Implicit Prejudice, Stereotypes, and the Self-Concept" (2013) 47 *Advances in Experimental Social Psychology* 233.

19   See John F Dovidio et al, "On the Nature of Contemporary Prejudice: The Causes, Consequences, and Challenges of Aversive Racism" in Victoria M Esses & Richard A Vernon, eds, *Explaining the Breakdown of Ethnic Relations: Why Neighbors Kill* (Oxford: Wiley-Blackwell, 2008).

leadership to call out the bigot cops is powerful and doing so is satisfying. But it is also a way to let ourselves and the police off the hook. When research isolates the effects of race from other factors, discrimination is revealed to be much more subtle and insidious.[20]

Implicit or subconscious bias is directly linked to the complexity and ambivalence of "aversive racism" (rationalizing an aversion to a particular racial group by appeal to rules and other seemingly neutral criteria).[21] People who behave in an aversively racial way may profess egalitarian beliefs and will often deny their racially motivated behaviour; nevertheless, they change their behaviour when dealing with a member of a minority group. Because aversive racism is neither conscious nor blatantly apparent to others, it is able to survive largely unchallenged by societal pressure for egalitarianism. Thus, outgroups, particularly racial minorities, can be subject to marginalizing social processes.

For instance, at every stage of the criminal justice system, Black Canadians and Indigenous people have been historically overrepresented, and the percentages are rising.[22] Aversive forms of discrimination can be manifested in the racialization of crime, hypersurveillance, racial hoaxes, White fear, and other micro- and macroaggressions. This can further create inhospitable social landscapes and poisoned environments, with debilitating consequences for the social and mental well-being of racialized people. When Western racial constructs and stigma are internalized this can contribute to ruptures in the psyche for people of colour, including ego depletion, flattened confidence, distorted systemic communications in public spheres, a tendency towards self-censorship in performance areas, and inauthentic presentations-of-self in evaluative settings.[23] Moreover, the cumulative intergenerational trauma of a lifetime of implicit racial

---

20 Sendhil Mullainathan, "Racial Bias, Even When We Have Good Intentions" *New York Times* (3 January 2015).

21 *Aversive racism* is a term first coined in the 1970s that has subsequently developed into a body of research studying the conduct of individuals who rationalize their aversion to a particular group by appeal to rules or stereotypes, and so, deny racially motivated behaviour. See John F Dovidio & Samuel L Gaertner, "The Aversive Form of Racism" in John F Dovidio & Samuel L Gaertner, eds, *Prejudice, Discrimination, and Racism* (San Diego: Academic Press, 1986) 61 [Dovidio & Gaertner, "Aversive"].

22 Howard Sapers, *Annual Report of the Office of the Correctional Investigator 2014–2015* (Ottawa: Correctional Investigator Canada, 2015) at 2.

23 Michael Inzlicht, Linda McKay, & Joshua Aronson, "Stigma as Ego Depletion: How Being the Target of Prejudice Affects Self-Control" (2006) 17:3 *Psychological Science* 262.

bias and negative stereotyping can theoretically contribute to diminished mortality and augmented morbidity.[24]

Implicit racial bias and racial stereotypes are obstacles to the access-to-justice that are so formidable and self-perpetuating that they cannot be overcome without deliberate and self-reflective intervention. Fair and impartial policing must incorporate an understanding that biased law enforcement occurs today predominately in the absence of explicitly "racist" thoughts and largely outside of conscious awareness and control. As we will demonstrate below in the second half of this chapter, the challenge moving forward to ensure fair and impartial policing services, and access-to-justice in courts and the criminal justice system more generally, is in developing effective debiasing interventions grounded in evidence-based and data collection-driven programs.

D.   THE SUBSTANTIVE EQUALITY LENS IN THE COURTS AND HUMAN RIGHTS TRIBUNALS

Canadian courts and human rights tribunals have demonstrated a growing acceptance of the science of bias and have shown a willingness to scrutinize seemingly "neutral" police behaviour to assess whether it falls within the phenomenon of aversive racial discrimination or profiling.[25] In the contemporary legal and human rights context, the way to "do diversity right" is to observe outcome-oriented standards of assessment associated with "substantive equality."

This, of course, was not always the case. Canada's unique history and conception of the relationship between the state and its constituent parts has gone through three phases of Canadian jurisprudence.[26] The first phase, stretching from the colonial period to the middle of the twentieth century, is marked by blatant exclusion and subordination. Here the adaption to diversity, or the original society-building idea of "doing di-

---

24   Lorne Foster, "Black and Mad and Black and Bad: Implicit Bias as a Psychosocial Determinant of Black Canadian Mental Health and Well-Being" in Merle Jacobs & Livy A Visano, eds, *"Righting" Humanity in OUR Time?* (Toronto: APF Press, 2015) 223.

25   In a seminal decision in *R v Brown*, 2003 CanLII 52142 at para 9 (Ont CA) [*Brown*], Morden JA stated that the Crown's concession that the phenomenon of racial profiling existed was "a responsible position to take because . . . this conclusion is supported by significant social science research." In *Peart v Peel Regional Police Services Board*, 2006 CanLII 37566 at para 94 (Ont CA) [*Peart*], Doherty JA stated that "racial profiling occurs and is a day-to-day reality in the lives of minorities affected by it."

26   Beverley McLachlin, "Racism and the Law: The Canadian Experience" (2002) 1 *University of Toronto Journal of Law and Equality* 7.

versity right," literally involved the exclusion of racial minorities as "the other." The legal response to this ethic of exclusion involved the use of the law to reinforce racial inequality and to prohibit marginalized communities from access to power and valued resources. The second phase, starting in the mid-twentieth century and terminating in the adoption of the *Canadian Charter of Rights and Freedoms* in 1982, was dominated by the goal of "equal opportunity." The legal response to the equal opportunity model involves the use of the law to end exclusion and to provide a broader access for racial minorities to society's major institutions — education, politics, economics, and so on. The legal adaption to diversity involves an openness to racial minority citizenship within the existing framework of society. This form of social membership maintained the prevailing racial hierarchy and reinforced structures of a White hegemony. Here, "doing diversity right" involved the participation of racial minorities in an institutional society that normalized Whiteness as a default position. The law positively seeking to enhance the equality and dignity of every individual characterizes the third and most recent phase. This post-*Charter* judicial paradigm is based on the idea of "substantive equality," and that outcomes in a multicultural and multi-racial population are directly applicable to the determination of discrimination.[27] Now the idea of doing diversity right increasingly involves an ethic of inclusion based on equitable participation and power-sharing between ethno-racial communities.

The Right Honourable Beverley McLachlin framed the challenge of racial discrimination in contemporary society from a substantive equality lens:[28]

> It requires us to recognize the context of historical, racial, and ethnic inequality and the myths and stereotypes that this context has produced. It requires us to disabuse ourselves of these preconceived notions, acknowledged or unacknowledged, to understand the reality that disadvantaged groups face, and to examine the claim of unequal treatment afresh based on this understanding.

In *R v Parks*, Doherty J, who continues to sit on the Court of Appeal, further stated:

> Racism, and in particular anti-black racism, is a part of our community's psyche. A significant segment of our community holds overtly racist views. A much larger segment subconsciously operates on the basis of negative racial stereotypes. Furthermore, our institutions, including the criminal justice system, reflect and perpetuate those negative stereotypes. These

27   *Ibid* at 7–24.
28   *Ibid* at 8.

elements combine to infect our society as a whole with the evil of racism. Blacks are among the primary victims of that evil.[29]

. . .

For some people, anti-black biases rest on unstated and unchallenged assumptions learned over a lifetime. Those assumptions shape the daily behaviour of individuals, often without any conscious reference to them. In my opinion, attitudes which are engrained in an individual's subconscious, and reflected in both individual and institutional conduct within the community, will prove more resistant to judicial cleansing than will opinions based on yesterday's news and referable to a specific person or event.[30]

Police services and officers across the country have historically been highly resistant to charges that they or their colleagues racially profile. Most officers likely have conscious goals to be egalitarian and do not intentionally allow racial bias to affect their actions. However, Canadian courts have progressively taken a "substantive equality" approach, which now acknowledges racial profiling as a form of discrimination that may be the product of subconscious and institutional racial bias, as well as the product of explicitly overt discrimination.[31] Racial profiling is recognized as a phenomenon that can occur through non-conscious stereotyping or in more subconscious, subtle, and subversive ways, as well as through overt prejudice.

Unlike explicit bias (which reflects the attitudes or beliefs that one endorses at a conscious level), implicit bias is recognized as bias in judgment and/or behaviour that results from subtle cognitive processes (e.g., implicit associations, implicit attitudes, and implicit stereotypes) that often operate at a level below conscious awareness and without intentional control. Implicit bias does not mean that people today are hiding their racial prejudices. More often, they literally do not know they have them.[32] Implicit bias occurs when someone like a police officer consciously rejects stereotypes and supports equality efforts in their professional conduct with the public, or in hiring, but also unconsciously holds negative associations in their mind.[33] Because implicit associations arise outside of

---

29   *R v Parks* (1993), 15 OR (3d) 324 at 342 (CA) [*Parks*].

30   *Ibid* at 343.

31   Sunil Gurmukh, "Summary of Canadian Racial Profiling Case Law Review" (2017) 14:1 *Journal of Canadian Diversity* 9.

32   Mahzarin R Banaji & Anthony G Greenwald, *Blindspot: Hidden Biases of Good People* (New York: Delacorte Press, 2013); Mullainathan, above note 20.

33   Cheryl Staats et al, *State of the Science: Implicit Bias Review* (Columbus, OH: Kirwan Institute for the Study of Race and Ethnicity, Ohio State University, 2014).

conscious awareness, these associations do not necessarily align with individuals' openly held beliefs or even reflect stances one would explicitly endorse.[34] In this respect, racial profiling reflects a new way of thinking about the issue of biased policing. What is new (in only the last few decades) is the mounting evidence that this form of racial discrimination is not the result of isolated acts of individual bad apples but part of a subtle and systemic bias in many police forces. There is now legal acknowledgement that an individual officer engaged in racial profiling may be subjectively unaware that she or he is doing so. Indeed, racial profiling does not necessarily reflect any explicit racial hostility at all. It may reflect the officer's legitimate perception of the reality of the world in which the officer operates.[35] However, in terms of a substantive equality lens, the intent, or motivation, or perceptions of racism are not determinative. It is important to look at the outcomes of behaviour and the results of a system.

As the Supreme Court noted in *Ontario (Human Rights Commission) v Simpsons-Sears Ltd*:[36]

> The *Code* aims at the removal of discrimination . . . an intention to discriminate is not a necessary element of the discrimination generally forbidden in Canadian human rights legislation.
>
> . . .
>
> [T]he proof of intent, a necessary requirement in our approach to criminal and punitive legislation, should not be a governing factor in construing human rights legislation aimed at the elimination of discrimination.[37]

The common assertion that unconscious or implicit racial bias runs contrary to the principle that our system of justice is predicated on the notion that "only those who act voluntarily should be punished." This is contrary to established principles of substantive equality and human rights. Post-*Charter* Supreme Court of Canada decisions have consistently confirmed that it is the impact or effect of the behaviour in question that is the essence of discrimination — intent to discriminate is not required.

People make choices that discriminate against one racial group and in favour of another on the basis of access to a repertoire of implicit and hierarchical stereotypes without even realizing that they are doing it and, perhaps even more strikingly, against their own conscious belief that

---

34 Sandra Graham & Brian S Lowery, "Priming Unconscious Racial Stereotypes About Adolescent Offenders" (2004) 28:5 *Law and Human Behavior* 483.

35 *Peart*, above note 25 at para 93.

36 [1985] 2 SCR 536.

37 *Ibid* at paras 13 and 14.

they are being unbiased in their decision making. This tendency leads people to be unwittingly complicit in the perpetuation of discrimination. Implicit bias might lead the line officer to automatically perceive crime in the making when she observes two young Latino-Canadian males driving in a predominately White neighbourhood or lead an officer to be under-vigilant with a female subject because he associates crime and violence with males. It may manifest among agency command staff who decide (without crime-relevant evidence) that an upcoming gathering of African-Canadian college students bodes trouble, whereas the upcoming gathering of White undergraduates does not.

E. THE SUBSTANTIVE EQUALITY LENS IN PUBLIC POLICY CONTEXT

The distinguishing feature of implicit racial biases in a policing and criminal justice context is that they are not accessible through normal introspection.[38] Neuroscience has discovered that the brain is capable of processing approximately 11 million bits of information every second, but our conscious mind can handle only 40–50 of those bits. This leaves the bulk of our mental processing to the unconscious level.[39] The unconscious mind is a reservoir of feelings, thoughts, urges, and memories that are outside of our general awareness, but nevertheless affect our conscious thoughts and behaviour.[40] The implication of the science is that even the best police officers may manifest bias because they are human, and even the best police services, because they hire humans, must be proactive in producing fair and impartial policing.

The convergence of behavioural and brain science on implicit forms of discrimination is translated into national and provincial public policy by our human rights codes. There is nothing novel in finding that non-conscious, seemingly neutral behaviours and well-intended rules that operate to discriminate against racialized Canadians are contrary to the *Code,* and nothing turns on how they are defined. Instead, the contours of "the new racism" drawn by our human rights codes prohibit the po-

---

38 Dovidio & Gaertner, "Aversive," above note 21.

39 Anthony G Greenwald et al, "A Unified Theory of Implicit Attitudes, Stereotypes, Self-Esteem, and Self-Concept" (2002) 109:1 *Psychological Review* 3; Staats et al, above note 33.

40 Raymond J Corsini & Danny Wedding, *Current Psychotherapies*, 9th ed (Belmont, CA: Brooks/Cole, 2011).

lice from treating persons differently in any aspect of policing because of their race, even if race is *only one factor* in the differential treatment.[41]

For example, in *Phipps v Toronto Police Service Board*,[42] an African-Canadian Canada Post employee was delivering mail in the affluent Bridle Path neighbourhood in Toronto on 9 March 2005 as a relief letter carrier. Mr Phipps was wearing the Canada Post issue uniform, carrying a mailbag, and delivering mail and flyers. While performing his usual delivery activities, he was stopped by Constable Shaw, a police officer with the Toronto Police Service, who was patrolling the neighbourhood in his cruiser, with a new recruit, Constable Diane Noto. Mr Phipps was asked to produce identification and showed Shaw his driver's licence and Canada Post identification. Constable Noto checked Phipps' identification against the police computer in the cruiser, which revealed nothing. Mr Phipps continued to perform his delivery duties and met up with another White letter carrier in the area, who advised Phipps that Shaw had questioned him about letter carriers in the Bridle Path area. The Human Rights Tribunal of Ontario (HRTO) concluded that Phipps' colour was a factor in Shaw's suspicion of Phipps and his decision to stop and question him and in the subsequent inquiries made regarding Phipps. The HRTO ruled that by stopping Phipps, questioning him, trailing him, and asking a White letter carrier to verify his identity, Shaw was guilty of racial profiling. The tribunal acknowledged "racial discrimination can be subconscious" and used this understanding "as a backdrop against which to assess the evidence before it, a useful and a necessary exercise given the subtle, pervasive and unconscious nature of racism."[43]

Social research has discovered implicit biases persist and are powerful determinants of behaviour precisely because people lack personal awareness of them; they can occur despite conscious non-prejudiced attitudes or intentions.[44] This process leads people to be unwittingly complicit in

---

41   See *Smith v Ontario (Human Rights Commission)*, 2005 CanLII 2811 (Ont Div Ct); *Dominion Management v Velenosi*, 1997 CanLII 1448 (Ont CA); *Peart*, above note 25 at paras 91 and 108; *Nassiah v Peel (Regional Municipality) Police Services Board*, 2007 HRTO 14.

42   *Phipps v Toronto Police Services Board*, 2009 HRTO 877.

43   Ontario Human Rights Commission, *Phipps v Toronto Police Services Board* (Factum of The Intervenor Ontario Human Rights Commission at para 35, online: www.ohrc. on.ca/en/phipps-v-toronto-police-services-board).

44   Dovidio & Gaertner, "Aversive," above note 21; Patricia G Devine, "Implicit Prejudice and Stereotyping: How Automatic Are They? — Introduction to the Special Section" (2001) 81 *Journal of Personality and Social Psychology* 757; Do-Yeong Kim, "Voluntary Controllability of the Implicit Association Test (IAT)" (2003) 66 *Social Psychology Quarterly* 83.

the perpetuation of discrimination. In the Phipps case, as in many cases alleging racial discrimination, there is no direct evidence of racial animus or dislike. As a result, the issue of whether the officer's actions amount to racial discrimination in violation of the *Code* falls on the determination of differential, disproportionate, and adverse impact in accordance with well-established principles applicable in circumstantial evidence cases.

To establish *prima facie* discrimination in circumstances alleging racial discrimination or racial profiling, the complainant must show three things: (1) that he or she is a member of a group protected by the *Code*; (2) that he or she was subject to adverse treatment; and (3) that a code-related ground was a factor in the alleged adverse treatment.[45]

In cases involving allegations of race discrimination or racial profiling, the *Ontario Human Rights Tribunal* (OHRT) has often referred to the following summary as establishing the applicable principles:[46]

(a) The prohibited ground or grounds of discrimination need not be the sole or the major factor leading to the discriminatory conduct; it is sufficient if they are a factor;

(b) There is no need to establish an intention or motivation to discriminate; the focus of the enquiry is on the effect of the respondent's actions on the complainant;

(c) The prohibited ground or grounds need not be the cause of the respondent's discriminatory conduct; it is sufficient if they are a factor or operative element;

(d) There need be no direct evidence of discrimination; discrimination will more often be proven by circumstantial evidence and inference; and

(e) Racial stereotyping will usually be the result of subtle unconscious beliefs, biases and prejudices.

F.   DEBIASING BEHAVIOUR AND REDUCING HARM

Post-*Charter* jurisprudence regarding equality and race is still in its infancy.[47] However, significant strides to address the conscious and unconscious ra-

---

45   See *Dang v PTPC Corrugated Co*, 2007 BCHRT 27, adopted in *Toronto (City) Police Service v Phipps*, 2010 ONSC 3884 at para 47 [*Phipps*]. In cases of racial profiling, as in *Phipps*, the key question for the tribunal is whether the applicant has shown that race, colour, and/or ethnic origin were factors in the treatment by the respondent.

46   See *Radek v Henderson Development (Canada) Ltd (No 3)*, 2005 BCHRT 302 at para 482.

47   McLachlin, above note 26 at 8.

cial biases of courts have been part of a more recent access-to-justice focus, particularly in the areas of racial profiling and jury selection.[48]

For instance, the Supreme Court of Canada held unanimously in *R v Williams*[49] that Mr Williams was entitled to ask potential jurors questions regarding racial bias. The Court found that there was ample evidence of widespread racism against Aboriginals and Blacks; that this racism included stereotypes that relate to credibility, worthiness, and criminal propensity; and that to forbid Mr Williams to challenge prospective jurors for racial bias would undermine his right to a fair trial by an impartial jury. The Court recognized that racism lies buried deeply in the human psyche, with "effects . . . as invasive and elusive as they are corrosive."[50] This requires as a matter of responsibility that positive steps be taken to discover and combat indirect and/or unintended racism.

Research has also confirmed the invasive, elusive, and corrosive nature of implicit racial bias in jury selection in the United States. A recent study by Anwar, Bayer, and Hjalmarsson examined the impact of jury racial composition on trial outcomes.[51] This study found evidence that: (1) juries formed from all-White jury pools convict Black defendants significantly (16 percentage points) more often than White defendants; (2) this gap in conviction rates is entirely eliminated when the jury pool includes at least one Black member; and (3) much of "legal decision-making" operates at a level below consciousness. The research concludes that the impact of jury race is much greater than what a simple correlation of the race of the seated jury and conviction rates would suggest. The findings imply that the application of justice is highly uneven and raises obvious concerns about the fairness of trials in jurisdictions with a small proportion of Blacks in the jury pool.

---

48 Some important initial cases shaping the substantive equality lens for racial profiling in the criminal justice system include: *Brown*, above note 25; *R v Richards*, 1999 CanLII 1602 (Ont CA); *Peart v Peel Regional Police Services*, 2003 CanLII 42339 (Ont SCJ). Another recent case discussed systemic racism in the criminal justice system in the context of sentencing: *R v Borde*, 2003 CanLII 4187 (Ont CA). In the context of jury selection, see also *Parks*, above note 29, and *R v Williams*, [1998] 1 SCR 1128, which recognize that racial beliefs are widespread enough in the broader community that in certain circumstances potential jurors can be asked direct questions about racial prejudice in jury selection.

49 *R v Williams, ibid.*

50 *Ibid* at para 22.

51 Shamena Anwar, Patrick Bayer, & Randi Hjalmarsson. "The Impact of Jury Race in Criminal Trials" (2012) 127:2 *Quarterly Journal of Economics* 1017.

Today blatant racial discrimination is typically suppressed by societal and personal norms and values. As a result, discrimination will not usually occur unless it can be explained away as being based on something other than prejudice.[52] Contexts in which this is prevalent are those where the norms and rules for appropriate behaviour are ambiguous or where justifications for the differential treatment — other than prejudice — are readily available.[53]

A study by Levinson examining implicit bias in legal decision-making found that judges and jurors in the United States unknowingly misremember case facts in racially biased ways.[54] Drawing upon studies from implicit social cognition, human memory research, and legal decision making, he argued that implicit racial biases affect the way judges and jurors encode, store, and recall relevant case facts. Paralleling Stuart Hall's reference model for cultural media studies, Levinson explained how this phenomenon of encoding perpetuates racial bias in case outcomes. To test the hypothesis that judges and jurors misremember case facts in racially biased and unconscious ways, he conducted an empirical study in which participants were asked to recall facts of stories they had read only minutes earlier. Results of the study confirmed the hypothesis that participants remembered and misremembered legally relevant facts in race-specific ways. For example, participants who read about an African-American story character were significantly more likely to remember aggressive facts from the story than participants who read about a Caucasian story character. Other results indicated that these racial memory biases were not related to explicit racial preferences. Levinson maintains the presence and power of implicit memory bias in legal decision making raises concerns about the legal system's ability to achieve social justice. The study suggests a multi-faceted response, including debiasing techniques and cultural change efforts, is needed in addressing aversive discrimination. Levinson's research holds that debiasing techniques, which use interventions such as diversity training to lessen the negative effects of implicit bias, hold promise for at least temporarily reducing the harms of implicit memory bias. This research further suggests the response with

---

52   Christian S Crandall & Amy Eshleman, "A Justification-Suppression Model of the Expression and Experience of Prejudice" (2003) 129 *Psychological Bulletin* 414.

53   Victoria M Esses & Joerg Dietz, "Prejudice in the Workplace: The Role of Bias against Visible Minorities in the Devaluation of Immigrants' Foreign Acquired Qualifications and Credentials" (Spring 2007) *Canadian Issues* 114.

54   Justin D Levinson, "Forgotten Racial Equality: Implicit Bias, Decisionmaking, and Misremembering." (2007) 57:2 *Duke Law Journal* 345.

the greatest permanent potential requires embracing cultural responsibility for the presence of negative racial stereotypes and coordinating efforts for change.[55]

In other words, a "best practice" for bias-neutral law enforcement is to openly acknowledge biases and then directly challenge or refute them.[56] Racial bias and stereotypes are obstacles to equity that are so formidable and self-perpetuating in our society and major institutions including criminal justice and policing that they cannot be overcome without deliberate and self-reflective intervention.[57] These adjustments are more likely to be successful if they incorporate evidence-based understandings, derived most effectively through valid and reliable race-data collection.

G. DEBIASING STRATEGIES AND DATA COLLECTION

Although cognitive bias research gives us a good insight into the causes and effects of racially biased policing, as we will demonstrate below the challenge moving forward on bias-neutral police services, and access-to-justice issues more generally, is in developing effective interventions grounded in evidence-based and data-driven programs. Data collection can provide a strong evidentiary means of support for debiasing strategies. Police debiasing strategies combined with race-data collection are crucial to fair and impartial policing.

Debiasing involves interventions at the individual and organizational level to avoid costly errors and negative impacts of biased judgment and decision making. For instance, debiasing techniques formulated to apply at the individual police officer level might include: (1) banning racial discrimination and profiling, (2) officer training (diversity, cultural sensitivity/responsibility/competence), (3) reducing officer discretion, and (4) adopting new technologies.[58]

At the organizational level, the elements of a comprehensive approach to producing fair and impartial policing might encompass (1) recruitment/hiring, (2) agency policy, (3) leadership supervision and accountability,

---

55   *Ibid.*

56   Carey Morewedge et al, "Debiasing Decisions: Improved Decision Making with a Single Training Intervention" (2015) 2:1 *Policy Insights from the Behavioral and Brain Sciences* 129.

57   *Ibid.*

58   Katherine B Spencer, Amanda K Charbonneau, & Jack Glaser, "Implicit Bias and Policing" (2016) 10:1 *Social and Personality Psychology Compass* 50 [Spencer et al].

(4) assessing institutional practices and policies, and (5) outreach to diverse communities.[59]

Many police departments are turning the corner in a commitment to adjusting their policies and procedures using debiasing tools to try to address biased policing and community complaints. Banning racial profiling, training officers, reducing discretion, and adopting new technologies are some of the more popular interventions aimed at bias-neutral police services. Fewer have committed to a more comprehensive approach that includes such interventions at the organizational level, such as recruitment and hiring, data transparency, program equity assessments, and bi-directional community engagement.

In terms of debiasing theory and methodology, all debiasing techniques, at an individual and service level, require "incentives," "nudging," and/or "education."[60] In policing, *incentives* and *nudges* occur at the performance management and evaluation level of the service. Incentivizing police performance against racial bias and discrimination can involve rewarding police officers for optimal behaviour through such devices as bonuses or promotions. Linking the equitable conduct of police officers to career advancement can be a strong performance motivator. Most of the individual and organizational debiasing techniques above can be incentivized. For instance, accountability and transparency in police governance may be leverageable to some extent through municipal budgeting tools. The same would apply for equity recruitment and hiring. However, incentivizing equity practices in policing is perhaps most effective when operationalized as an entrenched agency policy.

1) Banning Discrimination and Profiling Policies

Nudging police performance involves using disciplinary measures that make it more costly for suboptimal behaviour or racially biased decisions; this would also include measures to curb biased behaviour through such organizational management devices as bans or prohibitions on racial profiling. In the United States, federal legislation to prohibit racial profiling has been repeatedly introduced in Congress, but has not yet been enacted. In the absence of federal law to prohibit profiling, many states have adopted laws to address concerns about racial profiling within their borders. To date, thirty-two American states have adopted at least one

---

59   Lori A Fridell, *Producing Bias-Free Policing: A Science-Based Approach* (Cham, Switzerland: Springer International, 2017).

60   Morewedge et al, above note 56.

racial profiling law.[61] In Canada, various departments at the service level have also implemented mandates against racial profiling. Unfortunately, as described above, given the non-conscious operation of stereotypes, and that there is already a strong stigma against biased policing, it is unlikely that these bans are fully effective. Research by Spencer and her colleagues determined that most officers likely have conscious goals to be egalitarian and do not intentionally allow racial bias to affect their actions.[62] Therefore, enforcement of such bans is difficult because it requires determining which officers and which actions are influenced by stereotypes.[63] The answer to these questions require evidence-based analysis, and this can best be achieved through race-data collection efforts. In the absence of systemic and soundly constructed data collection and analysis, policies will be driven by assumptive policing techniques that are closed off to emerging social patterns. The resulting policy decisions are at the continual risk of being ineffective, unproductive, and incompetent.[64]

2) Debias Training

Linking bias-free policing to an incentive system or a disciplinary system is the primary debiasing technique for influencing fair and impartial police decision making. Another approach is education and training. Many police departments engage in different forms of training to improve officer performance and outputs on the public service delivery side. Agency-level policies and procedures on bias, officer discretion, and use of force often include training interventions. Most departments also train their officers on concepts that include racial bias, community-oriented policing, and cultural competence. In some cases, litigation or legislation mandates these trainings. However, there is a great amount of variability in the types and depth of training officers receive. There is also little empirical evidence about the kinds of training that are most effective in reducing bias in policing.[65] Education, to date, has received less focused

---

61 Dean Weld, *State Adoptions of Racial Profiling Laws: Exploring Functional, Social, and Political Determinants* (PhD Thesis, State University of New York, Department of Sociology, 2017) [unpublished] at 75–76.

62 Spencer et al, above note 58 at 59.

63 *Ibid.*

64 Joyce McMahon et al, *How to Correctly Collect and Analyze Racial Profiling Data* (Washington, DC: Department of Justice, Office of Community Oriented Policing Services, 2002) at 10.

65 Elizabeth L Paluck & Donald P Green, "Prejudice Reduction: What Works? A Review and Assessment of Research and Practice" (2009) 60 *Annual Review of Psychology* 339.

attention by policy makers than incentives and nudges because initial debiasing training efforts resulted in mixed success.[66] Some research also shows that in the case of diversity and cultural sensitivity training in other industries, there is no basis for confidence that these programs have meaningful, lasting effects.[67]

Indications are that education and training should be part of a police service long game. Some research contends that training can effectively debias decision makers over the long term through exposure to counter-stereotyping and stereotype negation techniques. For example, experiments by Morewedge and colleagues found that interactive computer games and instructional videos result in long-term debiasing at a general level. In a series of experiments, training with interactive computer games that provided players with personalized feedback, mitigating strategies, and practice reduced six cognitive biases by more than 30 percent immediately and by more than 20 percent as long as three months later.[68]

As stated above, traditional forms of prejudice can be combated by using direct and conventional attitude change and educational techniques designed to redress the conduct of ill-intended police officers. However, addressing contemporary forms requires alternative strategies designed not only for the few officers who are "bad apples," but also for the overwhelming number of well-intentioned police in this country who aspire to fair and impartial policing. Once an implicit association is activated, it is difficult to inhibit.[69] Training cannot easily undo the implicit associations that took a lifetime to develop. But cognitive bias research has shown that, with information and motivation, people can implement controlled (unbiased) behavioural responses that override automatic (biased) associations. The policy implication is that police agencies need to provide training that makes personnel aware of their unconscious biases so that they are able and motivated to initiate controlled responses to counteract them.

---

66   See Baruch Fischhoff, "Debiasing" in Daniel Kahneman, Paul Slovic, & Amos Tversky, eds, *Judgment Under Uncertainty: Heuristics and Biases* (Cambridge: Cambridge University Press, 1982) 422.

67   Paluck & Green, above note 65.

68   Morewedge et al, above note 56.

69   Nilanjana Dasgupta, "Implicit Attitudes and Beliefs Adapt to Situations: A Decade of Research on the Malleability of Implicit Prejudice, Stereotypes, and the Self-Concept" (2013) 47 *Advances in Experimental Social Psychology* 233.

3) Debiasing Police Technology

Some police services are adopting new technologies as a way of debiasing police practice. For example, IAPro software is growing in popularity as an early intervention technology that provides for the tracking of officer behaviour through data analysis that can produce various types of alerts that a problem exists. The software provides alerts by type of incident, i.e., an agency can set different thresholds for different incident types, such as citizen complaints, use-of-force incidents, or lack-of-service situations. The software provides for a monitored officer alert, which targets a specific employee or unit with an alert whenever the individual/unit is involved in an incident. A "top percentile alert" allows an agency to identify instantly people or units that appear in a designated top percentile for a specific time period. A "detail alert" is an alert by allegation and by use-of-force type. IAPro helps internal affairs personnel with caseload management through reminders that signal actions are required on a case or that a case is approaching overdue status. An overall alert can also be indicated; this alert is triggered regardless of incident type. Reports, graphs, and charts can be generated at the push of a button.[70]

IAPro internal affairs software can be juxtaposed against the "rise of the warrior cop" technology complete with surveillance cameras, drug-sniffing dogs, SWAT team raids, roadside strip searches, blood draws at DUI checkpoints, mosquito drones, tasers, privatized prisons, GPS tracking devices, zero tolerance policies, overcriminalization, and free speech zones.[71] New police tech can help both militarize or democratize the profession. However, data technology measuring the impact and performance of police has not yet fit very comfortably with the heightened surveillance of a post-9/11 securitization paradigm. Instead, to some extent, technology has contributed to a deep divide between the police officer's role and responsibilities as a sophisticated crime fighter on the one hand, and an ethical public servant on the other.

There is also some risk of overreliance on data technology by police services at the expense of the necessary analytic skills that can be provided by academics and outside experts. Police personnel are unlikely to have a background in analytical research methods, whereas professional researchers and academics are likely to lack knowledge of operational

---

70   Pamela Mills-Senn, "Tracking Officer Behavior" (2004) 31:4 *Law Enforcement Technology* 86.

71   Radley Balko, *Rise of the Warrior Cop: The Militarization of America's Police Forces* (New York: Perseus Book Group, 2014).

police procedures. Either party, then, is more likely to overgeneralize the questions and answers if they were to work in isolation. Combining the expertise of operational and research experts, working together, is perhaps the best way to accomplish an accurate and useful evaluation of the data.[72]

A report to the US State Department recommends that as much as possible police data collection and evaluation planning should blend police operational expertise with external research methods.[73] It counsels that the partnership between operational police expertise and external researchers should be established before the data collection begins. This will allow police to have input on operational constraints, and researchers to have input on what data will be required to reach meaningful conclusions. If the wrong data are collected, the best analysis in the world will be unable to reach useful or valid conclusions.

In addition, the US State Department report recommends the use of "multivariate analysis" to focus on accounting for all of the complexities of police procedures and operational methods, as well as the unique characteristics of the citizen populations served.[74] In race-data collection, the impact of many different influences on police-citizen encounters must be jointly taken into consideration before valid conclusions can be reached. Multivariate techniques allow researchers to look at relationships between variables in an overarching way and to quantify the relationship between variables. Here, researchers can control association between variables by using cross tabulation, partial correlation, and multiple regressions, and introduce other variables to determine the links between the independent and dependent variables or to specify the conditions under which the association takes place. This gives a much richer and realistic picture of police-citizen relations than looking at a single variable and provides a powerful test of significance compared to univariate and other techniques.

4) Data Collection and Debiasing Police Practice

Some research suggests that data collection is also an effective debiasing technique. Properly stated however, data collection and evaluation are not debiasing strategies; they are "best practices" for producing debias-

---

72 McMahon et al, above note 64 at 10.

73 *Ibid.*

74 *Ibid* at 11.

ing strategies in an age of aversive discrimination.[75] Because aversive racism is neither conscious nor blatantly apparent to others, it is able to survive largely unchallenged by societal pressure for egalitarianism. Data collection is a tool for detecting patterns of discrimination that operate undetected, below the level of conscious awareness.

Data is first needed to determine whether racial disparity exists or not. Importantly, the documentation of racial disparity, via high quality data collection, can increase the probability that otherwise undetected racial issues will be acknowledged and treated seriously by policing administrators, policy-makers, institutional stakeholders, and members of the public. If racial disparities are seen to exist and reach a discriminatory threshold, this can confirm the need for interventions, as well as provide a baseline of information in order to evaluate what interventions might be needed.

It is important to grasp the fact that data collection and evaluation can contribute to the unravelling of non-overt and adverse impact behaviours of well-intended police officers, as well as the overt discrimination of bad-apple cops. Subtle forms of discrimination can only be detected after looking at all of the circumstances to determine if a pattern of behaviour exists. Individual acts themselves may be ambiguous or explained away, but when viewed as part of a larger picture can lead to the inference that discrimination based on implicit association and unconscious stereotypes was a factor in the treatment a person received.

Valid and reliable data collection can surface the subtle, systemic, and aversive effects of modern discrimination. In this respect, data collection is critical for changing the way we think about biased policing in this country and preventing its occurrence. Race-data collection should be used as an evidentiary tool to help tailor debiasing strategies at the front line and organizational levels — from officer discretion, service delivery options, and new technologies to departmental transparency and accountability and equity recruitment and hiring. All strategic interventions to promote fair and impartial policing are more likely to be successful if grounded in evidence-based knowledge derived from a valid and reliable database.

Debiasing strategies for individuals and organizations should be developed collaterally with robust data collection and evaluation to determine their relevance and applicability for a specific police service or jurisdiction and for sound assessment of their sustainability. This approach can assist in discovering the answers to officer and service performance

---

75   Dovidio & Gaertner, "Aversive," above note 21.

questions and hypotheses; and in some cases, it can even predict future outcomes. Robust data collection provides a baseline starting point for rational and fact-based conversation about racial bias and discrimination, and about the policy implications of bias-neutral police practices and programs. Hence, this approach provides a strong, evidence-driven method for determining the effectiveness of debiasing techniques.

In addition, mandating data collection and data transparency would go a long way to diagnosing gaps and inefficiencies, and ascertaining the costs and benefits of service delivery formats and organizational efficiency, as well as reveal hidden patterns of racial disparity. Systematic and carefully crafted race-data collection and analysis is a major tool for unpacking, addressing, and preventing social problems, while promoting socio-economic productivity and inclusive citizenship.

In considering contemporary forms of discrimination in all of their subtlety and complexities, Banaji and Greenwald aptly observed it is incumbent on all of us to overcome our "racial blind spots" by adapting our beliefs and tailoring policies and procedures to "outsmart the machine" in our heads so we can be fairer to those around us.[76] The democratic challenge of fair play and fair competition in our major social institutions including policing now begins with understanding the subtle, systemic, and aversive effects of bias and stereotyping, and the determination to oppose it head on. Robust data collection can be a key equity-oriented strategic planning tool for understanding the contours and landscape of police-citizen encounters and access to substantive justice, without which the detection of equitable and inequitable conduct remains uncertain.

H.   WHAT KIND OF RACIAL DATA SHOULD BE COLLECTED BY THE POLICE?

Several countries and jurisdictions, including the United States and the United Kingdom, collect race-based data for equity purposes or as a means of preventing discrimination.[77] The collection of such data is becoming the norm. Canadian police and security agencies are encouraged by many segments of society to integrate relevant race-based data into their existing collection systems. Collecting race data and reporting is

---

76   Banaji & Greenwald, *Blindspot*, above note 32.

77   Lorne Foster, Lesley Jacobs, & Scott Wortley, *Research and Consultation Report for a Race-Based Collection Framework for Ontario*, Report for the Anti-Racism Directorate (ARD), Ontario Public Service, Government of Ontario (2017) [Foster, Jacobs, & Wortley].

also a show of openness and transparency on the part of agencies responsible for policing towards the communities served.

However, one of the greatest problems in assessing quality of policing is the lack of public data on impact and performance.[78] This problem is pervasive throughout Canada's policing and security sector, which explains why there is relatively little scholarly research in the field. Chan argued that such research is scarce because the police subculture operates on secrecy and loathes observation by outsiders.[79] As a specific feature of police culture, many officers come to rely on unquestioned racialized stereotyping as they confront the "mean streets" and battle crime, particularly where they perceive challenges to their authority and status. This may intensify a specific loathing towards outside observation around issues of race.

Canadian police services gather and retain an immense amount of micro- and metadata for crime analytics and to support the trend toward "intelligence-led policing,"[80] which shows that they are well positioned to also gather impact and performance data on the public service delivery side. The police also provide a tremendous number of diverse services for the community. Only some of these typically raise concerns about racial profiling and racial bias, in particular, those that involve safety and security. The police practices that are especially subject to scrutiny concern arrests and detentions, traffic stops, pedestrian stops, and criminal investigations. Our view is that racial data should eventually be collected for all of these aspects of policing.

There are many different sorts of information that might be gathered for the purposes of addressing concerns about racial bias and racial profiling. Our view is that there should be three basic categories of information gathered. One category is the demographics of those stopped. These demographics should include at minimum race, sex, and age. The second category is the reason or the context for police activity. For example, in the case of a traffic stop, the relevant information is the reason for the stop. The third category of information is the outcome for the person stopped, whether, for example, he or she was charged with a crime or given a ticket.

The precise fields of information, especially with regard to race, may well be calibrated for different communities. There is no one-size-fits-all

---

78 Neil Robertson, "Policing: Fundamental Principles in a Canadian Context" (2012) 55:3 *Canadian Public Administration* 343.

79 Janet Chan, "Changing Police Culture" (1996) 36:1 *British Journal of Criminology* 109.

80 Jerry H Ratcliffe, *Intelligence-Led Policing*, 2d ed (New York: Routledge, 2016).

for gathering racial data relevant to policing. In some communities, it is especially important to focus on whether or not the person subject to police activity was Black or Indigenous. In a different community the focus may be on whether or not the police officer perceives the person as Middle Eastern or South Asian. The decisions about racial categories should reflect the concerns of racialized minority communities about police activities. Racial data should not be gathered to assess the behaviour of racialized communities in Canada.

It is important to acknowledge the police who will be gathering this information about themselves. Canadian police services have a long history of gathering data in a professional manner. Collecting racial data to make them accountable should simply be another part of their job. Canadian police research suggests that data suppression and the lack of data transparency in areas of police performance and impact is the result of a deeply entrenched police subculture[81] that loathes observation by outsiders.[82] The racial data collected must be made public in order to inform debate over the extent to which racial profiling and racial bias is systemic.

With proper accountability, the security of Canadians can be safeguarded while protecting equity rights. In addition, oversight agencies mandated to monitor the activities of policing agencies need to play a role in reporting on equity issues and in encouraging appropriate corrective action, where necessary.

I.   WHY SHOULD A LAW ENFORCEMENT AGENCY BEGIN TO COLLECT AND PUBLISH RACE-BASED STATISTICS?

A report on data collection and analysis to the US State Department noted:[83]

> Data collection and evaluation is an appropriate way to address the concerns of racial profiling. Anecdotal evidence is an unreliable tool upon which to make policy decisions. However, in the absence of systematic and carefully crafted data collection and analysis, policies will be driven by anecdotal evidence. The resulting policy decisions may be inefficient at best, and at worst may, in the end, prove counterproductive.

---

81   Scot Wortley, "Northern Taboo: Research on Race, Crime, and Criminal Justice in Canada" (1999) 41:2 *Canadian Journal of Criminology* 261.

82   Akwasi Owusu-Bempah & Paul Millar, "Research Note: Revisiting the Collection of Justice Statistics by Race in Canada" (2010) 25:1 *Canadian Journal of Law and Society* 97.

83   McMahon et al, above note 64 at 10.

Early research in the United States found that collecting race-based statistics does help to address community concerns about the activities of the police and ascertain the scope and magnitude of racial profiling and racial bias.[84] The systematic collection of information regarding law enforcement performance can support community policing by building trust and respect for the police in the community. By providing information about the nature, characteristics, and demographics of police enforcement patterns, these data collection efforts have the potential for shifting the rhetoric surrounding racial profiling from accusations, anecdotal stories, and stereotypes to a more rational discussion about the appropriate allocation of police resources.[85]

Data collection for law enforcement is fundamental to a comprehensive early warning system that alerts management to problems of police misconduct.[86] By detecting and addressing instances of disproportionate treatment of persons of colour by the police, law enforcement organizations may be able to prevent the development of a systemic pattern of discriminatory practice.

Implementing a data collection system also sends a clear message to the entire police community, as well as to the larger community, that racial profiling is inconsistent with effective policing and equal protection and that the police have nothing to hide.[87]

J. BENEFITS OF DATA COLLECTION

The implementation of data collection systems have resulted in significant benefits for police services and communities in other countries with diverse populations. Studies conducted in both the United States and England have found that data collection processes can:

- Avoid rhetoric and accusation and promote more rational dialogue about appropriate policing strategies.
- Send a strong message to the community that the department is against racial profiling and that racial profiling is inconsistent with effective policing and equal protection.

---

84   Karl Lamberth, *Practitioners Guide for Addressing Racial Profiling* (Boston: Institute on Race and Justice, Northeastern University, 2005).

85   Deborah Ramirez et al, *A Resource Guide on Racial Profiling Data Collection Systems: Promising Practices and Lessons Learned* (Washington, DC: US Department of Justice, 2005).

86   *Ibid.*

87   Lamberth, above note 84.

- Build trust and respect for the police in the communities they serve through increased transparency and public accountability.
- Provide departments with information about the types of stops being made by officers, the proportion of police time spent on high-discretion stops, and the results of such stops.
- Help shape and develop training programs to educate officers about racial profiling and interactions with the community.
- Enable the development of police and community dialogue to assess the quality and quantity of police-citizen encounters.
- Alleviate community concerns about the activities of police.
- Identify potential police misconduct and deter it, when implemented as part of a comprehensive early warning system.
- Retain autonomous officer discretion and allow for flexible responses in different situations.[88]

K. BENEFITS OF GOOD DATA

Race-data collection efforts are an attempt to provide the tangible numbers that will enable police and community leaders to better understand their policing activities. Good data can:

- help identify and verify issues, theories and perceptions.
- help to proactively address issues, measure progress, and capitalize on opportunities.
- gain trust, develop effective, respectful consultations, and secure the support of key decision makers and stakeholders.
- reduce exposure to possible legal action and human rights complaints.[89]

L. CHALLENGES OF DATA COLLECTION

While jurisdictions can derive many benefits from implementing data collection systems, they also face several potential challenges. Such challenges may include the following:

- Concerns about extra-budgetary expenditures associated with collecting data;

---

88   Ramirez et al, above note 85.

89   Ontario Human Rights Commission, *Count Me In: Collecting Human Rights-Based Data* (Toronto: Ontario Human Rights Commission, 2010); Windsor Report, above note 5.

- Developing a robust benchmark against which the data can be compared;
- The potential burden an improved data collection procedure will have on individual officers in the course of a normal shift;
- The potential for police disengagement from their duties, which may lead to officers scaling back on the number of legitimate stops;
- The challenge of ensuring that officers will fully comply with a directive to collect stop data;
- Problems ensuring that data is recorded on all stops made, and that the data collected is correct;
- The difficulty of determining the race or ethnicity of the persons stopped; and
- Racial data on its own does not answer definitely whether racial profiling is systemic or not.[90]

M. A RACE DATA FRAMEWORK FOR EQUITY PURPOSES

Accurate and comprehensive race-data collection can:

- Help to ensure the integrity of social research;
- Be useful for describing social phenomena, as well as identifying questions requiring further investigation;
- Help promote informed public dialogue about appropriate policy strategies;
- Send a strong message to racialized communities that the police service is against racial discrimination and that discrimination is inconsistent with the vision of Canada as a multicultural democratic society based on social inclusion;
- Help build trust and respect for government through increased transparency and public accountability;
- Help identify issues or gaps in services, clarify issues, and suggest possible solutions or initiatives to deal with problems;
- Be used to monitor the effectiveness of anti-racism and anti-discrimination initiatives; and
- Provide a critical tool to effectively measure and comprehensively address aversive institutional and systemic barriers to racialized groups from the full enjoyment and exercise of human rights.

---

90 Ramirez et al, above note 85.

N. SEVEN USES OF RACE DATA

There are seven major uses of ethno-racial data collection for the purposes of racial equality, anti-racism, and inclusion that can be found in the research literature. These uses include: (1) Documenting the extent and nature of ethno-racial disparity; (2) Identifying the causes of ethno-racial disparity; (3) The development of evidence-based policies and programs; (4) The evaluation of anti-racism policies and equity strategies; (5) Increased system accountability; (6) Increased transparency and perceived system legitimacy; and (7) Improved public education and increased knowledge with respect to systemic racism and its consequences. A brief description of each of these potential uses is outlined below.[91]

1) Documenting Racial Disparity

Issues of race and racism continue to be highly contested in Canadian society including the policing and criminal justice sector. While some view racial bias or discrimination as an important and widespread social problem, others feel that racism has been greatly reduced or even eliminated over the past several decades. Ethno-racial data collection and dissemination is needed to inform this crucial debate in policing and criminal justice by documenting the extent and nature of racial disparities within police practice.

Importantly, the availability of race-based data or statistics can move the debate beyond simplistic denial. For example, beginning in the 1980s, members of Ontario's Black community alleged that they were much more likely to be stopped, questioned, and documented by the police than the members of other racial groups. Police officials originally refuted these claims and maintained that all civilians, regardless of race, receive equal police treatment. However, after the recent release and analysis of police street check and traffic stop data, police officials have largely conceded that Black Ontario residents are significantly overrepresented in officially documented cases of police-civilian contact. While community members and police officials may continue to debate the causes of this overrepresentation, police leaders no longer deny that this overrepresentation exists. Thus, as a result of data collection, the dialogue has shifted dramatically from a denial of racial difference to a discussion of whether racial disparities in police stops are caused by systemic racial bias or other, more legitimate, socio-legal factors.

---

91 Foster, Jacobs, & Wortley, above note 77.

In sum, data is first needed to determine whether racial disparity exists or not. Data can also be used to document the extent of racial disparity across different social sectors and changes in the level of disparity over time. Importantly, the documentation of racial disparity, via high quality data collection, can increase the probability that racial issues will be acknowledged and treated seriously by policing administrators, policy-makers, institutional stakeholders, and members of the public.

2) Explaining Racial Disparities

Once racial disparities have been documented or established, researchers and policy-makers should be compelled to identify explanations, theories, or mechanisms that may account for observed racial differences and disparities. Additional data collection and analysis can help test the validity of competing theories or explanations and determine the primary causes or reasons behind the racial disparities under study. For example, research has documented that students from some ethno-racial groups achieve lower grades than others and are subsequently less likely to graduate high school and pursue a post-secondary degree. What factors might account for racial disparities in educational outcomes? Some have argued that racial differences in educational outcomes reflect systemic barriers within the educational system including low expectations for minority students, biased streaming and disciplinary practices, lack of diversity among teaching staff, inadequate mentoring, and culturally biased curriculums. Others, however, have maintained that racial differences in school performance largely reflect racial differences in household income and poverty levels, housing quality, family structure, parental educational attainment, cultural capital, and attitudes towards education. These same validity tests and questioning are applicable to any and all police data collection studies as well. It must be stressed that data collection, combined with high quality multivariate analysis, can help identify the factors that have the largest or most significant impact on observed racial disparities. The identification of the most important factors or predictors of disparity can subsequently be used to inform policy development. The point is that data collection and analysis is not limited to the simple identification of racial disparities. Data can lead to a better understanding of why racial differences exist and what needs to be done to promote racial equity.

3) Evidence-Based Public Policy Development

As discussed above, race-based data does not only help with the identification of specific racial disparities, it can also help identify possible reasons for racial differences in important social outcomes. This, of course, is the very type of information that is required for the development of evidence-based public policy. In other words, high quality information on the nature, extent, and causes of racial disparities can be used to identify or develop stronger policing policies, programs, and protocols. Data can also help identify the types of strategies that might have the greatest impact with respect to reducing racial disparity and increasing social equality. Without such data, policing administrators and policy-makers are largely operating in the dark regarding the quality of police practice and performance — without the information they need to make informed decisions. It should be noted that a lack of data at the development stage also increases the probability of ineffective program implementation and increases the risk that taxpayer money will be used in an inappropriate fashion.

4) Policy and Program Evaluation

Modern police governance including the Canadian Association of Chiefs of Police (CACP) are firmly committed to combating systemic racism in police work by reducing racial disparities and promoting racial equity.[92] This includes "initiating or strengthening programs and strategies that promote bias-free policing, giving particular attention to public accountability, policy-making, management, supervision, equitable human resource practices, education, community outreach and partnerships."[93] Reflecting this commitment, a wide variety of police services across the country are now interested in developing and implementing specific strategies designed to meet anti-racism goals and objectives. As discussed above, the collection and analysis of race-based data can assist in the development of evidence-based policies and programs. However, the continued collection of such data is also needed to properly evaluate the effectiveness of anti-racism initiatives. Data can be used to establish baseline measures of disparity, establish specific goals or objectives

---

92   Canadian Association of Chiefs of Police (CACP), "Resolutions Adopted by the 99th Annual Conference in Vancouver, British Columbia, August 2004," August 7 Resolution #02/2004.

93   *Ibid* at 5.

with respect to disparity reduction, and determine whether goals are reached or not. Evaluation results can subsequently be used to identify what works and what is ineffective with respect to addressing racism and racial inequality. The results of evaluation research can also be used to identify program strengths and weaknesses and make good anti-racism policies even better. Evaluation results can be used to highlight effective practices and inform funding decisions.

5) Increased Accountability

Race-based data collection should not only be viewed as a research or planning exercise. Data can represent a form of accountability that may, in and of itself, reduce systemic racism and racial disparity. For example, through data collection and analysis, police organizations may, for the first time, come to realize the racially disparate impacts of their traditions and practices. This may produce changes to organizational culture and behaviours that will reduce racial inequities. The potential release and public discussion of racial data may also create incentives to develop and implement anti-racism policies and practices that are consistent with public expectations. Finally, data collection and monitoring may cause individuals to become more conscious of their own implicit and explicit prejudices and thus enable them to make decisions that are less likely to be racially biased.

6) Increased Transparency and Perceived System Legitimacy

Allegations of systemic racial bias in Ontario are not new. Critics have long argued that there needs to be more research conducted into the extent and nature of racism and the impact it has on minority communities. Increasingly, academics, activists, community organizations, and members of the public are calling for race-based data collection as a means of documenting racial disparity and evaluating anti-racism policies. In this context, disinterest or refusal to collect race-based data can be viewed with distrust. The failure to collect race-based data can be interpreted as disinterest in race-based issues or as an attempt to conceal racially biased practices and outcomes. By contrast, efforts to collect data on race-based outcomes indicate that governments and organizations are taking allegations of systemic racism seriously and trying their best to document and reduce racial inequities. Such efforts at transparency could serve to increase public confidence in the government and broader social system

— especially among minority citizens. Improvements in the perceived legitimacy of the state, in turn, can increase levels of civic engagement and cooperation with government officials.

7) Public Education

Finally, race-based data collection can contribute to public education. While people from minority communities often have personal experiences with both individual and systemic racism, members of the White majority often must learn about racism vicariously or through the results of social research. Race-based data collection, therefore, has the potential to educate people about the extent of current racial disparities in Canada and the negative impact that these disparities have on minority communities. Data can also be used to increase public understanding with respect to the causes of racial inequality and how it might be reduced. Importantly, improving the public's level of knowledge about racial disparity and its root causes could ultimately increase public support for anti-racism policies and programs.

8) The Importance of Legislation

A review of the experiences in the United States and the United Kingdom has brought to the forefront that the gold standard for implementing a race-data collection framework is through legislation.[94] The review provides an overview of legislation in the United States and United Kingdom that mandate race-based data collection. The United States has developed an extensive, consistent race-data collection system because the obligation to collect race data was required in a series of important civil rights laws that reflected concerns about racial inequalities and racial disproportionalities in sectors of government services that are fundamental to the daily lives of Americans. The United Kingdom's recent experience with race-data collection in the criminal justice system well illustrates how effective legislation can be at establishing the practice of race-data collection for equity purposes. This indicates that legislation is able to effectively create compliance mechanisms and financial incentives and penalties for race-data collection that are more challenging than when race-data collection is pursued through alternative, softer policy instruments.

---

94   Foster, Jacobs, & Wortley, above note 77.

O. CONCLUSION

This chapter explained how the factually complex and elusive nature of racial bias and discrimination has made race-data collection a required tool in policing. The tension and social inertia characterizing police-minority relations make it hard to stand back from issues and fashion an encompassing picture of what is going on. Adjustments to ensure bias-neutral policing are more likely to be successful if they incorporate evidence-based understandings derived most effectively through valid and reliable race-data collection. Systematic and carefully crafted race-data collection and analysis can be a major methodological advancement towards unpacking, addressing, and preventing police-community problems, while improving police productivity and promoting inclusive citizenship.

CHAPTER 11

A Double-Edged Sword

Carding, Public Safety, and the Impact of Racialized Police Practices

SCOT WORTLEY[*]

A. INTRODUCTION

Stop and search. Stop and frisk. Stop and account. Street checks. Field interrogations. Community engagements. Carding. Over the past two decades these terms have come to dominate both academic and public discourse on policing throughout North America and Europe. All of these terms refer to the police practice of stopping civilians — drivers, passengers, and pedestrians — for proactive investigation. Proactive investigation refers to the fact that officers usually decide to make these stops at their own discretion — they are not responding to a specific criminal event or reacting to a particular call for service. During such encounters, the police often ask civilians to produce formal identification and explain their presence in the community. Evidence also suggests that, during these stops, the police often "frisk" or pat-down civilians — under the pretense of officer safety — or ask civilians to submit to a consent search. Legal critics frequently challenge the lawfulness of such stops and argue that they violate basic civil rights. However, much of the debate centres around evidence that suggests that Blacks, Aboriginals, and other racial minority groups are much more likely to be subjected to police stop and search tactics than people of White or European backgrounds. This pattern is highly consistent with allegations of racial profiling. This paper will begin by briefly reviewing the research literature on police racial profiling in Canada. The paper will then discuss the potential utility of police stop and search tactics from a public safety perspective. It will

---

[*] Scot Wortley is an associate professor of criminology with the Centre for Criminology & Sociolegal Studies, University of Toronto.

be argued that the consequences of racial profiling far outweigh the potential benefits and that discretionary police tactics — including stop and search practices — require further monitoring in order to ensure transparency and public accountability. Unfortunately, the curtailing of "carding" by itself will not lead to a reduction in racialized police stop and search practices nor improve police-community relations.

B. CANADIAN EVIDENCE OF RACIAL PROFILING

Despite recent media attention, allegations of police racism are not new to Ontario. For example, during the 1970s and 1980s, long before the terms "racial profiling" and "carding" had been coined, Toronto's Black community frequently complained that they were disproportionately stopped and "harassed" by the police.[1] Such allegations have often been fiercely denied by police leaders.[2] Since the early 1990s a growing number of academics have attempted to address this debate through their research efforts.

Much of the research on racial profiling in Canada has consisted of qualitative interviews or focus groups with racialized individuals. Findings typically reveal that a high proportion of research subjects have experienced negative encounters with the police and often attribute these encounters to police racism.[3] For example, the Ontario Human Rights Commission (OHRC) gathered detailed testimonials from a non-random sample of over 800 people in Ontario — most of them Black — who felt that they had been the victims of racial profiling. The OHRC project provided vivid descriptions of specific racial profiling incidents and documented how these incidents negatively impact both minority individuals

---

1   David Cole & Margaret Gittens, *Racism Behind Bars: The Treatment of Black and Other Racial Minority Prisoners in Ontario Prisons — Interim Report of the Commission on Systemic Racism in the Ontario Criminal Justice System* (Toronto: Queen's Printer for Ontario, 1994).

2   Francis Henry & Carol Tator, *Racial Profiling in Canada: Challenging the Myth of "a Few Bad Apples"* (University of Toronto Press, 2006) [Henry & Tator, *A Few Bad Apples*].

3   Sulaiman Giwa et al, "Community Policing: A Shared Responsibility — A Voice-Centred Relational Analysis" (2014) 12:3 *Journal of Ethnicity in Crime and Justice* 218; Robynne Neugebauer, "Kids, Cops, and Colour: The Social Organization of Police-Minority Youth Relations" in Robynne Neugebauer, ed, *Criminal Injustice: Racism in the Criminal Justice System* (Toronto: Canadian Scholars Press, 2000) 83; Carl James, "Up to No Good: Black on the Streets and Encountering Police" in Vic Satzewich, ed, *Racism and Social Inequality in Canada: Concepts, Controversies and Strategies of Resistance* (Toronto: Thompson Educational Publishing, 1998) 157.

and communities.[4] Qualitative methodologies have also been used to study police officer perceptions of the racial profiling issue. For example, Owusu-Bempah recently interviewed fifty Black police officers from the Greater Toronto Area.[5] The majority of these police officers admitted that they themselves had been victims of racial profiling at some time during their careers and that they often worked with officers who engaged in racial profiling and/or condoned the practice.

Qualitative research efforts have recently been supplemented by a growing number of quantitative surveys that further document that African-Canadian and Aboriginal individuals are much more likely to be stopped and searched by the police than people from other racial backgrounds. These studies demonstrate that racial differences in police stop and search activities remain statistically significant after controlling for other theoretically relevant factors including age, gender, socio-economic status, education, driving habits, time spent in public places, criminal behaviour, gang involvement, and drug and alcohol use.[6]

Despite being published in peer-reviewed journals, and thus meeting the general standards of academic rigor, police officials and supporters often dismissed early Canadian research on racial profiling as "anecdotal" or "junk science."[7] What was needed, many argued, was large-scale, police-collected data that truly captured the nature of police activity. Unfortunately, such race-based data is typically not collected or disseminated in

---

4　Christopher Williams, "Obscurantism in Action: How the Ontario Human Rights Commission Frames Racial Profiling" (2006) 38:2 *Canadian Ethnic Studies* 1.

5　Akwasi Owusu-Bempah, *Black Males' Perceptions of and Experiences with the Police in Toronto* (PhD Thesis, University of Toronto, Centre for Criminology and Sociolegal Studies, 2014).

6　Scot Wortley & Gail Kellough, "Racializing Risk: Police and Crown Discretion and the Over-representation of Black People in the Ontario Criminal Justice System" in Anthony Harriott, Farley Brathwaite, & Scot Wortley, eds, *Crime and Criminal Justice in the Caribbean and Among Caribbean Peoples* (Kingston, Jamaica: Arawak Publications, 2004) 173; Scot Wortley & Julian Tanner, "Inflammatory Rhetoric? Baseless Accusations? Responding to Gabor's Critique of Racial Profiling Research in Canada" (2005) 47:3 *Canadian Journal of Criminology and Criminal Justice* 581; Scot Wortley & Julian Tanner, "Data, Denials and Confusion: The Racial Profiling Debate in Toronto" (2003) 45:3 *Canadian Journal of Criminology and Criminal Justice* 367; Robin Fitzgerald & Peter Carrington, "Disproportionate Minority Contact in Canada: Police and Visible Minority Youth" (2011) 53:4 *Canadian Journal of Criminology and Criminal Justice* 449; Steve Hayle, Scot Wortley, & Julian Tanner, "Race, Street Life and Policing: Implications for Racial Profiling" (2016) 58:3 *Canadian Journal of Criminology and Criminal Justice* 322.

7　Ron Melchers, *Inequality Before the Law: The Canadian Experience of Racial Profiling* (Ottawa: Research and Evaluation Branch, Royal Canadian Mounted Police, 2006).

the Canadian context. However, following a hotly contested freedom of information request that ultimately took them to the Ontario Court of Appeal, the *Toronto Star* newspaper eventually obtained information on approximately 2.95 million civilian "contact cards" that had been filled out by the Toronto police between 2003 and mid-2011 (an average of 310,000 contact cards per year over this period). It should be stressed that these contact cards are not necessarily completed after every police stop. They are only filled out when individual police officers want to record, for intelligence purposes, that they have stopped and questioned a particular civilian.[8]

Consistent with previous research, analysis of the contact card data reveals that Black people are grossly overrepresented with respect to police stop activity. Although they represent only 8 percent of the Toronto population, Black people were the target of almost 25 percent of all contact cards filled out during the study period. In other words, between 2003 and 2011, Blacks were 3.1 times more likely to appear in the contact card dataset than their representation in the general population would entail. Additional analysis reveals that, in some neighbourhoods, almost all young Black males have been carded and are thus officially "known to police." Furthermore, the data indicate that Black people were issued a disproportionate number of contact cards in all Toronto neighbourhoods regardless of the local crime rate or racial composition. Indeed, the findings indicate that although Blacks were overrepresented in contact cards collected in high-crime neighbourhoods, they were even more overrepresented in contact cards collected in low-crime, predominantly White neighbourhoods. This finding contradicts the argument that Black people are only stopped more than Whites because they are more likely to live or spend time in high-crime communities.[9]

The impact of the *Toronto Star*'s analysis should not be underestimated. Once hotly debated, the overrepresentation of Black people in police stop statistics can no longer be denied. The discussion has now turned from whether disproportionate minority contact exists, to what extent this overrepresentation is due to racial profiling or other, more

---

8   It should be noted that, in the vast majority of cases, contact cards were not filled out during police encounters that ended in arrest or criminal charges. In such cases an arrest report would have taken the place of the contact card.

9   Jim Rankin & Patty Winsa, "Known to Police: Toronto Police Stop and Document Black and Brown People Far More Than Whites" *Toronto Star* (9 March 2012) [Rankin & Winsa]; Jim Rankin, "Race Matters: When Good People Are Swept up with the Bad" *Toronto Star* (6 February 2010); Yunliang Meng, "Profiling Minorities: Police Stop and Search in Toronto, Canada" (2017) 11:1 *Human Geographies* 5.

legitimate, policing concerns. Furthermore, since they can no longer deny that investigatory stops do take place, police officials have turned to defending carding as a legitimate police practice that contributes to public safety.

C. POLICE STOPS, CARDING, AND CRIME PREVENTION

In recent years, North American police officials have come to increasingly defend "stop and frisk" and "carding" as effective crime prevention strategies. They have argued that these tactics are particularly effective with respect to combating street gangs and reducing gun violence.[10] Arguments in favour of stops/carding have included the following points:

- Police stop and search activities can result in the identification and confiscation of both illegal handguns and illegal drugs. Removing drugs, guns, and offenders from the street will ultimately reduce violent crime and save lives;
- Even when unproductive, police stops are a deterrent. Stopping and searching civilians, especially the residents of high-crime communities, will send the message that the police are taking violence and drug crime seriously. Offenders will come to know that the certainty of police detection and punishment is high and this will eventually deter them from carrying drugs or guns in public. This deterrent effect will reduce the likelihood of violent, gun-related crime and make communities safer;
- Stop and frisk tactics hold offenders accountable. Stopping civilians and demanding identification will help police officers identify offenders who have warrants out for their arrest. It will also help the police identify offenders who are in violation of parole, probation, and other court-imposed conditions (including pretrial release conditions). By uncovering breach-of-condition violations, stop and search tactics can increase control over offenders who do not respect community sanctions. This increased control will prevent more serious forms of offending;
- Gang members and drug traffickers often do not reside in the communities that they "terrorize." Stop and frisk practices can help identify trespassers and keep them out of public housing developments. Such practices will reduce both crime and fear of crime in affected communities;

---

10   See online: www.ctvnews.ca/video?clipid=777838.

- Stopping and documenting civilians (carding) can improve police intelligence. It can, for example, provide information on who resides in particular neighbourhoods or who frequents particular crime "hotspots." Carding can also help identify criminal "associates" and link offenders to potential witnesses, victims, and accomplices. Such intelligence can help the police solve crimes or decide what individuals or groups should be targeted for further investigation.

Unfortunately, such police arguments rarely consider the legality of these stop, question, and search tactics. Even if effective, should these tactics be condoned if they clearly violate basic *Charter* rights? After all, one could argue that if we eliminated all civil rights, and all rules of procedural justice, we would be in a better position to fight crime. Police would be better able to identify illegal activity and arrest offenders if they could only stop and search any person at any time for any reason. They could fight crime more effectively if they had the power to immediately conduct warrantless searches of homes and vehicles without having to explain their actions. But is that the type of society we want to live in?

Philosophical arguments aside, research evidence on the actual effectiveness of police stop and frisk tactics is quite limited. Canadian data is non-existent. Some American studies, however, do suggest that targeted, broken windows policing strategies — including stop and frisk tactics — are responsible for significant crime declines in cities like New York, New Orleans, and Los Angeles.[11] Skeptics, however, argue that most studies are inconclusive and have not taken into account other factors that may explain recent crime reductions. Skeptics also maintain that, over the past two decades, violent crime has also declined in many urban centres that do not employ stop and frisk tactics.[12] Interestingly, despite dire warnings, new regulations and the dramatic decline of stop and frisk activities in New York City have not resulted in significant increases in violent or property offending. In fact, crime rates have continued to decline

---

11   Anthony Braga, "Focused Deterrence and the Promise of Fair and Effective Policing" (2015) 14:3 *Criminology & Public Policy* 465; Anthony Braga, "Getting Deterrence Right? Evaluation Evidence and Complementary Crime Control Mechanisms" (2012) 11:2 *Criminology & Public Policy* 201; Steven Durlauf & Daniel Nagin, "Imprisonment and Crime: Can Both Be Reduced?" (2011) 10:1 *Criminology & Public Policy* 9.

12   Tracey Meares, "The Law and Social Science of Stop and Frisk" (2014) 10 *Annual Review of Law and Social Science* 335; Michael Tonry, "Less Imprisonment Is No Doubt a Good Thing: More Policing Is Not" (2011) 10:1 *Criminology & Public Policy* 137 [Tonry, "Less Imprisonment"].

to historic lows.[13] A similar situation seems to be emerging in Toronto. As the result of public pressure and the implementation of a new policy, the number of contact cards completed by the Toronto Police Service dropped by over 75 percent between 2012 and 2014.[14] However, Toronto's rate of violent crime continued to decline over this two-year period. By 2016 it was at its lowest level since the mid-1960s.[15]

While Canadian data is not available, we do know from American and British research that that police stop and frisk activities rarely uncover direct evidence of criminal activity. For example, between 2004 and 2012, the NYPD conducted approximately 4,135,000 stop and frisks.[16] Only 46,000 of these stops — a mere 1.1 percent — resulted in the seizure of illegal contraband and only one out of every thousand stops (0.01 percent) resulted in the seizure of an illegal firearm.[17] A similar picture emerges in England. As documented by Bowling and Phillips, the per capita police stop rate in England and Wales is approximately 6.5 times greater for Blacks than for Whites.[18] However, the hit rate for both Blacks and Whites is almost identical — about one percent of stops for both groups result in the discovery of illegal activity. The fact that these hit rates do not vary by race might be interpreted as an absence of racial bias. However, the hit rate figures, combined with the per capita stop and search rate, sheds light on another reality: every year innocent Black people in England and Wales are 6.5 times more likely than innocent Whites to endure an unnecessary stop and search encounter with the police. This fact could undermine public confidence in the police — a topic addressed further in the next section.

---

13   Preeti Chauhan et al, *Tracking Enforcement Rates in New York City, 2003–2014* (New York: John Jay College of Criminal Justice, 2015); Jesse Wegman, "Ray Kelly's Sour Grapes" *New York Times* (24 December 2015); Michael White, *Stop and Frisk: The Use and Abuse of a Controversial Police Tactic* (New York: New York University Press, 2016).

14   Rankin & Winsa, above note 9.

15   Jillian Boyce, *Police Reported Crime Statistics in Canada, 2014* (Ottawa: Canadian Centre for Justice Statistics, 2015).

16   Even though African Americans represent only 23 percent of New York City's population, they were involved in over half (52 percent) of the stops conducted by the NYPD over this period. By contrast, although Whites represent 46 percent of the NYC population, they were involved in only 10 percent of police stops.

17   Jose Torres, "Race/Ethnicity and Stop and Frisk: Past, Present and Future" (2015) 9:11 *Sociology Compass* 931.

18   Ben Bowling & Coretta Phillips, "Disproportionate and Discriminatory: Reviewing the Evidence on Police Stop and Search" (2007) 70:6 *Modern Law Review* 936.

D. THE CONSEQUENCES OF PROFILING

The social and psychological consequences of racial profiling have been extensively documented.[19] In sum, people who perceive that they have been the victim of racial profiling often feel humiliated, frightened, angry, frustrated, and helpless. Previous research further suggests that racial profiling is a quality of life issue and that frequent exposure to police stop and search activities can have a negative impact on mental health. The focus of this section of the essay, however, is to clearly document the consequences of racial profiling with respect to the criminal justice system.

First of all, logic dictates that there is a direct relationship between how closely people are monitored by the police and how likely they are to get caught for breaking the law.

In other words, if racial minorities are systematically stopped and searched more frequently by the police than Whites, they are also more likely to be detected and arrested for illegal activity than White people who *engage in exactly the same criminal behaviour.* Thus, racial differences in police stop and search activities may directly and significantly contribute to the overrepresentation of certain racial groups — Black and Indigenous Canadians in particular — within the Canadian criminal justice system.[20] In the United States, numerous academics have demonstrated that racially biased police stop and search practices, implemented as part of the war on drugs, directly contributed to the dramatic increase in the overrepresentation of Black and Hispanics within the American correctional system.[21] Critics further argue that differential law enforce-

---

19   David Harris, *Profiles in Injustice: Why Racial Profiling Cannot Work* (New York: New Press, 2002) [Harris, *Profiles*]; Jessica Hart et al, "Racial Profiling: At What Price?" (2008) 3:2 *Journal of Forensic Psychology Practice* 79 ["Hart et al, "Racial Profiling""]; David Tanovich, *The Colour of Justice: Policing Race in Canada* (Toronto: Irwin Law, 2006); Henry & Tator, *A Few Bad Apples*, above note 2; Ben Bowling & Leanne Weber, "Stop and Search in the Global Context: An Overview" (2011) 21:4 *Policing and Society* 480.

20   Scot Wortley & Akwasi Owusu-Bempah, "Crime and Justice: The Experiences of Black Canadians" in Barbara Perry, ed, *Diversity, Crime and Justice in Canada* (New York: Oxford University Press, 2011) 127; Akwasi Owusu-Bempah & Scot Wortley, "Race, Criminality and Criminal Justice in Canada" in Sandra Bucerious & Michael Tonry, eds, *The Oxford Handbook on Ethnicity, Crime and Immigration* (New York: Oxford University Press, 2011) 281.

21   Shaun Gabbidon & Helen Taylor Greene, *Race and Crime* (Thousand Oaks, CA: Sage, 2005); Marc Mauer, *Race to Incarcerate* (New York: The New Press, 1999); David Cole, *No Equal Justice: Race and Class in the American Criminal Justice System* (New York: The New Press, 1999); Michael Tonry, *Malign Neglect: Race, Crime and Punishment in America* (New York: Oxford University Press, 1995) [Tonry, *Malign Neglect*]; Coramae Richey

ment practices help explain why the majority of people convicted of drug crimes in the United States are Black and Hispanic, even though the vast majority of drug users and traffickers are White.[22]

The overrepresentation of racial minorities within the justice system, in turn, has been shown to cause immense social and economic harm to minority communities and families. Scholars often refer to such harm as collateral damage. The collateral damage associated with disproportionate minority incarceration, for example, can include economic hardship, social stigmatization, childhood trauma and underdevelopment, family dissolution, and poor physical and mental health.[23]

A second major consequence of racial profiling is that negative police stop and search experiences can undermine the legitimacy of the entire criminal justice system. Indeed, a growing volume of American,[24]

Mann, *Unequal Justice: A Question of Color* (Bloomington, IN: Indiana University Press, 1993).

22 Harris, *Profiles*, above note 19; Tonry, *Malign Neglect*, above note 21.

23 Michael Pinard, "Collateral Consequences of Criminal Convictions: Confronting Issues of Race and Dignity" (2010) 85 *New York University Law Review* 457; Bruce Western & Christopher Wildeman, "The Black Family and Mass Incarceration" (2009) 621 *Annals of the American Academy of Political and Social Sciences* 221; Holly Foster & John Hagan, "The Mass Incarceration of Parents in America: Issues of Race/Ethnicity, Collateral Damage to Children and Prisoner Re-entry" (2009) 623 *Annals of the American Academy of Political and Social Sciences* 179; Devah Pager et al, "Sequencing Disadvantage: Barriers to Employment Facing Young Black and White Men with Criminal Records" (2009) 623 *Annals of the American Academy of Political and Social Sciences* 195.

24 Jihong Zhao et al, "The Impact of Race/Ethnicity and Quality-of-Life Policing on Public Attitudes Toward Racially Biased Policing and Traffic Stops" (2015) 61:3 *Crime & Delinquency* 350 [Zhao et al, "Impact"]; James Unever, Shaun Gabbidon, & George Higgins, "The Election of Barack Obama and Perceptions of Criminal Injustice" (2011) 28:1 *Justice Quarterly* 23; Shaun Gabbidon, George Higgins, & Hillary Potter, "Race, Gender, and the Perception of Recently Experiencing Unfair Treatment by the Police: Exploratory Results from an All-Black Sample" (2011) 36:1 *Criminal Justice Review* 5 [Gabbidon, Higgins, & Potter, "Race, Gender"]; Jospeter Mbubu, "Attitudes Toward the Police: The Significance of Race and Other Factors Among College Students" (2010) 8 *Journal of Ethnicity in Criminal Justice* 201; George Higgins, Shaun Gabbidon, & Gennaro Vito, "Exploring the Influence of Race Relations and Public Safety Concerns on Public Support for Racial Profiling During Traffic Stops" (2010) 12:1 *International Journal of Police Science and Management* 12; Chris Gibson et al, "The Impact of Traffic Stops on Calling the Police for Help" (2010) 21:2 *Criminal Justice Policy Review* 139 [Gibson et al, "Traffic Stops"]; Lee Slocum et al, "Neighborhood Structural Characteristics, Individual-Level Attitudes, and Youths' Crime Reporting Intentions" (2010) 48:4 *Criminology* 1063 [Slocum et al, "Neighborhood"]; Shaun Gabbidon & George Higgins, "The Role of Race/Ethnicity and Race Relations on Public Opinion Related to the Treatment of Blacks by

British,[25] and Canadian[26] studies have firmly established that certain ra-

---

the Police" (2009) 12:1 *Police Quarterly* 102; Arthur Lurigio, Richard Greenleaf, & Jamie Flexon, "The Effects of Race on Relationships with the Police: A Survey of African American and Latino Youths in Chicago" (2009) 10:1 *Western Criminological Review* 29; George Higgins, Shaun Gabbidon, & Kareem Jordan, "Examining the Generality of Citizens' Views on Racial Profiling in Diverse Situational Contexts" (2008) 35:12 *Criminal Justice and Behavior* 1527; John MacDonald et al, "Race, Neighbourhood Context and Perceptions of Injustice by the Police in Cincinnati" (2007) 44:13 *Urban Studies* 2567; Ronald Weitzer & Steven Tuch, *Race and Policing in America: Conflict and Reform* (New York: Cambridge University Press, 2006); John Reitzel & Alex Piquero, "Does It Exist? Studying Citizens' Attitudes of Racial Profiling" (2006) 9:2 *Police Quarterly* 161; Wesley Skogan, "Asymmetry in the Impact of Encounters with the Police" (2006) 6 *Police and Society* 99 [Skogan, "Asymmetry"]; Wesley Skogan, "Citizen Satisfaction with Police Encounters" (2005) 8:3 *Police Quarterly* 298; Robin Engel, "Citizens' Perceptions of Distributive Justice and Procedural Injustice During Traffic Stops with Police" (2005) 42:4 *Journal of Research in Crime and Delinquency* 445; John Hagan, Carla Shedd, & Monique Payne, "Race, Ethnicity, and Youth Perceptions of Criminal Injustice" (2005) 70:3 *American Sociological Review* 381; Ronald Weitzer & Steven Tuch, "Racially Biased Policing: Determinants of Citizen Perceptions" (2005) 83 *Social Forces* 1009 [Weitzer & Tuch, "Racially Biased Policing"]; Tom Tyler & Cheryl Wakslak, "Profiling and Police Legitimacy: Procedural Justice, Attributions of Motive and Acceptance of Police Authority" (2004) 42 *Criminology* 253 [Tyler & Wakslak, "Profiling"]; Dennis Rosenbaum et al, "Attitudes Towards the Police: The Effects of Direct and Vicarious Experience" (2005) 8:3 *Police Quarterly* 343; Ronald Weitzer & Steven Tuch, "Perceptions of Racial Profiling: Race, Class, and Personal Experience" (2002) 40:2 *Criminology* 435.

25   Ben Bradford, "Convergence, Not Divergence? Trends and Trajectories in Public Contact and Confidence in the Police" (2011) 51 *British Journal of Criminology* 179 [Bradford, "Convergence"]; Ben Bradford, Jonathan Jackson, & Elizabeth Stanko, "Contact and Confidence: Revisiting the Impact of Public Encounters with the Police" (2009) 19:1 *Policing and Society* 20; Ben Bowling & Coretta Phillips, *Racism, Crime and Justice* (Harlow, UK: Pearson Education, 2002).

26   Liqun Cao, "Visible Minorities and Confidence in the Police" (2011) 53:1 *Canadian Journal of Criminology and Criminal Justice* 1; Scot Wortley & Akwasi Owusu-Bempah, "The Usual Suspects: Racial Profiling and Perceptions of Injustice in Canada" (2011) 21:4 *Policing and Society* 395 [Wortley & Owusu-Bempah, "The Usual Suspects"]; Scot Wortley & Akwasi Owusu-Bempah, "Crime and Justice: The Experiences of Black Canadians" in Barbara Perry, ed, *Diversity, Crime and Justice in Canada* (New York: Oxford University Press, 2011) 127; Christopher D O'Connor, "Citizen Attitudes Towards the Police in Canada" (2008) 31:4 *Policing: An International Journal of Policing Strategies & Management* 578; Scot Wortley, Ross Macmillan, & John Hagan, "Just Des(s)erts? The Racial Polarization of Perceptions of Criminal Injustice" (1997) 31 *Law and Society Review* 637 [Wortley et al, "Just Des(s)erts?"]; Scot Wortley, "Justice for All? Race and Perceptions of Bias in the Ontario Criminal Justice System: A Toronto Survey" (1996) 38:4 *Canadian Journal of Criminology and Criminal Justice* 439 [Wortley, "Justice for All"].

cial minority groups, including Blacks, Hispanics, and Aboriginals, have much more negative views about the police and the wider justice system than Whites. Furthermore, additional research suggests that much of the racial disparity in perceptions of the criminal justice system can be explained by disproportionate exposure to police stop and search activities. Indeed, a number of studies have now established that people who are frequently stopped and searched by the police have less trust in the justice system and are more likely to view criminal justice institutions as biased. Research also suggests that indirect or vicarious exposure to racial profiling (through the experiences of family members and friends) can also have a negative impact on perceptions of the police, criminal courts, and corrections.[27] Importantly, these same studies suggest that minority groups who have the highest level of involuntary contact with the police tend to have the most negative views of the police and the least trust in the justice system.[28]

Negative perceptions of the justice system and/or a lack of trust in the police have profound consequences for the functioning of the justice system. For example, a number of researchers have found that people with poor perceptions of the justice system are less likely to report crime to the police, cooperate with police investigations, and provide testimony in court.[29] Furthermore, a number of theoretical perspectives, including

---

27 Zhao et al, "Impact," above note 24; Bradford, "Convergence," above note 25; Gabbidon, Higgins, & Potter, "Race, Gender," above note 24; Wortley & Owusu-Bampah, "The Usual Suspects," above note 26; Gibson et al, "Traffic Stops," above note 24; Scot Wortley & Akwasi Owusu-Bempah, "Unequal Before the Law: Immigrant and Racial Minority Perceptions of the Canadian Criminal Justice System" (2009) 10 *Journal of International Migration and Integration* 447 [Wortley & Owusu-Bempah, "Unequal"]; Ronald Weitzer, Steven Tuch, & Wesley Skogan, "Police–Community Relations in a Majority-Black City" (2008) 45:4 *Journal of Research in Crime and Delinquency* 398; Skogan, "Asymmetry," above note 24; Weitzer & Tuch, "Racially Biased Policing," above note 24; Tyler & Wakslak, "Profiling," above note 24; Jeffrey Fagan & Garth Davies, "Street Stops and Broken Windows: *Terry*, Race and Disorder in New York City" (2000) 28 *Fordham Urban Law Journal* 457; Wortley et al, "Just Des(s)erts?," above note 26; Wortley, "Justice for All," above note 26.

28 Wortley & Owusu-Bempah, "Unequal," above note 27.

29 Rod Brunson, "Focussed Deterrence and Improved Police-Community Relations: Unpacking the Proverbial Black Box" (2015) 14:3 *Criminology & Public Policy* 507 [Brunson, "Black Box"]; Tonry, "Less Imprisonment," above note 12; Gibson et al, "Traffic Stops," above note 24; Slocum et al, "Neighborhood," above note 24; Tom Tyler & Jeffrey Fagan, "Legitimacy and Cooperation: Why Do People Help the Police Fight Crime in Their Communities?" (2008) 6 *Ohio State Journal of Criminal Law* 231; Hart et al, "Racial Profiling," above note 19; Rod Brunson, "Police Don't Like Black People:

Tyler's theory of legitimacy and compliance[30] and Sherman's defiance theory,[31] have clearly shown that people with poor perceptions of the justice system are less likely to obey the law.[32] In other words, individuals are better able to justify their criminal actions and neutralize their guilt when they feel that the justice system itself is fundamentally unfair or biased. Furthermore, because of their poor relationship and perception of the police, some minority individuals may feel that they have to take personal responsibility for their safety by resorting to street justice, thus further increasing the level of violence in disadvantaged minority communities.[33] In sum, racial differences in stop and search activities contribute to negative perceptions of the police and justice system among minority civilians. These negative perceptions, in turn, may result in a lack of cooperation with the police and courts and ultimately contribute to minority involvement in crime and violence.

E.   CONCLUSION — A DOUBLE-EDGED SWORD

Although research evidence is sparse and inconsistent, it is logical to assume that police stop and search tactics can sometimes lead to the identification of criminal offenders and could thus reduce crime — at least in the short-term. However, as the discussion above clearly illustrates, racial profiling is not a harmless phenomenon that can be condoned in the name of public safety. Indeed, racial biases with respect to police surveil-

---

African American Young Men's Accumulated Police Experiences" (2007) 6:1 *Criminology & Public Policy* 71; Eric Stewart, "Either They Don't Know or They Don't Care: Black Males and Negative Police Experiences" (2007) 6:1 *Criminology & Public Policy* 123 [Stewart, "Don't Know or Don't Care"]; Tom Tyler, *Why People Obey the Law* (Princeton, NJ: Princeton University Press, 2006) [Tyler, *Why People Obey*]; Ben Brown & WR Benedict, "Perceptions of the Police: Past Findings, Methodological Issues and Policy Implications" (2002) 25:3 *Policing: An International Journal of Police Strategies and Management* 543.

30   Tyler, *Why People Obey*, above note 29.

31   Lawrence Sherman, "Defiance, Deterrence and Irrelevance: A Theory of Criminal Sanction" (1993) 30 *Journal of Research on Crime and Delinquency* 445.

32   Scot Wortley & Julian Tanner, "Money, Respect and Defiance: Justifying Gang Membership in a Canadian City" in Frank van Gemert, Dana Peterson, & Inger-Lise Lien, eds, *Street Gangs, Migration and Ethnicity* (London: Willan, 2008) 192; Robert Kane, "Collect and Release Data on Coercive Police Actions" (2007) 6:4 *Criminology & Public Policy* 773; Tyler & Wakslak, "Profiling," above note 24.

33   Stewart, "Don't Know or Don't Care," above note 29.

lance activities can have a hugely detrimental impact on both minority communities and the operation of the criminal justice system.

It is these social consequences that have led many to call for the elimination of "carding" in Ontario. We must be careful what we ask for. To begin with, the elimination of carding does not mean the elimination of police stop and search tactics. A benefit of the current carding system is that the police actually document the street checks that they engage in. It is this documentation that has convinced many people that racial profiling is a problem that deserves policy attention. Would the public be as concerned with racial profiling if the contact card data did not exist? To ensure transparency and accountability, future policy must ensure that the Ontario police are required to record information on all proactive stops, not just those that are important to the development of a contact-driven, intelligence-based dataset. The police should be required to document the personal characteristics of all the civilians they stop (age, gender, race/ethnicity, address, etc.), the reason for the stop, the location of the stop, the date and time that the stop occurred, and the length of the encounter. Any actions taken during the stop should also be documented. Did the officer request ID? Did they conduct a record check? Did they conduct a search? Finally, officers should be required to document the outcome of the stop: did the stop result in an arrest, a citation, or a warning? Did the stop produce information helpful to an ongoing police investigation? Such information will help to investigate the effectiveness of police stop and search tactics and the possible impact they have on the general public. Without such data collection requirements it is quite possible that police stop and search activities will "go underground" and become even less transparent than they are now. Without official stop data, how police treat people from different racial and social backgrounds will become increasingly difficult — if not impossible — to document.

At the same time we must not completely handcuff the police. We must remember that minority communities sometimes suffer from violence and, like all people, desire police protection when it is needed. Arbitrary police stops, nonetheless, must be dramatically reduced. The use of documented police stops to evaluate officer performance is a failed practice. In cities like New York and Toronto such policies dramatically increased the number of stops being conducted, diminished the usefulness of these encounters, and greatly damaged police-community relations. A more targeted, community-driven approach is required.

The implementation of focused deterrence strategies is one possible solution. Proponents argue that focused deterrence strategies can reduce serious violence while simultaneously improving the often-strained relationship between the community and the police. To begin with, focused deterrence directly involves community leaders, social service providers, and regular citizens in the planning and implementation of violence-prevention initiatives. Partnerships between the police and community improve the transparency of law enforcement activity and provide local residents with both a voice and a role in crime prevention work. By using various analytical tools — including community stakeholders — to identify individuals, groups, and gangs central to local crime problems, these initiatives are highly focused on very high-risk people. In other words, they do not subject law-abiding citizens to indiscriminate police surveillance and investigation. Police also make concerted efforts to communicate with targeted individuals and warn them of the consequences of continued criminal behaviour. They are also made aware of community-based programs and services that will help them exit the criminal lifestyle. Community members tend to appreciate the fairness of offering youthful offenders the opportunity to change their behaviour rather than simply relying on arrest and prosecution. Finally, focused deterrence recognizes the important link between procedural justice and the perceived legitimacy of the justice system. Targeted offenders are treated with dignity and respect. Preliminary evaluation findings suggest that the focused deterrence approach has been successful at lowering crime rates and improving community confidence in police operations.[34] Such programs could represent the balance between public safety concerns and civil rights that Ontario deserves.

---

34   Nicholas Corsaro & Robin Engel, "Most Challenging of Contexts: Assessing the Impact of Focussed Deterrence on Serious Violence in New Orleans" (2015) 14:3 *Criminology & Public Policy* 471; Brunson, "Black Box," above note 29; Kenneth Land, "Something That Works in Violent Crime Control: Let the Focused Deterrence and Pulling Levers Programs Roll with Eternal Vigilance" (2015) 14:3 *Criminology & Public Policy* 515.

CHAPTER 12

Community Engagement in Policing

As a Dialogic Tool for Combating Racial Profiling

LORNE FOSTER & LESLEY JACOBS*

A. INTRODUCTION

Racial profiling by police has emerged as one of the most pressing concerns for members of racialized communities across Canada. Police services are struggling to respond to these concerns, seeking to balance, on the one hand, uneasiness about admitting that these concerns are genuine and the culpability implications for their members, and, on the other hand, taking seriously the rights of racialized Canadians in a context where the mandate of these services is to serve and protect all citizens.

This chapter advances the idea that community engagement can be an effective way to combat racial profiling and promote bias-neutral policing, both in terms of listening to the concerns of racialized Canadians, and as a strategy to help police officers better understand those concerns.

Community engagement theory is an approach to public administration that places the citizen at the centre of policy-makers' considerations, not just as a target, but also as an agent. Fundamental to any consideration of citizen engagement in policy-making and the design of public services is the recognition that the citizens in a democratic society have both rights and duties, and that democratic governance provides opportunities for citizens to participate actively in shaping their world. Community engagement theory recognizes the importance of the collaborative involvement of all stakeholders, including the marginalized and

---

* Lorne Foster is a professor of public policy and equity studies, as well as co-chair, Race, Inclusion and Supportive Environments, York University. Lesley Jacobs is a professor of law & society and political science, as well as the director of the Institute for Social Research, York University.

voiceless, to serve as a catalyst for problem solving and progressive social change.[1] This theory presumes a mutuality of influence and purpose that plays a vital role in advancing both the quality of governing practice and sustainable community development. Concepts such as "co-production" and "co-creation" have emerged to describe this systematic pursuit of sustained collaboration between government agencies and state actors like the police, with communities and individual citizens. Methodologically this requires a two-way, bidirectional approach to engagement that validates reciprocity and pluralism, and empowers all cultural voices within and outside state agencies, including policing, in goal setting, problem solving, decision making, and community building.

In policing, two-way engagement preserves the public role expectations of modern police as both "crime fighters" and "public servants." In this connection, community engagement and collaboration has a role to play beyond the law enforcement side of the profession. Attention to the public service values — such as respect for democracy, respect for diversity, and respect for professional ethics and integrity — is essential to a high-performing police organization that aspires to be transparent, accountable, and coherent in its policies and practices.

However, many police agencies have come increasingly to view their involvement with community engagement in a pragmatic rather than democratic lens. Community engagement has been predominately developed and utilized on the "crime fighter" side of policing, as opposed to the "public servant" side. Here, community engagement and partnerships aim at conscripting citizens into police enforcement goals and ground rules, and are considered valuable for prioritizing police administration problems and deployment planning. The crime fighting values of crime control and public order maintenance have taken precedence over the public service values that elevate democratic citizenship rights: respect for multicultural diversity and professional integrity and excellence (i.e., conducting business in a manner that will bear the closest public scrutiny).[2] Community engagement strategies emphasizing the performance goals of public service — including the balanced distribution of equitable services to growing multicultural communities and neutralizing police bias in an environment with multiple publics — has not as readily been embraced.

---

1   Anantha Kumar Duraiappah et al, *Have Participatory Approaches Improved Capabilities?* (Winnipeg: International Institute for Sustainable Development, 2005), online: www. iisd.org/pdf/2005/economics_participatory_approaches.pdf.

2   Canada, Treasury Board, *Values and Ethics Code for the Public Service* (Ottawa: Treasury Board of Canada Secretariat, 2003).

This chapter examines how the development of police policy-making and service design might benefit from thoroughgoing engagement with citizens and community groups. It argues that to effectively combat racial profiling and other forms of racial discrimination, and promote fair and impartial policing, modern police agencies should look for opportunities to utilize two-way community engagement on both sides of the protect and serve equation. Doing so can add more coherence to police service operations and contribute to a more dynamic understanding of professional policing in a diverse citizen democracy.

To ground the analysis, a two-way interactive model of community engagement is included through a case study of the Ottawa Police Service (OPS) Traffic Stop Race Data Collection Project (TSRDCP). This project stems from a settlement with the Ontario Human Rights Commission (OHRC) in 2013 in a case involving a racial profiling complaint against the OPS by a young Black man.[3] The authors both led the expert research team that designed and undertook the project.[4]

B. COMMUNITY ENGAGEMENT MOVEMENT IN MODERN POLICING

The concept of community engagement has become increasingly prominent in Canadian policing over the last few decades. Initial thinking around what effective community engagement would look like for Canadian police services appeared in a 1991 discussion paper from the solicitor general of Canada titled *A Vision of the Future of Policing in Canada: Police-Challenge 2000.*[5] In the same way as the traditionally paramilitary administration of policing came to be known as the "thin blue line" against crime, the solicitor general of Canada argued that community-based policing should

---

3   For a detailed description, see Ontario Human Rights Commission (OHRC), News Release, "Ottawa Police Agree to Collect Race-Based Data" (4 May 2012), online: www. ohrc.on.ca/en/news_centre/ottawa-police-agree-collect-race-based-data; Ottawa Police Service (OPS), "Traffic Stop Race Data Collection Project," online: www.ottawapolice.ca/ en/news-and-community/Traffic-Stop-Race-Data-Collection-ProjectTSRDCP.asp.

4   For a detailed description and results, see Lorne Foster, Lesley Jacobs, & Bobby Siu, "Race Data and Traffic Stops in Ottawa, 2013–2015: A Report on Ottawa and the Police District" (2016), online: www.ottawapolice.ca/en/about-us/resources/.TSRDCP_York_ Research_Report.pdf.

5   See Solicitor General of Canada, *A Vision of the Future of Policing in Canada: Police-Challenge 2000* (Ottawa: Solicitor General Canada, 1990).

be called the "new blue line."[6] This new community-based model of policing emphasized increased contact between the police and communities, organized around community engagement practices and outreach initiatives.

While traditional paramilitary conceptualizations of law enforcement emphasized a reactive approach to delivering goods and services, in which officers respond to calls for service from the public, government authorities and policing leadership began using the terms *engagement* and *participation* to theorize a proactive approach to interacting with community partners in order to address local order maintenance problems.[7] This new community policing philosophy emphasized a shift away from a strict paramilitary expert model of delivering crime-fighting services in urban Canada and a move towards a more collaborative knowledge model in which community partners play a significant role in the "co-production" of crime prevention between police and community.[8]

Community-based policing represents not so much a new policing alternative as a reconstitution of the original approach to public policing practised in eighteenth century England.[9] The central principle underlying community-based policing is that it involves a partnership between the community and its police[10] in identifying and ameliorating local crime and disorder problems.[11] Crime and disorder, in other words, are the joint property of both the community and the police, and this joint effort is carried out within an interactive, cooperative, and reciprocal relationship. Modern community policing is a philosophy that centres on the

---

6   Ontario, Ministry of the Solicitor General and Correctional Services & Canada, Department of the Solicitor General, *Community Policing: An Introduction to the Philosophy and Principles of Community Policing* (Ottawa: Supply and Services Canada, 1991); Ontario, Ministry of the Solicitor General and Correctional Services & Canada, Department of the Solicitor General, *Neighbourhood Foot Patrol: What It Is and How To Do It* (Ottawa: Supply and Services Canada, 1993).

7   Robert C Ankony, "The Impact of Perceived Alienation on Police Officers' Sense of Mastery and Subsequent Motivation for Proactive Enforcement" (1999) 22:2 *Policing: An International Journal of Police Strategies and Management* 120.

8   David H Bayley & Jerome H Skolnick, *The New Blue Line: Police Innovation in Six American Cities* (New York: The Free Press, 1986).

9   John Howard Society of Alberta, *The Role of Police* (1997), online: www.johnhoward. ab.ca/pub/C52.htm.

10   Dennis P Rosenbaum & Arthur J Lurigio, "An Inside Look at Community Policing Reform: Definitions, Organizational Changes, and Evaluation Findings" (1994) 40:3 *Crime and Delinquency* 299.

11   Randolph M Grinc, "Angels in Marble: Problems in Stimulating Community Involvement in Community Policing" (1994) 40:3 *Crime and Delinquency* 437.

involvement of citizens in the design, implementation, and evaluation of law-enforcement programs. As such, it offers a reform agenda that seeks to invest citizens with increasing responsibilities in the co-production of social order.[12] Here community policing means delivering public safety and security services in an equal and reciprocal relationship between police professionals, people using the services, their families, and their neighbours. The key components — community engagement and participation, as well as organizational transformation of the police and problem-solving activities — offer a reconstituted alternative to traditional and reactive policing strategies.

This modern reform agenda, inspired by the solicitor general's discussion paper, marks the official introduction of the concept of community engagement in law enforcement as a new terminology to describe how policing institutions might reform their service activities to better meet public safety needs. By the end of the 1990s, virtually every police force in Canada had incorporated the term *community policing* in their written mandates. This shift from a traditional paramilitary approach to community-based policing philosophy entails an expanded role of the police within the community and the community within policing.

· · ·

In 2010, the Ontario government and the Ontario Association of Chiefs of Police (OACP) released the Ontario Mobilization and Engagement Model for Community Policing (OMEM).[13] The OACP defined community engagement as "police actions that encourage participation of neighbours and citizens in increasing their own and [others'] safety, security and well-being."[14] In conjunction, the OACP also recognized that curbing disorder, fighting crime, and increasing feelings of personal safety require commitment from both the police and the public.[15] Hence, the

---

12   Paul McKenna, *Foundations of Community Policing in Canada* (Scarborough, ON: Prentice Hall Allyn & Bacon Canada, 2000).

13   Vince Hawkes, "Mobilizing and Engaging Your Community To Reduce Victimization and Reinvest Police Resources" (2016) 1:2 *Journal of Community Safety & Well-Being* 21, online: https://journalcswb.ca/index.php/cswb/article/view/11/27.

14   Ontario Association of Chiefs of Police (OACP), "Ontario's Mobilization & Engagement Model of Community Policing" (2016) at 1, online: www.oacp.on.ca/Userfiles/Files/NewAndEvents/CrimePreventionCampaign/COMMUNITY%20POLICING%20WHEEL-2.pdf.

15   Akwasi Owusu-Bempah, "Community Policing Strategies" in Roy McMurtry & Alvin Curling, eds, *Review of the Roots of Youth Violence: Literature Reviews* (Toronto: Government of Ontario, 2008) vol 5 at 270.

idea of community engagement and participation is now firmly set within an agenda for public safety and public protection, underscoring law enforcement and crime suppression.[16] This is formulated as a commitment to shared responsibility for safety, within the OACP definition of community engagement, and is associated with three strategic goals: engaging, mobilizing, and supporting communities; building sustainable strategic and collaborative partnerships; and prioritizing and addressing risk activities in communities and neighbourhoods in a collaborative manner.[17]

While community-based policing has always been a facet of policing in Canada, it is clear that it is now integral to long-term, service-level priorities and key strategic decisions. Involving the public and enlisting the assistance of community members in an order maintenance agenda allows for more flexibility in response to emerging law enforcement challenges. From a crime control perspective, community involvement and information sharing is a "value added" to the scope of policing that can be a relatively cost-effective means in many cases for improving external problem solving. Accordingly, community policing and engagement tools have been "mainstreamed" — becoming part of core police work, no longer confined to specialist teams or one-off programing.

C. PARTICIPATORY COMMUNITY DEVELOPMENT

1) The Pragmatic Dimension of Police-Community Engagement

The historical trajectory of policing in Canada and other democratic societies is informed by "participatory community development theory"[18] and the notion that modern police services are state actors that have reached their limits in problem solving. One aspect of this theory holds that in "global modernity" the imperative for participation and stakeholder involvement is growing because our major institutions are stretched thin in their ability to resolve complex social problems.[19] A modern state institution like policing cannot be successful without engaging the rest of the community in police organizational development and problem solving.

---

16   Herman Goldstein, *Problem-Oriented Policing* (Philadelphia: Temple University Press, 1990).

17   Ottawa Police Service, "2016–2018 Business Plan" (2015), online: www.ottawapolice.ca/en/news-and-community/20132015-Business-Plan.asp.

18   Denis Goulet, *Development Ethics: A Guide to Theory and Practice* (New York: Apex Press, 1995).

19   Arif Dirlik, *Global Modernity: Modernity in an Age of Global Capitalism* (2003) 6:3 *European Journal of Social Theory* 275.

Globalization adds a pragmatic dimension to police-community engagement. In today's world, the local and global are inextricably linked. Modern police are now exposed to local expressions of global geopolitics that sharpen the policing focus on crime control and disorder and precipitate trends towards a "surveillance society."[20] The changing nature of crime and elevated security threat levels post-9/11 have caused police services in Canada as well as the United States to seek methods that steer or nudge citizens in directions of security risk containment, or a "securitization paradigm,"[21] to address what is viewed as a "crisis of violence" within many recent and long-standing communities.[22] While some researchers argue that monitoring and controlling minority populations has always been a feature of police work, in the new world order, new fears of "the other," new "suspect populations," and new tools intended to control them have arisen in the face of instability associated with worldwide demographic shifts.[23]

The most marked advantage of police-community engagement and partnerships to date has been restricted to monitoring, tracking, and managing what police are or are not doing in relation to the emerging patterns of crime in the post-9/11 security ecosystem. On the enforcement side, community engagement is central to proactive strategies for neighbourhood watch, rapid response, crime detection, crime rates, and other tactics aimed at crime and public safety problems.

Globalization has led to trends in law enforcement towards intelligence-led policing (ILP) and problem-oriented policing (POP) — both in terms of risk analytics and assessment, and in terms of police case management systems.[24] This evidence-based approach, along with other leveraging of advanced technologies and strategic community policing partnerships, has helped to inform the crime fighting side of the profession. However, the public servant side of policing — in terms of the quality of officer performance and service outcomes — is often only weakly informed by evidence or actual community engagement. Outside of intermittent public

---

20   David Lyon, *Surveillance Society: Monitoring Everyday Life* (Buckingham, UK and Philadelphia: Open University Press, 2001).

21   Peter Hough, *Understanding Global Security*, 3d ed (London: Routledge, 2013).

22   Owusu-Bempah, "Community Policing Strategies," above note 15.

23   Leanne Weber & Benjamin Bowling, *Stop and Search: Police Power in Global Context* (New York: Routledge, 2012).

24   See Steve Darroch & Lorraine Mazerolle, "Intelligence-Led Policing: A Comparative Analysis of Organizational Factors Influencing Innovation Uptake" (2013) 16:1 *Police Quarterly* 3.

surveys conducted by some police services in Ontario every three to four years, such as those of the Windsor and Ottawa police, very little systematic evidence has emerged regarding public confidence in the police integrity and fair dealings with citizens.[25]

Community engagement is now a central consideration of all policing policy discourses in Canada and other developed societies. The effort of modern governments and police administrators has legitimized the community engagement movement in policing across the country as a logical response to social volatility and an important delivery system for integrated crime control services. The primary strategic objective has been to mobilize the willing cooperation of Canada's multicultural communities in the task of securing observance of laws. Pragmatic police-community engagement is designed to use a volunteer public and an auxiliary army to fill in the efficiency gaps and supplement the limitations of the paramilitary model of policing in a complex and diverse society. Contemporary intelligence-led policing has adopted the community-based policing model as a pragmatic external problem-solving strategy in many areas of crime control and prevention, public safety, and order maintenance. In this police-driven mode, community engagement and strategic partnerships are a rational approach to help fulfill the top-down administrative goals of police senior management.

2) The Democratic Dimension of Police-Community Engagement

Community development theory, however, also holds that as well as serving a pragmatic function, participation by citizens in the governance of their society is the bedrock of a deliberative democracy. Community engagement in policing is not only about order maintenance; it is about the empowerment of citizens. Free participation in decision making is essentially an ethical prerequisite of social development. As a broad principle, free participation in society's development implies that the "good society" requires popular mobilization of a kind that the top-down management recommended by the Ontario Association of Chiefs of Police has thwarted. The OACP's call for strategic partnerships for the "co-production" of public safety and security is a police-driven innovation that falls short of

---

25   See, for example, Ottawa Police Service, "2015 Public Survey on Policing Services" (2015), online: www.ottawapolice.ca/en/news-and-community/2015-Public-Survey-on-Policing-Services.asp; Windsor Police Service (WPS), "Community Satisfaction and Assessment Survey" (September 2013), online: www.police.windsor.on.ca/about/publications/Documents/WPS%202013%20Community%20Assessment%20Report.pdf.

the call for democratic "co-creation." As service production approaches in a policing context, co-production and co-creation are not synonyms for the same thing, but rather represent different points on a continuum of engagement.

Viewing engagement on a continuum acknowledges that in its most comprehensive form, the citizen is at the centre of policy-makers' considerations, not just as target, but also as agent.[26] The aim of comprehensive engagement is to develop policies and design services from the bottom up that respond more effectively to individuals' needs, build community capacities, and are relevant to their circumstances. Here, police-community engagement is reframed to regard the public as citizens whose agency matters and whose right to participate directly or indirectly in decisions that affect them should be actively facilitated. Such an approach honours the fundamental principle of a democratic state — that power is to be exercised through, and resides in, its citizens.[27]

Empowerment is the normative expectation of what Robert Lynd called a "thorough-going democracy" (a society committed throughout to democratic ends).[28] Empowerment fosters greater agency in citizens and communities by allowing them to act on issues that they define as important, which is a goal that everyone has reason to value. Empowerment allows citizens and communities to become agents and not merely beneficiaries of their own development. In this respect, empowerment and participation are deeply complementary and can be considered means and ends, processes and outcomes.[29]

Participatory development is not limited to professionals designing things efficiently for people. In a more thoroughgoing sense, it involves engaging people to think about and design their own futures using their own ingenuity and locally available resources. In practice, this kind of co-creation requires all who are involved to develop empathy, to share, and to accept equal partnership in the creation process. In a policing context, the movement from co-production to co-creation corresponds

---

26 See Sherry R Arnstein, "A Ladder of Citizen Participation" (1969) 35:4 *Journal of the American Planning Association* 216.

27 See Brenton Holmes, "Citizens' Engagement in Policymaking and the Design of Public Services: Executive Summary," Research Paper No 1 (Canberra: Parliament of Australia, Department of Parliamentary Services, 2011).

28 Robert S Lynd, "Power in American Society" in Arthur W Kornhouser, ed, *Problems of Power in American Democracy*, 2d ed (Detroit, MI: Wayne State University Press, 1957) at 6.

29 Jethro Pettit, "Empowerment and Participation: Bridging the Gap Between Understanding and Practice" (Paper delivered at the UNDESA Expert Group Meeting, UN Headquarters, NY, 10–12 September 2012).

to the transition from a one-way communication flow controlled by police authorities to a two-way communication between police and citizen stakeholders, where both are integral to processes and outcomes.

Robert Wallis, the president of the Australian Universities Community Engagement Alliance, argues that meaningful community engagement is more than "community participation, community consultation, community service and community development" and is better defined as "a two-way relationship leading to productive partnerships that yield mutually beneficial outcomes."[30]

Police-citizen engagement activities may be motivated from an administrative management perspective of the police authorities or from a democratic citizenship perspective. From the administrative stance, participation can build public support for police practices. It can educate the public about a law enforcement agency's activities undertaken to safeguard the social order. It can facilitate useful information gathering and dissemination regarding local neighbourhood conditions. It can also illicit community support and cooperation in the battle to suppress crime and maintain order in some at-risk communities. From a democratic citizen viewpoint, participation enables individuals and groups to influence police service decisions in a representational manner. In this respect, police-community engagement is not only about battening down the community hatches in a volatile age; it is also about the extension of citizenship rights. This reflects the desire of a public to cultivate and protect their own well-being.

These different types or possibilities of community engagement in policing depend on the motivation. From a police administration perspective, police-community engagement is a logical approach to solving social order problems. Whereas, from a democratic citizenship perspective, police-community engagement is approached, particularly by have-not citizens, as a means by which they can induce significant social reform and organizational change.

Perversely, police-driven encounters can sometimes function to frustrate the desire of a public to enhance or protect their own well-being. In some cases, police agencies deprive particular groups of the influence they need to protect themselves or indeed to extend protection to other groups that are being disadvantaged. The recurring issues of police use of force and racial profiling in major North American cities, as regularly

---

30   Robert Wallis, "What Do We Mean by 'Community Engagement'?" (Paper delivered at the Knowledge Transfer and Engagement Forum, Sydney, 15–16 June 2006) at 2.

described in major media, is particularly salient.[31] Police-minority tensions in various jurisdictions across North America — only recently from Ferguson, Missouri, to New York, New York, to the Canadian cities of Toronto, Montreal, and Ottawa — suggest that some police and racialized communities are at odds regarding the influence over the police policies and practices affecting their well-being. By participatory development standards, police practices that disadvantage people along racial lines are not as democratic as they might be, and the test of this is that influence over well-being ends up being poorly shared.

From an administrative management perspective, the goal of police-community engagement is the co-production of public safety and security for society. Co-production essentially redefines the relationship between public service professionals and citizens from one of dependency to mutuality and reciprocity. On such an account, citizens in receipt of services are valued resources and collaborators in safeguarding the system rather than mere beneficiaries of its protections. The users of police services are not defined entirely by their needs, but also by what they might contribute to the service efficiencies within the existing and established police-driven agenda.

The underlying and unspoken assumption of the police-driven order maintenance agenda is that an orderly society is a good society. Because of this assumption, police authorities often hugely underestimate the effect of historical mistrust on communities' willingness to engage[32] and miscalculate the depth of that mistrust.[33] This is particularly the case with some racialized communities who have a history of poor relations with the police. Some members of racialized minority groups experience police-community encounters with a great deal of trepidation, like an occupying force exercising territorial control over their beleaguered neighbourhoods. Concerns about stop and search practices and the related policies in Canada regarding street checks or carding have also given rise to major new areas of citizen anxiety over the last few years.[34] This ratcheting up of police-minority tension in urban centres throughout

---

31   See Weber & Bowling, above note 23.

32   Jill DuBois & Susan M Hartnett, "Making the Community Side of Community Policing Work: What Needs To Be Done" in Dennis J Stevens, ed, *Policing and Community Partnerships* (Upper Saddle River, NJ: Prentice Hall, 2002) 1.

33   Wesley G Skogan et al, *CAPS at Ten: Community Policing in Chicago — An Evaluation of Chicago's Alternative Policing Strategy* (Chicago: Illinois Criminal Justice Authority, 2004).

34   Scot Wortley & Akwasi Owusu-Bempah, "The Usual Suspects: Police Stop and Search Practices in Canada" (2011) 21:4 *Policing and Society* 395.

the continent attests to the fact that police can represent an intimidating presence to people of colour, reinforcing social distance rather than closing it. The paradox is that policing policy discourse that seeks to establish a sharper focus on crime control and disorder and propagate a "surveillance society" can actually undermine public trust and therefore be counterproductive to the very goals of public safety and police legitimacy that the authorities are trying to achieve.

Researchers have also challenged the narrow focus of police-driven community engagement programs. Police studies argue that community consultation tends to be passive and serves to legitimize predetermined objectives.[35] One study also highlights the problem of zero tolerance tactics being dressed up as community policing with disparate consequences for some vulnerable and minority groups.[36] The contemporary order maintenance agenda for community policing has allowed for even tighter centralized management of policing using easily measurable performance indicators, such as offences detected. However, evaluating the success of community policing through arrest rates does not fit well with the spirit of the approach, which prioritizes ongoing commitment to reducing local problems and the improved quality of participants' lives. While many people applaud community engagement and outreach, it can be used as a euphemism for an empty ritual instead of a marker of real citizen empowerment. Indeed, this may amount to fairly direct government micromanagement of policing.[37] While the research does not suggest that all police-community participation is manipulative, thoughtful observers agree that the model of policing that developed in the 1990s to the present tends to discourage genuine community participation in policing, particularly among minority ethnic and racialized communities.[38] As such, it constitutes a democratic deficit.

Beyond the organized police-community partnerships that reinforce crime suppression goals and increase a security focus, there is little in the way of organized community feedback to gauge the fairness or assess the professional ethics of police officers in dealing with a multicultural cit-

---

35   Clive G Harfield, "Consent, Consensus or the Management of Dissent? Challenges to Community Consultation in a New Policing Environment" (1997) 7 *Policing and Society* 271.

36   Gary Cordner, "The Survey Data: What They Say and What They Don't Say About Community Policing" in Lorie Fridell & Mary Ann Wycoff, eds, *Community Policing: The Past, Present, and Future* (Washington, DC: Police Executive Research Forum, 2004) 59.

37   Tim Newburn, ed, *Handbook of Policing* (Cullompton, Devon: Willan, 2003).

38   Andy Myhill, *Community Engagement in Policing Lessons from the Literature* (London: National Policing Improvement Agency, 2012) at 12.

izenry. Engagement mechanisms at an equity outcome and performance level — such as community participation in police officer recruitment, performance appraisal and promotion, and/or reviewing of complaints against the police — are beyond the scope of this paradigm.

From a democratic citizenship perspective, the goal of police-community engagement goes through co-production of policing processes to the co-creation of policing outcomes. This not only involves the co-operation of community stakeholder groups to effect police programming, but also the community co-construction of the service experience to suit their local context. Genuine police-community engagement in the co-creation of policies and services requires major shifts in the culture and governance of police agencies. It demands of police the development of new skills as enablers, negotiators, and collaborators. It demands of citizens a willingness to vigorously engage and the resource capabilities needed to participate and deliberate well. This, of course, is a tall order on both sides, but not an impossible undertaking, as we will illustrate below in our case study of the Ottawa Police Service, Traffic Stop Race Data Collection Project (TSRDCP).

D. THE LADDER AND THE PYRAMID OF PARTICIPATION

The term community engagement is typically one-dimensional in practice when, in reality, it can operate at different levels of complexity and involvement. Attempts have been made by researchers to theorize and reconcile various types of public participation.[39] One of the first pioneering typologies to appear was Arnstein's eight-step "ladder of participation" in 1969 (see Figure 12.1).[40]

In this typology, policing engagement and outreach can range from protecting the community (non-participation), to extending and reaching out to it (tokenism), to engaging it in genuine bidirectional relationships and interactions (citizen power). This entails an understanding of engagement on a continuum ranging from the most paternalistic forms of participation to the most participatory.

---

39 Arnstein, above note 26; Elizabeth M Rocha, "A Ladder of Empowerment" (1997) 17:1 *Journal of Planning Education and Research* 31; Desmond M Connor, "A New Ladder of Citizen Participation" (1998) 77:3 *National Civic Review* 249; Michelle Greenwood, "Stakeholder Engagement: Beyond the Myth of Corporate Responsibility" (2007) 74 *Journal of Business Ethics* 315.

40 Arnstein, above note 26.

FIGURE 12.1 Arnstein's Ladder of Public Participation[41]

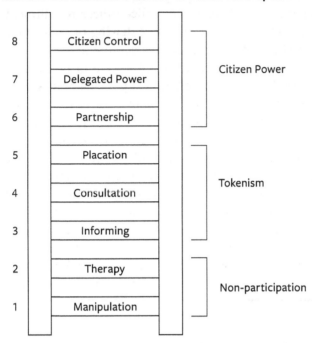

Arnstein defined citizen participation as the redistribution of power that enables the have-not citizens, presently excluded from the political and economic processes, to be deliberately included in the future.[42] Arnstein's ladder, as it is now called, emerged from her work in urban planning in the United States in the 1960s, framed by the issues of race and democratic citizenship rights. It set out to distinguish different levels of participation in relation to levels of, or access to, power in the context of a citizen democracy. As such, her work illuminates "normative" and "empirical" dimensions of community engagement. In the context of democratic society, what people normatively expect of participation is empowerment. Participation is a means of achieving self-determinative control over the factors and decisions that shape citizens' lives and is an exercise of their democratic citizenship rights. How public participation is organized and practiced empirically, however, can take many forms and often falls short of what is called authentic or durable empowerment.[43] Accordingly, Arnstein identified various forms of public partici-

---

41   *Ibid* at 217.

42   *Ibid.*

43   Jay Drydyk, "Durable Empowerment" (2008) 4:3 *Journal of Global Ethics* 231.

pation ranging in intensity from degrees of ritual non-participation, to degrees of tokenism, to degrees of actual citizen power.[44]

The bottom rungs of the ladder are: (1) manipulation and (2) therapy. These two rungs describe levels of "non-participation" that have been contrived by some to substitute for genuine participation. Their real objective is not to enable people to participate in planning or conducting programs, but to enable power-holders to "educate" or "cure" the participants. Rungs 3 and 4 progress to levels of "tokenism" that allow the have-nots to hear and to have a voice: (3) informing and (4) consultation. When proffered by power-holders as the total extent of participation, citizens groups may indeed hear and be heard. But under these conditions they lack the power to ensure that their views will be heeded by the powerful elite. When participation is restricted to these levels, there is no follow-through, no "muscle," hence no assurance of changing the status quo. Rung 5, placation, is simply a higher-level tokenism because the ground rules allow have-nots to advise, but retain for the power-holders the continued right to decide. Further up the ladder are levels of citizen power with increasing degrees of decision-making clout. Citizens can enter into a (6) partnership that enables them to negotiate and engage in trade-offs with traditional power-holders. At the top rungs, (7) delegated power and (8) citizen control, have-not citizen groups obtain the majority of decision-making seats or full managerial power.[45]

Each group of steps corresponds to changes in degrees of community engagement ranging from non-involvement through tokenism to citizen empowerment. As Arnstein herself acknowledged, the ladder is based on a conceptualization that "participation is a categorical term for power."[46] The ladder depicts participation as essentially a power struggle between citizen and ethno-racial communities trying to assert their rights and move up the ladder, and controlling organizations and institutions intentionally or unintentionally limiting their ascent to the top, barring the collective ability of citizens to claim control or power for themselves.

Arnstein was the first researcher to bring questions about the practice of community participation and engagement together with the questions about the quality of citizenship. In her view, two-way interactive citizenship involvement is important to the quality of life and society in several ways. It aids social cohesion and fosters social capital, it makes for more effective planning and delivery of public goods and services, and, perhaps most importantly, it is a right that is justified as an exercise of democratic citizenship.

---

44 Arnstein, above note 26 at 223.
45 *Ibid.*
46 *Ibid* at 216.

From the start, Arnstein recognized that the ladder of citizen control participation is an ideal type and heuristic device that does not correspond to any specific situation but rather needs to be re-addressed in every encounter. However, as an analytic typology, it helps to illustrate the point often missed: that there are significant gradations of community engagement in the context of a citizen democracy. Knowing these gradations makes it possible to cut through the hyperbole to understand the increasingly strident demands for participation from the marginalized and have-nots as well as the gamut of confusing responses from the elite power-holders. As such, the true import of this typology is that it provides a nuanced and dimensional understanding of the extent to which public participation can influence the relationship between differentiated communities and state agencies or similar authorities and how it can increase trust and boost citizen involvement and willingness to participate.[47]

1) The Police-Community Engagement Pyramid

In police studies, Andy Myhill turned Arnstein's ladder into a pyramid to depict the fact that the bulk of community engagement initiatives designed and offered by police agencies are conducted at the bottom rungs of the hierarchy.[48]

On the police-community engagement pyramid, an *information threshold* refers to a process of gathering and conveying knowledge for public benefit and well-being, while an *empowerment threshold* refers to the process of enabling public and community groups to increase their control over the factors and decisions that are relevant to their circumstances and influence the quality of their lives. At the empowerment end of the spectrum, communities increase their assets and attributes and build capacities to gain access, partners, networks, and/or a voice in order to gain control. It assumes that people are their own assets and the highest role of police-community partnerships is to catalyze or facilitate the community in acquiring power.

Myhill reviewed the research literature in the field in regard to the consistency of evidence to support the potential benefits of police-community engagements from an information to empowerment threshold — extending from reduced crime, reduced disorder, increased feelings of safety, improved police-community relations and community perceptions, and greater community capacity to changing officer attitudes and

---

47 *Ibid.*
48 Myhill, above note 38 at 1–111.

behaviour.[49] The review found that the majority of people will be situated at the bottom information-gathering/disseminating threshold of the hierarchy should they choose to be engaged at all. In addition, there are likely to be citizens and communities who do not even gain a basic level of reassurance from interaction with the police.

It can be argued that Myhill's contribution to Arnstein's ladder is that the pyramid adds a sense of scale as well as depth perception to police-community engagement. The police-community engagement pyramid reflects the fact that police-community engagements are dominated by police-driven interests in "information gathering" for order maintenance purposes. This engagement does not empower marginalized and have-not citizens, nor is it compelled to act upon the outcome of community contributions. Hence, much of the democratic potential and possibility for enriching police-community relations remains untapped.

FIGURE 12.2   A Typology of Community Engagement for Policing[50]

	PROMISE TO CITIZENS	PROMISE TO CITIZENS
Empowerment	You can take the final decision unless there is a clear jutsification preventing this	Public-initiated, police-supported, problem-solving initiatives
Partnership/cooperation	We will use your help, advice and expertise to the maximum possible extent	Local action meetings; crime audits; special constabulary; volunteering
Strategic consultation	We will keep you informed, adopt your priorities if possible, and provide feedback	A range of consultation methods, tailored to needs of citizens and communities
Monitoring/accountability	We will be transparent and accountable for the service we provide you	Independent Advisory Groups; citizen monitoring of police complaints process
Information/reassurance	We will make readily available balanced, objective information at a local level	A range of information channels, tailored to needs of citizens and communities

---

49   *Ibid* at 2.
50   *Ibid* at 18.

E. IMPLEMENTATION COMPLEXITIES AND QUALITATIVE DIMENSIONS OF ENGAGEMENT

Studies in various private and public sectors have also criticized Arnstein's typology over the years for the premise that community engagement and participation is a hierarchy, and the implication that those vulnerable or minority communities at the bottom of the ladder should be encouraged to progress towards the top.[51] The main idea driving this critique is that, contrary to the Arnstein ladder, citizen control is not the optimum form of participation, but rather just one policy goal among many. Moreover, the idea of "citizen control" participation is unsustainable and problematic. While large numbers of people may relish the opportunity to take part in decision making at revolutionary moments, what they prefer in the long term is not to replace leaders and officials but rather to hold them accountable in ways that allow the people to get on with their lives. This criticism raises the issue of the potential multitude of situational interests that actors may have in engagement, while de-emphasizing the citizenship values and power relationships that generate these interests in the first place.

Other researchers have found that different people will be comfortable at varying points along a continuum of participation,[52] with perhaps only a few having the skills, willingness, and time to sit at the more intensive end.[53] David Wilcox, for instance, retained the notion of a ladder (information, consultation, deciding together, acting together, supporting) but suggested added-on stages of participation, which may vary by different interests of stakeholders.[54] Kevin Collins and Ray Ison suggest it is time to jump off the ladder all together, and they propose a version of "social learning" (rather than participation) as a paradigm for the theory and practice of policy-making.[55] Over the years, various attempts to critique Arnstein's ladder tend to highlight the differentiated interests and implementation complexities of community engagement, while ignoring or challenging the necessity of its qualitative dimensions.

---

51   Kevin Collins & Ray Ison, "Dare We Jump off Arnstein's Ladder? Social Learning as a New Policy Paradigm" (Paper delivered at the Proceedings PATH (Participatory Approaches in Science & Technology) Conference, 4–7 June 2006, Edinburgh).

52   Patrick Bishop & Glyn Davis, "Mapping Public Participation in Policy Choices" (2002) 61:1 *Australian Journal of Public Administration* 14.

53   Chris Hayward, Lyn Simpson, & Leanne Wood, "Still Left out in the Cold: Problematizing Participatory Research and Development" (2004) 44:1 *Sociologica Ruralis* 95.

54   David Wilcox, *The Guide to Effective Participation* (Brighton: Partnership Books, 1994).

55   Collins & Ison, above note 51.

In police studies, for instance, there is a clear consensus that the implementation problems of community engagement have the potential to impact negatively on some communities or individuals, regardless of goodwill or intentions.[56] Poor implementation or the implementation failure of engagement is recognized as a pervasive problem with damaging effects.[57] This could happen through partner agencies, not managing community expectations adequately, or from sections of the community seeking to co-opt the police against others. Implementation deficiencies have been documented in areas such as performance management, tailoring and local flexibility, training and capacity building, partnering capacity, and resource allocations. Major community policing projects, programs, and strategies have generally suffered from at least some degree of implementation failure.[58] Studies constantly reveal shortcomings in implementation of engagement and problem solving.[59] Poorly implemented community engagement has been found to have the potential to be more damaging than not engaging at all.[60] The upshot is the ability of police agencies to implement effective and sustained engagement at an organizational level remains unproven.[61]

1) The Difference Between Implementation and the Quality of Engagement

From the start, Arnstein recognized a crucial distinction between the implementation and the quality of community participation. How well public participation can influence the relationship between minority communities and police agencies, and how it increases trust and boosts people's willingness to participate, are issues that go beyond the complexities of program implementation to the quality of citizenship.

Putting a wide range of processes on the axis of citizen power cuts straight through the complexities of organizing practices to the critical values at hand. The problem of determining what form or forms participation should take is not a merely pragmatic political problem, nor is it purely an implementation challenge for empirical social research. It is also, as Arnstein insists, a problem of normative ethics. Democratic principles

---

56 Myhill, above note 38 at 47.
57 *Ibid* at 2.
58 *Ibid* at 51.
59 Cordner, above note 36.
60 Myhill, above note 38 at 47.
61 *Ibid* at 3.

and values provide the ethical context for all engagement, even when the individual interests within are wide-ranging and differentiated.

Arnstein advocated for citizen control as a strategic principle of societal development and growth. For Arnstein, community engagement processes reach peak performance through citizens democratically exercising normative judgments as to how engagement goals are to be pursued. She was especially prophetic in proposing one particular ethical value: that community engagement in its highest form should serve to allow people to "induce significant social reform which enables them to share in the benefits of the affluent society."[62] Fundamental to this principle, the have-nots and marginalized are enabled in becoming agents, and not mere beneficiaries, of their own sustainable development.[63] As Narayan has noted, this lies at the bottom of what people mean now, five decades later, when what they expect of participation is "empowerment"[64]

Arnstein's ladder of citizen participation reveals that much "participation" does little to broker a reassignment of power and empowerment. In policing, as Myhill maintained, the majority of police-community engagement initiatives are situated at the bottom information-gathering and analytics threshold of the engagement hierarchy, in support of modern trends towards intelligence-led policing (ILP) and problem-oriented policing (POP) models. However, in contemporary Canadian society, the historical imperative of multicultural democracy and participatory community development demands a more equal power relationship where communities are "co-creators" of policies and practices, and the police "empower" residents to take control of their own neighbourhoods and the issues that impact them.[65]

. . .

In the final sections of the chapter, a model for this type of bidirectional police-citizen engagement is provided in the case study of the Ottawa Police Service (OPS) Traffic Stop Race Data Collection Project (TSRDCP). Citizen empowerment, particularly empowering racially marginalized citizens, is at the core and not on the periphery of this in-

---

62   Arnstein, above note 26 at 216.

63   Denis Goulet, *Development Ethics: A Guide to Theory and Practice* (New York: Apex Press, 1995).

64   Deepa Narayan, ed, *Measuring Empowerment: Cross-Disciplinary Perspectives* (Washington, DC: World Bank, 2005) at 4.

65   Lori Fridell, "The Defining Characteristics of Community Policing" in Fridell & Wycoff, eds, above note 36 at 1.

itiative. The TSRDCP provides an example of how to use community engagement to drive co-creation among police and racialized communities and enhance our citizen democracy.

F. OTTAWA'S TRAFFIC STOP RACE DATA COLLECTION PROJECT

The lack of reliable race data first received serious public attention with respect to concerns about police racial profiling in the late '90s in Canada.[66] This has led to a mounting call for stabilized relations between the police and racialized communities through evidence-based policy solutions.

The Traffic Stop Race Data Collection Project (TSRDCP) is a police-citizen partnership in the city of Ottawa to obtain reliable race data related to police-citizen encounters, and to inform professional standards of fair and impartial policing. The TSRDCP is the result of a settlement agreement between the Ottawa Police Services Board (Board) and the Ontario Human Rights Commission (OHRC) in 2013, stemming from a case involving a racial profiling complaint against the Ottawa Police Service (OPS) by a young Black man named Chad Aiken.[67] The project required police officers to record their perception of the driver's race, by observation only, for traffic stops over a two-year period from June 2013 to June 2015. This undertaking resulted in the largest race-based data collection project in Canadian policing history.[68]

Prior racial profiling studies in the United States and the United Kingdom suggest the two common and important goals of bidirectional police and minority community partnerships are (1) to create mutual understanding between police and the community about racial profiling; and (2) to provide a forum for each group to listen to the other's concerns. If the partnership is successful, then a third goal can be achieved: to develop working relationships that will arrive at joint solutions for neutralizing police racial bias.[69]

---

66 Some important initial cases shaping the substantive equality lens for racial profiling in the criminal justice system include: *R v Brown*, 2003 CanLII 52142 (Ont CA); *R v Richards* (1999), 120 OAC 344 (CA); *Peart v Peel Regional Police Services*, 2003 CanLII 42339 (Ont SCJ).

67 CBC News, "Ottawa Police Racial-Profiling Settlement Questioned" *CBC News* (4 May 2012), online: www.cbc.ca/news/canada/ottawa/ottawa-police-racial-profiling-settlement-questioned-1.1199823.

68 Full information, including the agreement, project updates, community consultation files, and the final report are available online: ottawapolice.ca/race.

69 Karl Lamberth et al, *Practitioners Guide for Addressing Racial Profiling* (Boston: Institute on Race and Justice, Northeastern University, 2005) at 6.

In order to achieve the three engagement goals, the Ottawa Police Service (OPS) incorporated the TSRDCP within its long-standing strategic community engagement platform, called Partnership in Action (PIA). Over the last decade the PIA strategic community engagement mandate has guided the OPS in identifying and building upon community involvement and partnership opportunities within policing in areas such as victim assistance, youth issues, and gang problems. Beyond the mobilization of particular communities, the PIA is concerned with how to link micro-assets to the macro-environment for sustainable community development within a pre-determined public safety and security framework.

The OPS is a Canadian service that has identified community engagement and input as a core component of quality policing services. It is considered one of the "broad priorities that will assist the Service in responding to the current and future challenges, issues and pressures facing the community and the OPS."[70] It is embedded in all the major organizational documents from the OPS business plan[71] and budget development draft[72] to the OPS Mission Statement,[73] all of which emphasize the development of community-based problem-solving partnerships at the neighbourhood level. As a police lever, it is a strategy directed towards expanding police organizational capabilities by engaging the rest of the community in policing solutions.

This fits well with a "top-down" management style that controls and dictates the terms of community engagement and partnerships for the purpose of more efficiently achieving policing goals. Community engagement is an important part of an information gathering process to inform police senior management decisions for maximizing external problem-solving and order maintenance. On the operational side, the OPS model of community engagement is considered highly adaptable and can easily be refocused to deal with emerging policing and community concerns.[74] Since community policing in the OPS is regarded as crucial to the statutory duties, sworn officers in Ottawa have long been accustomed

---

70 Ottawa Police Service, "A Plan Where Everyone Matters: 2013–2015 Business Plan" (2013) at 8, online: www.ottawapolice.ca/en/news-and-community/resources/2013_2015BusinessPlan.pdf [OPS Business Plan].

71 The enhancement of partnerships with the community is one of the four priorities of the OPS Business Plan, *ibid* at 11–20.

72 Ottawa Police Service, "Draft Budget" (2016), online: www.ottawapolice.ca/en/news-and-community/resources/Police_2016_draft_budget_book_2.pdf.

73 Ottawa Police Service, "Our Mission, Vision and Values," online: www.ottawapolice.ca/en/About-Us.asp?_mid_=16623.

74 OPS Business Plan, above note 70 at 5.

COMMUNITY DEVELOPMENT

The Mandate of the Community Development Section (CDS) is:

- To develop sustainable partnerships and engagement strategies within the community;
- To work with communities, agencies and members of the organization to identify problems, opportunities and potential solutions;
- To promote trust and confidence in policing by expanding and enhancing educational opportunities related to community policing.

Core Functions:

Partnership In Action (PIA): is the Ottawa Police Service framework for public consultation and wider community engagement. PIA is more than a traditional consultative approach because it aims to identify and build upon community involvement and engagement within policing. Furthermore, it is intended to develop, enhance and maintain strategic partnerships.

Community Policing Development: is the process by which police and other community members, partner to improve community well-being, safety and security through joint problem identification, analysis, response and evaluation. CDS provides ongoing support for OPS Community Police Centres in the areas of community engagement and mobilization, such as the coordination and management of the annual police week.

Community Engagement and Mobilization: is based on community support for whatever the process is trying to achieve. As such CDS provides support for actions and initiatives that police officers take to motivate and support community partners to deal more effectively with the root causes of crime and insecurity in their neighbourhoods. CDS provides expertise and support for police actions that encourage participation of community members, building capacity, and increasing safety, security and well-being.

to police-driven community engagement as a platform that is deeply embedded in all of the OPS policies and directives.

The OPS TSRDCP and racial profiling study is one such adaption, with a difference. The project is a direct outgrowth of existing community-oriented policing efforts and partnerships based on the principle that police should work with their communities on a shared responsibility for safety. However, it goes beyond the established crime suppression and order maintenance format towards community engagement that addresses and influences police performance integrity as well — a move from the usual crime fighting interests to public service values that affirm the transparency, accountability, and coherence of police policies and practices. Here the goal of police-community engagement goes through co-production of policing processes to the co-creation of policing outcomes. This not only involves the cooperation of racialized community stakeholder groups to be involved in police programming, but also the co-construction of the service experience to suit their local context.

For example, the TSRDCP first formed a Community Police Advisory Committee (CPAC) comprised of both sworn police officers and community members. The CPAC community advisors are for the most part selected members from the long-standing Ottawa Police Service Community Police Action Committee known as COMPAC, which in turn is comprised of a coalition of active ethno-racial community members who have regularly consulted and worked with the OPS on other community-policing initiatives. The launching of CPAC leveraged the existing relationships between the community and the OPS, and empowered the advisory committee to serve as a mediator between members of racialized communities concerned about racial profiling and the police.

The Community Police Advisory Committee helped establish the research focus of the TSRDCP, the shape of the research design strategy — down to the fundamental question of what race categories would be in the data field — and the scope of the final analysis and report of findings. The advisory committee had an impact on every stage of the research project, working together with the researchers to develop and refine the methods for data collection and consult on the application and dissemination of research project information.

After an initial "feeling out" process marked by cautious communications, police and community members came together to share experiences and ideas, challenge one another's perspectives on both the police and the community side, and ultimately deepen the discussion about race relations and racial profiling issues in the City of Ottawa.

This fits well with Janet Hutchinson and Michael Huberman's "community of learners" metaphor.[75] In this advisory setting, neither police members nor community members were afforded the luxury or expedience of simply "speaking to the converted" and were often forced to challenge their own taken-for-granted assumptions and beliefs. This stimulated bidirectional and dynamic advisory discussions that produced

---

75 Janet R Hutchinson & Michael Huberman, "Knowledge Dissemination and Use in Science and Mathematics Education: A Literature Review" (1994) 3:1 *Journal of Science Education and Technology* 27.

more substantive research planning and more stakeholder satisfaction with the design outcomes. This bottom-up approach also allows for more experimentation and a better feeling for what is needed at the grassroots level for fair and equitable police practice. What ensued is a fluid and emergent process cultivated and upheld primarily by front line stakeholders.

OPS community engagement before the TSRDCP has had a significant impact on various aspects of crime prevention and safety including programs for neighbourhood watch, violence against women, guns and gangs, and more. What differentiates the TSRDCP from other OPS community engagement initiatives lies in the crossover from a security-based agenda into an equity-based agenda. The TSRDCP extended the vision of community engagement and strategic partnerships beyond the usual parameters of effective law enforcement into areas of service impact and performance, adding more nuance and breadth to the community engagement model. Community engagement in the racial profiling project is a bottom-up approach that turns the lens back on the OPS and provides an opportunity for a kind of institutional self-examination and genuine commitment to progressive organizational change.

1) The Bottom-Up Management of TSRDCP

A "bottom-up" approach to community engagement is one that works from the grassroots: from a large number of people working together, causing a decision to arise from their joint involvement. A decision by a number of racialized groups to collaborate with the police on remedying racial profiling and other biased policing practices is a bottom-up decision. A bottom-up approach produces a series of incremental changes that represent an emergent process cultivated by bidirectional discourse and upheld by front line and everyday life realities.

The TSRDCP embraced a bottom-up management style that relied more on front line and grassroots feedback. Whereas other PIA projects are driven by a top-down engagement model, the TSRDCP is distinguished by a bottom-up engagement model, involving a process where members from all stakeholder groups are invited to participate in every step of the decision-making process. The composition of the advisory committee reinforced the bottom-up approach. Mutual participation allowed managers to communicate goals through milestone planning, and team members were encouraged to come up with the steps needed to reach the milestones on their own. The task performance was up to the advisory committee members and continued involvement throughout the project stages ensured that members felt involved in project development.

Bottom-up management allows all stakeholders and all levels from the grassroots to senior management to become a part of the process and helps make everyone feel invested in a large part of the goal. This was found to help build morale and improve productivity. Members and participants seemed more open to work and strive harder to reach goals and objectives when given the flexibility of finding the ways that work best for them. Bottom-up management styles allow for the full talents of stakeholders to be used. A lower-level employee may have unique insight on how to solve a common problem. Advisory members and members-at-large were provided opportunities to share their ideas about racial profiling and police biases, as well as their solutions. They could also, perhaps, pass them on to others, including front line police officers. This kind of collaboration appeared to improve processes by providing various venues that presented a safe space for working through issues.

2) Building a Two-Way Street

Actualizing effective community engagement requires two-way communication and dialogic consultation. The TSRDCP approach included the following issues for consideration:

- Identify any conflict of interest.
- Make sure that facilitators and scribes used at focus groups and workshops are clear about their role and have been briefed and/or trained.
- Ensure that the venues for the consultation sessions allow maximum participation by assessing the location for access by people with disabilities and by public transport.
- Ensure that privacy and confidentiality guidelines are adhered to in relation to comments collected during the consultation.
- Anticipate and plan for any specific support that may be needed to enable some groups to participate in the consultation.

The range of engagement methods to empower citizens included:[76]

- Project web page updates: ottawapolice.ca/race

---

76   Ottawa Police Service, *Traffic Stop Race Data Collection Project Update: Community Consultation Plan* (23 March 2015), online: http://ottawa.ca/calendar/ottawa/citycouncil/opsb/2013/05-27/item2.htm.

- Project intranet/wiki page updates for OPS members
- Project email box monitoring: racedata@ottawapolice.ca
- Project phone line monitoring
- Project updates to stakeholders and partners
- Project updates/reminders to OPS members
- Ride-alongs with community and media
- Questionnaires
- Community sessions/forums/dialogues
- Project update reports to the police services board
- Feedback and focus group sessions
- Co-host a focus group
- Sign-ups for a ride along with traffic police
- Project updates with feedback/survey mechanisms
- Community participation in quality assurance reviews
- Project update reports to the police board
- COMPAC and CPAC meetings
- OPA-OPS sessions for members
- Social media forums
- Project presentations

A sense of ownership plays a vital role in ensuring community empowerment. The TSRDCP and the research team sought to facilitate a sense of community ownership over the race data project in part to encourage confidence in Ottawa's racialized communities about the reliability of the research process and the data collected to strengthen the validity of the findings. In addition, confidence in the reliability and validity of the race data expedited more evidence-based discussion (over anecdotal and stereotypic experiences) between racialized communities and the Ottawa police. Important steps to facilitate a sense of community ownership were established and put in place.[77]

- Defining clearly the aims and parameters of the consultation.
- Engaging with the key participants and stakeholders in the consultation.
- Choosing the appropriate range of methods to engage all stakeholders in the consultation.
- Using strategies that maximize people's ability to participate.
- Ensuring coordination and avoiding duplication.

---

77 Ottawa Police Service, *Traffic Stop Race Data Collection Project Plan for Ongoing Engagement & Communications* (2 December 2013), online: www.ottawa.ca/calendar/ottawa/citycouncil/opsb/2014/01-27/item2a.pdf.

- Providing regular updates on project progress.
- Informing people about opportunities to provide input and feedback.
- Providing feedback on the outcome of the consultation and resulting decisions to all participants, and to groups with an interest.

These steps enabled the TSRDCP internal management and the researchers to capitalize on the relationships developed with CPAC members to raise the profile of the project, build and maintain interest, raise awareness, and stimulate dialogue on the issues. The result has been that community engagement not only benefited the TSRDCP's pioneering efforts to mine reliable data, it has also generated an important broader discussion about race, evidence-based policy-making, and bias-neutral policing in the city of Ottawa and beyond.

G. CONCLUSION

Participation by citizens in the governance of their society is the bedrock of a thoroughgoing democracy. However, there is an abundance of research literature confirming attempts to incorporate citizen participation in policy-making and service design are rarely productive. This chapter explores the public policy and the public administration of community engagement surrounding some major issues and antinomies, such as implementation versus quality control, public apathy versus service accountability, and administrative efficiencies versus democratic citizenship.

The analysis of this chapter is grounded by the case study of a police-community engagement where citizen empowerment is held up as the "goal" of participation. The TSRDCP is central to the search for bias-neutral policing and racial profiling remedies in the city of Ottawa, and it illustrates how modern policing might benefit from a more thoroughgoing engagement with community stakeholders. Two-way community engagement is used to drive co-creation, both in terms of the process and outcomes of policies and practices. This implies community ownership and action that explicitly aims at social and political change for equity purposes. Community empowerment, particularly empowerment for racially marginalized citizens, is at the core and not on the periphery of this project. This places the TSRDCP community engagement high along the partnership spectrum, as a democratic organizational enhancement.

CHAPTER 13

Ending Racial Profiling

BOBBY SIU[*]

A. INTRODUCTION

The purpose of this paper is to present a model of organizational changes in law enforcement agencies that, upon proper implementation, is expected to end racial profiling in police actions. The paper begins with a brief discussion on the prevalence of racial profiling and why ending it is critical. It is then followed by a presentation of the model with four pillars: strategic leadership, research, human resource management, and stakeholder engagement.

In each of these pillars, selected components with high potential to end racial profiling will be discussed. Specifically, strategic leadership will cover corporate value, policy, and culture; research will cover data collection and analysis on police actions, human resource management, and policing strategies; human resource management will cover staffing, training, and performance management; and stakeholder engagement will cover the engagement of community members and employees.

1) Prevalence of Racial Profiling

There are many ways to look at racial profiling and the literature shows a broad range of definitions. For the working purpose of this paper, racial profiling is defined as a formal or informal policy, strategy, and/or practice implemented by a law enforcement organization or its agents, for reasons

---

[*] Bobby Siu is an adjunct professor of public policy and public administration, York University.

they see fit, to identify individuals based on an association of race with criminality, which results in adverse impacts on racialized minorities.

In Canada, racial profiling had been noted, as early as 1992, by Stephen Lewis in his *Report to the Premier on Racism in Ontario*. The report drew our attention to the experience of racialized minorities (especially African Canadians) in discrimination in the criminal justice system. Such findings were further confirmed by the Commission on Systemic Racism in the Ontario Criminal Justice System (1995), the Association of Black Law Enforcers, and the African Canadian Legal Clinic.[1]

The overrepresentation of Aboriginal peoples as offenders in the criminal justice system has been well documented in the literature.[2] Similar patterns are noted for the Blacks and West Asians.[3] Disproportionate minority contacts by the law enforcement officers have also been noted in the US, Australia, and European countries. After examining police treatment of youth aged twelve to seventeen in Canada, Fitzgerald and Carrington concluded that racially discriminatory policing might be one explanation for disproportionate minority contacts.[4]

---

1   Ontario Human Rights Commission, *Paying the Price: The Human Cost of Racial Profiling: Inquiry Report* (Toronto: Ontario Human Rights Commission, 2003) at 9–10 [*Paying the Price*].

2   Carol LaPrairie, *Dimensions of Aboriginal Over-Representation in Correctional Institutions and Implications for Crime Prevention* (Ottawa: Solicitor General, 1992); Julian V Roberts & Ronald-Frans Melchers, "The Incarceration of Aboriginal Offenders: Trends from 1978 to 2001" (2003) 45 *Canadian Journal of Criminology and Criminal Justice* 211; Karen Beattie, "Adult Correctional Services in Canada, 2004/2005" (2006) 26:5 *Juristat*; Jodi-Anne Brzozowski, Andrea Taylor-Butts, & Sara Johnson, "Victimization and Offending Among the Aboriginal Population in Canada" (2006) 26:3 *Juristat*; Robin Fitzgerald & Peter Carrington, "The Neighbourhood Context of Urban Aboriginal Crime" (2008) 50 *Canadian Journal of Criminology and Criminal Justice* 523.

3   Jim Rankin et al, "Singled Out: An Investigation into Race and Crime" *Toronto Star* (19 October 2002) A1; Scot Wortley, "Justice for All? Race and Perceptions of Bias in the Ontario Criminal Justice System — A Toronto Survey" (October 1996) 38:4 *Canadian Journal of Criminology* 439; Scot Wortley & Julian Tanner, "Data, Denials, and Confusion: The Racial Profiling Debate in Toronto" (July 2003) 45:3 *Canadian Journal of Criminology and Criminal Justice* 367; Scot Wortley & Julian Tanner, "Inflammatory Rhetoric? Baseless Accusations? A Response to Gabor's Critique of Racial Profiling Research in Canada" (July 2005) 47:3 *Canadian Journal of Criminology and Criminal Justice* 581; Nene Ernst Khalema & Jenny Wannas-Jones, "Under the Prism of Suspicion: Minority Voices in Canada Post-September 11" (2003) 23 *Journal of Muslim Minority Affairs* 25.

4   Robin Fitzgerald & Peter Carrington, "Disproportionate Minority Contact in Canada: Police and Visible Minority Youth" (2011) 53 *Canadian Journal of Criminology and Criminal Justice* 449.

Human rights commissions, including the Alberta Human Rights Commission and the Ontario Human Rights Commission, reported allegations of racial profiling (such as police stops, unreasonable questioning, requests for identification, retaining personal information) in the law enforcement field and documented Ontario court cases related to racial profiling.[5] Similarly, the Commission des droits de la personne et des droits de la jeunesse in Quebec has received complaints of racial profiling since 2003, most of them related to police services.[6] Both the human rights tribunals and the courts have repeatedly recognized that racial profiling is systemic in nature and not an isolated incident.

The extent of allegations of racial profiling has been partially quantified by the Ontario Human Rights Commission. In 2007, it had 151 active complaints against 21 different police services with another 19 complaints before the Human Rights Tribunal of Ontario for adjudication. Although the complaints against police services constituted only 4 percent of all active human rights complaints, racial profile was still the largest single theme.[7] "Human rights complaints against police organizations are consistently the largest single sector of human rights complaints in Ontario."[8]

While some racial profiling cases had been formalized as human rights complaints and went through the tribunal process, the perception of racial profiling among diverse groups is much more widespread.

- The Ethno-Cultural Council of Calgary did a study on the perception of ethno-cultural groups and noted that 84 percent of respondents reported that they have personally experienced racial profiling, and 82 percent of them knew at least one person who

---

5   Alberta Human Rights Commission, "Racial Profiling Information Sheet" (2012), online: www.albertahumanrights.ab.ca/Documents/RacialProfiling.pdf; *Paying the Price*, above note 1; Ontario Human Rights Commission, *Submission of the Ontario Human Rights Commission to the Independent Police Review Director's Systemic Review of Ontario Provincial Police Practices from DNA Sampling* (April 2014) [OHRC Submission].

6   Louise Brossard & Evelyne Pedneault, *Racial Profiling and Systemic Discrimination of Racialized Youth: Report of the Consultation on Racial Profiling and Its Consequences — One Year Later: Taking Stock* (Quebec: Commission des droits de la personne et des droits de la jeunesse, 2012) at 9 [Brossard & Pedneault].

7   Shaheen Azmi, "Ontario Human Rights Commission Promotion Activities: The Experience of Responding to Racial Profiling by Police" in Shelagh Day, Lucie Lamarche, & Ken Norman, eds, *14 Arguments in Favour of Human Rights Institutions* (Toronto: Irwin Law, 2014) 305 at 309 [Azmi, OHRC Promotion Activities].

8   Ontario Human Rights Commission, *Human Rights and Policing: Creating and Sustaining Organizational Change* (Toronto: Ontario Human Rights Commission, 2011) at 13 [OHRC, *Human Rights and Policing*].

had experienced racial profiling in the last twelve months. The majority of African Canadians (96 percent) indicated that they had experienced at least one incident of racial profiling in the last year. Complaints about racial profiling from Aboriginal peoples in the Prairie provinces and by South Asians in British Columbia have also been noted.[9]

- Quoting the York University's Institute for Social Research's 1995 survey of over 1,200 adults in Toronto and the Toronto Youth Crime and Victimization Survey (2000) of 3,400 high school students, Wortley and Tanner observed that racialized minorities (especially Blacks) are much more likely to be stopped by police in the streets than their White counterparts.[10]
- A survey of Toronto residents in 2007 by Wortley and Owusu-Bempah concluded that Blacks are more likely to report police stops and searches than other racial minorities, while White and Asian respondents view profiling as a useful tool for fighting crime.[11]

While there are mounting allegations, formal human rights complaints, and research findings on racial profiling, there have been continuous, often heated, debates in the Canadian academic community about the same topic. These debates focused largely on research methodologies and data interpretation, and no consensus has been reached.[12] While these academic debates are instrumental to the advancement of knowledge, they are, to some extent, of peripheral importance in the real world because racial profiling, whether it is perceived or real, is of paramount importance to the public. As many police chiefs in the US have

---

9   Beth Chatten, ed, *Racial Profiling: The Lived Experience of Ethno-Cultural Community Members in Canada* (Calgary: Ethno-Cultural Council of Calgary, 2011) at i & ii.

10 Scott Wortley & Julian Tanner, "Discrimination or 'Good' Policing: The Racial Profiling Debate in Canada" (2004) 1 *Our Diverse Cities* 197 [Wortley & Tanner].

11 Scot Wortley & Akwasi Owusu-Bempah, "The Usual Suspects: Police Stop and Search Practices in Canada" (2011) 21:4 *Policing and Society* 395.

12 Alan D Gold, "Media Hype, Racial Profiling, and Good Science" (2003) 45:3 *Canadian Journal of Criminology and Criminal Justice* 391; Edward Harvey, "An Independent Review of the *Toronto Star* Analysis of Criminal Information Processing (CIPS) Data Provided by the Toronto Police Service (TPS)" (2003), online: www.torontopolice.on.ca/publications/2003.02.20-review/pptpresentation.pdf; Ronald-Frans Melchers, "Do Toronto Police Engage in Racial Profiling?" (2003) 45:3 *Canadian Journal of Criminology and Criminal Justice* 347; Ronald-Frans Melchers, *Inequality Before the Law: The Canadian Experience of "Racial Profiling"* (Ottawa: Royal Canadian Mounted Police, 2006); Ronald-Frans Melchers, "Comment on the Rejoinder of Henry and Tator to Satzevich and Shaffir" (2011) 53:1 *Canadian Journal of Criminology and Criminal Justice* 105.

acknowledged, addressing the public perception and concerns about racial profiling is important irrespective of whether racial profiling actually exists or not because it is imperative that the law enforcement sector restores public trust and improves police-community relations.[13]

B. WHY RACIAL PROFILING SHOULD END

Racial profiling must end because it is illegal, ineffective, offensive, destabilizing, and harmful. Racial profiling:

- Violates human rights legislation
- Is offensive to civil liberty
- Is an ineffective law enforcement strategy
- Heightens racial tensions and destabilizes society
- Has adverse impact on racialized minorities

1) Violation of Human Rights Legislation

Racial profiling violates Article 7 of the *Universal Declaration of Human Rights*, which states that "all are equal before the law and are entitled without any discrimination to equal protection of the law . . . ." It also violates Article 26 of the *International Covenant on Civil and Political Rights*, which states that " . . . the law shall prohibit any discrimination and guarantee to all persons equal and effective protection against discrimination on any ground such as race, colour, sex, language, religion, political or other opinion, national or social origin, property, birth or other status."

On 9 December 2002, the Ontario Human Rights Commission confirmed that racial profiling is a human rights issue and it is contrary to the principles of the Ontario *Human Rights Code*.[14] The *Code* recognizes the actualization of human potential and full citizenship is based on equality and human dignity. The Quebec Human Rights Tribunal confirmed that racial profiling "constitutes a special form of discrimination" that has "the effect of destroying or compromising the right to the recognition and exercise, in full equality, of human rights and freedoms, without distinc-

---

13 *Paying the Price*, above note 1 at 11; Russ Leach, "Addressing Racial Profiling: Creating a Comprehensive Commitment to Bias-Free Policing" (2006) at 153, online: www. theiacp.org/portals/0/pdfs/PCR_LdrshpGde_Part3.pdf [Leach].

14 *Paying the Price*, above note 1 at 1 and 3.

tion, exclusion or preference based on any of the grounds prohibited by the Charter."[15]

2)   Offensive to Civil Liberty

"Racial profiling is . . . offensive to fundamental principles of civil liberties and the Canadian *Charter of Rights and Freedoms*."[16] According to the BC Civil Liberties Association, "racial profiling's adverse effects far outweigh its alleged benefits in all areas where law enforcement or intelligence interact with society, including criminal, immigration and national security contexts and racial profiling undermines fundamental Canadian values."[17]

During its public consultation in 2009, the Commission des droits de la personne et des droits de la jeunesse in Quebec noted that some racial minority members believed that "they do not enjoy the same freedoms as the rest of the population, including the freedom to circulate, to have fun or to get together with other racialized youth. They feel as if they are on the margin of society, and are under scrutiny and targeted when they occupy public spaces."[18]

3)   Ineffective Law Enforcement Strategy

"Racial profiling is . . . ineffective as a law enforcement strategy . . . . "[19] Bourgue et al's study of various profiling strategies and tools used by law enforcement agencies concluded that, in light of "the absence of scientific support for the association between ethnic group membership and criminality and given the direct opposition of racial profiling to the spirit of the [Canadian Human Rights] Act," racial profiling is not justified. "The animosity between the citizens and the State as well as the social stigma

---

15   Brossard & Pedneault, above note 6 at 5.

16   Reem Bahdi, Olanyi Parsons, & Tom Sandborn, "Racial Profiling: BC Civil Liberties Association Position Paper" in Richard Marcuse, ed, *Racial Profiling* (Vancouver: BC Civil Liberties Association, 2010) 31.

17   Marcuse, ed, *Racial Profiling, ibid* at 2.

18   Paul Eid, Johanne Magloire, & Michele Turenne, *Racial Profiling and Systematic Discrimination of Racialized Youth: Report of the Consultation on Racial Profiling and Its Consequences* (Quebec: Commission des droits de la personne et des droits de la jeunesse, 2011) at 24 [*Racial Profiling and Systematic Discrimination*].

19   Bahdi, Parsons, & Sandborn, above note 16.

that would result from profiling constitutes sufficient repercussions to justify this position."[20]

The largest American study on the effectiveness of racial profiling in apprehending criminals was conducted in 1999 by the Department of Justice in which over 1.2 million searches, along with other studies, suggested that, because they are less likely than White people to possess contraband, it is not cost-effective to profile African- or Hispanic-Americans. Some of these studies showed that the racial differences are statistically significant. Consistently, all of these studies showed that racialized minorities are no more likely than White people to carry contraband.[21]

By focusing on racialized minorities, law enforcement agencies have been using precious resources in an unproductive manner. Lambert Consulting reported that after 1998, the customs service of the US Government abandoned racial profiling as a strategy in its searches. This resulted in a reduction of the workload of the previous disproportionate searches among Blacks and Hispanics. The surprising results showed that while the customs service cut its workload of searches by 75 percent of its 1998 level in 2000, the success rates for apprehending criminals among Whites, Blacks, and Hispanics in 2000 were identical with those in 1998. In essence, the searches in 2000 reduced 75 percent of the number of innocent people who would have been subjected to the indignity of a search.[22]

Leitzel, using the findings from American studies, also argued that racial profiling is counterproductive. It does not increase the apprehension of real criminals, as racialized minorities become unwilling to report crime, testify at trials, or convict defendants (when they serve on juries). It induces racialized minorities to disobey the law and makes racialized minorities distrust all police officers irrespective of whether individual police officers racially profile or not.[23]

---

20 Jimmy Bourgue et al, *The Effectiveness of Profiling from a National Perspective* (Ottawa: Canadian Human Rights Commission and the Canadian Race Relations Foundation, 2009).

21 David A Harris, *Profiles in Injustice: Why Racial Profiling Cannot Work* (New York: The New Press, 2002); *Paying the Price*, above note 1.

22 *Paying the Price*, above note 1.

23 Jim Leitzel, "Race and Policing" (March 2001) 38:3 *Society* 38.

4)   Heightening Racial Tensions and Destabilizing Society

Overall, racialized minorities are already more negative in attitude than Whites towards the criminal justice system, and they are less confident than Whites towards the police. Perceptions of racial bias are extensive among Blacks.[24]

The Ontario Human Rights Commission observed that racial profiling increases the level of distrust towards the police and a reluctance to work with law enforcement officers. This is because people are less cooperative with people they do not trust, and mistrust often leads to retaliation to perceived unfairness, which may put law enforcement officers and people at risk. Escalation of racial tension poses safety and security issues for the community and, if left unchecked, such situations may escalate to open conflicts.[25] Similarly, the BC Civil Liberties Association maintained that "racial profiling is a bad policy." It heightens "racial tensions ... by accentuating differences among citizens as a basis for unequal treatment," and it weakens "the fabric of our multicultural democracy."[26]

5)   Adverse Impact on Racialized Minorities

Racial profiling is harmful to racialized minorities, especially their youth segments. The Commission des droits de la personne et des droits de la jeunesse in Quebec consulted close to 150 young persons, their parents, and community representatives on the issue of racial profiling in 2009 and found that "prejudice acts as a driver for the discriminatory intervention or treatment that racialized minorities suffer . . . . The effect of this is not only to affect their confidence in the institutions, but also their self-esteem and their identification with Quebec society."[27] The commission recognized that the adverse impact of racial profiling on youth is greater than other age groups. Its harms could be greater for "their life choices and social integration" and concluded that "Québec cannot allow

---

24   Scot Wortley & Akwasi Owusu-Bempah, "Unequal Before the Law: Immigrant and Racial Minority Perceptions of the Canadian Criminal Justice System" (2009) 10 *Journal of International Migration and Integration* 447; Liqun Cao, "Visible Minorities and Confidence in the Police" (2011) 53:1 *Canadian Journal of Criminology and Criminal Justice* 1.

25   *Paying the Price*, above note 1; OHRC Submission, above note 5.

26   Marcuse, ed, *Racial Profiling*, above note 16 at 3.

27   *Racial Profiling and Systematic Discrimination*, above note 18 at 15.

some of its citizens to lose their trust in its public institutions, or even worse, to feel like foreigners in their own society."[28]

The Ontario Human Rights Commission has documented the adverse impact of racial profiling on individuals, families, communities, and the larger society in Ontario through an inquiry on the experiences of racial profiling that people perceived in a variety of contexts including housing, services, education, and private security. According to the commission, "those who experience profiling pay the price emotionally, psychologically, mentally and in some cases even financially and physically." The psychological effects of racial profiling include post-traumatic stress disorder and other forms of stress-related disorders, and perceptions of race-related threats. Racial profiling makes racialized minority groups feel like second-class members — marginalized, disenchanted, rejected, powerless, helpless, humiliated, and dehumanized — as they are subject to racial injustice at any time and are not in a position to change the situation. In turn, such experience has affected their aspirations, career choice, and opportunities for advancement.[29]

The Human Rights Tribunal of Ontario recognized that the impact of racial profiling goes beyond police stops; it can affect the investigation process (which adversely impacts Black suspects), and can contribute to the overrepresentation of Aboriginal peoples and Black Canadians in prison.[30]

C. ENDING RACIAL PROFILING

As literature suggests, the nature of racial profiling is not a collection of isolated incidents committed by a few "bad apples." It is systemic. The phenomenon has to be understood in the larger context of the organization and society in which it emerged and it is conclusively complex.[31] Upon implementation, this model aims at ending racial profiling and building a bias-free policing framework.

While the proposed model for bias-free policing in this paper may have simplified the solution to a complex phenomenon like racial profiling, it nevertheless captures the major thrust of what an organizational solution should have and that is a multi-pronged approach. The model focuses on the basic essentials of change ingredients: leadership, value, policy, culture, evidence, people, and their will. The model deliberately

---

28 Brossard & Pedneault, above note 6.

29 *Paying the Price*, above note 1 at 3–4 and 17–53.

30 OHRC Submission, above note 5.

31 *Racial Profiling and Systematic Discrimination*, above note 18 at 98 and 102.

leaves out the planning and operational aspect of bias-free policing, as it could be customized for each of the police services based on its resources and administrative systems as well as stakeholder groups that should have a say in how changes could be made.

This paper focuses on what police services can do at their organizational level. The position is supported with recommendations from experts, police associations, and governments, as well as examples of what has been put in place in the law enforcement sector. If police services start changing how things are done in their organizations and maintain the momentum in accordance with a bias-free spirit, racial profiling will be reduced or ended over time. Chief Russ Leach of the Riverside Police Department, California, listed establishing consistency and continuity in the pursuit of anti-racial profiling efforts as one of the core responsibilities for police departments.[32]

This proposed model has four pillars, and they all aim at ending racial profiling in a multi-pronged manner:

- Strategic leadership
- Research
- Human resources management
- Stakeholder engagement

In each of these pillars, a number of key components will be highlighted in illustrating how they can drive police services to a bias-free policing level, thus ending racial profiling simultaneously. Strategic leadership has (1) value, (2) policy, and (3) culture as its key components; research has data collection and analysis on (1) police actions, (2) police workforce and human resources management, and (3) policing strategies; human resources management has (1) staffing, (2) training, and (3) performance management; and stakeholder engagement has (1) community and (2) employees. These lists of components are not meant to be exhaustive or complete, but they are considered pivotal in making policing bias-free.

These components are also intended to reinforce each other as they are put in motion: each feeds energy to one another. In addition, when these components are put in place, they are more than likely to effect changes in organizational structure and processes, administrative policies and procedures, strategies and tactics, and how things are done in general in the police services. These last two aspects of the four pillars — inter-componental reinforcement and extra-componental impacts — will not be the substance of this paper.

---

32   Leach, above note 13 at 153–91.

TABLE 13.1   Model for Bias-Free Policing

BIAS-FREE POLICING FRAMEWORK

PILLAR 1: STRATEGIC LEADERSHIP	PILLAR 2: RESEARCH	PILLAR 3: HUMAN RESOURCES	PILLAR 4: STAKEHOLDER ENGAGEMENT
• Value of accountability • Anti-racial profiling policy • Culture of guardianship	• Police interventions • Police workforce and HR management • Policing strategies	• Management • Staffing • Training • Performance management	• Community • Employees

1) Pillar 1: Strategic Leadership

Strategic leadership means stewardship based on the ability to develop and implement a winning strategy for ending racial profiling based on these four pillars. Strategic leaders are committed to "walk the talk" and to create an organizational environment that is conducive to the success of the bias-free policing strategy; plan and carry out the strategic changes based on evidence-based information; influence, motivate, and engage people and mobilize resources to execute the strategy; and ensure the sustainability of a systemic approach to bias-free services through vigorous monitoring and enforcement.[33] As racial profiling affects the public, very often strategic leaders collaborate closely with political leaders and the government sector to end racial profiling, as shown in the following examples:

- The Ontario Association of Chiefs of Police (OACP) published *Anti-Racial Profiling Best Practices: A Self Audit to Minimize Corporate Risk* in 2009 as a proactive resource for police services in Ontario. The resource book provides ideas for police services to examine themselves and determine whether they are following best practices as put forward in the resource book.[34]
- The Toronto Police Service Board Chair and the Police Chief of the Toronto Police Service have continued to commit to allocating

---

33   *Ibid.*

34   Ontario Association of Chiefs of Police (OACP), *Anti-Racial Profiling Best Practices: A Self Audit to Minimize Corporate Risk* (Toronto: OACP Diversity Committee, 2009) at iv [OACP, *Anti-Racial Profiling*].

resources and providing efforts in leading, guiding, and assessing the organizational changes according to the Toronto Police Human Rights Project Charter even after the charter period ended in 2010. These police leaders have made public statements on the personal commitment to organizational changes.[35]

- In response to the rising public concerns over racial profiling in the US in the later 1990s, the Community Oriented Policing Services (COPS) established the Promoting Cooperative Strategies to Reduce Racial Profiling (PCSRRP) program. This grant program funded local law enforcement agencies to develop strategies in various topics including traffic stop data collection and analysis as well as reducing racial profiling through technology. Examples of COPS' funding supports included: (1) the Police Executive Research Forum (PERF)'s publication of a guide outlining departmental responses to biased-based policing; (2) the Regional Community Policing Institute's (RCFI) curriculum development and training materials related to racial profiling; and (3) sponsorship of local law enforcement agencies, such as the Boston Police Department, to produce roundtables on ethnics and integrity, focusing on race.[36]

- US Department of Justice organized conferences related to bias-free policing. It organized a conference ("Strengthening Police-Community Relationships") to address police conduct issues. Government officials, police, and civil rights advocates were brought together and identified racial profiling as one of the five key issues to deal with.[37]

Strategic leadership with a change agenda to end racial profiling signifies the commitment of leadership and organizational determination to adopt a new vision and direction and take on a new course of organizational development and, simultaneously, depart from its past ways of doing things. Strategic leaders effect change in three priority areas — value, policy, and culture — so as to prepare a conducive environment for ending racial profiling.

---

35   OHRC, *Human Rights and Policing*, above note 8 at 20–21.

36   Jack McDevitt, Amy Farrell, and Russell Wolff, *Promoting Cooperative Strategies to Reduce Racial Profiling* (Washington, DC: US Department of Justice, Office of Community Oriented Policing Services, 2008) at vii and 3 [*Promoting Cooperative Strategies*].

37   *Ibid* at 1.

a) Value of Accountability

To begin with, a bias-free policing strategy built on the four pillars necessitates a change in organizational values. There is a range of organizational values that enhance the effectiveness of this strategy, and they are accountability, transparency, integrity, quality services, collaboration, respect, fairness, impartiality, and public good. Among them, accountability may be singled out as the overarching value most important to help eliminate racial profiling.

The Community Oriented Policing Services of the US Department of Justice viewed accountability as one of the key components in ending racial profiling. "Accountability means holding officers responsible for their conduct, making sure that their behavior advances the goals of the department, and, at some level, making the actions of the officers and the values of the organization answerable to the wider community."[38] Accountability also means the "adherence to professional, legal, and ethical standards as well as the specific effectiveness of training." Russ Leah, Chief of Police at the Riverside Police Department, California, listed sustaining accountability mechanisms as one of the core responsibilities for police departments.[39]

The traditional top down command and control system in law enforcement agencies is not conducive to community-based policing. This system subjects officers to close supervision and extensive rules and regulations and eliminates their discretion, which fosters "suspicion" and a "demeaning perception of citizens" and perpetuates racial profiling.

A better way to reduce or end racial profiling is to focus on police accountability to the community. As police officers work in a broad range of fluid circumstances on a daily basis, a value-based supervision model equips officers to make professional judgment and value-guided discretion based on accountability; this is much more effective than merely demanding officers to follow rigid rules. In fluid circumstances, officers need more empowerment, coaching, training, and self-regulation. A new emphasis on this value-based approach will strengthen officers' accountability to the community as they can adapt their actions based on their judgment of the circumstances.[40]

---

38 *Ibid* at 7.

39 Leach, above note 13 at 153.

40 George Kelling, Robert Wasserman, & Hubert Williams, "Police Accountability and Community Policing" (1988) 7 *Perspective on Policing* 1 [Kelling, Wasserman, & Williams].

Accountability may be external or internal. External accountability means being answerable to the requests and complaints from the public on racial profiling. Internal accountability is based on officers' value-guided behaviour; compliance to the departmental directives and training messages; adherence to professional, legal, and ethical standards; establishment of early intervention systems and performance evaluation systems; effective training; equitable human resources management system; and departmental integrity in collecting and compiling data on racial profiling. One of the top priorities of any leaders in ending racial profiling is to sustain the value of accountability, among others, by putting in motion both the external and internal accountability mechanisms, which, in turn, are fostering a police accountability culture.[41] These mechanisms, be they research work, human resources management, and stakeholder engagement, will be discussed in other sections of this paper.

The President's Task Force on 21st Century Policing in the US recommmended that "law enforcement agencies should establish a culture of transparency and accountability in order to build public trust and legitimacy," and "community policing should be infused throughout the culture and organizational structure of law enforcement agencies." (2.4 Recommendation)[42]

The International Association of Chiefs of Police (IACP), in fostering officers' accountability, recommends police agencies eliminate racially biased policing by adhering to the bias-free policing strategy throughout agency culture and relying on citizen complaints as a gauge of perceptions of racial profiling.[43]

The Commission des droits de la personne et des droits de la jeunesse in Quebec, after its public consultation on racial profiling in 2009, strongly supports a community police model in which harmonious relations with the community and strategic partnership with the community are to be established and strengthened. Specifically, the commission implements an accountability process to document actions taken by police services against racial profiling in the cities and the provincial government, measures that ensure impartiality in the supervision of officers; mechanisms to detect and track signs of racial profiling among officers, anti-profiling watch committees made up of civilians, and alternative

---

41   Leach, above note 13 at 166.

42   President's Task Force on 21st Century Policing, *Final Report of the President's Task Force on 21st Century Policing* (Washington, DC: Office of the Community Oriented Policing Services, 2015) at 2, 85, 92 [President's Task Force].

43   Leach, above note 13 at 184–97.

methods of preventing and controlling crime. Accountability procedures are to be established at every organizational level so as to ensure
that each stakeholder is accountable for its actions. In Quebec, the Saint-
Michel and Riviere-des-Prairies districts of Montreal are positive examples of how community policing may reduce significantly the "pointless
questioning of young Blacks by the police."[44]

b) Anti-Racial Profiling Policy

Establishing an anti-racial profiling policy framework is fundamental
to the ending of racial profiling as such policy framework guides police
actions not only on a daily basis, but more importantly, the development
of organizational structure and processes, strategies and tactics, standards, and procedures. A policy framework must have at least the following principles:

- People's right to live and work in an environment free from racial
  profiling.[45]
- Protection of civil liberty of all groups within individual jurisdic-
  tion.[46]
- Procedural justice for all.[47]
- Alignment with the legal standards for police actions.[48]
- Only behaviour and evidentiary standards, not race, should guide
  police stop-and-search decisions.[49]

Developing a bias-free policing policy framework for setting in motion
the end of racial profiling has been recommended by governments, associations of chiefs of police, and police agencies. Here are a few examples:

- The Ontario Association of Chiefs of Police recommended law
  enforcement agencies to partner with the Ontario Human Rights
  Commission to develop a Human Rights Project Charter (accountability, public education, training, recruitment, promotion, etc.).[50]
- The International Association of Chiefs of Police (IACP) recommends to police agencies to eliminate racially biased policing by

---

44 *Racial Profiling and Systematic Discrimination*, above note 18 at 38–39 and 103.

45 OACP, *Anti-Racial Profiling*, above note 34 at 10.

46 The International Association of Chiefs of Police's recommendation as cited in Leach,
    above note 13 at 184–97; President's Task Force, above note 42 at 88.

47 President's Task Force, *ibid* at 2.

48 Leach, above note 13 at 161.

49 *Ibid.*

50 OACP, *Anti-Racial Profiling*, above note 34 at iv, v, and 52–54.

developing an unequivocal department policy "consistent with all laws and professional standards applicable to its jurisdiction," and "embed the ideals of bias-free policing within the department's mission statement."[51]

- In 2009, the Commission des droits de la personne et des droits de la jeunesse in Quebec recommended the cities and the police departments review their policies for deploying police and fighting crime in order to prevent discrimination and racial profiling.[52]

- The President's Task Force on 21st Century Policing in the US recommended that the adoption of "procedural justice as the guiding principle for internal and external policies and practices to guide their interactions with the citizens they serve." (1.1 Recommendation) The Task Force further recommended that law enforcement agencies should adopt and enforce policies " . . . prohibiting profiling and discrimination based on race, ethnicity, national origin, religion, age, gender, gender identity/expression, sexual orientation, immigration status, disabilities, housing status, occupation, or language fluency." (2.13 Recommendation) Furthermore, these agencies should adopt and enforce policies " . . . to identify themselves by their full name, rank, and command (as applicable) and provide that information in writing to individuals they have stopped. In addition, policies should require officers to state the reason for the stop and the reasons for the search if one is conducted." (2.11 Recommendation)[53]

- Chief Russ Leach of Riverside Police Department, California, recommended police departments establish clear and comprehensive policies banning racial profiling and missions that promote equal protection and equal service to all. This principle should apply to all law enforcement activities as well as police services.[54]

- Alpert, Dunham, and Smith, after investigating the allegations of racial profiling against the Miami-Dade, Florida, Police Department, recommended that "police departments must have clear policies and directives explaining the proper use of race in decision making."[55]

---

51   Leach, above note 13 at 185–91.

52   *Racial Profiling and Systematic Discrimination*, above note 18 at 30, 32, and 35.

53   President's Task Force, above note 42 at 2, 85, and 88.

54   Leach, above note 13 at 161.

55   Geoffrey P Alpert, Roger G Dunham, & Michael R Smith, "Investigating Racial Profiling by the Miami-Dade Police Department: A Multimethod Approach" (2007) 6:1

Law enforcement leaders are responsible for developing a policy framework prohibiting the practice of racial profiling.[56] In order to facilitate them to develop a police framework on anti-racial profiling, the Ontario Human Rights Commission published the *Policy and Guidelines on Racism and Racial Discrimination* (2005). This policy document acts as a model for law enforcement agencies to develop their own policies. It states that racial profiling is a form of racial discrimination, and the document contains a definition of racial profiling, methods of identifying it, importance of race-based data, adverse impacts on Aboriginal peoples and racialized minorities, examples of racial profiling activities, and roles and responsibilities of internal stakeholders.[57]

Anti-racial profiling policy and bias-free policing are now commonplace in most law enforcement agencies, particularly larger agencies in the US. Results from the 2003 Sample Survey of Law Enforcement Agencies (LEMAS), conducted by the Bureau of Justice Statistics, reveals that 43 of 48 (or 90 percent) of state police agencies responding to the survey reported having policy directives on anti-racial profiling. Based on the survey, 62 percent of municipal police departments and 63 percent of sheriffs' offices reported having anti-racial profiling policies.[58]

Some examples of anti-racial profiling policies are:

- The Peel Regional Police Service established a directive prohibiting racial profiling in accordance with the Ontario Human Rights Commission's *Policy and Guidelines on Racism and Racial Discrimination* and the findings of the Human Rights Tribunal of Ontario, HR-0954-05. It also has a diversity protocol prohibiting "racial profiling in all aspects of activity within the scope of our influence."[59]
- Dearborn Heights Police Department, Michigan, has a policy that prohibits racial profiling practices and does not compromise aggressive law enforcement.[60]
- Hamden Police Department, Connecticut, and Town and Country Police Department, Missouri, have clear mission statements on

---

Criminology and Public Policy 25 at 25 and 50–52 [Alpert, Dunham, & Smith].

56   Leach, above note 13 at 153–91.

57   Azmi, OHRC Promotion Activities, above note 7 at 313–16.

58   Leach, above note 13 at 159.

59   Ontario Association of Chiefs of Police (OACP), "Peel Region Police Directive" in OACP, *Anti-Racial Profiling*, above note 34 at 10–13.

60   Leach, above note 13 at 162–63.

protecting all persons "without prejudice or bias against race, religion, ethnic and national origin or sexual orientation."[61]

c) Culture of Guardianship

The organizational culture of each law enforcement agency provides a nurturing and reinforcing environment in which officers' attitudes and behaviours are moulded. According to the President's Task Force on 21st Century Policing[62] and Sue Rahr of the Washington State Criminal Justice Training Commission[63] in the US, the current American police culture is a warrior culture in which the police are trained and instilled with a fighting mindset. It is a "we" versus "them" mentality that drives most of their activities. One example of this mentality in Canada is illustrated in Satzewich and Shaffir's study of Hamilton Police Service's police subculture,[64] in which police officers saw themselves as distinct from community members. They felt they were the true victims of racism because community members labelled them as racial profilers.

In exerting their authority in fighting crimes, they see themselves as warriors sent to the community tasked with identifying and apprehending criminals. The warrior culture rationalizes the police's war with the people they are expected to protect and serve. Increasingly, the police tend to view constitutional rights as an impediment to public safety, although protecting constitutional rights is the mission of police in a democracy.

Furthermore, this culture is perpetuated by a police-training model that resembles a military boot camp; officers are encouraged to take orders without critical thinking or questioning and to make decisions based on compliance to organizational rules. This model encourages strong combative skills with much lesser priority placed on effective communication and de-escalation skills.[65]

This training model is a reflection as well as a reinforcement of a top-down leadership structure. The hierarchical organization fosters a

---

61   *Ibid* at 163.

62   President's Task Force, above note 42 at 2.

63   Sue Rahr & Stephen K Rice, *From Warriors to Guardians: Recommitting American Police Culture to Democratic Ideals*, New Perspectives in Policing Bulletin (Washington, DC: US Department of Justice, National Institute of Justice, 2015) [*From Warriors to Guardians*].

64   Vic Satzewich & William Shaffir, "Racism Versus Professionalism: Claims and Counter-Claims About Racial Profiling" (August 2009) 51:2 *Canadian Journal of Criminology and Criminal Justice* 199.

65   *From Warriors to Guardians*, above note 63 at 4–5.

climate of distrust between leaders and officers, especially when transparency is not the norm. This internal distrust spills over to the world external to police services. Distrust permeates the relationship between the police and community members. In this warrior culture, those who have power require their subordinates to be less critical and to follow orders without much flexibility.[66]

To end racial profiling, the current "warrior" police culture must be changed to one of "guardianship." A guardianship culture encourages the police to give the highest priority to protect democratic ideals, serve community members, and build trust and legitimacy. The current mindset must be discarded both within and outside the police agencies. The effective establishment of a guardianship culture depends largely on the commitment of police leadership in building a culture of transparency and accountability as well as developing a bias-free policing framework.

The shift from a warrior culture to a guardianship is recommended by the President's Task Force on 21st Century Policing in the US. It recommends that "law enforcement culture should embrace a guardian mindset to build public trust and legitimacy," (1.1 Recommendation) and "communities should support a culture and practice of policing that reflects the values of protection and promotion of the dignity of all, especially the most vulnerable." (4.4 Recommendation) Concrete policy items that follow these recommendations include making "all department policies available for public review and regularly post on the department's website information about stops, summons, arrests, reported crime, and other law enforcement data aggregated by demographics" (1.3.1 Action Item) and adopting "policies directing officers to speak to individuals with respect." (4.4.1 Action Item)[67]

The Washington State Criminal Justice Training Commission began a transformation in training from 2012 to the present under Executive Director Sue Bahr. The commission trains officers and deputies from across the state, covering 39 counties, 243 cities, and numerous tribal and state agencies. The new training model focuses on communication skills (along with physical skills in defence, firearms, and emergency), coaching, and encouragement. The objective is to train the police as "the guardians of democracy." The model has a motivational program focusing on a balance of officers' physical, emotional, and spiritual health. Currently, such

---

66 *Ibid* at 6–7.
67 President's Task Force, above note 42 at 2, 85, and 92.

a program is also implemented at the Arizona Law Enforcement Academy and among the rank and file at the New York Police Department.[68]

2) Pillar 2: Research

When allegations are made about racial profiling, at least three questions could be posed:

1) Is there any evidence that law enforcement officers practice racial profiling?
2) If so, why do these practices occur?
3) If not, why do people make allegations of racial profiling?

Without proper data, one could only speculate, and there would be no definitive conclusion on this speculation. Only when proper research is conducted, and valid and reliable data are collected and analyzed, can we then answer these three questions with some degree of confidence. To explore the issue of racial profiling, there are three main areas in law enforcement agencies that need to be studied: police actions, police workforce and human resources management, and policing strategies. Analyzing the data and information emerging from these studies can inform the development of appropriate solutions to end racial profiling.

a) Police Actions

First of all, it is important for law enforcement agencies to review their patterns of law enforcement agents' interventions. In the case of the police, traffic stops, pedestrian stops, ticketed, and searches, arrests are usually intervention activities in which racial profiling is detected. Data on these police actions may be collected and analyzed.

The collected quantitative data could be compared with external or internal benchmarks for the purpose of analysis. External benchmarks refer to data outside of police departments, and they usually mean composition of community population, driving population, driver population, or other populations. They may be difficult to interpret, but they offer an estimate on proportionate representativeness of drivers being intervened. Internal benchmarks refer to data of police interventions within a police unit or by an individual officer and compare them over time, across different units or officers, in the same or similar geographic areas. Inter-

---

68 *From Warriors to Guardians*, above note 63 at 7–9.

nal data may also be analyzed to determine "hit rates" (searches yielding anticipated results) for different racial groups.[69]

Qualitative information on racial profiling as obtained through investigation of complaints or allegations is also quite useful. As racial profiling is a form of racial discrimination that is "extremely subtle and insidious," it is difficult to identify and detect. Investigating and finding evidence to prove racial profiling is even more difficult as it involves psychological elements that are often not transparent. It is therefore important to identify indicators of racial profiling as well as develop guidelines for investigation.[70] Having more relevant qualitative data on policing is consistent with one of the recommendations put forward by Skogan and Frydl.[71] They believe that more research on public encounters, the experiences of individuals stopped by the police, police discretion, the use of police authority, street police behaviour, and crime control effectiveness may yield insights on the public view of police legitimacy.

Both quantitative data and qualitative information (such as types of stops, reasons or results of stops, racial groups stopped) help law enforcement agencies to monitor officers' activities, identify systemic disparities or barriers, develop or assess policing strategies and deployment of resources, make efforts to reduce perceptions of racial profiling, monitor racial profiling incidents or progress in anti-racial profiling initiatives, develop training resources, evaluate the performance and effectiveness of intervention programs, reduce racial profiling behaviour, and improve community relations. If the collected data do not show any indication of racial disparities in police actions, these data can provide a backdrop for establishing a constructive dialogue with the community that may help the police to find out the sources of community perceptions of racial profiling.

In its public consultation in 2009, the Commission des droits de la personne et des droits de la jeunesse in Quebec noted that there is a broad consensus in the communities that "data collection is an essential condition for better defining the forms and the scope of 'ethnocultural' discrimination .... This approach would enable managers and executives to detect possible discriminatory biases .... Moreover, without access to these data, it is impossible for managers to take stock of the results of measures that have been applied to prevent and counteract systemic

---

69 *Promoting Cooperative Strategies*, above note 36 at 41.

70 *Racial Profiling and Systematic Discrimination*, above note 18 at 97.

71 Wesley Skogan & Kathleen Frydl, eds, *Fairness and Effectiveness in Policing: The Evidence* (Washington, DC: National Academies Press, 2004) at 7–10.

discrimination . . . based on periodic reporting." A procedure for data collection and analysis must be established and agreed upon by researchers.[72]

b) Police Workforce and Human Resources Management

In addition to collecting information and data on police interventions, some of which may have been alleged to be racial profiled by some community members, research may be needed in other areas in law enforcement agencies as well. As racialized minorities have the tendency to perceive the underrepresentation of racialized minorities in the police workforce as an indicator of racial biases, having a closer look at the police workforce may be a start. A workforce analysis based on data on the racial composition or other diversity components (such as ethnicity, mother tongue groups, gender, and age) may provide valuable insights on how the workforce is reflective of the population that the police are serving.

Additional research may be conducted on how the police manage its human resources in areas such as recruitment efforts, selection criteria, training curriculum, training priorities, promotion processes, professional development, professional standards, succession planning, and performance management.[73] Information may be collected through internal data mining, documentary review, interviews, or focus groups. This information, upon collection and analysis, would be valuable as a basis for police-community dialogues as well as internal review by employees, both uniformed and civilian. Research findings may also help police management to develop internal policies and programs to better human resources management, which, in turn, may make the workplace more representative and equitable. For example, research results may note that racial profiling has not been comprehensively dealt with in training curriculum or that professional standards and the performance management system may need to be updated and upgraded, as racial profiling has not been traditionally treated as an explicit topic of coverage or as an indicator of performance.

c) Policing Strategies

Police actions in law enforcement are grounded in legislations. However, how they are carried out by officers is often determined by strategies developed internally by police management, whether they are at the police headquarters, district, or unit levels. Such strategies are open for research if there are allegations about racial profiling in police services.

---

72 *Racial Profiling and Systematic Discrimination*, above note 18 at 15 and 103.

73 Skogan & Frydl, eds, *Fairness and Effectiveness in Policing*, above note 71 at 7–10.

The deployment of police officers or specific police squads — emergency, anti-violence, drugs, or guns and gangs — in specific neighbourhoods could be analyzed upon collecting data on their effectiveness ("hit" rates), crime rates in neighbourhoods, intervention methods, and public reactions. Community policing strategies may also be studied in terms of officers' conflict resolution outcomes, liaison efforts, constructive community wellness initiatives, public perception of officers' treatment, etc. This information could be gathered through data mining, documentary reviews, surveys, participatory observations, interviews, or focus groups. Upon analyzing the data, the results may shed light on the extent of racial profiling and its impacts on the communities, as well as the internal allocation of resources and the cost-effectiveness in fighting crimes or serving the public.

For research purposes, there are additional qualitative information, such as organizational policies and procedures, and workplace cultures, that provide insights on barriers for removing racial profiling behaviour. Such qualitative information is supplementary to the quantitative data highlighting representation or distribution of racial groups according to types of police actions. The Ontario Human Rights Commission encourages law enforcement agencies to follow human rights principles in collecting human rights-based data as outlined in its "Count Me In! Collecting Human Rights-Based Data."[74]

d) Recommendations

Doing research on police actions has been overwhelming endorsed by governments and associations of police chiefs in both the US and Canada.

The International Association of Chiefs of Police recommended that law enforcement leaders should be teamed up with academic researchers to conduct research projects that are badly needed. [75] The association embraced the goal of such partnerships in every police agency across the US. Such partnership is also an integral part of the National Institute of Justice's Strategic Approaches to Community Safety Initiatives and Project Safe Neighborhoods. It also recommended that police agencies: eliminate racially biased policing through the use of quality and accurate

---

74 Ontario Human Rights Commission, "Count Me In! Collecting Human Rights-Based Data" (2009), online: www.ohrc.on.ca/en/count-me-collecting-human-rights-based-data.

75 International Association of Chiefs of Police, *Unresolved Problems and Powerful Potentials: Improving Partnerships Between Law Enforcement Leaders and University Based Researchers — Recommendations from IACP 2003 Roundtable* (Alexandria, VA: IACP, 2004).

stop-and-search data as performance indicators in early intervention systems; set the foundation for discussion with the community before the release of racial profile data; and use racial profiling data collection efforts and findings as a basis of dialogue with the community.[76]

i) USA

One of the President's Task Force on 21st Century Policing's recommendations was that "law enforcement agencies should be encouraged to collect, maintain, and analyze demographic data on all detentions (stops, frisks, searches, summons, and arrests)." (2.6 Recommendations) Deriving from this recommendation, one of its actionable items is to partner with universities and other organizations "to collect data and develop knowledge about analysis and benchmarks as well as to develop tools and templates that help departments manage data collection and analysis." (2.6.1 Action Item)[77]

Alpert, Dunham, and Smith, after investigating the allegations of racial profiling against the Miami-Dade, Florida, Police Department, recommended that "the department must maintain a data-collection and analytic system to monitor the activities of their officers as it pertains to the race of the citizen." Furthermore, they recommended that care should be exercised not to use the race of citizens as a tool for record checks, including records of interrogation for the detention and arrest of citizens.[78]

ii) Canada

The Commission des droits de la personne et des droits de la jeunesse in Quebec, after its public consultation on racial profiling in 2009, recommended that the municipal police services systematically collect and publish data related to the presumed racial identity of individuals during police actions in order to document the phenomenon and take the appropriate measures.[79]

The Ontario Human Rights Commission (2014) recommended police services to collect race-based data on police stops, searches, and DNA sampling practices. In addition, the commission recommended the collection of qualitative information on police perspectives and actions, through focus groups or interviews. In addition, the commission recommended that "police services across the province should install camera in

76   Leach, above note 13 at 184–97.

77   President's Task Force, above note 42 at 88.

78   Alpert, Dunham, & Smith, above note 55 at 25 and 50–52; Leach, above note 13 at 160.

79   *Racial Profiling and Systematic Discrimination*, above note 18 at 37.

police cruisers to allow for monitoring the interaction between the police and public."[80]

e)   Benefits and Challenges

The police can systematically collect data on traffic stops and other forms of police actions and computerize them. Hand-held computers and in-field reporting on mobile data terminals have made data collection easier and analysis faster. The adoption of these technological devices is to be reviewed carefully by both the end users (that is, police officers), the information technology professionals (that is, the civilians), and the minorities in the community. They need to confirm that these devices are easy to use, the information captured is reliable and is compatible with those from other systems, the tabulated data is usable for analysis, and the analytical results are meaningful to minority communities. Pilot testing of these devices and collected data is also an important step prior to the actual adoption of the technology and the data system.

Research in these three areas — police actions, workforce and human resources management, and policing strategies — yields many benefits for the police as well as the community.

- Data collection is an effective management tool as it promotes accountability. It is one of the necessary steps in dealing with racial profiling.
- Having these data and sharing them with the community enhances the credibility of the police and trust between the police and the community. Wortley and Tanner suggested that "a transparent effort to monitor and eliminate racial profiling . . . will ultimately improve the relationship between police and various racial minority communities."[81]
- It also symbolizes that the police are prepared to evaluate themselves and address issues emerging from the data.[82]
- Data also supports problem-solving strategies and partnership building as well as establishes new allies and brings more resources to the table.[83]

---

80   *Paying the Price*, above note 1 at 67–73.

81   Wortley & Tanner, above note 10 at 200.

82   Leach, above note 13 at 169–71; *Promoting Cooperative Strategies*, above note 36 at 41–42.

83   James Hussey, "Data-Management Issues in the Context of Protecting Civil Rights and Serving the Community" (2006) in Leach, above note 13, 209 at 212–15.

- Information on racial profiling based on cross-tabulation of police actions and those who have been stopped would make police officers more accountable.
- Using information technology, data on criminal activities and police actions are able to show their changing patterns and trends as well as hold police managers personally accountable for lowering crimes in different geographic areas.[84]
- Data of this nature would also make police actions more transparent to the public and allow the police to monitor the prevalence of racial profiling.[85]

However, there are also challenges for research activities of this nature:[86]

- At the start, it is difficult to enlist support from police officers, as they are suspicious of the value of data collection and how it impacts on the reputation of the police and their own performance and career.
- Community and other stakeholders are also reluctant to be involved in research of this nature, as they are not completely sold on its benefits. There are also the privacy issues that come with data collection, and the potential negative impacts on certain demographic groups.
- There are also numerous research methodological, data, technical, and logistic issues that require examination. Lingering concerns are still occurring about how traffic data collection could be integrated with other existing data systems and how the data are to be interpreted as relating to racial profiling. Technological devices for collecting information may not be compatible with each other and trying to include more data fields in existing software may pose additional challenges.[87]
- Furthermore, data collection demands financial resources and staff time. Employees in police services may find their workload increase due to data collection, interpretation, and analysis.
- Tangible impacts on ending racial profiling are not immediate even after research results are obtained, thus holding the attention and meeting the expectations of stakeholder groups is a challenge.

---

84 *Promoting Cooperative Strategies*, above note 36 at 28–29.
85 *Ibid* at 41–42.
86 *Ibid* at 47–49.
87 *Ibid* at 28–29 and 32–34.

- There are also issues related to the degree of organizational autonomy in the adaptation of technology and inter-agency conflicts based on unclear jurisdictional boundaries.[88]

But the benefits seem to outweigh the shortcomings. As Chief James Hussey of Cohasset Police Department, Massachusetts, noted, when police departments start to improve numerous data management action items, such as expanding the use of data collection tools, focusing on enhancing data quality and completeness, recognizing the limitations of data, and doing a better job in data interpretation, departments would reap more benefits in data collection.[89]

f) Prevalence of Data Collection

The International Association of Chiefs of Police (IACP) informed the police communities that racial profiling data collection and analysis is the current trend. More police leaders have determined that data-driven strategies have improved the management of police departments and such strategies are spreading across law enforcement agencies in the US and the world.[90] More and more states in the US are mandating traffic stop data collection for assessment. A number of local agencies are collecting racial profiling data on a voluntary basis and some are doing that due to court settlements, consent decrees, and memoranda of understanding.[91]

Currently, there is no up-to-date assessment of the spread of data collection related to racial profiling across the US. The 2003 Sample Survey of Law Enforcement Agencies (LEMAS) in the US, conducted by Bureau of Justice Statistics, does not have data regarding police accountability on racial profiling. However, racial or ethnic data collection is central to many accountability strategies now used in police departments. Agencies in the US are increasingly using traffic stop data as a way to evaluate individual officers' performance at work. In addition, law enforcement agencies can utilize citizen complaint processes and related data to assess the extent of complaints of racial biases in specific communities.[92]

Judging from the following data reports, it appears that racial data collection and analysis of traffic stops covered extensive law enforcement agencies in Massachusetts, Texas, and Illinois in the US.[93]

---

88 *Ibid.*
89 Hussey, above note 83 at 209–12 and 216–30.
90 *Ibid.*
91 Leach, above note 13 at 167.
92 *Ibid* at 160.
93 *Ibid* at 167–68.

- Data from approximately 250 law enforcement agencies in Massachusetts were analyzed by the Institute on Race and Justice at Northeastern University and its report was released in May 2004.
- The Texas Senate Bill 1074 required law enforcement agencies across the state to collect data and provide statistical summaries of traffic stop data. The Steward Research Group and the Texas Criminal Justice Coalition released a report in February 2005 analyzing data from more than 1,000 law enforcement agencies in Texas.
- Illinois released its *Illinois Traffic Stop Study* in July 2005, which analyzed the racial profiling data from nearly 1,000 municipal, county, and state police, and special jurisdiction agencies for the year 2004. The analysis was done by the Northwestern University Centre for Public Safety.

In spite of the above reports, it is still rather difficult to generalize the findings to the entire country. The Data Collection Resource Center of the Institute on Race and Justice at Northeastern University collects information on data collection efforts on a state-by-state basis. It notes that there are variations across states — some have legislation that require data collection and some only encourage it. Some states require data collection only from certain departments and most states require data collection for only a limited time frame. There are also variations among states on the types of data to be collected; some states require data on all traffic stops and some only require stops data under certain conditions (such as arrests). Some require pedestrian stops and some do not. Some require all agencies to collect data and some require only specific agencies to do so.[94]

Examples of racial data collection projects launched by individual police departments are listed below.

i)   USA

CompStat, a management accountability process developed by the New York City Police Department in 1994, has been adopted by a large number of law enforcement agencies across the US.[95]

Redlands Police Department, California, used hand-held iPAQ computers (with software from Hewlett-Packard) and digital recording systems to collect traffic stops data and a voice and video recording system that would provide information if allegations of bias were made. The

---

94   *Ibid* at 168.
95   *Promoting Cooperative Strategies*, above note 36 at 28.

department was able to integrate the new technology with the existing computer-aided dispatch (CAD) system.[96]

Tacoma Police Department, Washington, created a racial profiling task force with community engagement and developed a data collection system for reporting. Several adjustments were made to make the data collection system acceptable to community, police management, and police union members.[97]

Charlotte-Mecklenburg Police Department, North Carolina, addressed the issue of racial profiling by developing an "anti-arbitrary profiling" program and implementing a data collection plan (with input from fourteen community organizations). Using an intranet-based system, the department collected data on vehicle and pedestrian stops. An extensive training program was launched to help officers to enter stops data. The collection was field-tested, and after one year of data collection, the department analyzed the data with the assistance of a university research team.[98]

Dothan Police Department, Alabama, instituted a data collection that covers every police-citizen interaction and a bias-awareness training program for officers under a multi-stakeholder steering committee. Tablet PCs are used to collect data.[99]

Kansas City Police Department, Missouri, decided to collect more data than required by Missouri law with input from thirty-three community representatives and twenty-two police department members of various ranks. Hand-held computers (iPAQ) were used and integrated with the existing mobile data terminals (MDT) and desktop computers. Training of officers to collect data and field testing were also conducted.[100]

Oakland Police Department, California, established a racial profiling task force to develop a corporate policy and a comprehensive data collection system on racial profiling. Input was solicited from community groups. Hand-held PDAs and paper forms were used to collect data. The data was analyzed but the department was unable to determine whether racial profiling was the cause of racial disparities in data.[101]

---

96 *Ibid* at 30.
97 *Ibid* at 30–31.
98 *Ibid* at 42–43.
99 *Ibid* at 43–46.
100 *Ibid*.
101 *Ibid* at 46–47.

ii) Canada

Racial data collection on police actions related to alleged racial profiling in Canada is rather limited.

The first systematic data collection of racial profiling was done by the Kingston Police Service in 2003–4. The data was analyzed in terms of the frequency and nature of police interventions of persons based on their ethnicity.[102] The Ontario Association of Chiefs of Police viewed having knowledge of the race-based statistical study conducted by Kingston Police Service in 2005 as one of the best practices.[103]

The Ottawa Police Service has conducted racial data collection on traffic stops for a period of two years (2013–15) on an experimental basis. The collected data was analyzed by Lorne Foster, Les Jacobs, and Bobby Siu and the analytical report was submitted to the Ottawa Police Service in 2016. This data project is the largest traffic stops study in Canada as it covered more than 120,000 traffic stops.

The Commission des droits de la personne et des droits de la jeunesse in Quebec has been aware of the issue of racial profiling, and produced *Racial Profiling: Guidelines for Investigations* for complaint handling by employees and investigators.[104]

3) Pillar 3: Human Resource Management

Human resource management is an organizational function with a focus on recruiting and retaining people and developing and maximizing their potentials with the purpose of achieving organizational goals. Human resource activities, such as recruitment, hiring, promotion, performance appraisal, training, and development are carried out to enhance this function. In ending racial profiling, several human resource activities are useful to enable employees to achieve the organizational goal of bias-free policing, and they are staffing, training, and performance management.

a) Staffing

One of the premises in ending racial profiling is the ability of law enforcement agencies to demonstrate to the public that they are not racial-

---

102 William J Closs & Paul McKenna, "Profiling a Problem in Canadian Police Leadership: The Kingston Police Data Collection Project" (2006) 49:2 *Canadian Public Administration* 143; *Racial Profiling and Systematic Discrimination*, above note 18 at 36; OACP, *Anti-Racial Profiling*, above note 34 at 30–47.

103 OACP, *Anti-Racial Profiling*, *ibid* at v.

104 (Montreal: Commission des droits de la personne et des droits de la jeunesse, 2006).

ly biased in all their activities. The historical distrust that simmers or solidifies through time between racialized minority communities and police services may be reduced through equitable representation in the police workforce.[105] Having a diverse workforce would enhance effective police work and reduce racial profiling because it gives the public the impression that the police workforce is diverse and that the minorities in the police services can now provide the conduit between the communities and police departments, thus enhancing the opportunity for dialogues.[106] Having more racial minorities in the police workforce does not automatically end racial profiling, but it does provide a necessary step in restoring community trust and legitimacy. A police workforce that is reflective of the racial composition of the people it serves instills some degree of confidence in the fairness and impartiality of the police. To strengthen this potential of building dialogues and legitimacy, diversity must be reflected in the composition of employees at every level of their organizational hierarchy.[107]

Recruitment of minority group members for the police workforce is best conducted through community organizations, social and religious institutions, and media outlets for these ethnic and minority communities. It is critical that the police departments have cultivated good rapport with the key stakeholders (such as business owners and community representatives) in these communities.

However, there are challenges on the recruitment and hiring fronts: officers may not support diversity recruitment or hiring, traditional recruitment and marketing methods have been found to be ineffective, special mentoring for job candidates is still relatively absent, and there is a lapse in the time between the recruitment and hiring of minority members, all of which impact racial profiling.[108]

The American experience shows that the mistrust between minority communities and the law enforcement agencies does not dissolve as quickly as anticipated and, consequently, recruiting and hiring minority group members is difficult at the start. Even if they become police officers, their retention rates may be low because of a less-than-welcoming police culture and their difficulty in securing a promotion. Furthermore, the benefit of reducing racial profiling does not happen automatically just

---

105 *Promoting Cooperative Strategies*, above note 36 at 15.

106 Lorie Fridell et al, *Racially Biased Policing: A Principled Response* (Washington, DC: Police Executive Research Forum, 2001).

107 *Racial Profiling and Systematic Discrimination*, above note 18 at 103.

108 *Promoting Cooperative Strategies*, above note 36 at 19–20.

because law enforcement agencies have diverse and equitable representation of minority group members.[109]

Ensuring the police workforce is representative and equitable for racialized minorities is a central recommendation to police services from the associations of police chiefs and governments: the International Association of Chiefs of Police (IACP) recommends police agencies eliminate racially biased policing by promoting a diverse police force that is reflective of the community that the police department serves.[110]

In the US, the President's Task Force on 21st Century Policing recommends diversity in the police workforce "to reflect the demographics of the community," "to improve understanding and effectiveness in dealing with all communities,"(1.8 Recommendation) and to make the police workforce transparent, "all federal, state, local, and tribal law enforcement agencies should report and make available to the public census data regarding the composition of their departments including race, gender, age, and other relevant demographic data." (2.5 Recommendation)[111]

Chief Patrick Oliver, a retired chief of Fairborn Police Department, Ohio, recommends that recruitment strategies be developed and tailored to ethnic and minority communities.[112]

The Ontario Human Rights Commission recommends "organizations or institutions that have, or are alleged to have a problem with racial profiling should undertake measures to improve recruitment, retention and promotion of employees who are members of racialized groups." It had the same recommendation for the Ontario Provincial Police in 2014.[113]

Some examples of staffing that aim at racial equity in the workplace:

- The Toronto Police Service initiated actions that are conducive to employment equity: completion of a workforce survey and recruitment of underrepresented group members to the police service. It is working towards a more representative workforce. In addition, the Toronto Police Service has also implemented a process to screen out job applicants with racial biases.[114]

---

109 *Ibid* at 15.

110 Leach, above note 13 at 184–97.

111 President's Task Force, above note 42 at 2, 86, and 88.

112 Patrick Oliver, "Personnel Management Issues in the Context of Protecting Civil Rights and Serving the Community" in Leach, above note 13, 193 at 197–98.

113 *Paying the Price*, above note 1 at 72.

114 OHRC Submission, above note 5.

- The Peel Regional Police have already been working towards a more representative workforce reflecting the composition of the population they serve.[115]
- Jersey City Police Department, New Jersey, aimed to hire more racialized minorities by refining their recruitment strategies to include marketing campaigns, speaking tours in high schools, advertising in shopping malls, media advertising, etc.[116]
- Indianapolis Police Department, Indiana, kicked off a recruitment campaign with a press conference; advertised on TV, radio, and billboards; organized events; disseminated information to local media; and co-hosted a breakfast for ministers. They also organized orientation sessions and organized ride-alongs. Officers also provided special tutoring (mentoring) lessons to help candidates go through the hiring process including the written assignment, oral examination, and physical agility test.[117]
- Lansing Police Department, Michigan, targeted youths from minority backgrounds for recruitment, and they trained officers to do the recruiting. They set up booths in schools and provided students with brochures and CD-ROMs on choosing a career in law enforcement. They did a survey of grade 11 students and launched focus groups with students on their perceptions of police officers and the attractiveness of a policing career. Using the results, they designed their recruitment strategy targeting youths. They launched several advertising strategies: TV, radio, billboards, and newspapers.[118]
- Farmington Police Department, Connecticut, used its own employees who have connections with ethnic and racial minority communities to be the recruiters at job fairs and community events.[119]

b) Training

i) Training in Bias-Free Policing

When the policing sector determines to eliminate racial profiling in its activities, the focus on bias-free community policing is in order. Accordingly, the roles of police officers have to be changed from traditional law

---

115 *Ibid* at 40.
116 *Promoting Cooperative Strategies*, above note 36 at 16.
117 *Ibid* at 18.
118 *Ibid* at 18–19.
119 Oliver, above note 112 at 198.

enforcement and suppression to taking on the role of peacekeeping and community service in addition to the traditional ones. Such change in the roles of the police necessitates changes in police training for both the new recruits and the in-service officers. First of all, the "tone" or approach has to change from one of the imposition of rules from above to one of cultural and attitudinal changes. Secondly, the contents of training have given higher priority to the discretionary power of the police officers as they take into consideration the community dynamics when they act. Thirdly, additional skills have to be stressed including communication, problem solving, public presentation, conflict resolution, and negotiation.[120]

Training police officers, supervisors, and managers involves inculcating an attitude of bias-free policing, diversity, and cultural awareness; understanding stereotyping, prejudice, and ethno-cultural dynamics of communities; and providing legal and ethical standards, as well as instruction on handling stops, racial profiling data collection, and protocols. Training based on a positive and no-accusatory approach is more effective than a compliance-based approach. The training message must be consistent with other messages communicated within the police department. This means that it has to be coordinated and free from internal contradictions. Front-line officers or supervisors must have the same anti-racial profiling message as that directed from police managers. Palmiotto, Birzer, and Unnithan put forward a training curriculum with emphasis on community policing along similar lines.[121]

In recommending an anti-racial profiling training model for the Ontario Provincial Police (OPP), the Ontario Human Rights Commission recommended that the training model must:[122]

- Design and deliver the training by trainers with expertise in the field of racial profiling;
- Engage local racialized and marginalized communities in designing, delivering, and evaluating the training;
- Convey the importance of good community relations;

---

120 Edwin Meese, III, "Community Policing and the Police Officer" (Washington, DC: US Department of Justice, Office of Justice Programs, National Institute of Justice, 1993) at 2 and 6–7.

121 Leach, above note 13 at 164; Michael J Palmiotto, Michael L Birzer, & N Prabha Unnithan, "Training in Community Policing: A Suggested Curriculum" (2000) 23:1 *Policing: An International Journal of Police Strategies and Management* 8.

122 OHRC Submission, above note 5.

- Describe the nature of racism, including its impact on Aboriginal and Black communities;
- Explain that racial profiling violates the Ontario *Human Rights Code, Charter of Rights and Freedoms, Police Services Act,* and police policies and procedures, with references to relevant caselaw;
- Incorporate role-play and scenario-driven learning modules to improve its street level application and articulation;
- Address the angry reactions from people who perceive that they have been racially profiled and do not let such reactions result in further differential treatment by officers;
- Communicate the message that racial profiling is not acceptable and will result in disciplinary penalties, up to and including dismissal from work; and
- Explain why respect for human rights is aligned with the objectives of the Ontario Provincial Police.

It is important that this training model should also be integrated with training in investigative detention, consent searches, customer service and conflict de-escalation, mediation, and resolution.

a.   Benefits

There are several reasons why staff training is critical to the ending of racial profiling:

- The value of accountability, bias-free policing policy, and corporate culture of "guardianship" could only be internalized by officers through a continuous effort to increase their level of awareness and empathy towards racial groups and to update and upgrade their knowledge and skills in interacting and working with them. Training also can instill positive organizational values, liaison, problem solving, and judgment skills.
- Policing involves a balance between the protection of public safety, security, and the civil liberties of individuals. Police training therefore has to tackle this issue for new police recruits as well as in-service police officers.[123]
- Training may allow officers to learn that racial profiling is an ineffective way to apprehend criminals; instead they may learn other more effective tactics.[124]

---

123   *Promoting Cooperative Strategies,* above note 36 at 34.
124   Fridell et al, above note 106.

ii) *Perspectives on Bias-Free Policing Training*

Government, police services, and associations of police chiefs in both Canada and the US are endorsing and supporting bias-free policing or anti-racial profiling training for the police services. The Human Rights Tribunal of Ontario sees the importance of anti-racial profiling training in combating conscious or unconscious biases for officers or investigators.[125] Similarly, the Toronto Police Service's Police and Community Engagement Review (PACER) report states that "the training of officers is an essential part of ensuring the Service achieves the organizational aspirations of treating everyone in an impartial, equitable, sensitive and ethnical manner."[126]

Leaders are responsible to implement a sound training regimen that reinforces departmental policies. The Chief of Police at the Riverside Police Department, California, Russ Leach, listed implementing a sound training program as one of the five core responsibilities for police departments.[127] The Ontario Association of Chiefs of Police views having training plans on anti-racial profiling for police managers, supervisors, and officers as one of the best practices, as well as having a working understanding of caselaw and sociological literature as it applies to racial profiling.[128]

Formal recommendations on bias-free policing training:

- The International Association of Chiefs of Police (IACP) recommends police agencies eliminate racially biased policing through developing "comprehensive and effective training programs" for those engaged in stop-and-search activities, and ensure that the training is "ongoing, comprehensive, relevant, and compelling."[129]
- The President's Task Force on 21st Century Policing recommended that "both basic recruit and in-service training" should incorporate content around "recognizing and confronting implicit bias and cultural responsiveness" (5.9 Recommendation) and that "both basic recruit and in-service" require "training in a democratic society." (5.10 Recommendation) In line with this recommendation is an actionable item: "law enforcement agencies should

---

125 OHRC Submission, above note 5.

126 Toronto Police Service, *Toronto Police Service: The Police and Community Engagement Review (The PACER Report) Phase II — Internal Report and Recommendations* (Toronto: Toronto Police Service, 2013) [*PACER Report*].

127 Leach, above note 13 at 153–91.

128 OACP, *Anti-Racial Profiling*, above note 34 at v.

129 Leach, above note 13 at 153–97.

implement ongoing, top down training for all officers in cultural diversity and related topics that can build on trust and legitimacy in diverse communities. This should be accomplished with the assistance of advocacy groups that represent the viewpoints of communities that have traditionally had adversarial relationships with law enforcement." (5.9.1 Action Item)[130]

- The Commission des droits de la personne et des droits de la jeunesse in Quebec, after its public consultation on racial profiling in 2009, recommended that the police training programs provide anti-racism training and that the police college promote diversity training. They felt that both management and non-management employees should have this kind of training and that "cities and police departments take steps to ensure that their practices in recruiting, promoting and evaluating police take into account intercultural competencies."[131]
- The Ontario Human Rights Commission recommended that "organizations or institutions that have, or are alleged to have a problem with racial profiling should engage in ongoing effective training initiatives on racism, race relations and racial profiling" and that these kinds of training should be provided to "new staff with sufficient support to ensure that they learn appropriate practices and not resort to racial profiling," and that "in conjunction with local communities, police services should develop educational materials, particularly aimed at youth, explaining citizens' rights."[132]
- Toronto Police Service's Police and Community Engagement Review recommended: "That the Service continue to ensure all uniform Officers and investigators receive training that includes, but is not limited to: . . . prevention of discrimination, racism and Black racism . . . . All training will involve community participation in training design, delivery and evaluation."[133]
- Alpert, Dunham, and Smith, after investigating the allegations of racial profiling against the Miami-Dade, Florida, Police Department, recommended that "officers must be trained and educated in the overall impact of using race as a factor in deciding how to respond to a citizen."[134]

---

130 President's Task Force, above note 42 at 95–96.
131 *Racial Profiling and Systematic Discrimination*, above note 18 at 41 and 103.
132 *Paying the Price*, above note 1 at 72–73.
133 *PACER Report*, above note 126.
134 Alpert, Dunham, & Smith, above note 55 at 25 and 50–52.

iii) Prevalence of Police Training

a.   USA

One example of police training is found in Muscatine Police Department, Iowa, where officer training on diversity and cultural awareness has been carried out.[135]

The extent of police training regarding racial profiling and related issues has not been documented and the comprehensiveness and rigour of this kind of training in the US is not clear.[136] However, in 2002, the Bureau of Justice Statistics (BJS) reported that "Ninety-six percent of law academies addressed this topic [racially-based policing] during academic training, 40 percent during practical skills training, and 31 percent during field training."[137] The 2003 Sample Survey of Law Enforcement Agencies (LEMAS) in the US, conducted by BJS, did not measure the prevalence of training, therefore no national data was available on this front.[138]

b.   Canada

Since 2007, the Ontario Human Rights Commission worked with the Ontario Police College and established a new recruit-training framework (with racial profiling as a key component). Between 2007 and 2012, this collaboration also resulted in joint training. Several police services in Ontario (Pembroke, London, Thunder Bay, Owen Sound, Hamilton, and Windsor) have training of this nature.[139]

iv) Police Training Resources

a.   USA

- Brookline Police Department, Massachusetts, has its philosophy of integrity, fairness, cultural awareness, and community involvement, and its police training was developed to align. The department developed simulation training using the Range 3000 XP4 Force Con-

---

135   Leach, above note 13 at 164.

136   *Promoting Cooperative Strategies*, above note 36 at 35.

137   MJ Hickman, *State and Local Law Enforcement Training Academies, 2002* (Washington, DC: US Department of Justice, Office of Justice Programs, Bureau of Justice Statistics, 2005). Leach, above note 13 at 153–91.

138   Leach, *ibid* at 160.

139   Azmi, OHRC Promotion Activities, above note 7 at 323–24.

trol Simulator (an interactive training system) and training films (with racial profiling scenarios).[140]

- Metropolitan Nashville Police Department, Tennessee, implemented a racial profiling training program for both police officers and community people instructing officers to avoid racial profiling and informing the community of police practices and policies regarding traffic stops. The department used the Safe and Legal Traffic Stops (SALTS) training curriculum developed by the Florida-based Institute of Police Technology and Management. The department used Perspectives on Profiling from the Museum of Tolerance in Los Angeles for community education.[141]
- Phoenix Police Department, Arizona, implemented a process of information seeking, processing, and refinement, and developed preventive strategies. This process included interviewing internal stakeholders and conducting training workshops for them using the Perspectives on Profiling curriculum ("Knowledge Café"), plus holding public forums for youths with role-playing exercises and focus groups (with the objective of developing prevention strategies for racial profiling). [142]
- Sheriff Sue Rahr of the King County Sheriff's Office, Washington, developed the LEED Training model in 2011. LEED stands for Listen and Explain with Equity and Dignity. Officers trained under this model take time to listen to people, explain how the process unfolds, and why particular decisions were made so that the equity of decisions is transparent and the dignity of the participants is intact.[143]
- US Department of Justice has developed training material to promote awareness of Arab, Muslim, and Sikh cultures; conducted various regional train-the-trainer seminars; and sponsored the development of *The First Three to Five Seconds*, a video that highlights Arab and Muslim cultural features.[144]

b. Canada

- The Peel Regional Police Service has developed a training package on racial profiling that is available in an electronic format upon

---

140 *Promoting Cooperative Strategies*, above note 36 at 36–37.
141 *Ibid* at 37–38.
142 *Ibid* at 38–39.
143 *From Warriors to Guardians*, above note 63 at 3.
144 Leach, above note 13 at 164.

request. It has a discussion on racial profiling, a group exercise, a summary of Kingston Police Service's data collection project, legal cases on racial profiling, public interaction, a discussion on the differences between criminal profiling and racial profiling, and strategies for avoiding racial profiling.[145]

- In facilitating more extensive training for the police services, the Ontario Human Rights Commission published the *Human Rights and Police: Creating and Sustaining Organizational Change*. It is a manual focusing on organizational change practices and was supported by testimonials from the Ontario Association of Chiefs of Police, the Ontario Association of Police Services Boards, the Ontario Police College, the Toronto Police Service, and the Ontario Provincial Police.[146]
- The Toronto Police Service has developed an e-learning training module on racial profiling for police officers, and it is available for use through the Canadian Police Knowledge Network.[147]

v) Challenges

While police training on bias-free policing or anti-racial profiling is beneficial in many ways, there are challenges in training officers, especially at the start when officers do not buy into the concept. They do not see the need and the topic of racial profiling elicits strong emotion among officers. Community members also do not trust training initiatives organized by police services.

There is also a tendency for the training goals to be diffused and not focused enough as more stakeholders are involved in the planning process and put forward a broader range of ideas. Keeping these stakeholders committed to training may not be easy, as they may not witness the training outcomes and impacts immediately. Learning through training may not yield actual behavioural results for some officers as anticipated.

There is also the difficult choice of having internal or external training programs, having a simplistic or multi-pronged approach, and placing an accountability mechanism upfront.[148] All these tend to delay the implementation of police training.

---

145 OACP, *Anti-Racial Profiling*, above note 34 at 15–25.
146 Azmi, OHRC Promotion Activities, above note 7 at 323–24.
147 OHRC Submission, above note 5 at 44.
148 *Promoting Cooperative Strategies*, above note 36 at 35 and 39–40.

c) Performance Management

i) *Focus on Procedural Justice and Community Policing*

A performance management system will enable officers to improve their skills and perform in accordance to the expectations of the police department. As Bayley, Davis, and Davis proposed, human rights should be the operational principle for all aspects of policing including human resources management.[149] Along the same line of thought, Branly et al proposed a performance management model that is based on the concept of community policing with focus on procedural justice.[150]

Community policing is founded on partnership, collaboration, and mutual trust between the police and the community with the objective of reducing crime, and improving the quality of life and police-community relations. The focus of this model is the principle of procedural justice that requires the police to be bias-free (fairness), treat all community members with dignity (respect), explain what they do and why (transparency) to community members, and provide them with an opportunity to express their views (voice).

This model is critical for ending racial profiling because, if done properly, the performance management system may enable supervisors to provide timely feedback to officers on their performance, coach them, monitor their performance, detect their biases, develop measures to improve their performance, and/or empower them to adopt a value-guided approach in community policing.

Effective law enforcement depends on whether the community perceives the police as procedurally just or not. Procedural justice means the extent to which the criminal justice procedures are fair, impartial, and respectful and are seen by community members as such. Although the police do not represent the entire criminal justice system, the public nevertheless view the police as the "face" of the system. Research on procedural justice suggests that public perceptions of the police are affected by the process of police-citizens interaction rather than by the outcome of the interaction. When the police-public interaction is seen by the community as not procedurally just, its authority is no long viewed as

---

149 David Bayley, Michael Davis, & Ronald Davis, *Race and Policing: An Agenda for Action*, New Perspectives in Policing Bulletin (Washington, DC: US Department of Justice, Office of Justice Programs, National Institute of Justice, 2015) at 9–10 [*Race and Policing*].

150 Shannon Branly et al, *Implementing a Comprehensive Performance Management Approach in Community Policing Organizations: An Executive Guidebook* (Washington, DC: Office of Community Oriented Policing Services, 2015) at 2–3 [Branly et al].

legitimate. Under this scenario, citizens are less than willing to cooperate or collaborate with the police in enforcing the law. The consent of citizens in police actions is critical. Therefore, in building a trusting relationship with the community, the police have to incorporate the principles of procedural justice in their performance management.[151]

The principles of procedural justice must be embedded in the corporate culture of police departments as well as their entire operation (including management). Police leaders and managers are to perform in accordance to procedural justice and treat police officers respectfully and impartially and maintain a bias-free work environment ("internal procedural justice"). Racial tensions should be rooted out, minority employees are to be given an opportunity to voice their concerns, and value statements and codes of ethics are to be developed for guiding police conducts. Only when procedural justice is operationalized internally in police departments can it be extended to an external environment in which police officers interact respectfully and impartially with community members ("external procedural justice"). In community policing, the priority is *service* (to people), not *compliance* (to rules). The performance management of the police is therefore fundamental to actualizing the principles of procedural justice.[152]

Under the auspices of the Community Oriented Policing Services, US Department of Justice, Branly et al recommend three major changes in performance management:[153]

1) Police agencies' current performance and evaluation systems (their purposes, processes, and contents) are to be assessed with the objective of determining whether there are connections between performance management, accountability, and disciplinary systems.

2) The strengthening of supervisor-employee relationships through two-way communication, making supervisors more visible in the field, emphasizing treating each respectfully and fairly, and enabling officers to have their voice in the organization.

3) The emphasis on talent and career development at all levels by recruiting qualified supervisors, selecting supervisors fairly, training supervisors to be effective leaders, equipping supervisors with coaching and mentoring skills, using an individual development plan

---

151 *Ibid* at v, vii, and 1.
152 *Ibid* at vii–viii; *Race and Policing*, above note 149 at 10–12.
153 Branly et al, above note 150 at 5–8 and 31–51.

as a personalized tool for every employee, and using the 360-degree evaluation process for each employee.

Establishing a performance management system with a focus on procedural justice (as described above) has been supported and advocated by the chiefs of numerous police departments including Chief Tim Dolan (retired) of Minneapolis Police Department; Chief Will Johnson, Arlington Police Department (Texas); Chief Charlie Deane (retired), Prince William Country Police Department (Virginia); Chief Janee Harteau, Minneapolis Police Department; and Chief Robert White, Denver Police Department.[154]

Some examples of performance management that focus on procedural justice in community policing:[155]

- Madison Police Department, Wisconsin, pioneered the community policing approach and Milwaukee Police Department has a detailed code of conduct.
- Denver Police Department reviewed and restructured its performance evaluation system in 2011–13.
- Minneapolis Police Department's goals and metrics performance facilitated monthly dialogues among supervisors and between supervisors and officers.
- Brooklyn Park Police Department, Minnesota, instituted end-of-shift debriefing sessions with the entire squad.
- Los Angeles Police Department has a mentoring program for job candidates.
- Boise Police Department, Idaho, has a 360-degree review system for supervisors.

d) Early Intervention System

The Community Oriented Policing Services, US Department of Justice, has identified an "early intervention system" as a proactive tool to prevent racial profiling. This system assumes that unless racial profiling behaviours of officers are identified by supervisors and are rectified through counselling and training, police officers may continue these behaviours without knowing that they are problematic. The system produces data that provide information on the context and patterns of police behaviours.[156]

---

154 *Ibid* at 53–58.
155 *Race and Policing*, above note 149 at 10.
156 *Ibid* at 10–12.

Essentially, an early intervention system has the following steps:[157]

- Determining specific indicators for measuring performance of officers;
- Measuring selected indicators of officers' performance and identifying patterns and trends through police intervention data and allegation information;
- Determining departmental thresholds of tolerance for each indicator as a baseline for performance intervention;
- Identifying police officers whose performance indicators exceed the departmental threshold(s);
- Determining whether performance intervention is needed for the officers (intervention may consist of counselling, training, closer supervision, more performance assessment, or re-assignment); and
- Continuous monitoring and review of officers' performance to determine extent of effectiveness.

This system enables law enforcement organizations to identify the sources of racial profiling activities — individual police officers, departmental units, institutions, or a mix of both. With results from this system, police organizations would be able to determine the solutions. However, having a well-designed data system for tracking different aspects of police actions for the purpose of reducing or ending racial profiling may require adequate resources and alignments with the current administrative system of the police. And, after collecting the data, the law enforcement organizations still need to determine the thresholds for police interventions and with good justifications.[158]

As a supplement to the quantitative tendency of an early intervention system, Kelling, Wasserman, and Williams proposed to sample and audit police activities by interviewing witnesses and other parties about police arrests or survey stakeholders on their satisfaction with the police. While the early intervention system has a tendency to quantify data on police activities, the proposed audit system focuses on the quality, not quantity, of officers' performance. In essence, audits are accountability checks after the fact.[159]

Kelling, Wasserman, and Williams maintained that when police officers make mistakes, they should be supported by better coaching from their supervisors. However, when incompetence and irresponsibility of

---

157 *Promoting Cooperative Strategies*, above note 36 at 7.

158 *Ibid* at 7–8.

159 Kelling, Wasserman, & Williams, above note 40 at 5–7.

officers occur, discipline is needed.[160] The International Association of Chiefs of Police (IACP) recommends police agencies eliminate racially biased policing by "using appropriate disciplinary mechanisms for officers who show a pattern of willful racial profiling."[161]

In implementing the early intervention system, a number of challenges emerged. To begin with, police officers have been resisting the implementation of such a system as it has been viewed as a threat to their jobs. Some are concerned about the issues of data privacy, confidentiality, and legality. Some community members also distrust the system as it may just "whitewash" racial profiling activities of officers. There are also technical issues related to the compatibility and integration of technological hardware as well as administrative issues related to stakeholders' approval of system usage.[162]

Some examples of police services adopting the early intervention system: Arlington Police Department, Texas; police department for the City of St Paul, Minnesota; and Denver Police Department, Colorado.[163]

e) Encouragement System

Another way to achieve the results of ending racial profiling is to develop an encouragement system in which police actions that engage with the community, build partnerships, and collaborate on building community wellness are to be encouraged. There are several police activities that have not been traditionally included in the evaluation of police performance, such as dispute resolution, crime prevention, problem solving, and maintenance of order and peace. These activities could be incorporated as indicators of bias-free community policing. Police behaviours could be evaluated on a regular basis by measuring these indicators.

The President's Task Force on 21st Century Policing in the US has this line of thinking. It recommended that community policing should be infused in the corporate culture of law enforcement agencies and in line with this is a proposed action: "law enforcement agencies should evaluate officers on their efforts to engage members of the community and the partnerships they build. Making this part of the performance evaluation process places an increased value on developing partnerships." (4.2.1 Action Item) Similarly, patrol deployment practices should "allow

---

160 *Ibid* at 6–7.
161 Leach, above note 13 at 184–97.
162 *Promoting Cooperative Strategies*, above note 36 at 12–14.
163 *Ibid* at 9–12.

sufficient time for patrol officers to participate in problem solving and community engagement activities." (4.2.2 Action Item)[164]

Peer review could also be used as a supplementary method for monitoring and evaluating officers' performance. Currently, only a few police departments use this method for police accountability. While the exact mechanism of operation has not quite worked out, police services may develop procedures for assessing officers' engagement with communities through peer reviews.[165]

In aligning officers' performance with the standards set by police departments, rewards could be used when police officers have a track record of engaging with the community and practicing bias-free policing.

4) Pillar 4: Stakeholder Engagement

Stakeholder groups are organizations or individuals who have a vested interest in law enforcement issues, as decisions may impact on them directly or indirectly. They may be categorized as external and internal. For racial profiling issues:

- External stakeholder groups are organizations or individuals outside law enforcement agencies. They may include schools, community organizations, neighbourhood councils, social service agencies, ethnic or racial minority organizations, advocacy groups, parent associations, teachers and school principals, shopping malls owners, police colleges, associations of police chiefs, government departments, and the public at large.
- Internal stakeholder groups are organizations or individuals inside law enforcement agencies. They may include police chiefs, police boards of governors, police associations, police officers, sergeants, detectives, superintendents, and civilian employees.

The purposes of engaging stakeholder groups are to solicit opinions and suggestions from them, work together to identify problems and find solutions, foster better accountability, and create an emotional attachment and sense of ownership for all stakeholders. Stakeholder groups could be pivotal in the development of organizational structures and processes for effecting changes, and this may include the development of an accountability framework or a task force, committee, or office that is responsible for planning, communicating, implementing, coordinating,

---

164 President's Task Force, above note 42 at 92.

165 *Race and Policing*, above note 149 at 10–12.

reporting, monitoring, assessing, and decision making on matters related to ending racial profiling. Bayley, Davis, and Davis believe that such engagement with stakeholder groups, especially at the community level, is critical in ending racial profiling.[166]

a) Community Engagement

To be successful in ending racial profiling, stakeholder groups, such as racialized minority communities, are to be engaged. Getting minority communities to be involved could be done by providing opportunities for them to voice their concerns and to provide input in the decision-making process on policy and other important matters in police departments, establishing channels of two-way communication between communities and police departments, and being transparent on issues of importance to them.

Bayley, Davis, and Davis suggested that community engagement means a shift in the current policing culture from one that focuses on fighting against criminals to "engaging with communities to help those at risk or in need." In operational terms, it means having police officers familiarize themselves with the history of the communities, be specific on what community policing means, explain to community members what the police are doing, regularly assess how people feel towards the police, implement a user-friendly complaint procedure, and be transparent about allegations of police misconduct, investigation results, and disciplinary outcomes.[167]

Communication is a key ingredient in engagement, and it is a two-way street. The onus is on police services, including their leaders, to inform community members about the police's anti-racial profiling initiatives including policy development, training strategies, accountability, and police officers' ethical codes.[168] At the individual level, officers should inform citizens of why they are being stopped and their rights. Conversations with community members must be conducted with respect and should be impartial. At the collective level, police managers should publicize policies and mission statements on bias-free policing, listen to the public concerns, and work on solutions with the community.

Community members also have an obligation to voice their concerns and put forward their ideas and suggestions. At the individual level, community members should be able to express their feelings and inform police officers of their community priorities. At the collective level, community members should be able to inform the police about the

---

166 *Ibid* at 9–10.

167 *Ibid.*

168 Leach, above note 13 at 153–91.

history and dynamics of their communities. Each party can learn from the other.[169] The chief of police at the Riverside Police Department, California, Russ Leach, listed communicating with community members as one of the five core responsibilities for police departments.[170]

Clear communication to key stakeholder groups and the public at large regarding the organizational efforts made to end racial profiling is crucial to its success. This is because they have a vested interest in knowing the progress as well as the results of these efforts. Clear communication conveys the message of transparency, and stakeholder groups and the public at large appreciate it greatly. On a topic such as racial profiling, clarity in communication strengthens good relationships without stirring up the historical police-community distrust.

To be meaningful and effective, communication must also be accessible. To accomplish this, the language and media for communication become crucial, as they have to be tailored for different segments of the population. Most racialized minorities are immigrants and they might not be proficient in the Canadian official languages. Their information may depend largely on relatives or friends (in other words, word-of-mouth); they may also be obtaining their information through a range of media, including ethnic media. Social media are increasingly used by the younger age groups of racialized minorities.

This engagement process is important for several reasons: The legitimacy of a police department depends on whether the public views it as working in their best interest. Police departments need to work with the communities to eliminate the historical distrust between themselves and minorities, demonstrate that the enforcement of law is fair and unbiased, and develop legitimacy for their work. When trust and legitimacy are developed and consolidated between these two parties, it will make law enforcement more effective. Without public support, police work is less effective because law enforcement depends largely on information provided by the public. Without the collaboration of the community, the police get less information from the community members. This makes it more difficult to do their job well.[171]

Community engagement can promote positive perception of the police especially when communication and engagement are carried in good faith and genuine spirit. Racial minorities have a tendency to view police behaviour as negative due to past experiences. Racial profiling is seen not

---

169   *Ibid* at 167.

170   *Ibid* at 153.

171   *Promoting Cooperative Strategies*, above note 36 at 21–22 and 55–56.

as isolated individual incidents, but as a pervasive problem affecting their daily lives. When the relationship between the police and minority communities is negative, any police stops, no matter how legitimate they are, are viewed as suspicious or problematic by these minorities. Therefore, it is imperative that the police-minority relations be improved through more dialogues, more minority involvement in police work, and more minority voices in the public.[172]

However, there are several challenges in community engagement. As the mistrust of the police is very deep-seated, an improvement of police-minority relations through engagement is not a quick fix; it should be treated as a long-term strategy. Investing efforts in bringing minority communities to the discussion table is one essential step in forging a relationship with them in a sustainable manner. The willingness to engage the community and listen to minorities' concerns is to be demonstrated on a continuous basis. In addition, there is often a lack of buy-in from police officers (regarding minority inputs on police operation), lack of focus on racial profiling issues, and lack of training expertise in racial profiling.[173]

Governments and associations of police chiefs are very supportive of community engagement as a way to build bias-free police services. They recommended community outreach, building relationships, public consultation and collaboration, changing policing policies and strategies, community involvement in police training and problem solving, and utilization of community media. The President's Task Force on 21st Century Policing in the US has a series of recommendations related to community engagement:[174]

- "Law enforcement agencies should develop and adopt policies and strategies that reinforce the importance of community engagement in managing public safety." (4.1. Recommendation)
- These agencies "should build relationships based on trust with immigrant communities." (1.9 Recommendation)
- "Law enforcement agencies should engage community members in the training process." (5.2 Recommendation)

Action items listed in the report include:

---

172 *Ibid* at 21.
173 *Ibid* at 26.
174 President's Task Force, above note 42 at 85 and 92–95.

- To "conduct research to develop and disseminate a toolkit on how law enforcement agencies and training programs can integrate community members into this training process." (5.2.1 Action Item)
- In the US, "law enforcement agencies should involve the community in the position of developing and evaluating policies and procedures." (1.5.1. Action Item)
- "When serious incidents occur, including those involving alleged police misconduct, agencies should communicate with citizens and the media swiftly, openly, and neutrally, respecting areas where the law requires confidentiality." (1.3.2 Action Item)

The Commission des droits de la personne et des droits de la jeunesse in Quebec, after its public consultation on racial profiling in 2009, recommended that (1) the administrators of police departments work with community partners to fight effectively against crime, and (2) with respect for the rights of citizens, the government and the municipalities allocate adequate funding for this purpose in their budgets.[175]

The International Association of Chiefs of Police (IACP) recommended police agencies eliminate racially biased policing through an ongoing outreach program:[176] Governments, associations of police chiefs, and police services also established joint partnerships in driving bias-free policing. Here are some examples:

- The partnership in the Human Rights Project Charter between the Toronto Police Services Board, the Toronto Police Service, and the Ontario Human Rights Commission was a good example of stakeholder partnership. It was a three-year project (2007–10) "aimed to identify and eliminate any discrimination that may exist in the employment and service policies of the Toronto Police Services Board and the practices of the Toronto Police Service." The project focused on accountability, public education, recruitment, selection, and training. Even after 2010, these three parties continue their collaboration by acting jointly as sponsors and meet regularly to oversee the continuous efforts in effecting organizational changes.[177] The Ontario Association of Chiefs of Police views this partnership as one of the best practices.[178]

---

175   *Racial Profiling and Systematic Discrimination*, above note 18 at 42, 102, & 103.
176   Leach, above note 13 at 184–97.
177   OHRC, *Human Rights and Policing*, above note 8 at 16 and 20.
178   OACP, *Anti-Racial Profiling*, above note 34 at v.

- The Commission des droits de la personne et des droits de la jeunesse in Quebec remains attentive to the community organizations that it encountered during consultation and continues to work in collaboration with them so that their knowledge and expertise could be utilized.[179]
- As a way to outreach and engage community members, the Toronto Police Service publicized its commitment to fair and equitable policing to more than 400,000 homes in Toronto through a newspaper insert.[180]
- The Windsor Police Service Board works with the African-Canadian community on issues centred around the latter's complaints (such as police encounters and recruitment).[181]
- Buffalo Police Department, New York, partnered with United Neighborhoods in developing study circles. These study circles facilitated training and provided guides to deal with racial profiling. They also arranged discussion meetings and action forums (aimed at finding solutions) between youths and the police.[182]
- Rochester Police Department, New York, implemented enhanced community education programs (e.g., cadet program, clergy response team, medical information sharing), improved communication, and recruiting qualified minority candidates.[183]
- New Haven Police Department, Connecticut, conducted the "Community Justice Dialogue Project," which improved police-community conversation. The project was guided by an advisory committee made up of a broad range of stakeholders. The project was carried out in several locations.[184]
- Charlotte-Mecklenburg Police Department, North Carolina, has an online complaints procedure to make it easier for community members to voice their concerns.[185]

b) Employee Engagement

It is important that police officers and civilians in police organizations are involved in the development and implementation of any initiatives

---

179 *Racial Profiling and Systematic Discrimination*, above note 18 at 42, 102, & 103.
180 OHRC Submission, above note 5 at 39.
181 *Ibid* at 14.
182 *Promoting Cooperative Strategies*, above note 36 at 22–23.
183 *Ibid* at 23.
184 *Ibid* at 25–26.
185 *Race and Policing*, above note 149 at 10.

that address and eliminate racial profiling. As police officers are on the front line interacting with community people, their understanding of the issue of racial profiling as well as their conduct in carrying out their police duties are seen or felt by those who interact with them. When police officers do not recognize racial profiling and are not convinced of the value of anti-racial profiling initiatives or the way that they are carried out, they will not co-operate and these initiatives will fail.

Very often police leaders see the urgency of restoring community trust over the issue of racial profiling or the perception of it. However, this urgency, along with good rationales, may not have been convincingly communicated to police officers and have resulted in resistance at the rank-and-file level. The lack of alignment between the mindset of police officers and that of police leaders spells the end of any initiatives that aim to eradicate racial profiling or the community perception of it.

In order to ensure that police officers are aligned with organizational priority in addressing the issue of racial profiling, they need to be involved in all stages of anti-racial profiling initiatives — conception, development, implementation, and evaluation. Their concerns about workloads, community tension, police reputation, individual responsibility, ease of execution, and many others are to be dealt with and resolved. Police officers need to dispel their suspicion, be on the side of police leaders, and guide the developmental process so as to meet their needs and interests. They need to see the initiatives as beneficial to them (or at least not harmful for them) as well as the public good.[186] For these reasons, police representatives of all ranks as well as police associations or unions are to be involved in these initiatives upfront so that their voices can be heard.

In addition to police officers, civilians working in police organizations responsible for communication, public liaison, legal issues, data system, and technology have also been on board on anti-racial profiling issues. The efforts to align the messages and synchronize the sequences of releasing information are best carried out in consultation and collaboration with the civilians in charge of communication and public liaison. There are also legal issues related to racial profiling and the ways the police interface with community members. Legal counsels need to be knowledgeable about these issues prior to giving the police advice. As for data system and technology, civilians in these fields know issues related to data and technical compatibility, privacy and confidentiality, and data transferability. Involvement from them in the different stages of

---

186 *Promoting Cooperative Strategies*, above note 36 at 54–55.

anti-racial profiling initiatives would avoid false starts and save a lot of resources and efforts.

Engagement of uniformed and civilian employees in police services has not been high on the priority list in police efforts to end racial profiling. It is a topic that has been barely mentioned in both academic and professional literature. In spite of this, the Ontario Association of Chiefs of Police views having an internal communication vehicle where the chief of police could provide positive guidance to personnel on the issue of racial profiling as one of the best practices.[187] One of the actionable items as proposed by the President's Task Force on 21st Century Policing in the US is "law enforcement agencies should involve employees in the process of developing policies and procedures" in order to achieve internal legitimacy. (1.4.1 Action Item)[188]

D. CONCLUSION

For a complex issue like racial profiling, finding a way to end it is not easy. Given the current scenario of continuous debates on whether it actually is happening or not, a proposed model of bias-free policing necessarily has to assume that racial profiling exists. This assumption is based on currently available evidence, especially from the US. The existence of racial profiling is still subject to rebuttal if more solid evidence emerges. Irrespective of where one stands on this issue, the perception of racial profiling, especially among racial minorities, is abundantly clear, both in Canada and the US. Consider the negativity that racial profiling has brought — illegality, offence to civil liberty, an ineffective tool for fighting crime, heightened racial tension, and adverse impacts for minorities. Identifying solutions to racial profiling, or the perception of it, is worthwhile and, indeed, urgent.

The four pillars as proposed in this model — strategic leadership, research, human resource management, and stakeholder engagement — have to be strong and supportive of each other. Without this mutual reinforcement, the impact of the model will be minimal in ending racial profiling. For example, even if police leaders are working full steam in changing their policing approach, without community engagement, their attempts will be viewed with suspicion and may be seen as illegitimate. Without employee support, bias-free policing could only be half-heartedly carried out. Similarly, if police officers are not trained in anti-racial profiling, it would be

---

187   OACP, *Anti-Racial Profiling*, above note 34 at v.
188   President's Task Force, above note 42 at 85.

difficult to see a culture embedded with the value of accountability or a culture of guardianship for policing. All the components in each pillar are to be implemented and coordinated in a seamless manner.

Ending racial profiling is an incremental and long-term process. In this paper, many recommendations on supporting bias-free policing, anti-racial profiling, and community policing have been put forward by associations of police chiefs, police departments, human rights commissions, and other government agencies, after they have examined the issue of racial profiling. Police services in Canada and the US have been developing policies, programs, and initiatives to end racial profiling and to promote bias-free policing. These examples serve to confirm the value of ending racial profiling. While results on the outcomes and impacts of these efforts remain rather limited and strong evidence on the value of bias-free policing is still pending, governments and police services acknowledge that bias-free policing is the way to go. It is hoped that Canada will begin in earnest to end racial profiling, not only by promising more changes, but by placing more efforts and resources in practical actions.

Race Data and Traffic Stops in Ottawa, 2013–2015

A Report submitted to Ottawa Police Services Board and Ottawa Police Service

DR. LORNE FOSTER, DR. LES JACOBS, & DR. BOBBY SIU

October, 2016

TABLE OF CONTENTS

EXECUTIVE SUMMARY

This report provides a city overview of the findings of the Ottawa Police Service's Traffic Stop Race Data Collection Project (TSRDCP), a pioneering community-based research project that involved undertaking the largest race based data collection in Canadian policing history. The project arose from an agreement between the Ontario Human Rights Commission (OHRC), the Ottawa Police Services Board (Board), and the Ottawa Police Service (OPS). The OHRC and the OPS believe that race-based data collection is part of an organizational approach to ensuring bias-neutral policing services. Full information regarding the agreement is available online at ottawapolice.ca/race.

The Traffic Stop Race Data Collection Project required police officers to record their perception of the driver's race, by observation only, for traffic stops over a two-year period from June 27, 2013 to June 26, 2015. A total of 81,902 records of traffic stops were examined for this report. Each record included complete information on race, sex and age, along with complete information on police districts, reasons for traffic stops and outcomes. The record did not include the time of day nor the neighbourhood where the stop occurred. The officers entering the race data reported perceiving the race of the driver prior to the stop in 11.4% of the cases.

This research project addresses three issues:

INCIDENCES OF TRAFFIC STOPS – Do drivers of different race groups have disproportionately high incidences of traffic stops, when compared with their respective driver populations in Ottawa? Research findings showed that:

- The study examines 81,902 traffic stops where officers recorded their perception of the driver's race: 69.3% White (56,776), 12.3% Middle Easterner (10,066), 8.8% Black (7,238), 4.7% E.Asian/SE Asian (3,875), 2.7% S. Asian (2,195), 1.9% Other racialized minorities (1,545), and .3% Indigenous Peoples (207).
- In Ottawa, Middle Easterner and Black groups, irrespective of their sex and age, are the two race groups with disproportionately high incidences of traffic stops. Middle Easterner Drivers were stopped 10066 times, which constituted about 12.3% of the total stops over the two year period. However, these drivers represent less than 4% of the total driving population in Ottawa. This means that Middle Easterner Drivers were stopped 3.3 times more than what you would expect based on their population. Black Drivers were stopped 7238 times, which constituted about 8.8% of the

total stops over the two-year period. However, these drivers represent less than 4% of the total driving population in Ottawa. This means that Black Drivers were stopped 2.3 times more than what you would expect based on their population.

- With the exception of Indigenous peoples, men aged 16-24 of all race groups (including White) have disproportionately high incidences of traffic stops. The disproportionalities ranged from 64.21% (E. Asian/ S.E. Asian) to 1100.39% (Middle Easterner).
- Middle Easterner Male Drivers aged 16-24 were stopped 2302 times, which constituted about 2.8% of the total stops over the two year period. However, these drivers represent less than 0.25% of the total driving population in Ottawa. This means that young Middle Easterner male drivers were stopped 12 times more than what you would expect based on their population. Black Male Drivers aged 16-24 were stopped 1238 times, which constituted about 1.5% of the total stops over the two year period. However, these drivers represent less than 0.2% of the total driving population in Ottawa. This means that young Black male drivers were stopped 8.3 times more than what you would expect based on their population. White Male Drivers aged 16-24 were stopped 6172 times, which constituted about 7.5% of the total stops over the two year period. However, these drivers represent about 4.3% of the total driving population in Ottawa. This means that young White male drivers were stopped 1.7 times more than what you would expect based on their population.

REASONS FOR TRAFFIC STOPS – Do racialized minority drivers experience disproportionately high incidences of specific reasons for traffic stops when compared with their White counterparts in Ottawa? Research findings showed that:

- The findings showed that the reason most used by police officers in traffic stops is "provincial and municipal offenses". It was used in 79,603 of the 81, 902 traffic stops (97.19%). Police officers did not utilize "provincial and municipal offenses" for traffic stops in a disproportional manner for any racial minority groups.
- When compared with the White group, "criminal offences" reason has been used disproportionately by police officers for five of the six racialized minority groups. The data is inconclusive about Indigenous peoples with regard to this issue because the number of stops citing "criminal offenses" was too low to draw any conclusions.

- Similarly, "suspicious activities" reason has been used disproportionately by police officers for four racialized minority groups — Indigenous peoples (99.37%), Black (148.40%), Middle Easterner (133.70%), and other racialized minorities (132.78%).

OUTCOMES OF TRAFFIC STOPS – Do racialized minority drivers experience disproportionately high incidences of specific outcome of traffic stops when compared with their White counterparts in Ottawa? Research findings showed that:

- All race groups (including White) have received similar proportions of charges (44.65%) from police officers after traffic stops.
- All race groups (including White) have received similar proportions of warnings (41.29%) from police officers after traffic stops.
- Indigenous peoples (37.77%), Black (47.28%), Middle Easterner (36.84%), and other racialized minorities (28.21%) groups experienced disproportionately high incidences of "final (no action)" outcomes of traffic stops.

This study is a correlational study on the relationship between race, sex, age, and traffic stops in Ottawa. It does not deal with the issue of causality. That is to say, it does not explain why and how these factors are related or not related. For this reason, the findings only provide a big picture of traffic stops in the entire capital city of Ottawa, covering a two-year period from 2013 and 2015 – a picture which provides a fresh and pioneering perspective on race and traffic stops in Canada.

RECOMMENDATIONS

It is recommended that the Ottawa Police Services Board and Ottawa Police Service:

(1) Determine the sources of the disproportionately high incidences identified in this study through additional research on psychological, organizational, and social issues within the Ottawa Police Service – systemic biases in police practices; police leadership and corporate culture; organizational policing strategies and tactics; human resources policies and practices; institutional mindsets about the association between race and crime; the diversity of the Ottawa Police Service workforce; and race relations dynamics with the diverse communities that constitute the City of Ottawa.

(2) Develop and implement solutions to address the anomalies of disproportionately high incidences through a review of research findings
gathered through the implementation of Recommendation # 1 in consultation with stakeholder groups, race and ethnic communities, and
the public.

(3) Increase positive police-community contact by holding monthly, or
regular, relationship-building meetings; train officers and community members together; promote joint police and community committee work particularly in advisory areas; and hold "critical incident"
discussions and trainings and annual conferences on police-community relations.

(4) Continue collecting race data in traffic stops with improved tools
and processes; monitor regularly traffic stops issues; place data reports as a regular agenda item on meetings at the level of staff, senior
management, and board; and communicate data related to race and
traffic stops regularly to the public through quarterly bulletins, press
releases, annual reports, and other media.

(5) Build on its extensive and successful experience with community engagement and develop a multi-year action plan to address the issues
of racial disparities in traffic stops raised in this report.

(6) Make readily available the data collected for this research project on
race and traffic stops. The raw data made available should allow for
analysis that goes beyond the scope and methodology of this report,
but within the legal limits of the *Freedom of Information and Protection of Privacy Act* and the *Municipal Freedom of Information and Protection of Privacy Act.*

AVAILABILITY OF DATA – The traffic stop data used for this report is
available at http://www.ottawapolice.ca/en/news-and-community/Traffic-
Stop-Race-Data-Collection-ProjectTSRDCP.asp

Part I

Project Findings

INTRODUCTION

This report provides a city overview of the findings of the Ottawa Police Service's Traffic Stop Race Data Collection Project (TSRDCP).

Background

This race data collection project is derived from the letter of understanding signed between the Ontario Police Service Board and the Ontario Human Rights Commission on April 27, 2012. This settlement agreement was based on the complaint put forward by Chad Aiken, a young Black man, who was pulled over by a police officer in Ottawa. He believed that he was racially profiled and alleged that his right to equal treatment with respect to services without discrimination because of age, colour, ethnic origin, and race.

According to the Minutes of Settlement, the Ottawa Police Service Board agreed to collect race data in traffic stops. It agreed to "begin collecting the data on or before June 27, 2013. The data shall be collected for no less than two (2) full years ("the data collection period"). The data collection period may be extended if recommended by the expert."

Project Design

Since the Fall of 2012, in preparing for the race data collection project, the Ottawa Police Services has retained the consulting and research services of Dr. Lorne Foster, Dr. Les Jacobs, and Dr. Bobby Siu of York University (York University Research Team).

In developing the framework for the project, Ottawa Police Service and York University Research Team, along with other stakeholder groups, discussed a range of project components including consultations with communities, internal stakeholders, Ottawa Police Association, and the Ontario Human Rights Commission; data requirements; information technology; data collection mechanisms, policies and procedures; data storage; roles and responsibilities; quality assurance; methodology and data limitations; education and training; communications; and schedule of project activities.

Communication, community and stakeholder consultation

Communication is crucial in gaining support from the employees of the Ottawa Police Service, the Ottawa Police Association, community members, and the public at large. Prior to rolling out the data collection process, York University Research Team advised the Ottawa Police Service to communicate clearly senior management's commitment to the project, and the messages were to be cascaded through the middle management to the constable level.

An Ottawa Police Service's project team, led by Inspector Pat Flanagan, was created to carry out the project and provide regular communications updates; and working in partnership with key stakeholders and project partners to ensure meaningful community participation throughout the project.

Project stakeholders include:

- Ottawa Police Services Board;
- Ontario Human Rights Commission;
- Ottawa Police Association;
- Ottawa Police Service Community Police Action Committee (COMPAC); and
- Traffic Stops Race Data Collection Project (TSRDCP) Community Police Advisory Committee.

The Ottawa Police Service also has extensive community outreach strategies and communications tools for reaching community partners and the general public. The cornerstone of OPS community engagement efforts is its Partnership in Action (PIA) framework that aims to identify and build upon community consultation within policing. Under the auspice of the Partnership in Acton framework for strategic community engagement and partnerships, the Traffic Stops Race Data Collection Project was able to leverage many existing community relationships established over the years by the OPS, for race data project development purposes. Hence, throughout this project, the internal and external stakeholders, as well as many Ottawa Police Service's community partners were engaged in all stages of the data collection process.

In addition, Ottawa Police Service engaged the public in dialogues on racial profiling issues, and encouraged people to provide ideas and inputs on the project. It has also made project plans, project information, and progress updates regularly available for the public through its website on the project as well as social media. Special community updates were conducted on a regular basis through the community police advisory committee. In addition, community engagement opportunities have been broadened through social media, phone line, e-mail connection, "community ride along with officers", surveys and focus groups, public dialogue session ("Let's Chat Sessions"), and internal sessions for members of the police service.

DATA COLLECTION

As this is the first time that the Ottawa Police Service has collected race data in traffic stops, numerous factors had to be considered: state of information technology and data system, officers' capabilities of data collection, data quality assurance, communication, and engagement.

Data system

Through consultation with communities and stakeholder groups, data types were identified, seven race categories, which correspond to the typology of Statistics Canada, along with their breakdowns in sex and age. Community members' recommendations for collecting data on reasons and outcomes of traffic stops based on race have also been incorporated into the project design. Data breakdowns by police districts in Ottawa have also been provided.

The computer technology used by the Ottawa Police Service was modified to accommodate these data needs. The data collection process was also made more user-friendly and less prone to errors. These modifications enabled the Ottawa Police Service to increase its data quality.

Data collection capabilities

Police officers are responsible for collecting traffic stop data. The technical modifications to include required race categories and other traffic stop data required additional skill development, which the Ottawa Police Service provided through on-line training with a toolkit and coaching. There were also pilot test sessions for detecting errors so that the training model could be improved. York University Research Team was not engaged in the actual training of police officers, but did provide advice on how best to upgrade their data collection skills.

Data quality assurance

A project of this nature depends on the quality of data collected. To ensure high quality data, supervisors were trained through orientation, videos and regular briefings on the data collection mechanisms and detection of collection errors. The Ottawa Police Service also monitored the quality of data collected on a daily basis at the initial stage of data collection, followed by weekly monitoring to identify anomalies. In the early stage of data collection, several types of data entry errors and omissions were detected, and adjustments were made, resulting in significant improvement.

RESEARCH FINDINGS ON OTTAWA

During the two-year period between June 27, 2013 and June 26, 2015, the Ottawa Police Service had non-erroneous data in 120,617 traffic stop records. The traffic stops data was collected by police officers. As this research required the presence of data on Ottawa residents, with their complete information on race, sex and age, along with complete information on police districts, reasons for traffic stops and outcomes, the number of traffic stops which is useable for this research is 81,902.

This analysis of traffic stops with respect of the representation of race groups, with sex and age breakdowns, and the distribution of race groups among reasons for traffic stops and outcomes of traffic stops is based on this data set of 81,902 traffic stops.

Section A: Incidences of Traffic Stops

The first objective of this research is the determination of whether there are any disproportionately high incidences of race groups, broken down by sex and age, in traffic stops in Ottawa.

For working purposes, data on Ottawa residents was divided into seven race groups (Indigenous peoples, White, Black, East Asian/Southeastern Asian, South Asian, Middle Easterner, and Other Racialized Minorities). They were then divided into male and female which were then subdivided into three age groups: 16-24, 25-54, and 55 and over. In total, there are 42 race subgroups.

The benchmark for measuring disproportionately high incidences of traffic stops is the segment of population in Ottawa, which drive to work using private vehicles (based on the "commute-to-work" population data in the National Household Survey, 2011). There were 286,145 drivers out of a total of 707,665 in the population in Ottawa. Diagram 1 provides a graphic representation of the driver population based on race in Ottawa.

DIAGRAM 1:   Race of Driver Distribution In Ottawa, Based on National Household Survey, 2011

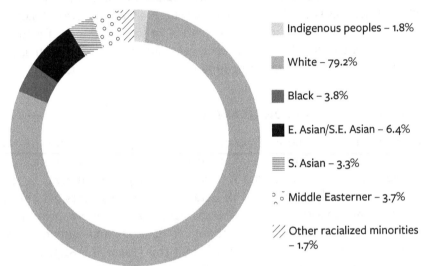

Indigenous peoples – 1.8%

White – 79.2%

Black – 3.8%

E. Asian/S.E. Asian – 6.4%

S. Asian – 3.3%

Middle Easterner – 3.7%

Other racialized minorities – 1.7%

A comparison of the driver segments (commuters-to-work) and the population of all seven race groups showed that the White group is the only race group whose driver segment is proportionately higher than its population (3.69%), whereas that of the Black group is disproportionately lower than its population (-22.95%). Other racialized minority groups are all proportionately lower than their populations (from -6.18% to -12.12%). This has implications later in our analysis of traffic stops.

As the catalyst of this research study was a concern about racial profiling in traffic stops in Ottawa, special attention is therefore focused on the disproportionately high incidences of traffic stops among race groups, broken down by sex and age.

PROPORTIONS OF DRIVER SEGMENTS AND POPULATIONS, BY RACE, IN OTTAWA

RACE GROUPS	DRIVER SEGMENTS	POPULATIONS	DIFFERENCES IN PROPORTIONS
Indigenous peoples	1.82%	1.94%	-6.18%
White	79.23%	76.41%	3.69%
Black	3.76%	4.88%	-22.95%
E. Asian/ S.E. Asian	6.41%	6.97%	-8.03%
S. Asian	3.31%	3.69%	-10.29%
Middle Easterner	3.73%	4.11%	-9.24%
Other racialized minorities	1.74%	1.98%	-12.12%
Total	100.00%	100.00%	

The White group is the only race group with a positive percentage, and this means their driver segment is proportionately high.

The "20% rule" suggested that the Black group's difference is disproportionately low, and the differences of other racialized minority groups are just low.

These incidences are indicated by percentages of 20% or over in the differences between traffic stop data and commute-to-work data. When race groups are described as having "disproportionately high incidences in traffic stops" (20% and over), this means they are over-represented in traffic stops when their shares of traffic stops are greater than their shares in the "commute-to-work" driver segments. A zero percentage (0%) in the proportionality of incidences in traffic stops for a race group means the group's proportion in traffic stops corresponds to its proportion in the driver segment (who commute to work).

Ottawa

Findings

Among the 81,902 traffic stops of Ottawa residents, in addition to race, the findings allow for a breakdown of incidences of traffic stops based on age groupings and sex groupings. The findings, summarized in Diagram 2, show that almost two-thirds of traffic stops involved drivers between the ages of 25 and 54.

DIAGRAM 2: Age of Driver Distribution Among Traffic Stops

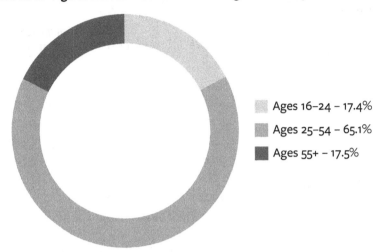

Ages 16–24 – 17.4%
Ages 25–54 – 65.1%
Ages 55+ – 17.5%

The findings, summarized in Diagram 3, show that only one-third of drivers stopped were women.

DIAGRAM 3: Sex of Driver Distribution Among Traffic Stops

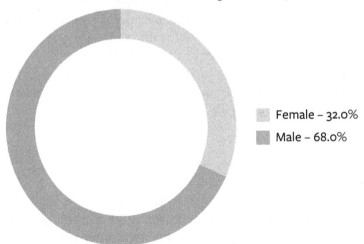

Female – 32.0%
Male – 68.0%

The study examines 81,902 traffic stops where officers recorded their perception of the driver's race: 69.3% White (56,776), 12.3% Middle Easterner (10,066), 8.8% Black (7,238), 4.7% E.Asian/SE Asian (3,875), 2.7% S. Asian (2,195), 1.9% Other racialized minorities (1,545), and .3% Indigenous Peoples (207). The officers entering the race data reported perceiving the race of the driver prior to the stop in 11.4% of the cases. Diagram 4 provides an overview of the breakdown of the race of the driver based on the seven race groupings used in the project. The majority (69.3%) of traffic stops involved White drivers.

DIAGRAM 4: Race of Driver Distribution Among Traffic Stops

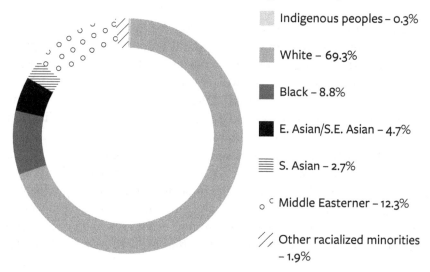

Indigenous peoples – 0.3%

White – 69.3%

Black – 8.8%

E. Asian/S.E. Asian – 4.7%

S. Asian – 2.7%

Middle Easterner – 12.3%

Other racialized minorities – 1.9%

Diagram 5 provides a comparison between race of driver distribution among traffic stops and the National Household Survey.

DIAGRAM 5: Comparison of Race of Driver Distribution Among Traffic Stops and NHS

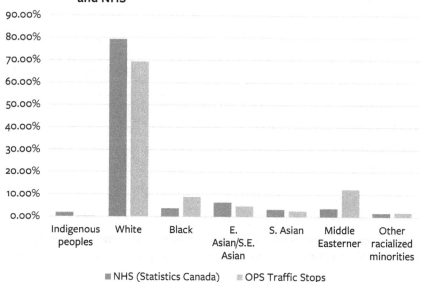

In Ottawa, Middle Easterner and Black groups, irrespective of their sex and age, are the two race groups with disproportionately high incidences of traffic stops. Middle Easterner Drivers were stopped 10066 times, which constituted about 12.3% of the total stops over the two year period. However, these drivers represent less than 4% of the total driving population in Ottawa. This means that Middle Easterner Drivers were stopped 3.3 times more than what you would expect based on their population. Black Drivers were stopped 7238 times, which constituted about 8.8% of the total stops over the two-year period. However, these drivers represent less than 4% of the total driving population in Ottawa. This means that Black Drivers were stopped 2.3 times more than what you would expect based on their population.

Middle Easterner group's disproportionally high incidences are 229.44% on average, and those of the Black group are 134.80% on average. They are the only two racialized minority groups (among all seven race groups) that have disproportionately high incidents of traffic stops. All other racialized minority groups (except other racialized minorities) have proportionately low incidents of traffic stops. E. Asian/ S.E. Asian group (-26.14%) and Indigenous peoples' (-86.09%) disproportionalities in traffic stops are even lower. The White group's incidences of traffic stops (-12.51%) are proportionately low too.

PROPORTIONALITIES OF INCIDENCES OF TRAFFIC STOPS, BY RACE, IN OTTAWA

(Arranged in descending order)

RACE GROUPS	PROPORTIONALITIES OF INCIDENCES OF TRAFFIC STOPS	RATIO OF SHARE OF TRAFFIC STOPS TO SHARE OF POPULATION $(1 + X-Y/Y)$
Middle Easterner	229.44%	3.3
Black	134.80%	2.3
Other racialized minorities	8.61%	1.1
White	-12.51%	0.9
S. Asian	-19.06%	0.8
E. Asian/ S.E. Asian	-26.14%	0.7
Indigenous peoples	-86.09%	0.1

Negative percentages denote low proportionalities. Positive percentages denote high proportionalities. Shaded positive percentages denote disproportionately high incidences of traffic stops.

In total, among the 42 race subgroups for which traffic stop data is available, there are 17 subgroups with disproportionately high incidences of traffic stops in Ottawa:

- Middle Easterner – 6 subgroups: all age groups among men and women.
- Black – 5 subgroups: all age groups among men and women except Black women aged 55 and over.
- Other racialized minorities – 3 subgroups: all age groups among men.
- White – 1 subgroup: men aged 16-24.
- E. Asian/S.E. Asian – 1 subgroup: men aged 16-24.
- S. Asian – 1 subgroup: men aged 16-24.

Middle Easterner and Black groups constituted eight of the top 10 subgroups with disproportionately highest incidences of traffic stops (ranging from 1100.39% for Middle Easterner men aged 16-24 to 78.97% for Black women aged 16-24).

RACE SUBGROUPS THAT HAVE DISPROPORTIONATELY HIGH INCIDENCES OF TRAFFIC STOPS IN OTTAWA

(Arranged in descending order)

RACE	SEX	AGE	DISPROPORTIONALITIES OF HIGH INCIDENCES OF TRAFFIC STOPS
Middle Easterner	Male	16-24	1100.39%
Black	Male	16-24	731.78%
Middle Easterner	Male	25-54	235.87%
Black	Male	25-54	196.13%
Middle Easterner	Female	16-24	189.60%
Middle Easterner	Male	55+	165.77%
Black	Male	55+	114.31%
Black	Female	16-24	78.97%
Other racialized minorities	Male	16-24	77.86%
White	Male	16-24	72.99%
S. Asian	Male	16-24	66.40%
Middle Easterner	Female	25-54	65.08%
E. Asian/S.E. Asian	Male	16-24	64.21%
Middle Easterner	Female	55+	34.11%
Other racialized minorities	Male	55+	33.23%
Black	Female	25-54	25.25%
Other racialized minorities	Male	25-54	20.51%

Middle Easterner and Black groups are highlighted.

It is also noted that men aged 16-24 of all the race groups, except Indigenous peoples, have disproportionately high incidences of traffic stops as well. Diagram 6 summarizes the findings for White, Black and Middle Eastern Male Drivers aged 16-24.

DIAGRAM 6: Comparison of Drivers 16-24 Based on Race

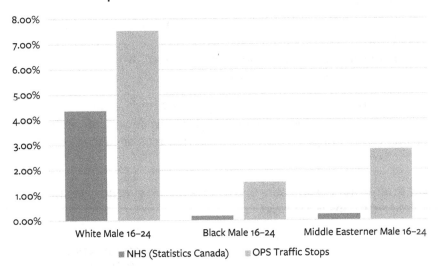

PROPORTIONALITIES OF INCIDENCES OF TRAFFIC STOPS AMONG RACE SUBGROUPS, MALE AGED 16-24, IN OTTAWA

(Arranged in descending order)

RACE	SEX	AGE	PROPORTIONALITIES OF INCIDENCES OF TRAFFIC STOPS	RATIO OF SHARE OF TRAFFIC STOPS TO SHARE OF POPULATION $(1 + X\text{-}Y/Y)$
Middle Easterner	Male	16-24	1100.39%	12
Black	Male	16-24	731.78%	8.3
Other racialized minorities	Male	16-24	77.86%	1.8
White	Male	16-24	72.99%	1.7
S. Asian	Male	16-24	66.40%	1.7
E. Asian/S.E. Asian	Male	16-24	64.21%	1.6
Indigenous peoples	Male	16-24	-75.98%	0.2

Race groups with disproportionately high incidences of traffic stops are highlighted. Indigenous peoples is the only race group with disproportionately low incidences of traffic stops.

Discussion

Middle Easterner Male Drivers aged 16-24 were stopped 2302 times, which constituted about 2.8% of the total stops over the two year period. However, these drivers represent less than 0.25% of the total driving population in Ottawa. This means that young Middle Easterner male drivers were stopped 12 times more than what you would expect based on their population. Black Male Drivers aged 16-24 were stopped 1238 times, which constituted about 1.5% of the total stops over the two year period. However, these drivers represent less than 0.2% of the total driving population in Ottawa. This means that young Black male drivers were stopped 8.3 times more than what you would expect based on their population. White Male Drivers aged 16-24 were stopped 6172 times, which constituted about 7.5% of the total stops over the two year period. However, these drivers represent about 4.3% of the total driving population in Ottawa. This means that young White male drivers were stopped 1.7 times more than what you would expect based on their population.

Middle Easterner men aged 16-24's disproportionality reached 1100.39% for its subgroup; and that of Black men aged 16-24 reached 731.78%. Note that there was not a high incidence of traffic stops for Indigenous men aged 16-24. Consider the threshold of "20% and over" used in this study to denote disproportionately high incidences of traffic stops and the proportionately low percentages of the driver segments of Middle Easterner and Black groups, these disproportionalities are statistically high. This may be due to one or more of the following factors:

- The level of criminal and non-criminal activities (provincial and municipal offenses) in the neighbourhoods in which traffic stops occurred
- Mindsets of police officers associating criminality, race, sex and age
- The level of mistrust between police officers and community members
- The race data in traffic stops is based on the "other-identification" method — the perception of the officer conducting the traffic stop — and the benchmark data is based on "self-identification"

None of the above could be proved or disproved by the data available for this study. Additional information and data are needed.

SECTION B: REASONS FOR TRAFFIC STOPS

The second objective of this research is the determination of the extent to which the reasons why police officers traffic stopped varied by race groups, and whether there are any marked differences between the White group and each of the racialized minority groups.

To meet this objective, Ottawa Police Service identified three major reasons for traffic stops: (a) criminal offenses, (b) provincial and municipal offenses, and (c) suspicious activities. Police officers identified the reason for each traffic stop.

- "Criminal offenses" – offenses based on the *Criminal Code* of Canada. Examples: stolen vehicles and impaired driving.
- "Provincial and municipal offenses" – Offenses related to provincial laws and municipal by-laws. Examples: Offenses related to the Highway Traffic Act such as speeding and light/stop sign running, licence plate sticker validation.
- "Suspicious activities" – Activities deemed to be dubious by police officers.

Ottawa

Findings

The findings showed that, in Ottawa, the reason most used by police officers in traffic stops is "provincial and municipal offenses". It was used in 79,603 of the 81, 902 traffic stops (97.19%). The rationale of "suspicious activities" was used in 1837 stops (2.24%) and "criminal offenses" in 462 stops (0.56%). The findings are summarized in Diagram 7.

DIAGRAM 7: Reasons for Traffic Stops Among Race Groups

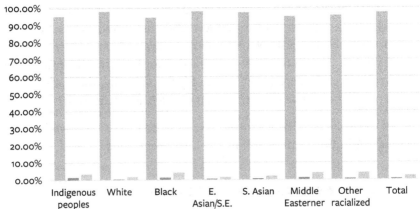

Police officers did not utilize "provincial and municipal offenses" for traffic stops in a disproportionate manner for any racial minority groups. As a reason, the findings suggest that "criminal offenses" has been disproportionately used by police officers for five of the six racialized minority groups when compared with the White group. The data is inconclusive about Indigenous peoples with regard to this issue because the number of stops citing "criminal offenses" was too low to draw any conclusions. "Suspicious activities", as a reason for traffic stops, has been used disproportionately by police officers for Indigenous peoples (99.37%), Black (148.40%), S. Asian (23.56%), Middle Easterner (133.70%), and other racialized minorities (132.78%).

PROPORTIONALITIES OF REASONS FOR TRAFFIC STOPS, BY RACIALIZED MINORITY GROUPS, IN OTTAWA

RACIALIZED MINORITY GROUPS	CRIMINAL OFFENSES	PROVINCIAL AND MUNICIPAL OFFENSES	SUSPICIOUS ACTIVITIES
Indigenous peoples	299.44%*	-2.83%	99.37%
Black	257.94%	-3.53%	148.44%
E. Asian/ S.E. Asian	56.48%	0.05%	-14.80%
S. Asian	88.35%	-0.74%	23.56%
Middle Easterner	209.40%	-3.09%	133.70%
Other racialized minorities	60.55%	-2.52%	132.78%

Disproportionately high incidences of reasons for traffic stops are highlighted.

*This calculation is based on 3 incidences when criminal offenses were cited as the reason for the stop of an Indigenous driver. This number is too low to support any inferences about disproportionality.

Discussion

Any inferences about the uses of criminal offenses or suspicious activities as reasons for traffic stops should be undertaken with great caution, given the small numbers in both of these categories compared to the provincial and municipal offenses. However, as a phenomenon, racial disparities on the reasons for traffic stops are evident.

This phenomenon may be related to the locations of traffic stops and circumstantial factors. Police officers may, for example, be responsive to the situational updates of neighbourhoods and are therefore mindful of unusual activities. Not having information on the sites, times and circumstances of these traffic stops, it is hard to speculate about the factors behind the disproportionalities of traffics stops for a number of racialized minority groups.

SECTION C: OUTCOMES OF TRAFFIC STOPS

The third objective of this research is the determination of the extent to which the outcomes of traffic stops varied by race groups, and how disproportionate these variations are between each of the racialized minority groups and the White group.

To meet this objective, Ottawa Police Service identified three major outcomes of traffic stops: (a) "final (no action)", (b) "warned", and (c) "charged".

- "Final (no action)" outcomes - Police officers did not give warnings or lay charges to the drivers after the traffic stops. No further action was taken by officers.
- "Warned" outcomes - Police officers gave verbal or written warnings to the drivers after the traffic stops.
- "Charged" outcomes - Police officers laid charges (such as speeding or distracted driving) to the drivers after the traffic stops.

In traffic stops, being charged is considered to be more severe than being warned, which, in turn, is considered to be more severe than no action on the part of police officers.

The analysis of proportionalities is based on a comparison of the outcomes of traffic stops as experienced by each of the racialized minority groups with the White group. The outcomes for the White group acted as a benchmark to measure the extent of deviations of outcomes for the racialized minority group.

Ottawa

Findings
In Ottawa, most outcomes of traffic stops are either "warned" (41.20%) or "charged" (44.65%). "Final (no action)" outcomes constituted 14.15%. But there are variations in outcomes among race groups. Diagram 8 provides an overview of the outcomes based on the race groupings.

DIAGRAM 8: Outcomes of Traffic Stops Among Race Groups

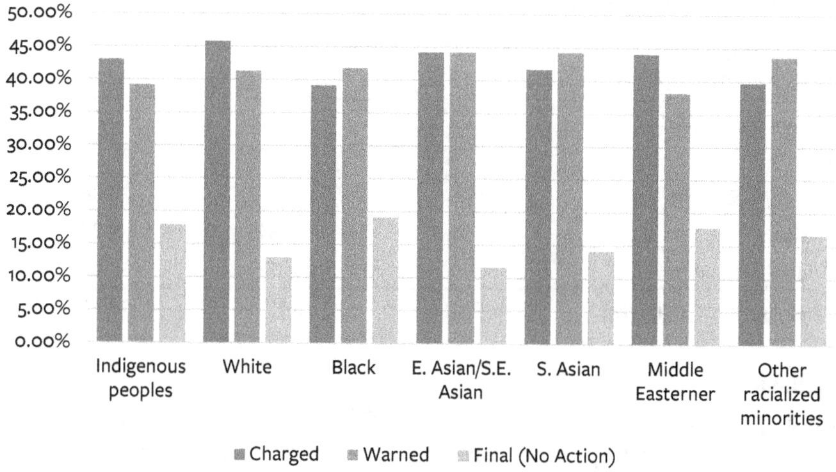

Legend: ■ Charged ■ Warned ▨ Final (No Action)

The ranges in outcomes among race groups are observed as follows:

- "Final (no action)" outcomes ranged from 11.59% (for E. Asian/S.E. Asian) to 19.11% (for Black).
- "Warned" outcomes ranged from 38.18% (for Middle Easterner) to 44.24% (E. Asian/S.E. Asian).
- "Charged" outcomes ranged from 39.10% (for Black) to 45.75% (for White).

A review of the three outcomes showed that it is only in the "final (no action)" outcomes that disproportionately high incidences are observed among racialized minority groups. When compared with the White group, the disproportionately high incidences of "final (no action)" outcomes are found in Black (47.28%), Indigenous peoples (37.77%), Middle Easterner (36.84%), and other racialized minorities (28.21%) groups.

There are no disproportionately high incidences in the "warned" and "charged" outcomes among racialized minority groups when they are compared with the White group. In other words, other race groups (including the White group) experienced more or less the same fate in terms of warnings and charges as the result of traffic stops.

PROPORTIONALITIES OF OUTCOMES OF TRAFFIC STOPS, BY RACIALIZED MINORITY GROUPS, IN OTTAWA

RACIALIZED MINORITY GROUPS	FINAL (NO ACTION)	WARNED	CHARGED
Indigenous peoples	37.77%	-5.19%	-6.03%
Black	47.28%	1.26%	-14.54%
E. Asian/ S.E. Asian	-10.60%	7.10%	-3.38%
S. Asian	8.51%	7.18%	-8.89%
Middle Easterner	36.84%	-7.50%	-3.68%
Other racialized minorities	28.21%	5.69%	-13.14%

Discussion

The disproportionally high incidences of "final (no action)" among the four racial minority groups shows that, when stopped, they were more likely to face no further police actions when compared with the White group. It has also been noted that no disproportionately high incidences of "warned" and "charged" outcomes are found among racialized minority groups when compared with the White group.

The lack of disproportionate differences in warnings and charges for racial minority groups in Ottawa when compared with the White group suggests that, as individuals, when stopped, racial minority groups are treated more or less the same as the White group, as far as warnings and charges are concerned. Some variations are noted, but they are not disproportionately high or low.

The disproportionately high incidences of "final (no action)" outcomes noted among the four racialized minority groups — Indigenous peoples, Black, Middle Easterner, and other racialized minorities — suggests that, after the intervention of traffic stops, police officers found that their reasons ("criminal offenses", "provincial and municipal offenses" or "suspicious activities") identified prior to their decisions for traffic stopping racialized minority groups were not as relevant or strong as those used for traffic stopping the White group. In other words, there was a greater propensity that these four racialized minority groups were traffic-stopped for nothing serious enough to be warned or charged, when compared with the White group.

Does this finding imply that police officers are disproportionately lenient towards these four racialized minority groups? There is a possibility that they might be. There are circumstantial situations as well as personal discretion of police officers, which might impact on their decisions. However, the data from this study does not allow such conclusion.

A More Integrated Picture

The above research findings have been presented in a compartmental manner. In this section, all three aspects of the traffic data, with a focus on the disproportionately high incidences, are presented. This allows a better understanding of the research findings as they relate to race groups.

This study sets the margin of errors using the "20% rule" in the design of the research project. As a rule, it filters out most common errors in data collection prior to data analysis, and allows a "cushion" for a relatively conservative analysis before coming to a conclusion. The disproportionalities of high incidences of traffics stops and their reasons and outcomes experienced by racialized minority groups are therefore considered relatively high.

These high disproportionalities of incidences indicated especially the severity of over-representation of two racialized minority groups – Middle Easterner and Black – in traffic stops. In addition, the data also showed that "criminal offenses", as a reason, has been disproportionately used by police officers in traffic-stopping mainly three more racialized minority groups – E. Asian/ S.E. Asian, S. Asian, and other racialized minorities. Moreover, "suspicious activities", as a reason, has been utilized by police officers to traffic stop Indigenous peoples and other racialized minorities, whereas E. Asian/ S.E. Asian and S. Asian are spared.

The fact that some racialized minority groups have higher probabilities of being traffic stopped, when compared with the White group, does not mean that as individuals they are more likely to be warned or charged. When compared with the White group, the data shows that individuals from racialized minority groups do not have disproportionately higher incidences of being warned or charged. In fact, four racialized minority groups groups – Indigenous peoples, E. Asian/ S.E. Asian, S. Asian – have disproportionately high incidences of "final (no action)" outcomes. The latter essentially means that they have a higher chance than the White group that the reasons for traffic-stopping them under the premises of "criminal offenses" or "suspicious activities" and, as a matter of fact, "provincial and municipal offenses", are not substantiated or not strong enough to justify warnings or charges. However, it should be noted that because certain racialized minority groups – Black and Middle Easterners – are stopped disproportionately high, the corresponding total amount of charges laid by the Ottawa Police Service against Black and Middle Easterner drivers are also high. One may argue that, upon drilling deeper into the traffic stop data, as collective entities, these groups may receive far

DISPROPORTIONATELY HIGH INCIDENCES OF TRAFFIC STOPS, REASONS AND OUTCOMES, BY RACE GROUPS IN OTTAWA

RACE GROUPS	INCIDENCES OF TRAFFIC STOPS	REASONS FOR TRAFFIC STOPS				OUTCOMES OF TRAFFIC STOPS	
		CRIMINAL OFFENSES	PROVINCIAL AND MUNICIPAL OFFENSES	SUSPICIOUS ACTIVITIES	FINAL (NO ACTION)	WARNED	CHARGED
Indigenous peoples		299.44%		99.37%	37.77%		
White							
Black	134.80%	257.94%		148.40%	42.28%		
E. Asian/S.E. Asian		56.48%					
S. Asian		88.35%					
Middle Easterner	229.44%	209.40%		133.70%	36.84%		
Other racialized minorities		60.55%		132.78%	28.21%		

Disproportionalities of high incidences are expressed in percentages (capturing only those +20% and over).

The benchmark for traffic stops is the population size of "commute-to-work" drivers of individual race groups.

The benchmarks for reasons for traffic stops and outcomes of traffic stops are proportions of the White group in relationship to racialized minority groups.

Blank cells mean that there are no disproportionately high incidences in the respective categories.

Middle Easterner and Black groups' disproportionalities are highlighted.

more tickets for provincial offences than estimates based on their population numbers warrant.

The experiences of E. Asian/S.E. Asian and S. Asian groups are different from other racialized groups. When compared with the White group, they have been traffic-stopped disproportionately high on the basis of "criminal activities"; but their outcomes have not been disproportionately high on "final (no action)". Such absence of high disproportionality on being "let go" does not create the impression that police officers have been "harassing" them through traffic stops. They have been warned or charged just as any other race groups. This may explain why those in the E. Asian/S.E. Asian and S. Asian groups are typically less concerned than other racialized minority groups towards police conducts regarding traffic stops.

CONCLUSION

This study is a correlational study on the relationship between race, sex, age, and traffic stops in Ottawa. It does not deal with the issue of causality. That is to say, it does not explain why and how these factors are related or not related. For this reason, the findings only provide a big picture of traffic stops in the entire capital city of Ottawa, covering a two-year period from 2013 and 2015 – a picture which provides a fresh and pioneering perspective on race and traffic stops in Canada.

Incidences of Traffic Stops

The research findings showed that Middle Easterner and Black groups have been disproportionately traffic-stopped by police officers. In the analysis of driver segments by race earlier in the report, it has been shown that Middle Easterner and Black groups have proportionately fewer drivers and the White group has more drivers. Therefore, the disproportionately high incidences of traffic stops experienced by these two racialized minority groups are especially glaring.

The findings also showed that young men aged 16-24 of other race groups (including the White group), but not those of Indigenous peoples, have disproportionately high incidences of traffic stops. This suggested that race, sex and age do play a key role in the patterns of traffic stops. Exactly how these factors influence police officers' decisions to traffic-stop remains undetermined by the data. The correlation of race, sex, age and traffic stops is definitely clear. In this sense, racial disparities in traffic stops exist.

Overall, in Ottawa, seventeen of the 42 (or 40%) race subgroups have disproportionately high incidences, and their disproportionalities ranged from 20.51% (men aged 25-54 in the other racialized minorities group) to 1100.39% (Middle Easterner men aged 16-24). Most police districts have more than ten race subgroups, and they are mostly of racialized minority backgrounds. These disproportionately high incidences of traffic stops among these race subgroups may be viewed as anomalies. It is important to note that these anomalies are extensive in number and severe in disproportionality. The data collected for this study are not able to determine the sources of these anomalies, but other research has tended to emphasize police leadership and culture, policing strategies and tactics, human resources management, community relations, and stereotyping and prejudice.

The research findings which emerged from this study showed that racial disparity in traffic stops are accentuated by a mix of race, sex and age. But, the findings are not able to substantiate the factors behind the traffic stops. This implies that, to ensure clarity in answering the central question on racial profiling and traffic stops, greater in-depth research is needed:

- A more comprehensive study on the police organizations and cultures, their strategies and tactics of policing, training and development, and human resources management as they relate to traffic stops.
- A deeper research on the psychological makeup and decision-making process of how police officers do traffic stopping.
- A more thorough examination of the changing social environment as it related to community development and race dynamics.

These areas are not exhaustive, but they are relevant areas to explore and illuminate the findings of this study.

Reasons for Traffic Stops

The research findings on the reasons used by police officers in traffic stops showed the overwhelming prevalence of "provincial and municipal offenses". However, when compared with the White group, five racialized minority groups have been disproportionately stopped by police officers using the "criminal offenses" reason, and four racialized minority groups – Indigenous peoples, Black, Middle Easterner, and other racialized minority groups — have been disproportionately stopped for an additional reason of "suspicious activities".

These findings suggested that, compared with the White group, racialized minority groups have a great propensity to be suspected by police officers of doing something problematic or criminal. While these reasons constituted very small percentages of reasons used, they have created more opportunities for racialized minority groups to be traffic stopped. The data does not provide the factors that gave rise to police suspicion or police perception of criminal offenses. Integrating these findings with other more qualitative research is needed to determine how police officers come to suspect people or how they perceive criminality in people or their conducts. Intersecting research of this sort provides a space where quite possible explanations for the high disproportionalities of racialized minority groups in traffic stops could be deciphered.

Outcomes of Traffic Stops

The data on the outcomes of traffic stops showed that all race groups (including the White group) experienced similar proportions of warnings and charges. There were minimal racial disparities there. But Indigenous peoples, Black, Middle Easterner, and other racialized minorities groups have disproportionately high incidences in the "final (no action)" outcomes. This may result in a perception that traffic stops are merely a form of police harassment, as police officers may see no justifications for warning or laying charges. This situation warrants additional thoughts on how traffic stops, as a police practice of law enforcement, could be made more effective.

The most surprising finding in terms of outcomes of traffic stops is the disproportionately high incidences of the "final (no action)" outcome for Indigenous peoples, Black, Middle Easterner, and racialized minorities groups, when compared with the White group. It means these four groups have been traffic stopped, but no warnings have been made nor any charges laid.

RECOMMENDATIONS

It is recommended that the Ottawa Police Services Board and Ottawa Police Service:

1. Determine the sources of the disproportionately high incidences identified in this study through additional research on psychological,

organizational, and social issues within the Ottawa Police Service – systemic biases in police practices; police leadership and corporate culture; organizational policing strategies and tactics; human resources policies and practices; institutional mindsets about the association between race and crime; the diversity of the Ottawa Police Service workforce; and race relations dynamics with the diverse communities that constitute the City of Ottawa.

2. Develop and implement solutions to address the anomalies of disproportionately high incidences through a review of research findings gathered through the implementation of Recommendation # 1 in consultation with stakeholder groups, race and ethnic communities, and the public.

3. Increase positive police-community contact by holding monthly, or regular, relationship-building meetings; train officers and community members together; promote joint police and community committee work particularly in advisory areas; and hold "critical incident" discussions and trainings and annual conferences on police-community relations.

4. Continue collecting race data in traffic stops with improved tools and processes; monitor regularly traffic stops issues; place data reports as a regular agenda item on meetings at the level of staff, senior management, and board; and communicate data related to race and traffic stops regularly to the public through quarterly bulletins, press releases, annual reports, and other media.

5. Build on its extensive and successful experience with community engagement and develop a multi-year action plan to address the issues of racial disparities in traffic stops raised in this report.

6. Make readily available the data collected for this research project on race and traffic stops. The raw data made available should allow for analysis that goes beyond the scope and methodology of this report, but within the legal limits of the *Freedom of Information and Protection of Privacy Act* and the *Municipal Freedom of Information and Protection of Privacy Act*.

Part II
Technical Notes

NOTE 1: RACE CATEGORIES

For the purpose of conducting this research, race data are divided into several race categories: Indigenous peoples, White, Black, East/Southeast Asian, South Asian, Middle Easterners, and other racialized minorities. The following chart is created for the purpose of cross-referencing the 7 Ottawa Police Service's race categories and the 12 race categories of the National Household Survey, 2011, along with some examples of these race categories.

OTTAWA POLICE SERVICE - RACE CATEGORIES N: 7	NATIONAL HOUSEHOLD SURVEY, 2011 - RACE CATEGORIES N: 12	EXAMPLES
Indigenous peoples	Aboriginal persons	First Nation (North American Indian), Metis, Inuk (Inuit)
White	White	People of European origins
Black	Black	People of African and Caribbean origins
East Asian, Southeast Asian	Chinese	Chinese
	Filipino	Filipino
	Korean	Korean
	Japanese	Japanese
	Southeast Asian	Indonesian, Laotian, Malaysian, Singaporeans, Thais, Vietnamese, etc.
South Asian	South Asian	East Indian, Pakistani, Sri Lankan, Bangladeshi
Middle Easterner	Arab/West Asian	Afghan, Armenia, Egyptian, Iranian, Iraqi, Lebanese, Palestinian, Moroccan
Other Racialized Minorities	Latin American	Mixed races, Pacific Islanders, and people from Latin and South America
	Other (Specify)	

NOTE 2: METHODOLOGY

This report consists of two types of analysis: one is representation analysis on incidences of traffic stops, the other one is distribution analysis of the reasons for and outcomes of traffic stops.

Representation Analysis on Incidences of Traffic Stops

The race data collected by the Ottawa Police Service on traffic stops is designed to answer the question: Which race groups, if any, are proportionately over-represented in the traffic stops?

Two sets of race data were required — one is the race data in the traffic stops records from the Ottawa Police Service, the other is the race data in the commute-to-work segment of the labour force data as collected by the National Household Survey (NHS), 2011. The second data set was used for benchmarking purposes.

The National Household Survey was a voluntary survey undertaken by Statistics Canada in which approximately 4.5 million households received a questionnaire. The survey provides social and economic information, covering such topics as: immigration, citizenship, place of birth, ethnic origin, visible minorities, religion, Aboriginal peoples, labour, education, place of work, commuting to work, mobility and migration, language of work, income, earnings, housing and shelter costs. The commuter data has been weighted to enable benchmarking against the traffic stop data. The National Household Survey was accessed at the York University Research Data Centre.

Based on the feedback from community members, a further breakdown of race data by sex (male and female) and age groups (aged 16-24, 25-54, and 44 and over) allowed for the analysis to be drilled down to the level of race subgroups. The reason why the term "representation" is used to describe this analysis is that our analysis uses an external benchmark for data comparison.

"Commute-to-work" persons are persons who usually drove to work during the week of May 1 to May 7, 2011 according to the data collected in Question 47(a) of the National Household Survey of 2011. By implication, these drivers are the employed, although the question allowed people who held no jobs since January 1, 2010 to answer. This means that the data includes an undetermined number of persons who are unemployed and not in the labour force. However, the data does not include drivers who drive for non-work purposes.

Being drivers in this data set does not mean that they drive all the time, 24 hours a day, and 365 days a year. The benchmark is not perfect for measuring against the driving population captured in the Ottawa Police Service's traffic stops records because that population encompasses drivers for both work and non-work purposes. However, as there are no available comparable data on "non-work" drivers or driving population (people driving on the streets) by race groups within the entire boundaries of Ottawa under the jurisdiction of the Ottawa Police Service, the York University Research Team utilized the best benchmark available to provide a proxy for measuring the extent of representation of race in traffic stops in Ottawa. This benchmark is more suitable for this kind of analysis than other data sets, based on its driver population size and the geographic boundaries the data covered. The use of the National Household Survey's "commute-to-work" data for this study will unlikely end the debate on benchmarking for studies of racial biases in traffic stops in Canada.

This analysis required a comparison of the two data sets – drivers recorded in traffic stops and commute-to-work drivers – by race, sex, and age in Ottawa and its six police districts (as based on the census tract boundaries of the Ottawa Police Service).

Essentially, the traffic stop data, broken down by race, sex and age (as expressed in percentages of the total population in Ottawa and individual police districts) was then compared with the "commute-to-work" segment of the Ottawa residents (as expressed in percentages of the total "commute-to-work" population in Ottawa).

The values of the differences in comparison, holding race, sex and age constant, were expressed in positive or negative percentages. Positive percentages denote over-representation (that is, high incidences) of race groups in traffic stops, and negative percentages denote under-representation (that is, low incidences) of race groups in traffic stops.

How much attention one should pay to these percentages in these two data sets was determined by the "20% rule". This rule should not be construed as a measurement of statistical significance. Rather, it is an indication of the unlikelihood of errors when the 20% difference is reached, either positive or negative. It is used to increase the confidence level of how we interpret the data. Data, either higher than +20% or lower than -20%, is viewed as better in quality. Percentages that are in range between +20% and -20% are considered less robust in data quality.

For our working purposes in interpreting the data, a zero percentage (0%) in the proportionality of incidences in traffic stops for a race group means the group's proportion in traffic stops corresponds to its proportion in the driver population (who commute to work). Data that is in the range between +19.99% and 0% is termed as "high incidences" and -19.99% and 0% is termed as "low incidences". Data that is +20% or over are termed as "disproportionately high incidences", and -20% or less are termed as "disproportionately low incidences".

The following diagram may help to put proportionalities of incidences in perspective:

Although the "20% rule" allows our data analysis to be more robust, it has a conservative implication. It puts aside a pool of "high incidences" and "low incidences" between +19.99% and -19.99% as a cushion of research errors, and reserves "disproportionalities" to those incidences with percentages of differences +20% or higher and those -20% or lower.

Distribution Analysis of Reasons for and Outcomes of Traffic Stops

Disproportionately low incidences (or disproportionately under-represented)	Low Incidences (or under-represented)	High Incidences (or over-represented)	Disproportionately high incidences (or disproportionately over-represented)
-infinity	-20% 0%	+20%	+ infinity

The race data collected by the Ottawa Police Service on traffic stops also provide answers to the following two questions:

- Which race groups, if any, have disproportionately high incidences in specific reasons for traffic stops?
- Which race groups, if any, have disproportionately high incidences in specific outcomes of traffic stops?

This distribution analysis of reasons for traffic stops focuses only on race. The data are not broken down by sex and age. The reason why the term "distribution" is used in this analysis is that our analysis focuses on the internal distribution patterns of data, using an internal benchmark (and that is, the White group) for measurement, and not an external benchmark.

(a) Reasons for traffic stops
In this analysis, three categories of reasons are used: criminal offenses, provincial and municipal offenses (or non-criminal offenses) and suspicious activities.

- "Criminal offenses"
- "Provincial and municipal offenses"

- "Suspicious activities"

These three categories cover all the reasons why police officers traffic-stop. To answer the question on the proportions of race groups distributed among these three categories, it follows a two-tiered calculation: First, holding each race group constant, the percentages of traffic stops in which police officers used each of these categories of reasons is calculated. Second, holding each category of reasons constant, the percentages of each race group in these categories are then compared with those of the White group. As there is a perception that racial profiling exists, the White group is therefore used as the benchmark. The differences in percentages between each of the racial minority groups and the White group under each of the reasons are expressed in percentages.

Once again, using the "20% rule", this research considers only the differences between the White group and each of the racialized minority groups that are +20% or higher. Incidences with "+20% or higher" percentages are termed as "disproportionately high incidences". Data on these incidences are more robust and are relatively error-free.

(b) Outcomes of traffic stops

In this analysis, three categories of outcomes are used: "final (no action)", "warned" and "charged". These three categories cover all the outcomes of traffic stop.

- "Final (no action)"
- "Warned"
- "Charged" – includes criminal and non-criminal offenses

To find out the proportions of race groups distributed among these three categories, the distribution of each of these three outcomes is tabulated for each race group and these proportions are expressed in percentages. As there is a perception that racial profiling exists, the White group is the benchmark. The percentage of each of the racial minority groups under these three outcomes is then compared with that of the White group under each of the same three outcomes. The differences of these two data sets are expressed in percentages.

Once again, using the "20% rule", this report focuses on the differences between the White group and each of the racialized minority groups which are +20% or higher in percentages. The outcomes of traffic stops with these percentages are considered to be "disproportionately high incidences".

Benefits

The methodology used in this study has several benefits:

- Unlike other methodologies, this methodology provides an overview of how race groups fare in traffic stops, covering not just a limited sample of people in a few locations in Ottawa, but all drivers-to-work in the entire City of Ottawa. Research results based on local studies or those with limited sample usually beg for more studies to determine their capability of generalization.
- Data generated from this methodology are simple statistics based on a simple comparison of race groups using traffic stops data and data on those who drive to work.
- This methodology shows, in a relatively simple way, the anomalies among race groups traffic-stopped by police officers. These anomalies are measured in percentages of differences, and they are not skewed by the size of the race groups. The "20% rule" enables the readers to determine which anomalies among race groups are less prone to errors. The rule also enables Ottawa Police Service to set priorities in addressing these anomalies as they have been quantified. While this methodology does not determine the causation of traffic stops, the anomalies suggest areas for deeper analysis.

Limitations

Scholars have been attempting to "prove" or "debunk" racial profiling. Not only is the concept vague or ambiguous at times, it is also a concept without much of a consensus among scholars. Therefore, in demonstrating the existence or the extent of racial profiling, numerous approaches and research tools have been adopted, mostly on traffic stops in the U.S., and to a much lesser extent in Canada. These studies brought forward some new insights, and yet, they have been criticized for their inadequate methods, measuring tools, and/or benchmarking.

This status quo of research in racial profiling reflects largely the multiple "moving parts" of the subject matters. Research is also hindered by the lack of comparable data or information (for benchmarking purposes), the availability or limitations of feasible tools, the sensitivity of the subject matters, and the difficulty of having a representative sample of the driving population, time-wise and location-wise.

The methodology utilized in this study is not able to escape from some of the above-mentioned realities. Here are highlights of a few limitations:

- It provides a correlational (not causal) relationship on race and in-cidents of traffic stops. It does not examine the motives of police officers behind the traffic stops and offers no definitive explana-tions on why certain race groups are over-represented in traffic stops or why they are more prone to be stopped based on specific reasons or have certain outcomes based on the traffic stops.

- It compares Ottawa Police Service's traffic stops data based on the "other identification" method (that is, police officers identified the races of the drivers) with Statistics Canada's "commute-to-work" driver population data based on the "self-identification" method (that is, drivers identified their own races). Studies in racial iden-tification suggested that these methods often yielded different results, and "other identification" method is preferred only under limited circumstances.

- The external benchmark used in the methodology is the "commute-to-work" segment of the labour force data collected in the Nation-al Household Survey, 2011. This benchmark is based only on the individuals who drive to work, not when they use their cars for non-work purposes. In addition, it is not clear the extent to which the data cover unemployed individuals and those not in the labour force.

NOTE 3: OTTAWA POLICE SERVICE'S TRAFFIC STOPS DATA SET

This report is based on the traffic stop data collected by the Ottawa Po-lice Service from June 27, 2013 to June 26, 2015 (2 years). All traffic stops undertaken by the Ottawa Police Service during this period were the subject of the data collection project. The individual police officer con-ducting the stop entered the data fields. A total of 120,617 traffic stops was reported. Of these, 106,576 records of traffic stops have race data. The officers entering the race data reported perceiving the race of the driver prior to the stop in 11.4% of the cases.

The analysis in this report only uses of 81,902 of these traffic stops. Not all of the 106,576 traffic stops records containing race data were used for analysis because of the following reasons:

- As the analysis covers only persons 16 years and older, all traffic stops with drivers under 16 years of age have been filtered out. There were 11 stops involving drivers under 16 years of age among the 106,576.

- The representation analysis involved only traffic stop records with complete information on the fields of sex, age, and geographic locations in addition to race. Stops with incomplete information for any of these fields have been filtered out. There were 100,792 stops with all of these fields complete.
- These 100,792 stops involved 84,893 unique driver identifications. The significance of multiple stops of a single driver and the reliability of the unique driver identifications contained in the data set is beyond the scope of the present analysis.
- As data on the commute-to-work drivers in Ottawa is based on Ottawa residents only, all traffic stops with non-Ottawa residents have been filtered out. The data set of 100,792 included 18,890 stops of non-Ottawa residents.

As a result of these filters, the representation analysis in the report is based on 81,902 traffic stop records. For the sake of consistency, the distribution analysis of the reasons for and outcomes of traffic stops used the same data set.

It is important to note that when the data is broken down by race, sex, and age, or by police districts with reasons for or outcomes of traffic stops, there are cases in which the numbers in various tabulated data cells become small (as in the case of Indigenous peoples). Such small numbers reduce data reliability and impact on data interpretation.

Although the data collection process was subject to extensive quality control management over the two year period ensuring its reliability, Brown and Primeau in an independent 2016 report based on interviews with 57 OPS officers found that some frontline officers reported that on occasion they deliberately entered some inaccurate race data out of concern about how the findings based on the data might impact their employment.

Table of Cases

Index